D1229001

CONTENTS

Introductio

↑damage
noted ecb
6/18/13

SPECIAL EDITION

USING
Microsoft® Office
Visio® 2007

DATE DUE

Steven Holzner

®

800 East 96th Street
Indianapolis, Indiana 46240

SPECIAL EDITION USING MICROSOFT® OFFICE VISIO® 2007

Copyright © 2008 by Que Publishing

All rights reserved. No part of this book shall be reproduced, stored in a retrieval system, or transmitted by any means, electronic, mechanical, photocopying, recording, or otherwise, without written permission from the publisher. No patent liability is assumed with respect to the use of the information contained herein. Although every precaution has been taken in the preparation of this book, the publisher and author assume no responsibility for errors or omissions. Nor is any liability assumed for damages resulting from the use of the information contained herein.

ISBN-13: 978-0-7897-3686-4
ISBN-10: 0-7897-3686-1

Printed in the United States on America

First Printing: October 2007

10 09 08 07   4 3 2 1

Trademarks

All terms mentioned in this book that are known to be trademarks or service marks have been appropriately capitalized. Que Publishing cannot attest to the accuracy of this information. Use of a term in this book should not be regarded as affecting the validity of any trademark or service mark.

Windows and Visio are registered trademarks of Microsoft Corporation.

Warning and Disclaimer

Every effort has been made to make this book as complete and as accurate as possible, but no warranty or fitness is implied. The information provided is on an "as is" basis. The author and the publisher shall have neither liability nor responsibility to any person or entity with respect to any loss or damages arising from the information contained in this book.

Bulk Sales

Que Publishing offers excellent discounts on this book when ordered in quantity for bulk purchases or special sales. For more information, please contact

U.S. Corporate and Government Sales
1-800-382-3419
corpsales@pearsontechgroup.com

For sales outside of the U.S., please contact

International Sales
international@pearsoned.com

This Book Is Safari Enabled

The Safari® Enabled icon on the cover of your favorite technology book means the book is available through Safari Bookshelf. When you buy this book, you get free access to the online edition for 45 days.

Safari Bookshelf is an electronic reference library that lets you easily search thousands of technical books, find code samples, download chapters, and access technical information whenever and wherever you need it.

To gain 45-day Safari Enabled access to this book:

• Go to http://www.quepublishing.com/safarienabled
• Complete the brief registration form
• Enter the coupon code UHKI-4NRJ-4GXQ-YHJ5-H3MU

If you have difficulty registering on Safari Bookshelf or accessing the online edition, please email customer-service@safaribooksonline.com.

Library of Congress Cataloging-in-Publication Data

Holzner, Steven.
  Special edition using Microsoft Office Visio 2007 / Steven Holzner.
    p. cm.
  Includes index.
  ISBN 0-7897-3686-1
  1. Computer graphics. 2. Microsoft Visio. 3. Business—Data processing.
I. Title.
  T385.H6775 2007
  006.6'8682—dc22
                              2007036850

Associate Publisher
Greg Wiegand

Acquisitions Editor
Loretta Yates

Development Editor
Kevin Howard

Managing Editor
Gina Kanouse

Senior Project Editor
Lori Lyons

Copy Editor
Cheri Clark

Indexer
WordWise Publishing
Services, LLC

Proofreader
Water Crest Publishing

Technical Editor
John Marshall

Publishing Coordinator
Cindy Teeters

Book Designer
Anne Jones

Composition
Nonie Ratcliff

CONTENTS

ABOUT THE AUTHOR

Steven Holzner is the award-winning author of 106 books. His books have sold more than two million copies and have been translated into 18 languages around the world. He has been a contributing editor at *PC Magazine*, and has been on the faculty of MIT and Cornell University, where he got his PhD. Steven is a Visio expert and uses it constantly in his work.

DEDICATION

To Nancy, as always!

ACKNOWLEDGMENTS

The book you hold in your hands is the product of many people's hard work. I'd especially like to thank Loretta Yates, acquisitions editor; Kevin Howard, development editor; Lori Lyons, senior project editor; Cheri Clark, copy editor; Nonie Ratcliff, compositor and Sarah Kearns, proofreader.

WE WANT TO HEAR FROM YOU!

As the reader of this book, *you* are our most important critic and commentator. We value your opinion and want to know what we're doing right, what we could do better, what areas you'd like to see us publish in, and any other words of wisdom you're willing to pass our way.

As an associate publisher for Que Publishing, I welcome your comments. You can email or write me directly to let me know what you did or didn't like about this book—as well as what we can do to make our books better.

Please note that I cannot help you with technical problems related to the topic of this book. We do have a User Services group, however, where I will forward specific technical questions related to the book.

When you write, please be sure to include this book's title and author as well as your name, email address, and phone number. I will carefully review your comments and share them with the author and editors who worked on the book.

Email: feedback@quepublishing.com

Mail: Greg Wiegand
           Associate Publisher
           Que Publishing
           800 East 96th Street
           Indianapolis, IN 46240 USA

READER SERVICES

Visit our website and register this book at www.informit.com/title/9780789736864 for convenient access to any updates, downloads, or errata that might be available for this book.

INTRODUCTION

In this introduction

Welcome to Visio 2007! Visio is an exceptionally powerful application, and this book is designed to cover it as much as is possible with any book. The whole Visio story is here.

Visio is the premier drawing software available today. Want to set up flowchart slides for that all-important meeting? Visio's your answer. Want to specify what goes where in your office layout? Visio's your ticket.

For just about any drawing you can commit to paper—electronic circuits, plumbing diagrams, data-flow drawings, website maps, Windows XP user interfaces (creating mock-ups of windows, dialog boxes, and wizards)—Visio is the way to go.

And Visio 2007 is more powerful and bigger than ever before. You may be coming to this book from a previous version of Visio. If so, you're going to find that Visio 2007 has more to offer you—more capabilities and resources—than you could imagine.

WHO IS THIS BOOK FOR?

This book is for you if you want to get the whole Visio story.

If you're a beginner, you'll find that this book doesn't assume any Visio knowledge, and that all the steps for the tasks you'll see here are spelled out in detail. Want to drag and configure shapes onto the Visio drawing surface? You'll see everything, step by step. Want to add text to a shape, or set some data associated with a shape? It's all here.

This book is also for you if you have some experience with Visio. If you have already been using Visio but want to complete your skill set, this book has been designed to give you what you want. Maybe you're ready to go beyond the basics and want to become a full-fledged expert. Want to create custom stencils? You'll find that here. Want to write your own ShapeSheet formulas? No problem.

Advanced users will feel right at home as well, because this book has been written to be crammed with tips, special notes, and timesaving insights. Want to use Visio to reach out on the Internet and make a map of any website for you? Check out Chapter 14. Want to create a Gantt chart from data you have in Microsoft Project? Take a look at Chapter 13.

In short, this book has been designed for anyone interested in Visio 2007—beginner, novice, intermediate user, advanced user, or power user.

WHAT'S IN THIS BOOK?

This book was written to encompass all of Visio 2007—no easy task. Just about everything you can do in Visio 2007 is here. You'll find Visio 2007 themes; how to connect to databases, Excel, Project, Outlook, and even general websites; how to create and customize Visio 2007 data graphics and PivotDiagrams; and more.

Here's a breakdown, chapter by chapter:

- 1, **"Essential Visio"**—This chapter welcomes you to Visio, and establishes basic Visio skills such as creating drawings, drawing with shapes, and handling stencils.

- 2, **"Working with Shapes"**—In this chapter you first create Visio drawings by dragging shapes from stencils to the drawing surface, then customize and print those shapes.

- 3, **"Connecting Shapes and Adding Text"**—Some essential skills in Visio when it comes to shapes are to connect those shapes, showing relationships, and adding text to labels shapes—as well as rotating and resizing that text.

- 4, **"Guides, Rulers, and Custom Shapes"**—Visio comes with a built-in grid for aligning shapes, as well as other tools, such as rulers and guides. You'll also see how to create custom shapes in this chapter.

- 5, **"Groups, Pages, and Layers"**—This chapter covers themes, groups, adding shapes to groups, and cutting up Visio drawings into layers.

- 6, **"Building Your Own Stencils, Templates, and Reports"**—This chapter covers how to make your own custom stencils, add shapes to custom stencils, and create custom templates.

- 7, **"Controlling Shape Behavior and Marking Up Drawings"**—This chapter is all about making 2D shapes 1D, customizing double-click behavior, locking shapes, marking up drawings, and using digital ink in Visio.

- 8, **"Linking and Embedding Objects and Publishing to the Web"**—You can insert objects in Visio drawings, as well as linking to those objects and embedding those objects. Also in this chapter: publishing drawings on the Web.

- 9, **"ShapeSheets and Macros"**—ShapeSheets are datasheets for shapes. Here, you'll find how to open ShapeSheets, work with ShapeSheets, and write ShapeSheet formulas. Also included: writing and running Visio macros.

- 10, **"Using Visio with Other Applications"**—One of Visio 2007's strong points is connecting with other applications. This chapter covers importing and exporting data, as well as using data links, data graphics, and the Visio database tools.

- 11, **"Creating Block Drawings and Charts"**—This chapter is all about creating block drawings, tree drawings, concentric drawings, and charts and graphs.

- 12, **"Creating Organization Charts and Flowcharts**—Creating organization charts, importing and exporting data, and creating flowcharts are covered here.

- 13, **"Scheduling Projects and Handling Brainstorming Sessions"**—This chapter is all about scheduling projects, creating calendars, Gantt charts, scheduling timelines, and creating brainstorming drawings.

- 14, **"Creating Software Development Drawings"**—This chapter covers UML drawings, UML state drawings, data-flow drawings, user interfaces, and designing of websites.

As you can see, there's a lot coming up in this book. Visio is a big topic, and there's plenty of in-depth coverage included to encompass it.

CONVENTIONS USED IN THIS BOOK

Here's a quick look at a few structural features designed to help you get the most out of this book. To begin with, you'll find the following features:

TIP

> Tips are designed to point out especially quick ways to get the job done, good ideas, or techniques you might not discover on your own.

NOTE

> Notes offer even more insight into features or issues that may be of special interest, without distracting you from the meat-and-potatoes answers you're looking for.

CAUTION

> Cautions, as you'd expect, warn you away from potential pitfalls and problems, and point out fixes for common issues.

Que's *Special Edition* conventions are designed to be completely predictable. It's easy to understand what you're reading and what you're supposed to do.

For example, whenever you should press multiple keys together, in this book they are written separated by a plus sign, like this: Ctrl+B. That means hold down the Ctrl key, press the B key, and then release both keys.

Terms introduced and defined for the first time are formatted in *italic*.

Actions that you are supposed to perform or text that you are supposed to type in are formatted in bold type, as in the following example:

1. Select File > Page Setup. This opens the Page Setup dialog.

Okay, that's it—we're ready to start. Turn to Chapter 1 now to start digging into Visio 2007.

CHAPTER

1

ESSENTIAL VISIO

In this chapter

WELCOME TO VISIO 2007

What's the guiding principle behind Visio? Easy: A picture is worth a thousand words. Think of all the media you deal with each day—newspapers, television, magazines, presentations, and so on. They all present information graphically.

Have a table of data? What's going to be more visually appealing—tall columns of numbers, or a colorful pie chart? What's going to communicate a point better—a description of an electrical circuit, or a diagram of the circuit itself? Even discussing a new layout for your office is best done graphically.

Visio is the application that comes to your aid in creating those kinds of graphical aids. You might think of Visio with some trepidation, but in fact you can use Visio on many different levels, including a very easy level. And that's the level you'll see in this chapter as you build the foundation you'll need for the rest of the book.

All you really need to do to use Visio at its most basic is to fire it up and drag the shapes you want onto the drawing surface. Simple. And that's how we're going to start off using Visio, because even simple use can be powerful, and it will prepare you for the more advanced material to come.

You're also going to get an introduction to the Visio terms and concepts—such as templates and stencils—that you'll need throughout the book. A familiarity with these terms and concepts is going to serve you well in this book.

SO WHAT IS VISIO?

What does Visio 2007 actually look like? You can see it in Figure 1.1.

Figure 1.1
This is the Visio 2007 startup screen.

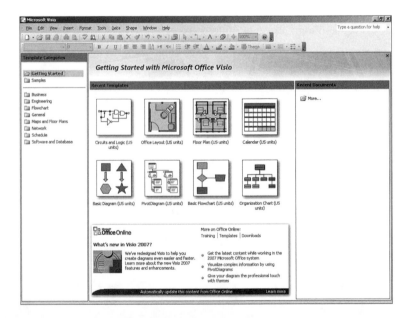

The figure shows a typical startup screen you see when you start Visio. In the center, Visio displays the recent templates—collections of drawing shapes—you've used. If you haven't used any templates yet, that part of the window will be blank.

At right, there's a pane labeled Recent Documents that contains your most recent drawings for easy access. If you don't have any drawings yet, that folder won't show up.

At left, in a column headed Template Categories, you'll see several items, which you're going to see in some detail in this book.

At the top in the left column is an item named Getting Started, which is selected by default when you start Visio. That item provides an overview of Visio, as you can see in the figure. To get back to that overview at any time, you can also select the menu item File > New > Getting Started.

Below the Getting Started item is a Samples item. When you select this item, you'll see a display of sample drawings that gives you an idea of what Visio can do. More on this item later.

Underneath the Samples item you'll see the various drawing categories that Visio supports. There are eight such categories, and you're going to get to know them well in this book. That's Visio Professional you see in Figure 1.1, and here are the supported categories (you won't see all these categories if you have Visio Standard):

- **Business**—Contains organizational and other business diagrams, such as audit templates.
- **Engineering**—Contains electrical, piping, process control, and other engineering templates.
- **Flowchart**—Contains various flowchart templates.
- **General**—Contains templates that hold basic shapes—stars, rectangles, circles, and the like.
- **Maps and Floorplans**—Contains templates you can use to create maps and design the layout of furniture and rooms.
- **Network**—Contains network templates you use to create computer networks, from intranets to web server installations.
- **Schedule**—Contains templates for timelines, Gantt charts, calendars, and the like.
- **Software and Database**—Contains templates for database design, program design, and so on.

It's important that you get the basic terminology down right from the start—for example, just what is a template, and how does it differ from a stencil? To see the answer, let's create our first drawing so that the rest of the overview in this chapter will make sense. This example will be an office floor plan to get the ball rolling.

A VISIO EXAMPLE

In the Getting Started window, click the Maps and Floor Plans template category, giving you the result shown in Figure 1.2.

Figure 1.2
The Maps and Floor Plans template category.

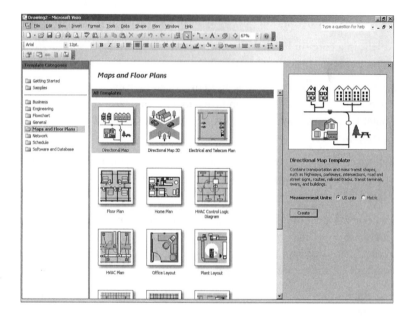

Okay, you're now taking a look at the available templates for creating maps and floor plans. Double-click the Office Layout template, giving you the result shown in Figure 1.3.

Figure 1.3
The Office Layout template.

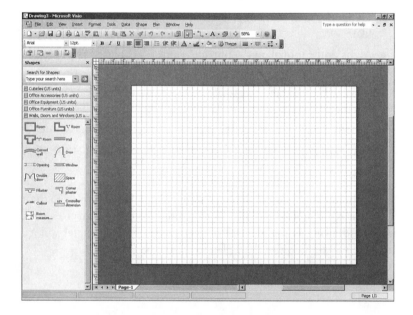

Now you've selected a template—the Office Layout template—from the Maps and Floor Plans category. So far so good.

Next, select the Office Furniture tab at left. This opens the *stencil* shown in Figure 1.4. Templates are collections of stencils, and stencils are collections of shapes.

Figure 1.4
The Office Furniture stencil.

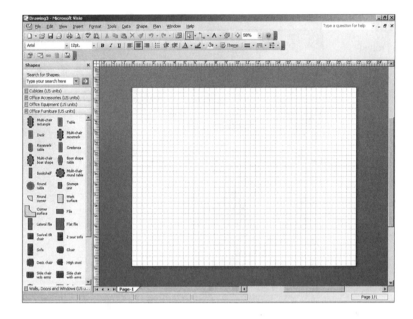

Great, now you've drilled down from a template category to a template, to a stencil full of shapes.

The shapes available in this stencil appear in the Shapes pane at left. Drag the Multi-Chair Round Table icon onto the drawing surface, creating a round table with chairs, as shown in Figure 1.5.

That's the prototypical Visio action—dragging a shape from the Shapes pane onto a drawing surface. And now you've gotten a start on creating a Visio drawing. Not bad.

Here are the terms you've seen so far:

- **Template Category**—A collection of related templates, such as the Engineering template category, which contains circuit, piping, fluid control, and other engineering templates.

- **Template**—A collection of related stencils, each of which contains shapes. Each stencil appears with its own tab in the Shapes pane after you select a template. For example, the Office Layout template contains the stencils Cubicles; Office Accessories; Office Equipment; Office Furniture; and Walls, Doors, and Windows. Templates also contain information about the drawing page, the units used, and the styles available.

- **Stencils**—A collection of related shapes. A template is a collection of stencils, and each stencil displays a set of shapes you can drag onto your drawing surface.

- **Shape**—The actual drawing object you drag onto the drawing surface. Visio drawings are made up of collections of shapes. For example, you've already seen how to use the multi-chair round table shape.

Figure 1.5
Drawing a round table with chairs.

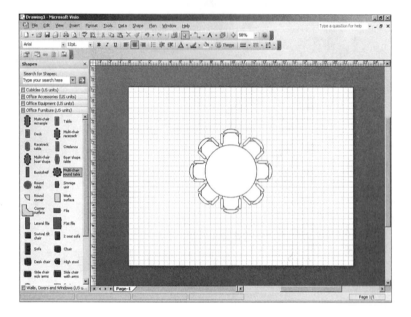

That's the way it works—you drill down from a template category (a collection of templates) to a template (a collection of stencils) to a stencil (a collection of shapes) to the shape(s), which you drag onto the drawing surface.

And that, in essence, is the Visio drawing process. It's all about finding the shapes you want to use, and dragging them onto the drawing surface. Of course, that's just the beginning—we haven't discussed how to connect shapes, configure them, or create your own shapes. But now you've seen the basics of Visio at work.

While we're discussing terms, here's one more: drawing. What you create in Visio are *drawings*, although you'll sometimes see them called *diagrams*. *Drawing* is the official Visio term, but you actually do very little drawing, unless you've chosen a shape that lets you draw freehand. That's why some people call drawings *diagrams* instead.

PROFESSIONAL VERSUS STANDARD VISIO

Visio 2007 comes in two versions: Standard and Professional. In fact, that's a simplification from previous versions—you used to be able to purchase Standard, Professional, Technical, and Enterprise versions of Visio.

All those options confused people, however, and led to customer dissatisfaction. Tracking down which features were in which version was a tedious process. And, worse yet, what if the features you wanted were divided among different versions? Did you have to buy *both* the Technical and the Professional versions to get what you wanted?

Microsoft revamped this picture for Visio 2007 into two versions: Standard and Professional. What's the difference?

Visio 2007 Standard edition is designed for business people, from product managers to business analysts. This version gives you the capability to create business diagrams and charts in order to diagram business processes, organizational charts, schedules, timelines, trends, and the like. You can also create office layouts and maps with the Standard edition.

Visio 2007 Professional edition is designed for more technical users. It contains all that the Standard edition has, and adds functionality. The Professional version is used by database designers, IT managers, electrical engineers, network managers, Internet and web professionals, software developers, Web site administrators, and other technical professionals. You'll find additional template categories in Visio 2007 Professional to deal with these additional areas.

Here are some features the Professional Edition provides that the Standard Edition lacks:

- **Additional templates**—Besides the more technical template categories, the Professional edition comes with some additional new templates that make it easier to display complex data graphically. These include the PivotDiagrams, Value Stream Map, Information Technology Infrastructure Library, and Work Flow Diagram templates, which are discussed later in this book.

- **Examining data in the Data Graphics pane**—This pane lets you convert plain text data into something with graphical pizzazz.

- **The Data Selector Wizard**—Importing data is made much easier with the Data Selector Wizard, which leads you step-by-step through the process of importing data from other applications such as Microsoft Access, SQL Server, and Microsoft Excel, as well as some non-Microsoft applications.

- **PivotDiagrams**—PivotDiagrams are special diagrams that let you display complex data from various perspectives. They're collections of shapes arranged in tree format, which allows you to analyze associated data from different views.

Which Visio is right for you? If you're a business professional involved in managing projects, sales, and strategies, or a casual user, Visio Standard is right for you. If you're a technical professional involved with technical subjects like electrical engineering, software development or planning, Web design, and the like, Visio Professional is the one you want.

What's New in Visio 2007?

You might have already used previous versions of Visio, and might be wondering what's new in Visio 2007. Here's an overview of the major changes, which you're going to see more of throughout this book.

Better organization of template categories—Previously, Visio had more template categories. Now, they've been redesigned and reorganized. There are fewer template categories, and each one contains more templates in a better organization.

More templates—Even though there are fewer template categories, there are more templates. Most template categories contain more templates than they did formerly. And the stencils in most templates have been reorganized in a way that makes more sense.

Recent template list—The recent template list, which has been added to the Getting Started page, displays your most recently used templates. If you have a set of templates you use often, you can create a new drawing just by double-clicking one of those recent templates. Presto.

Just two versions—As mentioned, Visio used to come in Standard, Professional, Technical, and Enterprise versions; now it comes in just Standard and Professional versions. (Actually, Enterprise still exists, but it is bundled with Microsoft's programming suite of applications, Visual Studio.)

Sample diagrams and data—The Professional version comes with sample diagrams that give you an idea what Visio is capable of. These samples are tied to data stored in Excel, and you also have access to that data directly—clicking a button opens the data set in Excel.

Themes—A theme sets the visual characteristics of a drawing, such as drawing colors. You may have already seen themes in Windows, and themes in Visio are much the same. Themes are new in Visio 2007, and they make it easy to create drawings with the same colors, font styles, and so on. Using a theme, you don't have to individually configure each drawing to follow the properties of another drawing.

Sharing data—Visio 2007 comes with more power to import data from other applications, such as Excel or Microsoft Project. As Visio comes to be used by more and more teams, this is going to be an increasingly popular feature. You can put data on a SharePoint server, such as Microsoft Project data, and share it among various people using Visio. You can even email Visio drawings now using Outlook, and other people can see those drawings even if they don't have Visio.

Connecting shapes more easily—Visio makes it easier than before to connect shapes, by handling the process automatically. You can let Visio connect shapes by itself, as well as align shapes automatically. You can also make connections later by using the connectors (coming up soon) associated with each shape, and just pointing to them.

Saving data in XPS—Visio can store data using the XML Paper Specification (XPS). That's a standard data format for storing data meant for exchange between applications. When you store your data in XPS format, other XPS-aware applications can use it, allowing you to export that data with ease to other applications.

WHAT'S NEW FOR VISTA?

Visio works under Windows Vista in a slightly different way than under Windows XP. There are two main areas of difference: graphical and security.

The graphical differences are mostly eye candy—there's no task you can perform under Windows Vista that you can't perform under Windows XP. Vista supports the Aero Glass visual interface, and it looks nicer than what's available in Windows XP.

There are some benefits to using Windows Vista rather than XP. For one, Graphics will appear faster on the screen. Although this is not a serious difference between Windows versions, it means that under Vista, Visio appears snappier, and more responsive. And some fonts and lines are rendered better in Windows Vista, which can give Visio a more professional appearance.

Vista also supports some additional sweets. One of those is called Freeze Dry, which saves an application's window size, cursor position, and other current program settings. If you have to reboot for some reason, Freeze Dry can restore Visio faster than you'd see under Windows XP.

In addition, Vista lets you search for documents using all kinds of metadata, such as the author of a Visio document. This means that locating and sorting your Visio data can be easier under Vista. Both Windows XP and Vista can display thumbnail images of your drawings when you take a look at a directory.

Microsoft Office is also more robust under Vista. If Office determines that an operation you're asking for is going to make it crash, it stops and tells you what the problem is instead of just going ahead and crashing.

A big difference in using Visio under Vista is the security differences. Those differences can be great if you need them—but they can also get in the way of individual users. On the other hand, many of these security features run automatically, so they don't present obstacles. Let's take a look at them.

Vista makes a big distinction between users and administrators on your machine. Most accounts work in user mode—which means that some things you used to do in Visio no longer function without additional work. For example, you'll have to get permission to access your data directories. Security is a big part of Vista, and some awkwardness is the unavoidable result.

You can also write and use macros in Visio using the Tools > Macros > Record New Macro menu item. A macro is a collection of commands, and using macros means that you don't have to enter all those commands individually—you can just run the macro. The point here is that macros must be digitally signed under Vista, but not under XP. That's another hoop you have to jump through to satisfy Vista's security system.

In fact, some macros will simply not work under Vista, although they worked under XP. A typical example of this is when a macro deletes a file—you have to have the correct privileges under Vista to be able to delete a file. So if you're creating macros in Vista, be prepared to spend some time working out the kinks.

Vista is also very particular about accessing data. If, for example, you want to access data on a network drive, you're probably going to get requests for passwords. And you have to have permission rights, or administrator rights, on the network drive to access that data. One

1

way to handle this problem is to set trusted locations in Visio so that the permissions are set up automatically. More on creating trusted locations later.

All right, now you've gotten an overview of Visio. It's time to start digging into the details.

THE VISIO DETAILS

Take a look at Figure 1.6, where you see Visio at work creating a business organizational chart.

Figure 1.6
Drawing a business organizational chart.

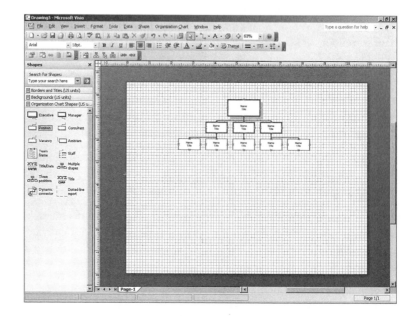

Let's take apart this display.

At top, you can see Visio's title bar, which displays the text "Drawing5 - Microsoft Visio." Under the title bar is the menu bar, with the Visio menus: File, Edit, View, Insert, Format, Tools, Data, Shape, Window, and Help. In addition, there's another, nonstandard menu in the menu bar—Organization Chart—which is there because you're creating an organization chart. This menu contains items specific to organization charts, such as Arrange Subordinates, Move Subordinates, and Import Organization Data.

Under the menu bar you'll see toolbars. The toolbars—there are three of them in Figure 1.6—contain buttons that give you shortcuts for menu items. For example, to save your drawing, click the Save button—which shows a diskette icon—in the top toolbar.

At left, as you already know, is the Shapes window. Currently, it's showing the Organization Chart template, which has the following stencils (as you can see in the figure): Borders and Titles, Backgrounds, and Organization Chart Shapes. The shapes in the stencils are called master shapes—the ones that appear on the drawing are simply called shapes. Master shapes don't go anywhere; they stay on the stencils.

The rest of the window is taken up by the drawing window, which contains the drawing under construction (sometimes called a form). You can see rulers at the top and side of this window, and they're there to help you position shapes.

TIP

Want to turn off rulers or the grid on the drawing surface? Deselect the check mark in front of the View > Rulers or View > Grid menu items.

Let's look at these items—menus, toolbars, and so on—in more detail.

THE TOOLBARS

Visio comes stocked with more than a dozen toolbars—although only a few are displayed at once. How can you tell which toolbars are visible at any time? Right-click the toolbar area, and a list of toolbars will appear, as shown in Figure 1.7.

Figure 1.7
The toolbars.

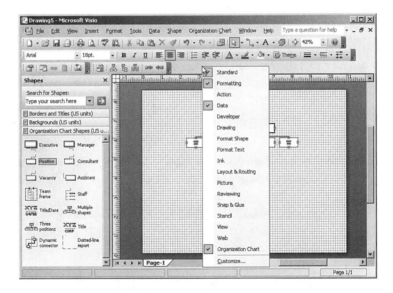

After you've right-clicked the toolbar, you can select which toolbars you want to display by selecting the toolbars you want. Toolbars with a check box next to their name will appear in the Visio window.

Each toolbar has buttons in it, and an easy way to determine what the buttons do is to let the mouse hover over a button. That action causes a tool tip to appear, as shown in Figure 1.8, giving a description of the button, just as you'll see in other Windows applications.

Figure 1.8
A tool tip in a toolbar.

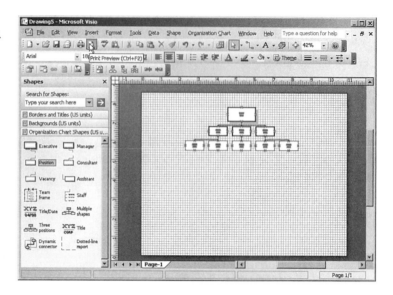

Want to turn off tool tips? Select Tools > Options and click the View tab. Then deselect the tool tips (called ScreenTips in Visio) you don't want to see, such as the Stencil Window ScreenTips item.

You can turn tool tips for toolbars off as well—right-click a toolbar and select Customize, then click the Options tag. Finally, deselect the Show ScreenTips on Toolbars check box.

CREATING A CUSTOM TOOLBAR

So how do you create your own toolbar? You can do that in Visio.

To create your own toolbar, select the View > Toolbars > Customize menu item, which displays the Customize dialog box shown in Figure 1.9.

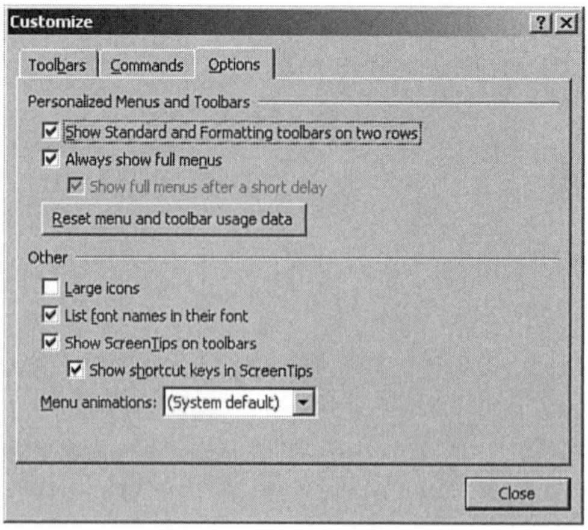

Figure 1.9
The Customize dialog.

Click the Toolbars tab, as shown in Figure 1.10.

Figure 1.10
The Toolbars tab of the Customize toolbar dialog.

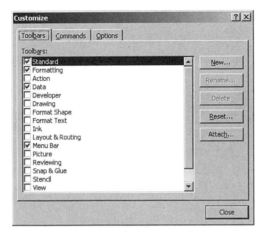

Now click the New button, opening the New Toolbar dialog. Accept the suggested name of "Custom 1" and click the OK button, creating the new Custom 1 toolbar, as shown in the bottom of the Customize dialog in Figure 1.11.

Figure 1.11
Creating a new toolbar.

Okay, you've created a new toolbar, and you can see it (it's small) next to the Customize dialog in Figure 1.11.

To add buttons to this new toolbar, right-click it and select the Customize menu item. Then click the Commands tab in the Customize dialog box.

The Customize dialog displays categories of commands at left, and the actual commands (buttons) in each category at right, as shown in Figure 1.12, in which the Windows and Help category is selected.

Figure 1.12
Adding buttons to the
new toolbar.

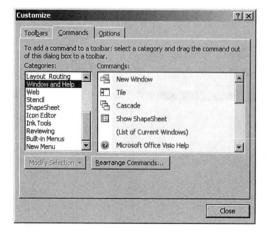

Drag a button onto the new toolbar, such as the Microsoft Office Visio Help button,
adding that button to the toolbar—as shown in Figure 1.12.

Finally, click the Close button in the Customize dialog, and drag your new toolbar onto the
toolbar space at the top of the Visio window, adding that toolbar to the others, as shown in
Figure 1.13 (the new toolbar has only a Help button on it, and appears after all the other
toolbars).

Figure 1.13
Adding the new tool-
bar to the toolbars
region.

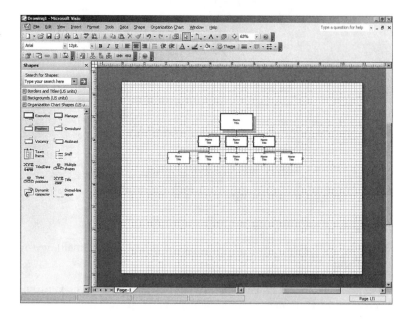

Congratulations—now you've created a new toolbar, customized it, and added it to the
other toolbars. Not bad.

MOVING TOOLBARS

As you've just seen, you can create new toolbars, customize them, and move them to the toolbar region of the Visio window. Can you do the reverse, and move toolbars away from the toolbar region?

You sure can—just drag a toolbar using the mouse. For example, you can drag the Organizational Chart toolbar from the toolbar region at the top of the Visio window and let the toolbar "float," as shown in Figure 1.14.

Figure 1.14
Floating a toolbar.

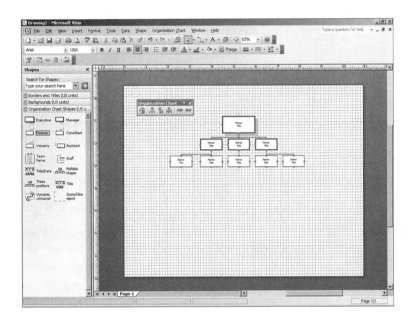

Floating toolbars like this give you the option of placing them in more convenient reach of the mouse. If you've got a lot of toolbar clicks to make, this is an option to consider.

However, we're not done yet—you can also dock a toolbar against any edge of the Visio window that you want to. All you have to do is drag a toolbar to the edge of the window that you want it to dock to, and the toolbar will connect itself to that edge.

You can see an example in Figure 1.15, where the Organization Chart toolbar has been docked to the right edge of the Visio window.

You can also drag the toolbars around in the toolbar area. Want the Formatting toolbar to come before the Standard toolbar? Just drag it where you want it.

As you can see, you can move toolbars around at will in Visio, making them float or dock as you like.

Figure 1.15
Docking a toolbar.

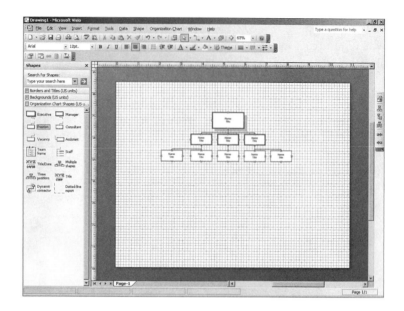

MODIFYING TOOLBARS

What if you just want to add a button to a toolbar, or delete one? That's simple in Visio.

Want to hide a toolbar? Visio has many of them, and they can cut down on your drawing space; so if you want to hide a toolbar, you can do it. Just right-click the toolbar area and deselect the check box next to the toolbar you want to hide.

For example, the Organization Chart toolbar has been removed from Visio in Figure 1.16 (compare to Figure 1.13).

Figure 1.16
Removing the
Organization Chart
toolbar.

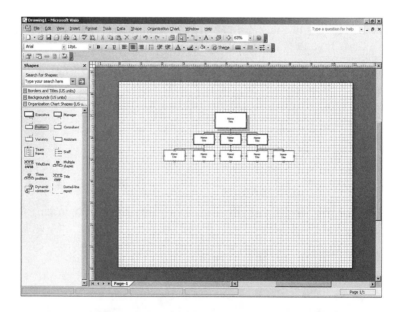

What about changing the buttons on a toolbar? You can do that too. Just right-click a toolbar and select the Customize option, opening the Customize dialog shown in Figure 1.17.

Figure 1.17
Customizing a
toolbar.

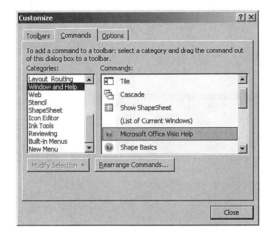

Select a category of toolbar button in the left pane of this dialog, and a button in the right pane of the dialog. For example, the Microsoft Office Visio Help button is selected in Figure 1.17.

Then just drag the new button to the toolbar you want. For example, you can see the Microsoft Office Visio Help button in the Organization Chart toolbar shown in Figure 1.18.

Figure 1.18
Adding a button to
a toolbar.

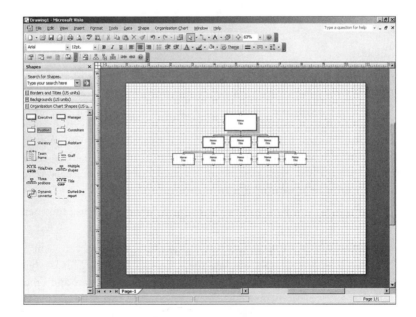

Okay, you've added a button to a toolbar. But what if you now decide that you don't actually want that button there? You can remove buttons from toolbars easily.

To delete a button from a toolbar, just right-click the toolbar, and select Customize. Then simply drag the button you want to remove off the toolbar, and it will be deleted.

For example, you can see the Organization Chart toolbar restored, without the Help button, in Figure 1.19.

Figure 1.19
Deleting a button from a toolbar.

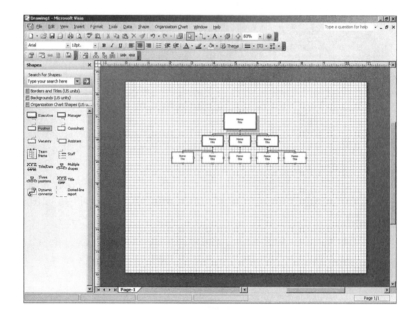

THE MENUS

Visio comes provided with a good set of menus; for example, you can see the Visio File menu in Figure 1.20.

Here's an overview of the Visio menus and the items they contain:

- **File**—The standard File menu, used for opening and saving files. Use the File > New > Getting Started item to get to the Getting Started page. You can also select any shape using the File > Shape submenu, which has submenus for each template category. You can also print from the File menu.

- **Edit**—The standard Edit menu. In Visio, you can also use this menu to copy shapes and entire drawings.

- **View**—The View menu lets you decide which windows you want to see. Already selected are the Shapes window, the Rulers, and so on. This is where you'll see action when it comes time to look at the Pan and Zoom window and others.

Figure 1.20
The Visio File menu.

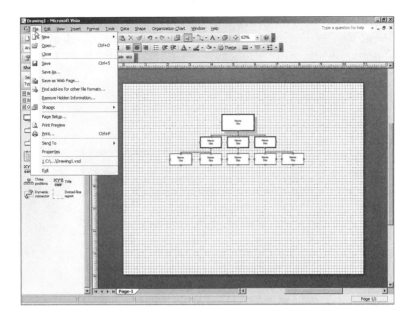

- **Insert**—You use this menu to insert new objects into the current drawing, such as a new page (drawings can be multipage). You can also insert clip art and text boxes (more on text boxes coming up later in the book).

- **Format**—The Format menu lets you set the format of text, lines, corner rounding, and other aspects of shapes.

- **Tools**—The Tools menu contains tools for working with shapes and the drawing. You can set Visio's color palette, rulers, and grids. There are also other standard items, such as Spelling, Customize, and Options.

- **Data**—This menu appears only in the Professional edition, and it's all about importing data from other sources into your Visio drawing. The Data > Link Data to Shapes item opens the Data Selector Wizard, which lets you import data from a variety of sources.

- **Shape**—This is the menu that handles the shapes in your drawing. You can group, flip, rotate, and align shapes using this menu. You can also fragment and intersect shapes using this menu.

- **Window**—This is the standard Windows window menu, which lets you move between windows. In Visio, each drawing has its own window, so you can navigate between drawings using this menu.

- **Help**—The Help menu offers, as you can guess, help. There are many different items in this menu—the one you'll want most often is Help > Microsoft Office Visio Help.

In addition, other menus may appear from time to time, depending on what you're doing in Visio. For example, you can see the Organization Chart menu in Figure 1.6.

There are plenty of menu items in each menu, which brings up another topic: You can customize the menus in another way—by having Visio display a short version of each menu, showing only the most-used menu items at first, and displaying a double arrowhead to let you select the full menu.

To use short menus, select the Tools > Customize menu item, opening the now-familiar Customize dialog, shown in Figure 1.21.

Figure 1.21
Customizing menus.

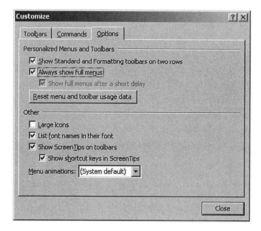

Click the Options tab in the Customize dialog, as shown in Figure 1.21. Then deselect the Always Show Full Menus check box.

This will make Visio display short menus, as shown in Figure 1.22, where you see the short form of the Edit menu.

Figure 1.22
A short version of the Edit menu.

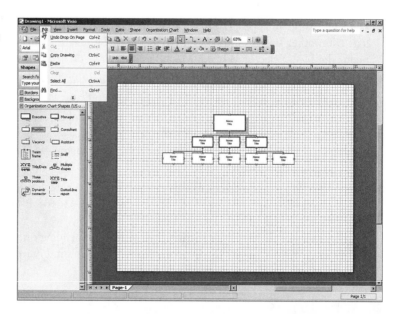

Note that this short form of the menu displays only the most commonly used menu items, as well as a double-headed arrow at the bottom of the menu. Selecting that double-headed arrow will make Visio display the full version of the menu.

In other words, you can shorten the menus if you like, getting the full version when needed. Personally, I don't find any real reason to shorten the menus—the items I want are always hidden.

THE DRAWING WINDOW

The drawing window shows the drawing under design. It appears at the right in Figure 1.23.

Figure 1.23
The drawing surface in Visio.

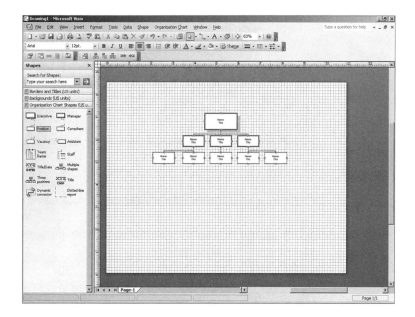

This drawing window is the subject of much discussion in this book, as you can imagine.

The drawing surface is where you drag your shapes to, and you can see various business organization shapes on the drawing surface in Figure 1.23. The drawing surface is customizable in several ways. For example, if you don't need a grid to align your shapes to (we'll see how to set the scale of that grid later), you can remove the grid. To do that, deselect the check mark in front of the View > Grid menu item. Simple. You can see the results in Figure 1.24.

The rulers you see at top and at left in the drawing window give you an idea of shape placement for printing purposes. You can also remove the rulers if you don't want them by deselecting the View > Rulers menu item. Figure 1.25 shows the rulers are gone.

Figure 1.24
The result of having removed gridlines from the drawing surface.

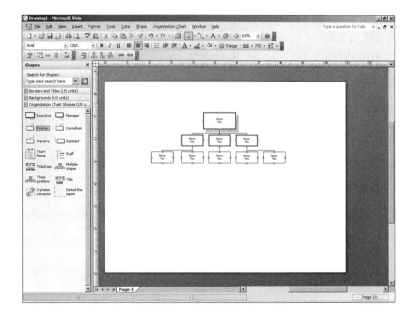

Figure 1.25
Removing rulers from the drawing surface.

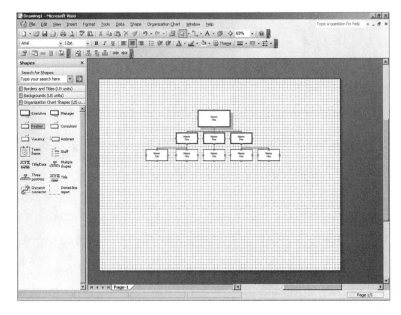

Note also the page tabs at the bottom of the drawing surface. Drawings can be multipage, and the tabs let you move from page to page. You're going to see multipage drawings later in this book.

1

TIP

When you drag shapes around the drawing surface, you might want to restrict their movement to vertical or horizontal to make aligning them with other shapes easier (you can also use the items in the Shape menu to align shapes). To make sure that shapes move in only pure vertical or horizontal directions, hold down the Shift key as you drag the shape.

There are all kinds of additional windows you're going to see that work with the drawing window, and those additional windows are accessed through the View menu.

For example, say that you're working with a large drawing, and not all of it is visible at once in the drawing window. In that case, you might want to move your viewpoint around in the drawing window, a process known as *panning*. Alternatively, you might want to zoom in on part of a drawing to get more detail—just called *zooming* in Visio.

To perform both these operations, you can use the Pan & Zoom window in Visio, which you open with the View > Pan & Zoom Window menu item. Selecting that item opens the Pan & Zoom window, shown in Figure 1.26.

Figure 1.26
The Pan & Zoom window.

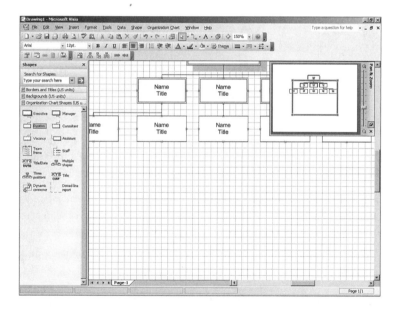

To pan and zoom, you just use the mouse and the scale in this window. For example, to zoom in, you move the scale "thumb" (the small draggable handle in the scale) upward. You can see a zoomed-in version of the drawing under design in Figure 1.26.

To close the Pan & Zoom window, you just click the × in that window. Note also the thumbtack icon in that window. You can use that icon to enable "auto-hide" of that window, as well as the other windows you can display in the drawing window (such as the Shape Data window, the Size & Position window—all coming up later in this book).

When you click the thumbtack icon (AutoHide), that collapses the window when it is not in use against the current edge of the drawing window that it's docked to. That moves the window out of the way for you, collapsing it to a tab, as shown in Figure 1.27. The thumbtack is a toggle that turns the AutoHide feature for that window on or off. It is a feature that is available in a number of other windows.

Figure 1.27
Hiding the Pan &
Zoom window.

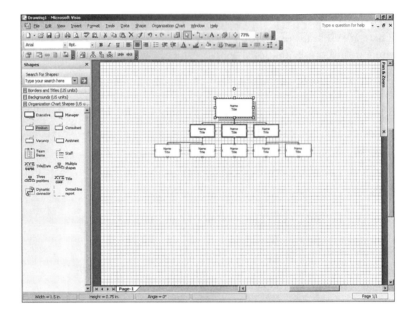

To expand the Pan & Zoom window again, just let the mouse ride over the collapsed tab. That's an easy way of configuring your workspace—docking additional windows in the drawing window and collapsing/expanding them as needed.

You can also zoom a drawing using the View menu. To do that, open the View > Zoom submenu, shown in Figure 1.28. When that submenu is open, you can select a zoom factor—100%, 150%, and so on—to zoom in to the drawing window.

More on the subwindows you can use in the drawing window is coming up when we start discussing the details of inserting shapes into a drawing.

Here's a useful subwindow for the drawing window: the Size & Position window. When you drag shapes around the drawing surface, it's hard to know exactly where you're positioning them. You can use the Size & Position window to tell you where they are or to set a specific position, width, height, or angle.

The default scale used in the drawing window is in inches. To see where a particular shape is placed in the drawing window, select that shape and then select the View > Size & Position menu item to display the Size & Position subwindow in the drawing window, as shown in Figure 1.29.

Figure 1.28
Zooming using the
View menu.

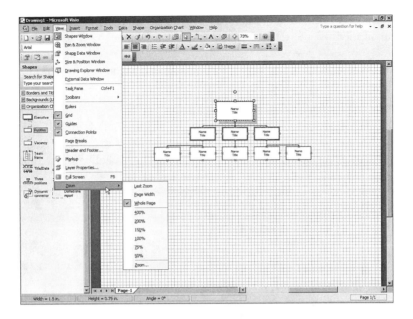

Figure 1.29
The Size & Position
subwindow.

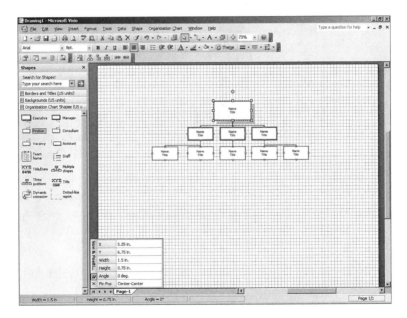

You can see the precise position of the selected shape in the Size & Position window. As shown in Figure 1.29, the upper-left point of the selected shape (the top box in the organization chart) is at 5.25 inches horizontally and 6.75 inches vertically. Its width is 1.5 inches, and its height is 0.75 inches. When position becomes important, that kind of data can be very helpful. And in fact, when you print drawings, you can set up a scale, such as 1 inch equals one foot, or 0.1 inch equals one mile.

Having said that, it's important to know that Visio isn't a CAD (computer-aided design) application. It's not really designed for the micro precision that CAD applications can give you. Visio will give you a reasonable amount of accuracy, but it's not really designed to give you industrial-level precision; for that, you need a true CAD application.

THE SHAPES WINDOW

You're going to read a great deal about the Shapes window in this book. That's where most of the action is in Visio. The Shapes window displays the current template of stencils, and you can see an example displaying the Part & Assembly Drawing template in Figure 1.30.

Figure 1.30
The Shapes window.

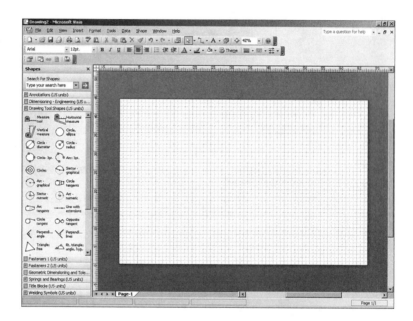

As you know, templates are collections of stencils, which are themselves collections of shapes. The stencils are displayed using tabs, as you can see in the Shapes window at left in Figure 1.30, and clicking a tab displays the matching stencil. And there can be many stencils in a template, as shown in Figure 1.30.

Is it possible to hide the Shapes window? Yes it is, although it's hard to see why you'd want to. To close the Shapes window, you can click the × in its upper-right corner. Want it back? To open the Shapes window again (or to open most windows you have closed inadvertently), use the View menu. In this case, choose the View > Shapes Window menu item. This action restores the Shapes window.

The Shapes window gives you many options for working with shapes. For example, if you have a set of favorite shapes, you can store them in a special stencil named Favorites.

Here's how it works. First, select the shape that is your favorite in the Shapes window, and right-click it, and open the context menu that appears.

Select the Add to My Shapes menu item, which opens a submenu. Select the Favorites menu item in that submenu to add your selected shape to the Favorites stencil.

That's fine—you've added your favorite shape to the Favorites stencil. Now how do you access the Favorites stencil when you want to?

You can open the Favorites stencil by selecting the Shapes > My Shapes > Favorites menu item. Selecting that menu item opens the Favorites stencil in the Shapes window, in addition to the stencils already there, as shown in Figure 1.31. Very cool.

Figure 1.31
The Favorites stencil.

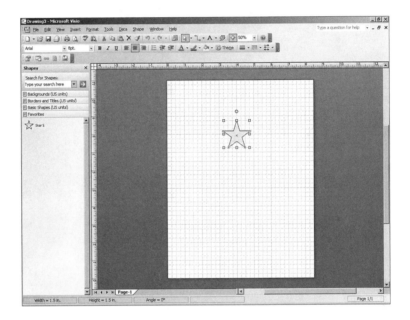

So in this way, you're already getting the idea that Visio lets you manage your own shapes and stencils. If you want to close the Favorites stencil, just right-click its tab and select the Close menu item.

Being able to organize your favorite shapes into a Favorites stencil is very powerful, and acts as a shortcut—now your favorite shapes will always be available to you.

GETTING HELP

Visio is particularly good at offering help. You'll often see help buttons in dialog boxes, such as the one at the lower left in the Tools > Options dialog shown in Figure 1.32.

Clicking that help button brings up context-sensitive help—that is, help about the Options dialog in this case, as you can see in Figure 1.33.

Figure 1.32
A context help
button.

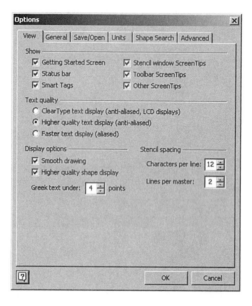

Figure 1.33
Context-sensitive
help.

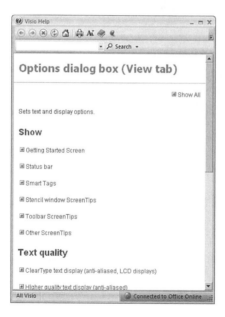

You'll find help buttons like the one in the Options dialog studded throughout Visio.

If you want more general help, select the Help > Microsoft Office Visio Help menu item, opening the Visio Help dialog shown in Figure 1.34.

Figure 1.34
The general Help dialog.

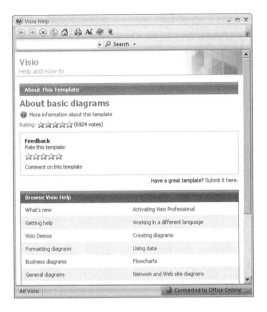

The general Help dialog gives you a Browse Visio Help section, which isn't usually of too much help if you're looking for help on a specific topic. Instead, you can click the book icon in this dialog's toolbar to open Help's Table of Contents, as shown in Figure 1.35.

Figure 1.35
The Help Table of Contents.

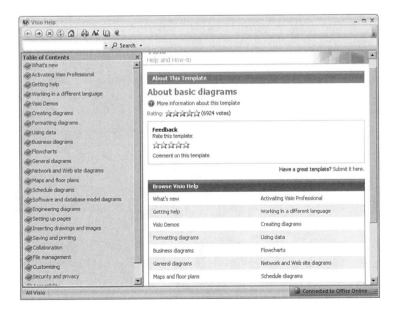

This is more like it—now you can get help on many specific topics—engineering diagrams, schedule diagrams, file management, and the like.

You can also search for help on a particular topic—just enter the term you're searching for, such as "my shapes," into the search box and click the Search button. That will bring up a series of matches, as shown in Figure 1.36.

Figure 1.36
Searching for a term.

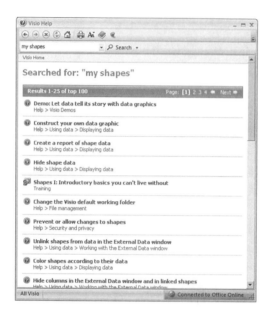

There's another way of getting help—you can type questions into Visio's question box, which appears at the upper right in the Visio window. For example, you can see the question "What are stencils?" entered into the question box at the upper right in Figure 1.37.

Figure 1.37
The question box.

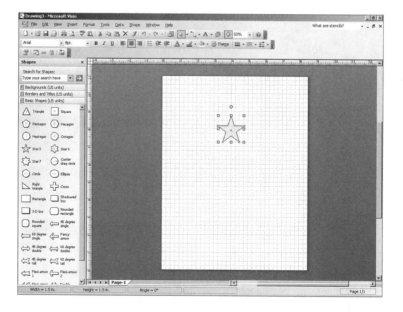

When you press Enter, Visio tries to figure out your question, and displays the topics it found, as shown in Figure 1.38.

Figure 1.38
The answer to a question.

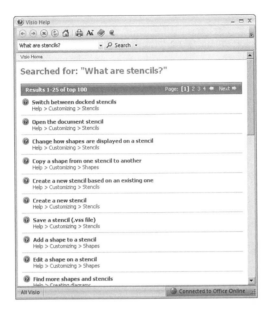

That's quite an asset—the ability to ask a natural language question and get an answer. As you can see, Visio tries hard when it comes to providing help.

Okay, that's the basics. Now let's get started with the process of creating and saving Visio drawings.

CREATING A DRAWING THE USUAL WAY

There are various ways of creating drawings in Visio, and we'll start with the normal, usual way:

1. Start by opening Visio if it's not already open. This displays the Getting Started page by default, with the Template Categories displayed at left, as shown in Figure 1.1.

2. Click a template category to select it. This displays the templates in that category in the center of the Visio window.

3. Double-click a template. This creates a drawing using that template. If you want to set the units to other than US units—the only other option is Metric—make that selection at the right in Visio before double-clicking the template you want to use.

That's the process in general. Some templates, such as the Calendar template, require a little initialization. For example, the Calendar template asks you for the date of the calendar.

There are a few more things that happen automatically here that you should know about. First, Visio chooses the default pointing tool for you—the arrow mouse cursor. There are other options you'll get familiar with in this book, such as the Multiple Select and Area Select tools.

Visio also sets up the drawing surface to a default 8 1/2×11 inches, sets the drawing style to portrait (as opposed to laying the drawing on its side, which would be a landscape-oriented drawing), and sets the printing scale to 1:1. Visio also selects an appropriate font, color, and point size.

HANDLING STENCILS

When you select a template category and then a template, Visio opens the stencils in that template for use in your drawing. There are many ways of handling stencils in Visio, and we'll discuss them here.

ARRANGING STENCILS

When you open a template, the stencils in that template appear in the Shapes window. Those stencils are arranged using tabs, and when you click those tabs, the stencils move around so that the one you selected is displayed. You can see an example in Figure 1.39, where the Borders and Titles stencil was clicked, which sent the Basic Shapes stencil to the bottom of the Shapes window.

Figure 1.39
Arranging a stencil window.

You can also treat the stencils as separate windows, which means that you can dock them wherever you want them. To dock a stencil window in the drawing window, for example, all you have to do is to drag the stencil you want to the drawing window, as shown in Figure 1.40. You can dock the stencil against any edge in the drawing window.

Figure 1.40
Docking a stencil window.

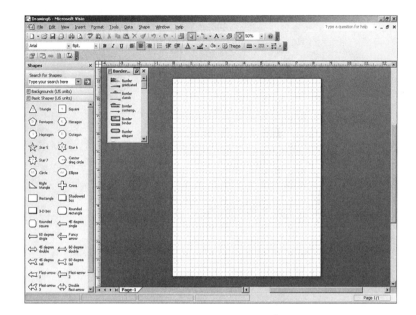

Besides docking a stencil window, you can just let it float free, as its own window.

In fact, you can dock the whole Shapes window wherever you want it. Take a look at Figure 1.41, for example, in which the Shapes window has been moved to the right side of Visio. Cool.

CLOSING STENCILS

You can also close stencils at any time. There are no × buttons in stencils, but closing them is easy. Just right-click the stencil tab (that's its title bar) and select Close.

Close a stencil by mistake? Take a look at the next section to see how to reopen it.

OPENING STENCILS

Visio does its best to present useful stencils in its templates, but there are going to be many times when you'll want a stencil that is part of another template. For example, you might be drawing an office layout, and have an octagonal table to add. There are no octagonal tables in the Office Layout template—but there is an octagon shape in the Basic Shapes stencil, which is part of the Basic Diagram template, part of the General category.

Figure 1.41
Docking the Shapes window.

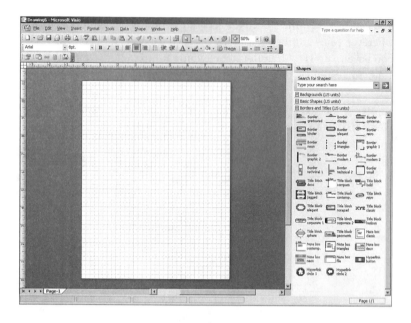

So how do you add a stencil to the Shapes window? How would you, for example, add the Basic Shapes stencil to the Shapes window when you're working with the Office Layout template? You follow these steps:

1. Select File > Shapes. This opens a submenu of the template categories, as shown in Figure 1.42.

Figure 1.42
Selecting a stencil.

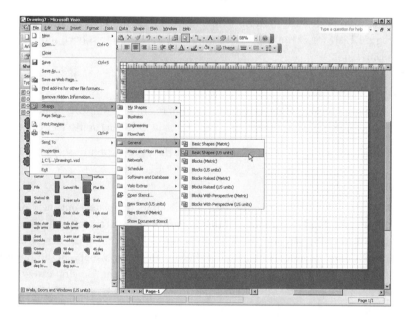

2. Open the template category submenu that your stencil is in, which is General here.

3. Doing so opens the stencils in the General template, including the one you want, the Basic Shapes stencil. Select that stencil, and it's added to the stack of stencils in the Shapes window, as shown in Figure 1.43.

Figure 1.43
Using a new stencil.

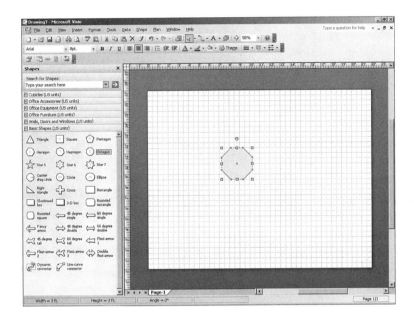

Now you can use the new stencil to draw shapes with, just as you could use the stencils already in the template. For example, as you can see in Figure 1.43, we're drawing an octagonal table using the Basics Shapes stencil inside the Office Layout template. Nice.

CHOOSING A MOUSE POINTER

Before working with shapes, you can choose an appropriate mouse pointer. You might think that the default mouse pointer, which you've already worked with, might just be called "the default mouse pointer," but Visio has another name for it: the "Area Select" pointer. And there are other mouse pointers you can choose—but note that they all look the same, just the usual mouse-pointer arrow.

You choose a mouse pointer from a drop-down list in the Formatting toolbar, as shown in Figure 1.44.

The Area Select pointer—that is, the default pointer—lets you select individual shapes by clicking on them—and also lets you select multiple shapes by dragging a rectangle around them, as shown in Figure 1.45. Note that when you're dragging a rectangle to select multiple shapes, the mouse pointer turns into a plus (+) sign.

Figure 1.44
Choosing a mouse pointer.

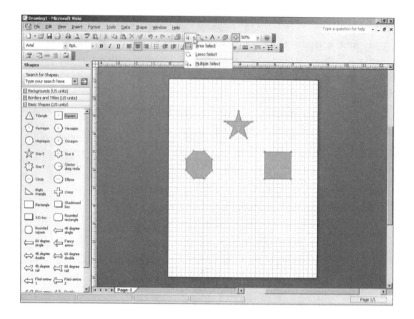

Figure 1.45
Making a selection with the Area Select mouse pointer.

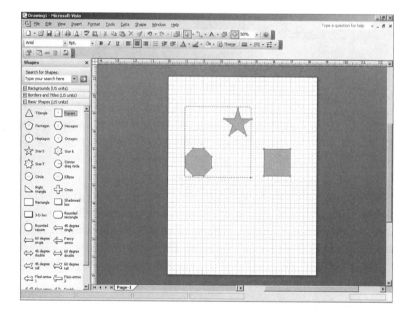

When you select multiple shapes, you can work with them together, all at once. For example, if you wanted to move multiple shapes at once, you would select them all and then drag them to their new location.

The Lasso Select mouse pointer lets you draw, lasso-like, and select shapes that way, which is useful if you don't want to select all the shapes within a rectangle. You can see the Lasso Select pointer at work in Figure 1.46.

Figure 1.46
Making a selection with the Lasso Select mouse pointer.

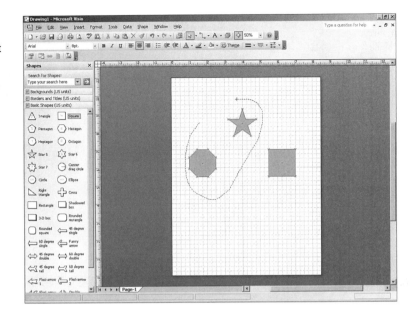

The Lasso Select pointer is a good one when you have a dense drawing in which there are all kinds of shapes, and you don't want to select shapes using a rectangle because you want to omit some shapes that would otherwise be selected that way.

The Multiple Select option gives you even more freedom—when you use this option, you can select multiple shapes just by clicking them. That is, if you want to select five shapes in different locations in your drawing, just click them, one after the other. That action selects just those shapes.

The Multiple Select option modifies the two other types of pointers (the Area Select pointer and the Lasso Select pointer). It's an on/off option—you have to select it or deselect it by clicking this option in the drop-down pointer selection box.

You can see the Multiple Select option at work in Figure 1.47, in which it's been used to select two shapes, the octagon and the square, with the Area Select pointer. Visio draws a rectangle enclosing those two shapes—and the rectangle also encloses the star in the middle. However, the star is not selected—only those shapes with a red (black in the figure) border are selected.

You can verify this by dragging the selected shapes to a new location, as shown in Figure 1.48. Only the shapes actually selected are dragged—when you release the mouse pointer, they will move to their new location, and the star will stay where it is.

Figure 1.47
Making a selection
with the Multiple
Select mouse pointer.

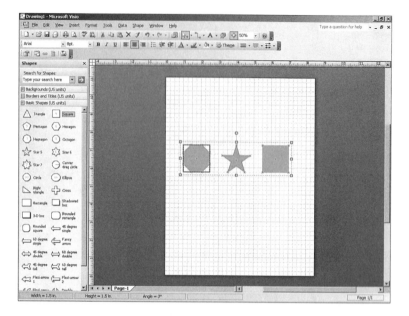

Figure 1.48
Dragging a selection
with the Multiple
Select mouse pointer.

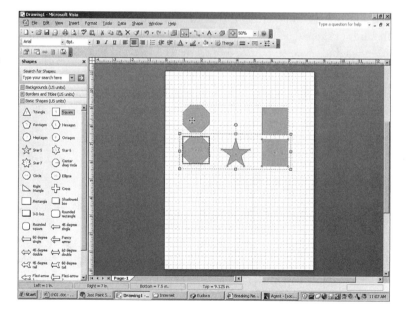

HANDLING SHAPES

Visio drawings are composed of shapes and connections between those shapes. They're
what makes Visio Visio—without shapes, you'd have nothing in your drawings. There's a lot
to cover about handling shapes in this book, and we're going to start here, in this first chapter, with the essential skills you need to know.

ADDING SHAPES

You've already seen the basics of adding shapes to drawings. You move the mouse pointer over a shape in a stencil, press the left mouse button, and then drag that shape onto the drawing surface.

As you drag the shape over the drawing surface, Visio displays that shape in outline. You drop the outline where you want it in the drawing, and that outline is replaced with the shape itself. The shape in the stencil—the master shape—is not affected no matter how many times you drag it onto the drawing surface.

When you add a shape to the drawing surface, it's selected, and you can resize or rotate it, as covered later in this section.

There's another way of getting shapes from a stencil to the drawing surface: copy and paste. You can right-click a shape in a stencil and select the Copy item from its context menu. Then you right-click the drawing surface and select Paste from the context menu that appears. The shape is then displayed at the location where you right-clicked the drawing surface.

Here's another trick: You can select multiple shapes from a stencil at the same time. You do that typically when you're starting a new drawing, and you know the shapes you want to use. To select multiple shapes in a stencil at the same time, hold down the Shift key as you click those shapes. They will be selected (turning a darker color). Then drag any one of those shapes onto the drawing surface, and all the shapes will follow.

When you drop the multiple shape selection onto the drawing surface, those shapes will appear stacked, as shown in Figure 1.49. They're ready for your use in your drawing—all you have to do is to drag them into position.

Figure 1.49
Dragging multiple shapes from a stencil to the drawing surface.

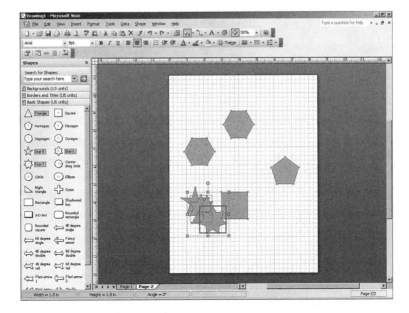

RESIZING SHAPES

When you drag a shape onto the drawing surface in Visio, it appears at a standard size. For example, if you drag a five-pointed star from the Basic Shapes stencil to the drawing surface, that star will appear with its standard size on the drawing surface.

That's fine if that size works for you, but of course you can resize the shape if its current size isn't right. You do that with the *sizing handles* that appear around the shape when you select it. Sizing handles are those eight little green boxes that appear in a rectangle around a selected shape. And you can use them to resize shapes.

All you have to do to resize a shape is to let the mouse pointer rest on a sizing handle, and the cursor will change to a double-headed arrow, as shown at the lower right in the selected star in Figure 1.50 (note that in addition to the eight sizing handles, there's a rotation handle at the top of the selected figure).

To resize the star, just drag a sizing handle. Simple.

Figure 1.50
Using sizing handles.

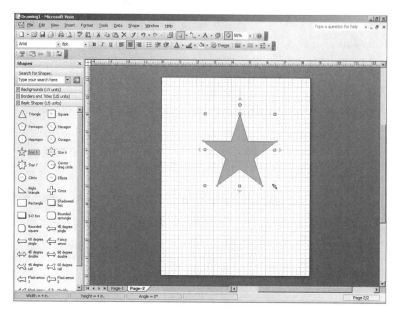

ROTATING SHAPES

You can also use rotation handles to rotate shapes. When you select a shape in Visio, eight sizing handles appear—as does one rotation handle. The rotation handle appears at the top of the selected shape, above the sizing handles. The sizing handles appear as green boxes, and the rotation handle appears as a green circle.

You can drag that rotation handle around in a circle, and the selected shape will rotate accordingly. You can see an example in Figure 1.51, in which the user is rotating the star figure.

Figure 1.51
Using rotation handles.

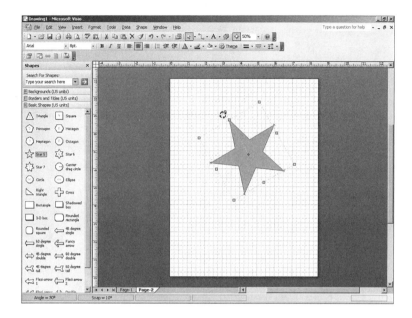

By default, shapes rotate in 15° increments. For finer rotation, move the mouse further from the shapes rotation point as you rotate. You can also use items in the Shape menu to rotate shapes in 90° increments. To do that, you use items in the Shape > Rotate or Flip submenu. Here are the menu items that appear when you select Shape > Rotate or Flip:

- Rotate Right
- Rotate Left
- Flip Right
- Flip Right

DELETING SHAPES

You can also delete shapes from drawings. Just select the shape, as shown in Figure 1.52.

Then press the Delete key to delete the shape and it's gone, as shown in Figure 1.53.

You can also delete a shape by selecting it and then selecting Edit > Cut, or by right-clicking a shape and selecting Cut from the context menu that appears.

Figure 1.52
A selected shape.

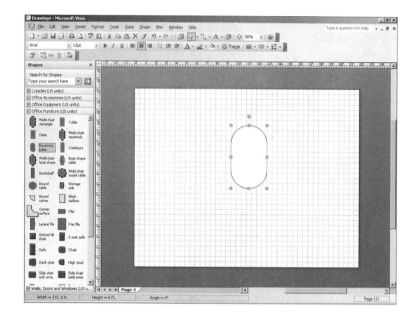

Figure 1.53
The shape has been deleted.

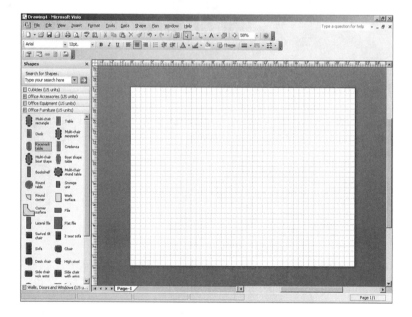

Some shapes have more involved behavior when you delete them. For example, take a look at the multi-chair round table shape in Figure 1.54.

This shape is actually a composite of table and chairs, as you can see if you click the table and then press the Delete key. The result is that you end up with only the chairs, as shown in Figure 1.55.

Figure 1.54
A multi-chair round table.

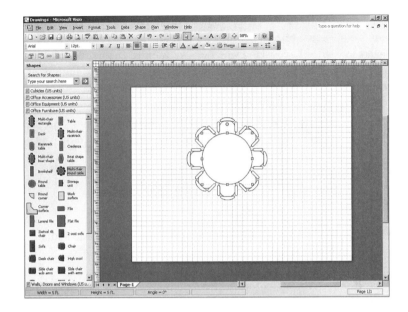

Figure 1.55
Multi-chairs.

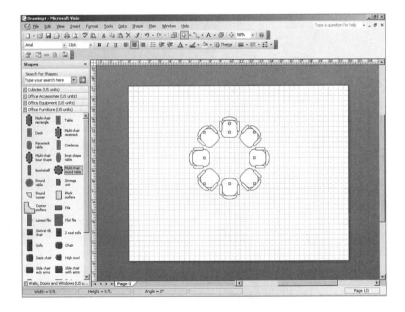

SEARCHING FOR SHAPES

You can also search for shapes in Visio. There are so many shapes in so many stencils in so many templates that being able to search for shapes by name is practically essential.

How do you search for a shape? You use the search box at the top of the Shapes window. This search box has the label Search for Shapes, as shown in Figure 1.55. Just type your search term into that box and click the button with the right arrow to search.

1

For example, you can search for shapes with the term "star" in their names by entering "star" in the search box. When you do that for the first time, you may see the dialog that appears in Figure 1.56, asking whether you want to enable the Indexing Service on your machine, which helps search files faster. Click the Yes or No button, depending on your decision.

Figure 1.56
Indexing your search.

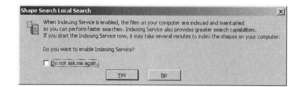

When the search is complete, a new stencil is created with the matches to your search term, as shown in Figure 1.57.

Figure 1.57
Finding star shapes.

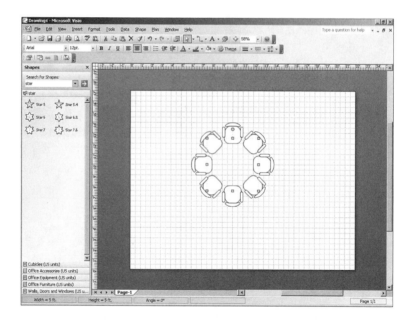

HANDLING DRAWINGS

There's a great deal of support in Visio at the drawing level as well, and you'll get an overview in this, the foundation chapter. To create new drawings, you can use the File > Getting Started item and then select a template category, followed by a template. Or you can select File > Template Category > Template directly. After you've got your new page, you can zoom in, use multiple pages, save drawings, and do much more.

ZOOMING IN

As your diagrams get more complex, the need to zoom in on parts of those diagrams increases. There are several ways to handle zooming in your drawing, including the Pan & Zoom window, which you've already seen briefly.

The first way to zoom a drawing is to use the Zoom drop-down box, shown in Figure 1.58. This box appears in the toolbar.

Figure 1.58
The Zoom drop-down box.

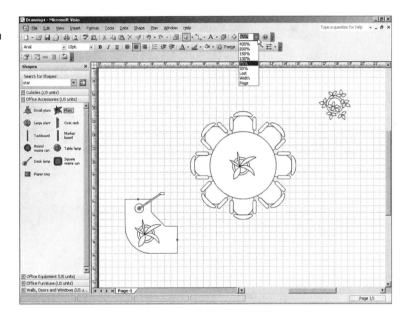

This box offers the following preset zoom levels:

- **400%:** Zoom to 400%.
- **200%:** Zoom to 200%.
- **150%:** Zoom to 150%.
- **100%:** Zoom to 100%.
- **75%:** Zoom to 75%.
- **50%:** Zoom to 50%.
- **Last:** Use the last zoom setting.
- **Width:** Display the width of the page.
- **Page:** Display the entire page.

You can see a drawing zoomed to 75% in Figure 1.58. The Zoom box is a painless way to zoom drawings—but do you have to be satisfied with the preset values?

No, you don't—you can type your own value (as a percentage) into the Zoom box and press Enter. When you do, the drawing is zoomed to your value. Cool. You can see an example in Figure 1.59, in which a drawing has been zoomed to 60%.

Figure 1.59
Zooming to 60%.

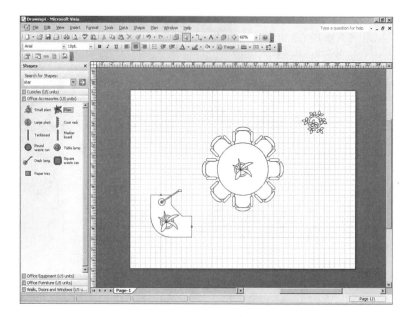

You can also zoom using the Zoom menu item, View > Zoom. Select that menu item, and you'll get the same preset values as with the toolbar Zoom box—as well as a Zoom menu item that you can use to type your own custom zoom value into.

Another way to zoom, and possibly the most convenient, is to hold down the Ctrl key and use the wheel on your mouse (if your mouse has a wheel, that is). Scrolling forward (roll the wheel away from you) zooms in; scrolling backward (roll the wheel toward you) zooms out.

And if you hold down both the Ctrl and the Shift keys, the mouse pointer turns into a magnifying glass. Then you can do one of the following:

- Click the left mouse button to enlarge the view.
- Click the right mouse button to reduce the view.
- Click the left mouse button and drag. The resulting magnification depends on the size of the box that you create as you drag—the smaller the box, the greater the magnification.

You can also use the Pan & Zoom window, shown in Figure 1.60. The rectangle inside the Pan & Zoom window is red, and it shows the visible part of the page.

To use the Pan & Zoom window, select View > Pan & Zoom Window, which makes that window appear.

Figure 1.60
Using the Pan &
Zoom window.

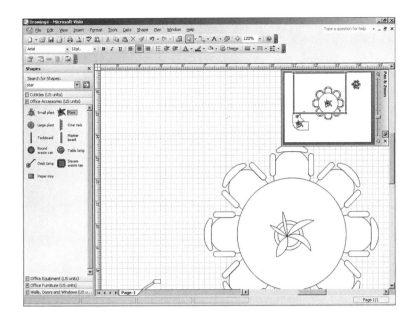

To zoom in on specific areas of the drawing, move the mouse pointer over the red rectangle until the mouse pointer turns into a four-headed arrow. Drag the red rectangle to wherever you want to view in the drawing and release the mouse pointer. You can also click outside the red rectangle, which will cause Visio to create a new red rectangle centered on the location you've clicked.

If you want to, you can zoom in or out with the red rectangle as well. All you need to do is move the mouse pointer to an edge or corner of the red rectangle until the mouse pointer becomes a two-headed arrow. Then press the mouse button and drag the mouse to resize the view by resizing the red rectangle.

When you modify or resize the red rectangle, Visio will shift your view of the drawing to match the area enclosed by the red rectangle.

HANDLING MULTIPLE PAGES

As you're going to see in this book, drawings can extend to several pages. How do you create and add a new page to a drawing? You can right-click the page tab (currently reading Page-1 at the bottom left of the drawing window in Figure 1.60) and select the Insert Page context menu item.

Doing so opens the Page Setup dialog box, which you're going to see more about later, shown in Figure 1.61.

Figure 1.61
Creating a new page.

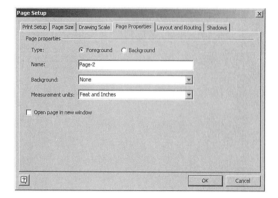

This dialog lets you configure the new page, including its printing properties and scale. For now, accept the defaults and click OK. That creates the second page of the drawing, and adds a new tab with the caption Page-2.

Now you can use the tabs to navigate between the pages. More on multipage drawings is coming up when we discuss printing drawings.

USING THE DRAWING EXPLORER

There's a tool you should know about when it comes to working with drawings: the Drawing Explorer. This tool is the Visio database for your entire drawing, even if it has multiple pages.

The Drawing Explorer keeps track of the number of pages, the shapes used in each drawing, the subshapes used in each shape, the layers in a drawing (drawings can be divided into layers, as you're going to see—and that's a good idea when you have a complex drawing and want to print out only certain layers, such as the pipes for the plumbers, circuits for the electricians, and so on), the styles and fill patterns used in the drawing, and more.

You can open the Drawing Explorer using the View > Drawing Explorer Window. That window is shown in Figure 1.62.

The Drawing Explorer displays its data in hierarchical form, much as the Windows Explorer does. You can see a set of nodes corresponding to all the objects in your drawing. There's a surprising amount of information here, showing the subobjects that make up each shape, for example.

You can right-click each object in the Drawing Explorer to get a context menu showing you the options connected with that object. You can configure or delete most of the objects, insert pages, delete shapes, examine and modify shape data, and adjust the layer the object appears on, all with the Drawing Explorer.

You can do most of what you can do with the Drawing Explorer by right-clicking objects in the drawing window itself. However, these capabilities have all been collected into one place in the Drawing Explorer.

Figure 1.62
The Drawing
Explorer.

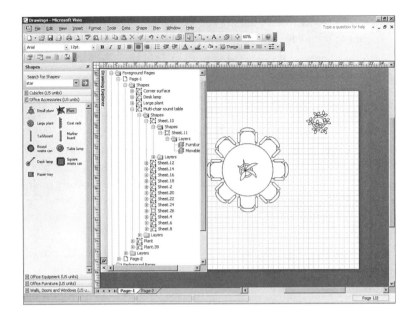

SAVING DRAWINGS

You've put in a lot of work on your drawing—hours and hours. The last thing you want is to lose all that, so it's time to take a look at saving that drawing.

Saving a drawing is simplicity itself in Visio. Just follow these steps:

1. Choose File > Save As. This selection opens the Save As dialog shown in Figure 1.63. If this is the first time you've saved the drawing, selecting File > Save or clicking the diskette icon in the toolbar will also open the Save As dialog.

Figure 1.63
The Save As dialog.

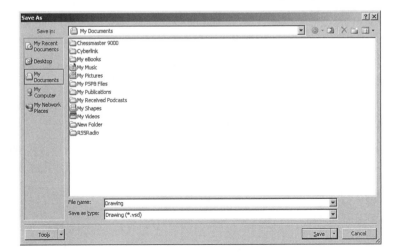

2. Select a folder to save the drawing in. Double-click folder icons to open them and navigate to the folder you want to store the drawing in.

3. Enter the name of the drawing in the File Name text box. There's no need to enter the extension, which is .vsd for Visio drawings. That extension will be filled in automatically, depending on the setting in the Save as Type box.

4. Select a file type in the Save as Type box. The default file type is .vsd for Visio drawings. If you're saving a drawing (as opposed to, say, a stencil), leave the type set to .vsd.

5. Click Save. Clicking the Save button saves the drawing.

After you've saved a drawing, you can save it again (after working on it, for example) by selecting File > Save, clicking the diskette icon in the toolbar, or typing Ctrl+S.

You can save files in many formats in Visio; here's the list:

- Drawing
- Stencil
- Template
- XML drawing
- XML stencil
- Visio 2002 drawing
- Visio 2002 stencil
- Visio 2002 template
- Scalable Vector Graphics (SVG)
- Scalable Vector Graphics compressed
- XML Paper Specification (XPS)
- AutoCAD drawing
- AutoCAD interchange
- Web page
- Compressed Enhanced Metafile (EMZ)
- Enhanced Metafile (EMF)
- Graphics Interchange Format (GIF)
- JPEG file
- Portable Network Graphics (PNG)
- Tagged Image File format (TIF)
- Windows Bitmap (BMP)
- Device Independent Bitmap (DIB)
- Windows Metafile (WMF)

You can also enable AutoSave, which will cause Visio to save your drawings automatically. To do that, select Tools > Options to open the Options dialog and click the Save/Open tab.

Next, enter a number of minutes in the Save AutoRecover Info Every box, as shown in Figure 1.64. Then click OK.

Now if Visio crashes, or your session is otherwise terminated, Visio will recover your drawing using the most recent AutoSave information.

Okay, now you've saved a drawing—congratulations. Now how do you open it back up?

Figure 1.64
Setting up AutoSave.

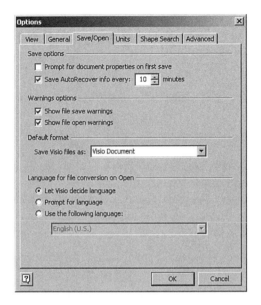

OPENING DRAWINGS

You can open drawings with the File > Open menu item, or with the folder icon in the tool-bar, which opens the Open dialog, as shown in Figure 1.65.

Figure 1.65
Opening a file.

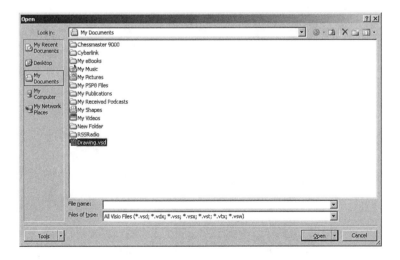

Navigate to and select the file to open. If you're opening a drawing from a previous version of Visio, Visio will update the drawing to the current version. You can also open more than one drawing at a time—if you do, you can access the various drawings using the Window menu. Any drawing you open or create remains open in Visio until you close it.

If you do open a drawing from a previous version of Visio, there can be issues with stencils that aren't supported anymore. Visio will inform you of the problem, and let you choose alternative stencils.

Note the Files of Type box at the bottom of the Open dialog; you can open all types of files: drawings, stencils, templates, workspaces, SVG, AutoCAD, GIF, JPG, TIF, BMP, WMF, and others.

SAVING A DRAWING AS A CUSTOM TEMPLATE

You can also save templates in Visio. You already know all about templates—a template can be viewed as a collection of settings that someone else can use in Visio. When corporations use Visio among many employees and analysts, they often use custom templates to preserve available stencils, page setups, printing settings, and so on. You're going to see more about how to create custom templates in this book, but here's a sneak peek for now:

1. Select File > Open to open a drawing. If you want to base your template on a current drawing, open that drawing.

2. Select File > Shapes to open any stencils you want as part of the custom template. Add the stencils you want to include in the drawing by opening them now.

3. Select a file type in the Save as Type box. The default file type is .vsd for Visio drawings. If you're saving a drawing (as opposed to, say, a stencil), leave the type set to .vsd.

4. Select File > Page Setup. This makes the Page Setup dialog appear, as shown in Figure 1.66.

Figure 1.66
The Page Setup dialog.

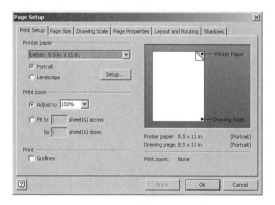

5. Select the Print Setup, Page Size, and Drawing Scale tabs to make changes. This allows you to customize the page setup for your template.

6. If you want to, create a background page. Drawings can have background pages, and if you create one now, your template will contain that page.

7. Select File > Save As. Now it's time to save your template.

8. Select the folder in which to save your template.

9. Enter a name for your template. You don't have to include an extension—that will be added in the next step.

10. Select Template in the Save as Type box. This will give your template file the extension `.vst`.

11. Click Save. This saves your template file.

Want to create a drawing from your new custom template? Use the File > New > New Drawing from Template menu item, and navigate to your `.vst` file.

CHAPTER 2

WORKING WITH SHAPES

In this chapter

HANDLING VISIO SHAPES

Shapes are the building blocks you use in your drawings: diagrams, graphs, charts of all kinds. They're the visual elements that make up Visio drawings. This chapter gives you the story on Visio shapes, including the complex shapes that have additional data connected with them, additional handles, and so on. This is central information for anyone wanting to master Visio.

You're also going to see how to print Visio drawings in this chapter. There's more to the subject than you might think—drawing scales and printing scales are different, for example. There's a lot of Visio coming up in this chapter, and we'll start by examining what's in a shape.

WHAT'S IN A SHAPE?

You're already familiar with some basic shapes in Visio, but there's a lot more going on. Microsoft calls Visio shapes SmartShapes, and there's something to that—shapes often have advanced behavior, or special data connected to them.

For example, take a look at the pie chart in Figure 2.1. You can't just draw a pie chart like any other shape such as a star or an octagon and then size it to fit your requirements—pie charts have slices that you need to size individually. You can right-click a pie chart and select the Set Number of Slices menu item or the Set Slice Sizes menu item to configure the pie.

Figure 2.1
A pie chart.

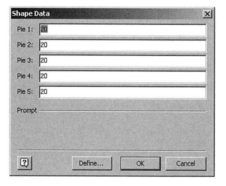

That's just one example. You can also set the "vanishing point" of 3D objects like cubes, giving them a sense of perspective, and you can associate data with shapes, such as tracking numbers, inventory numbers, or serial numbers—all of which you can print.

There are many different aspects of shapes that we'll take a look at, starting with open and closed shapes.

HANDLING OPEN AND CLOSED SHAPES

You can break down Visio shapes into various categories, such as open and closed shapes. You can see a few closed shapes in Figure 2.2—a square, a star, and a circle.

Figure 2.2
Some closed shapes.

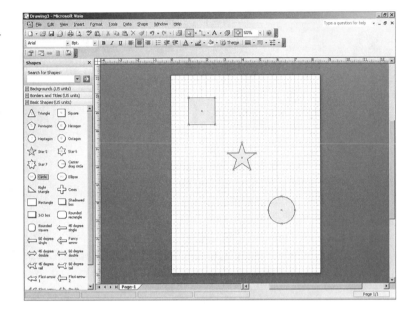

Closed shapes can be filled with color, as well as patterns, as shown in Figure 2.3 (you'll see how to do this in this chapter). You can even give Visio shapes shadows.

Figure 2.3
Closed shapes filled with color and patterns.

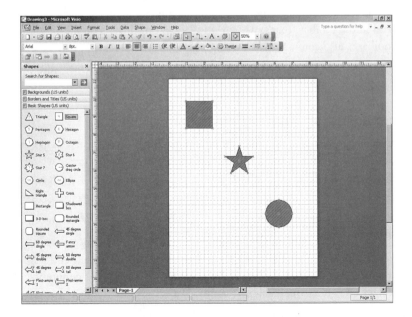

On the other hand, open shapes can't be filled. Some examples of open shapes appear in Figure 2.4.

Figure 2.4
Some open shapes.

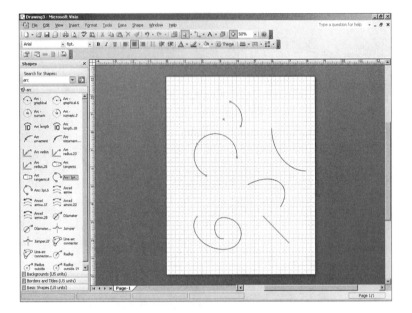

How can you draw open shapes using Visio? There are two ways. The first way is to use the built-in shapes in various stencils. There are arcs and lines built into some of the available stencils. The second option is to use the Visio drawing tools, which allow you to augment shapes. You can access the drawing tools with the Drawing toolbar, which you can make visible with the View > Toolbars > Drawing menu item, or by clicking the Drawing Tools icon in the toolbar (that's the icon to the right of the A icon in the toolbar). The Drawing toolbar is also coming up in this chapter.

Open shapes, in contrast to closed shapes, cannot be filled with color or patterns—but they can have shadows.

HANDLING ONE- AND TWO-DIMENSIONAL SHAPES

Visio shapes can also be broken into one- and two-dimensional shape categories. One-dimensional shapes have *endpoints*, and two-dimensional shapes have *handles*—such as eight sizing handles and a rotation handle.

For example, you can see a line shape in Figure 2.5—a one-dimensional shape. You can see that it has two endpoints—which are not the same as the handles a two-dimensional shape has.

You can manipulate one-dimensional shapes by dragging their endpoints. For example, you can extend and rotate the line in Figure 2.5 by dragging the endpoints. Want to make a longer line? Just stretch the endpoints. Want to rotate the line? Just drag an endpoint to match. You can also rotate one-dimensional shapes with the Shape menu's Flip or Rotate submenu, or with the Action toolbar (which you display by right-clicking the toolbar and selecting Action).

Figure 2.5
A one-dimensional shape.

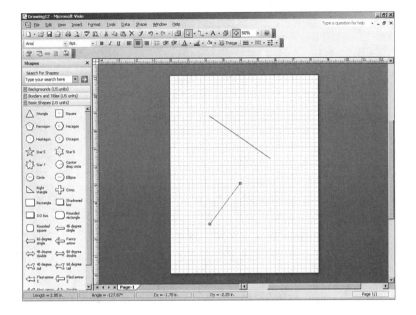

In contrast, two-dimensional shapes have handles associated with them—sizing handles, rotation handles, and the like. You can see some two-dimensional shapes in Figure 2.6.

Figure 2.6
Two-dimensional shapes.

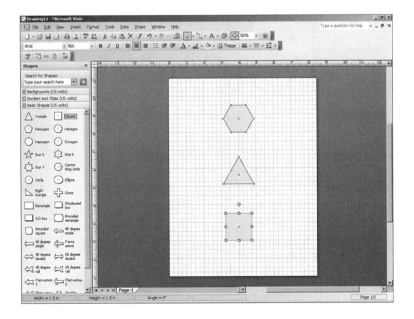

When you select a two-dimensional shape, it's enclosed in a selection frame, as shown in Figure 2.7. As you know, there are eight sizing handles here, and one rotation handle. Other shapes have more handles, as you'll see in the next section.

Figure 2.7
Two-dimensional shape handles.

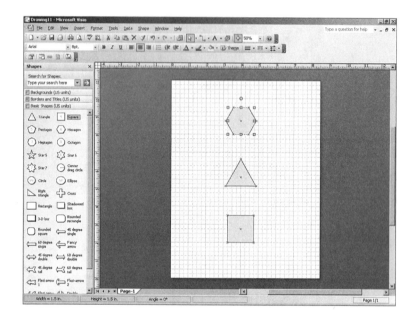

You can also select multiple two-dimensional shapes at the same time, as shown in Figure 2.8.

Figure 2.8
Selecting two-dimensional shapes.

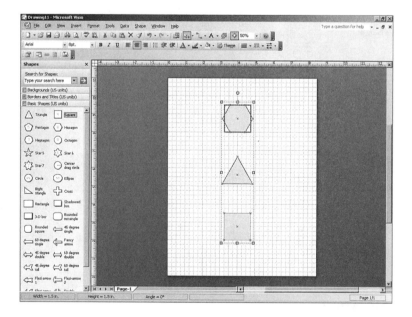

When you select multiple two-dimensional shapes, magenta squares appear around the shapes you've selected, and a selection frame appears. The selection frame may enclose non-selected shapes—for example, the triangle in Figure 2.8 is not selected, so it doesn't have a magenta square around it, as the hexagon and square do (hard to see in black-and-white). The primary shape (the hexagon, in this case) has a thicker magenta square around it.

Visio also has figures that look as though they're three-dimensional. In fact, of course, they're really two-dimensional, appearing on computer screens as they do. You can see an example in Figure 2.9, using the General template category's Blocks with Perspective template.

Figure 2.9
Three-dimensional shapes.

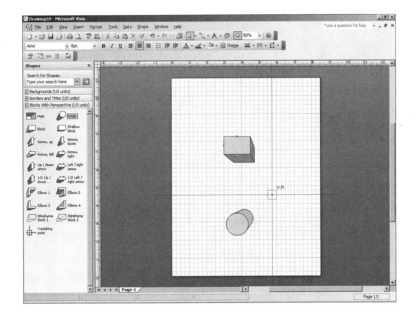

You can see a 3D block and cylinder in Figure 2.9. There's a sense of perspective in the figure, as you can see. The 3D figures are oriented toward the drawing's *vanishing point*, or VP, which is also shown in Figure 2.9. You can move the VP around simply by dragging it in the drawing, and the 3D shapes will reorient themselves to match.

DISPLAYING ALL HANDLES

Some shapes, such as arcs and freeform drawings, have additional handles. Those handles are not visible by default, but you can make Visio display them. To do that, select Tools > Options to display the Options dialog, and click the General tab, as shown in Figure 2.10.

To show all the handles associated with all shapes, select the Show More Shape Handles on Hover check box, as shown in Figure 2.10.

Figure 2.10
The Options dialog.

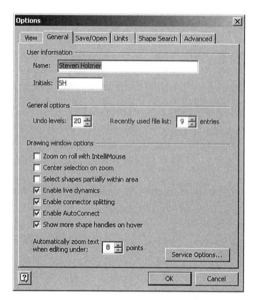

Now you can see all the handles associated with shapes, such as the third handle associated with arcs, as shown in Figure 2.11. In addition to the two endpoints, there's also a resize handle shaped like a diamond.

Figure 2.11
Arc handles.

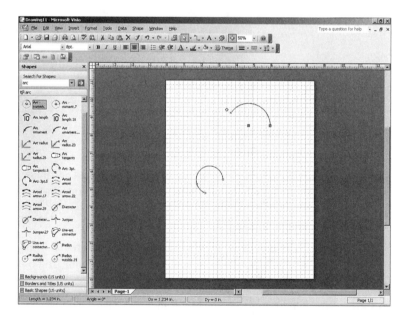

Want to see a whole bunch of handles? Make sure the Show More Shape Handles on Hover check box is selected and use the freeform drawing tool in the Drawing toolbar. You can see a freeform shape in Figure 2.12, complete with all its handles.

You can use the handles in Figure 2.12 to bend the freeform figure as you like.

Figure 2.12
Freeform handles.

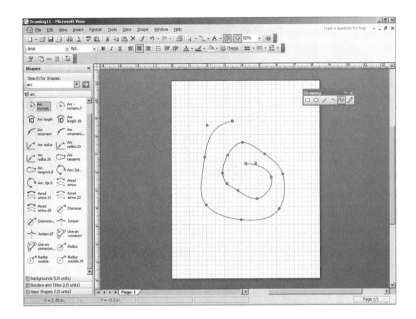

MANIPULATING SHAPES

After dragging a shape from a stencil to the drawing surface, you have literally dozens of options. You can move the shape as you need to, you can nudge the shape, you can position it exactly, you can delete it, you can copy it. All that and more is coming up next.

MOVING SHAPES

When you create a drawing full of shapes, you usually move those shapes around a lot until you get things just the way you want them. You already know how to move shapes—you just drag them. As you move those shapes, the shape's position appears in the rulers, as shown in Figure 2.13. The vertical and horizontal position of the shape is recorded by (unfortunately) very faint dotted lines in the ruler, which are not easy to make out in the figure. Dotted lines appear for the shape's top, middle, and bottom, as well as its rightmost point, its middle point, and its leftmost point.

If you want a shape to be 2 inches from the bottom of the drawing, you can place it there using the ruler.

Later in this book, you'll see how to "snap" shapes to the grid, rulers, and other elements. You use the Snap & Glue toolbar, which appears in Figure 2.14, to snap shapes; in the figure, shapes have been snapped to the grid, which means that when you move a shape, it jumps from gridline to gridline automatically.

Figure 2.13
Moving a shape.

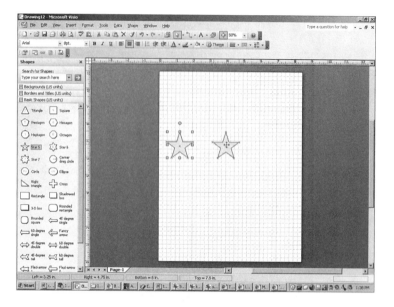

Figure 2.14
Snapping to the grid.

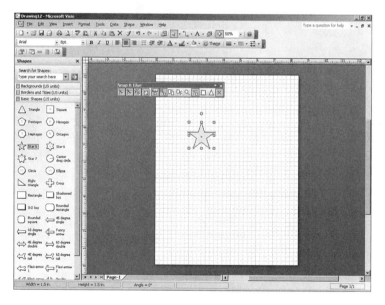

You can also *nudge* shapes in Visio. Nudging shapes works with the keyboard arrow keys.

To nudge a shape, follow these steps:

1. Select the shape. Click the shape to select it.

2. Use the arrow keys. Using the up-, down-, left-, and right-arrow keys will nudge the shape a small distance in the corresponding direction. The distance is usually small enough to make it difficult to move the shape the same amount using the mouse.

3. Deselect the shape. Click outside the shape's selection frame to deselect the shape.

If you want to, you can make the distance by which the figure is nudged even smaller—just hold down the Shift key as you nudge the shape.

Want the ultimate in moving a shape? Use the Size & Position window. To open this window, select View > Size & Position Window, which opens that window, shown in Figure 2.15.

Figure 2.15
Using the Size &
Position window.

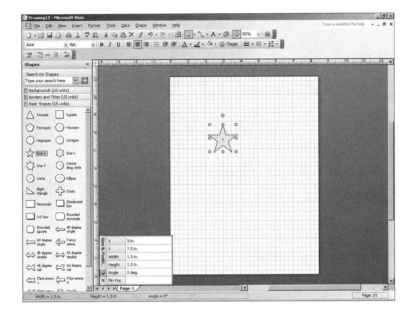

After selecting a shape, you can use the Size & Position window to set the shape's x and y position, as well as its width and height, in the units you're using. It's the ultimate in positioning—you can enter the shape's x and y location, as well as its width and height, as precisely as you want.

Using the mouse is one way to position and size shapes in Visio, but if you want total control, use the Size & Position window.

SIZING SHAPES

Another thing you commonly do when you create drawings is to (re)size your shapes. Getting that table and that desk just the right size for your office layout can be crucial.

You can use the sizing handles that appear when you select a shape to size the shape. Just select a shape and drag the sizing handles to size the shape as you want it. For example, Figure 2.16 shows a star shape being resized using the sizing handles.

If you look carefully, you can see the new size of your shape in the rulers as you move the sizing handles.

In addition, you can use the Size & Position window to size a shape. Just select the shape, open the Size & Position window with the View > Size & Position Window menu item, and enter the new width and/or height of the shape to whatever degree of accuracy you want.

Figure 2.16
Sizing a shape.

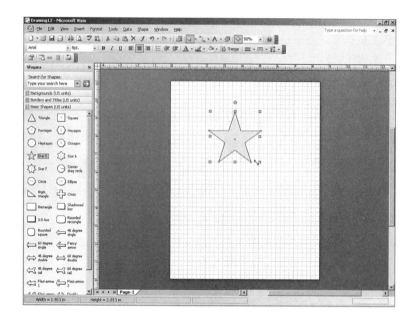

CONTROLLING SHAPES

It's time to go beyond the basic shape operations into the more advanced Visio. Besides sizing handles and rotation handles, Visio supports control handles, control points, vertexes, connection points, and more. We're going to dig into those topics next.

USING CONTROL HANDLES

Control handles let you set some aspect of a shape that's not the shape's size or position or rotation. Every shape's control handles—if there are control handles—have a purpose, and that purpose differs by shape. You can use the mouse to see the tool tip associated with the control handle.

For example, you can see a bar chart in Figure 2.17, created with the Charts and Graphs template of the Business template category. There's a control handle—a small diamond, which is yellow on the screen—above the mouse pointer in Figure 2.17.

You can use the control handle just above the mouse pointer to adjust the width of the bars in the bar chart—its tool tip reads "Modify bar width." All you have to do to set the bar width is drag the control handle to the right or left, modifying the width of the first bar in the bar chart—the other bars are adjusted to have the same width.

The other control handle in the bar chart, at the upper left, adjusts the height of each bar in the chart.

That's one type of control handle; here's another type, used with 3D shapes such as you create with the General template category's Block Diagram with Perspective template. The default is to give all such shapes the same vanishing point, but you can select a shape and drag the vanishing point to a new location for just that shape.

Figure 2.17
Control handles.

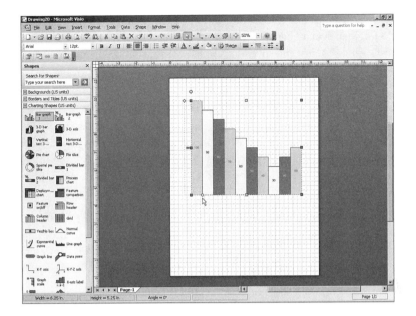

This is shown in Figure 2.18, in which the block has an individually set vanishing point. Note that when you drag the vanishing point for an individual shape, the vanishing point turns into a control handle, as shown in the figure. You can drag that control handle to set the shape's vanishing point. Cool.

Figure 2.18
Setting the vanishing point.

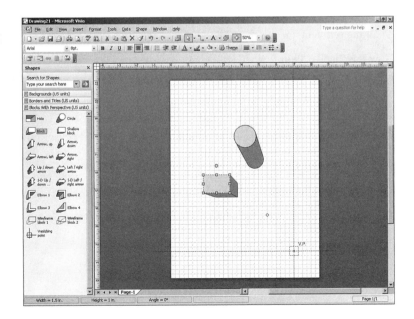

2

Control handles like these work in different ways for different shapes. To find out what they do for a particular shape, let the mouse hover over a control handle and look for the tool tip, such as "Adjust pie slice" or "Adjust corner rounding," Control handles let you adjust some aspect of a complex shape that's not needed by more simple shapes, so look out for them—small yellow diamonds.

USING CONTROL POINTS

You use control points to adjust figures drawn with the Drawing toolbar—lines, rectangles, ellipses, arcs, freeform figures, and so on. Control points are used to bend those shapes the way you want them. When you let the mouse hover over a control point, the tool tip says "Bend shape."

For example, the freeform figure in Figure 2.12 displays a set of control points you can use to adjust the shape of the figure. Just dragging one of those control points lets you adjust the figure to your liking. In other words, all you need to do is draw with one of the drawing tools, and you can then adjust what you've drawn using the figure's control points.

In fact, the drawing tools can also be used to control a shape's shape. What does that mean? Say for example that you want a pentagon with one side that bulges out in a circle—you can use the drawing tools to create such a shape.

First, draw the pentagon, using the Basic Diagram template of the General template category. Then make sure that the Drawing toolbar is visible—select View > Toolbars > Drawing, or click the Drawing icon in the toolbar to display the Drawing toolbar.

Next, select the drawing tool you want to use to modify the pentagon—the ellipse drawing tool in this case—and click the shape you want to modify. Visio will display control points on all the segments of the shape, and you can use those control points to bend the shape.

How the shape is bent depends on which drawing tool you've selected. When you've selected the ellipse drawing tool, the shape will be bent in the shape of an ellipse, as shown in Figure 2.19.

This is a very important part of working with Visio—the capability to modify shapes using the drawing tools. There are thousands of shapes built into Visio—and now you can modify them as well.

Want a pentagon with bulging sides? You can do it. Want a circle with some straight sides? No problem. Want a triangle with one side you draw freeform? No worries—all through the use of control points.

Figure 2.19
Using control points
to create shapes.

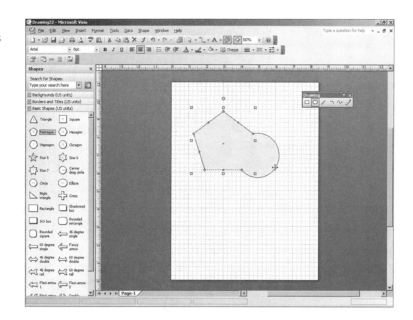

USING VERTICES

Besides control points, shapes also have *vertices*, which you can use to adjust the angles of a shape.

You can use vertices when you have selected a drawing tool from the Drawing toolbar, or if you have asked Visio to display all the handles every shape has (to do that, select Tools > Options to display the Options dialog, then click the General tab and select the Show More Shape Handles on Hover check box). Vertices appear in on top of corners, and have the tool tip "Adjust corner."

You can use vertices to adjust the angle at which line segments meet. For example, you might want to adjust the angle of a corner of a pentagon. To do that, draw the pentagon, using the Basic Diagram template of the General template category. Then either make sure that the Drawing toolbar is visible—select View > Toolbars > Drawing, or click the Drawing icon in the toolbar—or ask Visio to display all handles.

Then find a corner of the pentagon shape that you want to modify and click that corner. A vertex will appear (along with the control points in the shape) and you can drag that vertex as you want, adjusting the angle.

You can see an example in Figure 2.20, in which one corner of the pentagon has been stretched. Cool.

Figure 2.20
Using vertices.

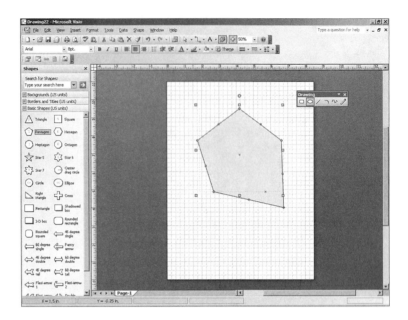

Like control points, vertices give you a way of controlling your shapes. It's amazing to think that all the corners of the thousands of shapes in Visio come fitted with vertices, ready for you to use to adjust those corners.

USING ROTATION HANDLES

You already know that shapes have rotation handles when selected, but there's more to rotation handles than we've covered so far.

Rotation handles are those round, green handles that appear when you select a shape. They start at the top of the shape, and you can use them to rotate shapes.

To rotate a shape with a rotation handle, just drag the rotation handle in the direction you want to rotate—clockwise or counterclockwise. The shape rotates to match.

Here's the part you haven't seen before. Every rotation handle also has an accompanying *center of rotation* pin. That's the axis around which the shape rotates. The center of rotation appears in the center of the shape by default.

However, you can move the center of rotation, just by dragging it with the mouse. That means you can set the axis around which the shape will rotate.

For example, take a look at Figure 2.21. The center of rotation for the star shape has been dragged to its right side, as you can see in the figure. Dragging the rotation handle now makes the star rotate around the new center of rotation.

Figure 2.21
Using rotation
handles.

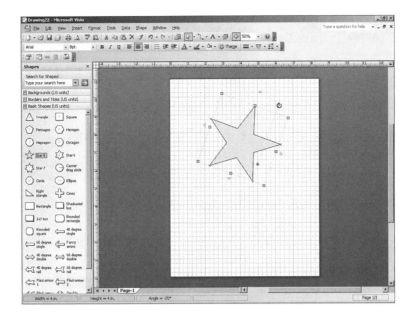

ALTERING ARCS WITH ECCENTRICITY HANDLES

All elliptical shapes in Visio have eccentricity handles, which let you set the eccentricity, or off-centeredness, of the arc that is part of the ellipse.

When you draw an arc, you can use eccentricity handles to modify how it curves between its endpoints. Eccentricity handles are visible only when you use the pencil drawing tool, part of the Drawing toolbar, or when you have the Show More Shape Handles on Hover option on.

Using eccentricity handles, you can set the curvature of arcs in Visio. They're not the easiest handles to access, however. First, use the arc drawing tool to draw an arc. Then select the arc, and you'll have two endpoints and a control point to bend the arc. Double-click the control point, and Visio will add two eccentricity handles, as shown in Figure 2.22.

If you want to change the angle of the arc, drag the eccentricity points. To change the arc's eccentricity, drag either eccentricity handle away or toward the control point. Using the arc's handles, you can manipulate how that arc curves.

USING CONNECTION POINTS

Now we come to a very important Visio topic—*connectors*. Connectors connect shapes, and they're a big part of Visio. You use them to connect the various components of your drawing, and some new capability has been added in Visio 2007.

You'll see a great deal more on connectors in the next chapter, but since they rely on connection points, which are related to control points and so on, you'll get a sneak preview of connectors now.

Figure 2.22
Eccentricity handles.

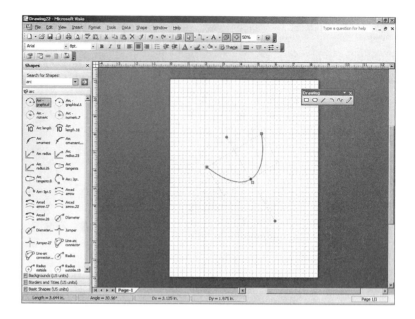

Let's get started. To start, you can display a shape's *connection points*. These points are small blue ×s that you can attach connectors to. You draw connectors from connection point to connection point. Connection points usually appear at corners of shapes.

To make the connection points visible in your shapes, select View > Connection Points (this option should be selected by default). Now you can see the connection points on various shapes, such as the ones in Figure 2.23 (they're the small ×s at the corners of the shapes).

Figure 2.23
Connection points.

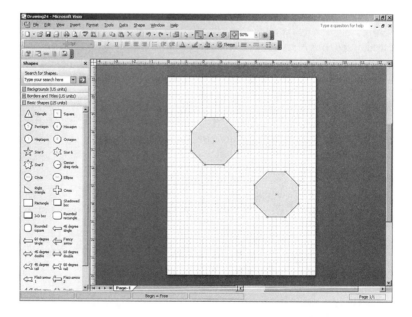

Fine, those are the connection points that you can connect. How do you connect them? You use the Connector tool, which you can select in the toolbar—it's the button just to the right of the selection tool (the mouse cursor button). When you select this tool, the mouse cursor changes to the crooked arrow shown in Figure 2.24.

Figure 2.24
The Connector tool's mouse cursor.

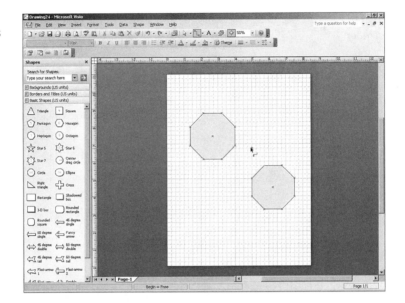

To draw a connector between two connection points, just click the first connection point, and drag the new connector to another connection point and release the mouse button. That draws a new connector, as shown in Figure 2.25.

Figure 2.25
A connector.

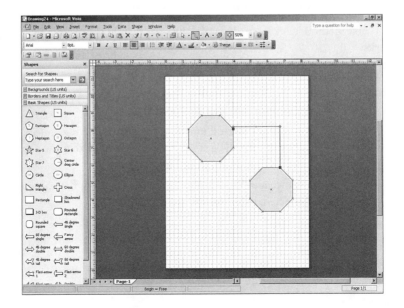

And that's the basics—you make the connection points visible, and use the Connector tool to actually draw the connector.

Want to add some text to your connection? Just double-click the connector and Visio will display a text box that you can enter text into, as shown in Figure 2.26.

Figure 2.26
Text for a connector.

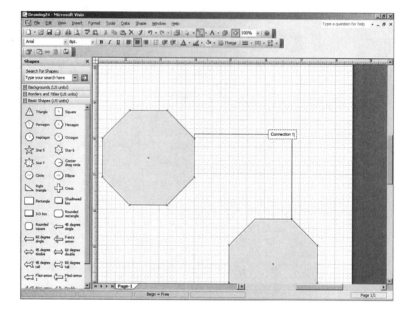

You can also use automatic connection points, starting in Visio 2007, and there are several ways to do that. When you create connectors automatically, Visio uses the default connector style, right-angle connectors.

The first method lets you create connectors as you add shapes to a diagram. Here's how it works:

1. Place a shape on the drawing surface. This is the shape that you're going to connect to.
2. Drag the shape you want to connect to the first shape. You'll see four light blue triangles; these are automatic connection points.
3. Move the second shape around until one of the automatic connection points on the original shape turns dark. This is the connection point that the second shape will connect to. You can see this in action in Figure 2.27.
4. Drop the second shape. Visio connects the shapes using the automatic connection point you've selected, as shown in Figure 2.28.

Figure 2.27
An automatic
connector.

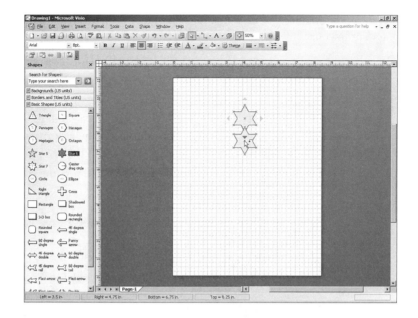

Figure 2.28
Using an automatic
connector.

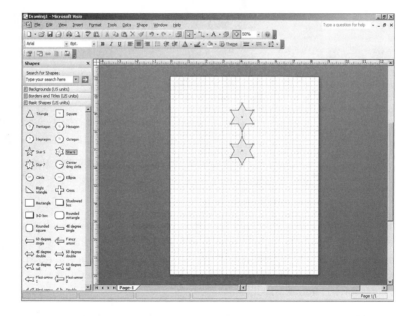

That's one method of using automatic connectors, and it's an easy one—just drag a shape over an existing shape, choose the automatic connection point you want to use, and drop the dragged shape.

Here's another method. This is a good technique if you already have existing shapes that you want to connect:

1. Select the shape you want to connect from. Visio displays automatic connection points.

2. Hover over the automatic connection point you want to use. Visio darkens the connection point.

3. Make sure that the target shape appears with a red box around it. Visio selects the target shape it thinks you want to connect to automatically by surrounding it in a red box, as shown in Figure 2.29.

4. Click the dark blue automatic connection point. Visio draws the connector between the shapes.

Figure 2.29
Selecting the target shape.

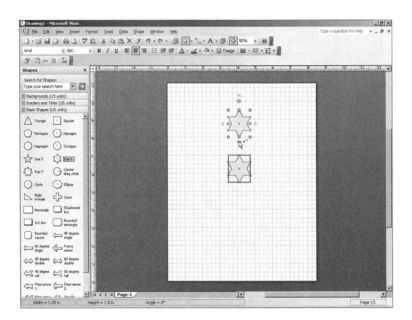

This technique, then, is a good one when you want to automatically connect existing shapes. Just select the source shape, select an automatic connection point by darkening it, make sure that the target shape is outlined in a red box (indicating that Visio will connect to that target shape), and click the darkened automatic connection point. Visio connects the shapes for you automatically.

And there's another method as well. Say you have a shape already on the drawing surface, and want to draw a shape connected to that original shape. Here's how you can do it:

1. Make sure that the original shape is on the drawing surface. This is the shape that Visio will connect to.

2. Select the second shape—the one you want a connection to—in the Shapes window. Do this by highlighting the second shape in the Shapes window.

3. Hover the mouse over the original shape until the automatic connection points appear. These automatic connection points are light blue.

4. Move the mouse until one of the automatic connection points turns dark blue. That's how you select where the second shape will connect to.

5. Release the mouse button. Visio draws the shape selected in the Shapes window, and connects it to the original shape automatically, using the automatic connection point you've selected.

This is an easy shortcut—just select the shape you want to draw in the Shapes window, select the automatic connection point you want to connect to, and release the mouse button. Visio will draw the shape you've selected, and connect it to the original shape, using the automatic connection point you've selected. Nice.

Some templates bend over backward to let you connect shapes, such as the Organization Chart template in the Business template category. When you start using this template by dropping a shape onto the drawing surface, you'll see the dialog shown in Figure 2.30, informing you that to connect shapes, you only have to drop a shape onto the "superior" shape.

Figure 2.30
A prompt on how to connect shapes.

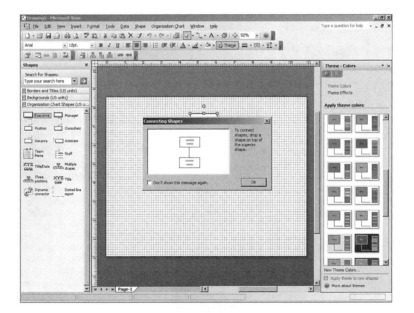

That means that when you drop, say, a Manager shape onto a superior Executive shape, the Executive shape is treated as superior, and the Manager shape is moved down one level and connected to the Executive shape.

You can see the results in Figure 2.31, where we've dropped three Managers onto the same Executive shape. The three Managers are connected to the Executive, while being one level down in the organization.

Figure 2.31
Adding manager shapes.

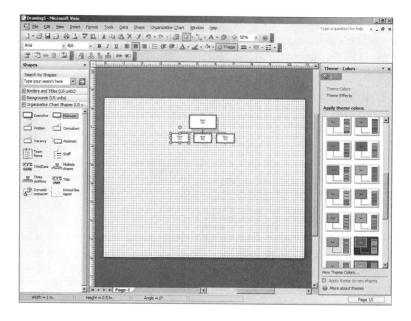

SEARCHING FOR SHAPES

You already know that you can use the search box to search for shapes, but there's more to the process than first meets the eye. The search box lets you search for matching shapes by name, as shown in Figure 2.32, in which we're searching for star shapes.

Figure 2.32
Searching for star shapes.

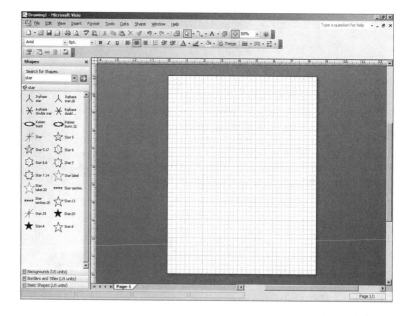

The shapes that Visio finds that match your search are displayed in a new stencil, as shown in Figure 2.32, and you're free to use those matched shapes as you would any other—just drag them from the new stencil to the drawing surface.

That's how you perform a shape search using Visio—but did you know that, by default, Visio searches the Internet for shapes, as well as your local Visio installation? If you want to, you can turn off Internet searching.

To configure shape searches, select Tools > Options, and click the Shape Search tab, as shown in Figure 2.33.

Figure 2.33
Configuring shape searches.

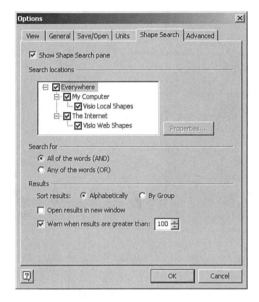

If you don't want Visio to search the Internet for shapes, simply deselect the check box next to The Internet, which will restrict shape searches to your local machine.

Under the Search For heading, you can select whether you want Visio to search for matches to all your search terms, or search for any of the words you specify. The first case means that you want Visio to match all your search terms (for example, "five pointed star"), and the second case means that you want Visio to display matches to any of the words you've asked it to search for.

You can also direct Visio to report the results alphabetically (the default), or ordered by group. When you search by group, you'll see the results broken up by stencil.

In fact, you can direct Visio to search for shapes similar to a shape you've already used. For each shape, Visio maintains a record of search terms that the shape will match—for example, a five-pointed star has the search terms "star," "five," "5," "pointed," and "basic" associated with it in Visio.

So if you search for shapes similar to a five-pointed star, Visio will search for shapes that match any of the terms "star," "five," "5," "pointed," or "basic"—which is a lot of shapes.

How do you perform a search by type of shape in Visio? You right-click a shape on the drawing surface, select Shape, then select Find Similar Shapes, as shown in Figure 2.34.

Figure 2.34
Searching for similar shapes.

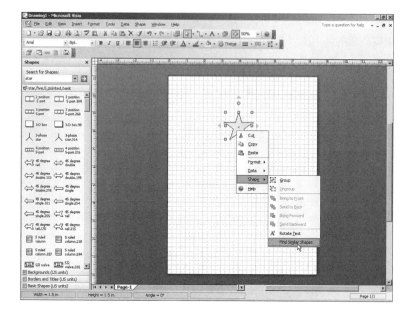

You can also see the results of the search in Figure 2.34, in the open stencil. Visio has found more than 200 "similar" shapes—some of which aren't very similar at all (the matches include shapes for bus-stop sign, airport signs, and the like).

However, the matches also do include a number of similar shapes (six-pointed stars, seven-pointed stars), so the search was worthwhile. You'll just have to scroll down in the results stencil to find the matches you want.

INTRODUCING THEMES

While discussing what you can do with shapes, we can introduce themes. Themes let you give shapes a consistent appearance across many different drawings.

Themes have two formatting options. First, there are Theme Colors, which control the colors used in your drawings. Each shape gets a coordinated color treatment. Second, there are Theme Effects, which you can use to change characteristics of the color within the shape—shapes might use a graduated color scheme, or a starburst pattern, for example. Or you can change shapes from having sharp points to having rounded corners, for example.

APPLYING THEMES

You can apply these two options using the Themes pane in Visio. You can display the theme pane by clicking the Theme button in the Formatting toolbar (it's easy to find this button—it's the one with the word "Theme" on it). Or you can select Format > Theme. Or you can right-click the toolbar and select the Task Pane context menu item, which, unexpectedly, opens the Theme pane.

The Theme pane appears in Figure 2.35, at right.

Figure 2.35
The Theme pane.

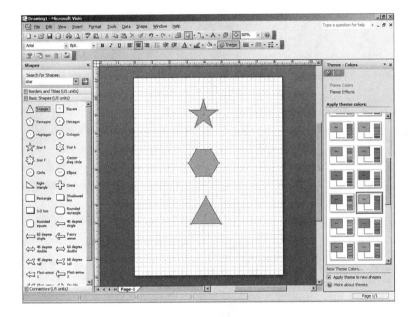

You can select between the two theme options—Theme Colors and Theme Effects—by clicking those terms at the top of the Theme pane. For example, selecting Theme Colors allows you to specify the colors of the shapes in your drawing, as in Figure 2.35, in which the shapes are filled in with a rose color (back and white in the figure, of course).

You can also select Theme Effects, as shown in Figure 2.36.

In Figure 2.36, we've selected the rounded corners theme, and as you can see in the figure, the shapes have indeed been given rounded corners. Very cool.

The theme previews you see in the Theme pane are small—you can enlarge them by selecting the drop-down arrow in a preview and selecting the Show Larger Previews menu item, showing the larger previews you see in Figure 2.37.

Note the Apply Theme to New Shapes check box at the bottom of the theme pane—that's there to select theme behavior as you add additional shapes to your drawing. If this check box is selected, the current theme will be added to any new shapes you draw.

Figure 2.36
Theme effects.

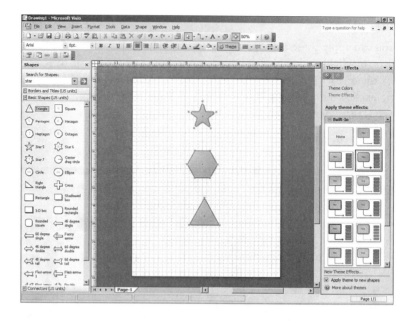

Figure 2.37
Using bigger theme previews.

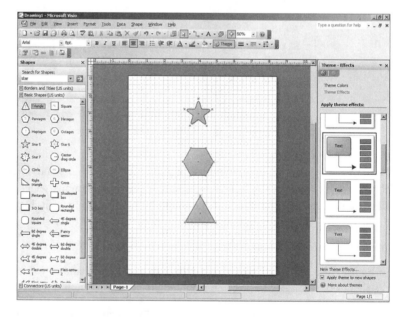

TIP

Some shapes won't accept themes by default. To change that, you can right-click the shape and select Format > Allow theme.

APPLYING MULTIPLE THEMES

You can also use multiple themes in the same drawing, as shown in Figure 2.38, in which the top shape uses one theme color, and the bottom two shapes use a different theme color.

Figure 2.38
Using two themes.

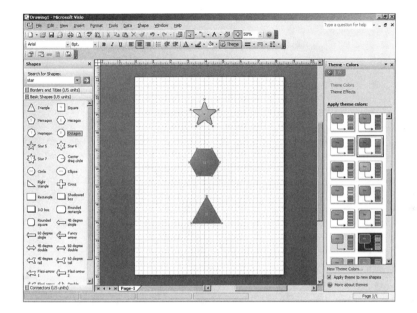

Here's how you do this. You select a theme, which in this case applies to all the shapes in the drawing. Then, you turn off further theme changes to the shapes that you want to remain as they are (with the current theme). You do that by deselecting the Allow Themes item in the Format context menu. In other words, right-click the shape in which you want to preserve the current theme, and deselect the check box in front of Format > Allow Themes. Then select the new theme for the rest of the drawing—and the shape you've "frozen" will not reflect the new theme.

More on themes is coming up in this book. Note that you also have more options here—you can modify a theme as applied to any shape with the items in the Format menu.

Here are the items in the Format menu that apply to shapes:

- **Text**—Lets you set the text and font associated with the shape.
- **Line**—Lets you set the line thickness and color the shape is drawn with.
- **Fill**—Lets you set the fill pattern for the shape.
- **Shadow**—Lets you set a drop shadow for the shape.
- **Corner Rounding**—Lets you set how rounded the corners of the shape will be.

These items apply even when you've applied a theme to a shape, so you can customize the shape by, for example, setting the roundness of its corners.

You can also use the Format Painter, a useful tool, to "paint" the format of one shape to another. Here's how it works: Select the shape whose format you want to paint, and click the Format Painter tool in the Formatting toolbar—it's the button showing a paintbrush icon.

When you select the Format Painter tool, the mouse pointer shows a paintbrush, as shown in Figure 2.39.

Figure 2.39
Using the Format Painter.

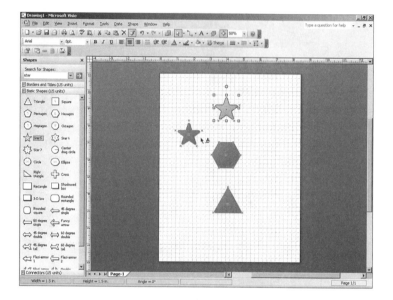

You can then paint any shape with the new format just by clicking it, as shown in Figure 2.40.

Figure 2.40
Painting a format.

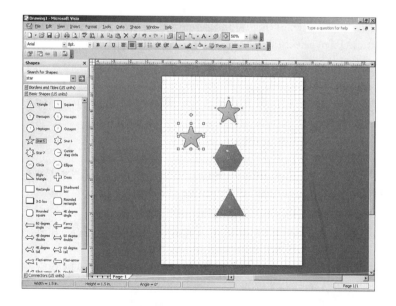

Okay, that puts us in good shape on shapes. Now it's time for the second topic in this chapter: printing your drawings.

PRINTING YOUR DRAWINGS

Typically, when you print a Visio drawing, you can just print it, and you'll get the results you anticipate. If your drawing doesn't vary from the template, 8 1/2×11 inches, you'll have no problem. But what if your drawing is larger than a printed page? Or what if it's a lot smaller than a page? Or wider? That's the kind of issues we'll take a look at here.

It's important to realize that the Visio printer paper size and the Visio drawing page size are independent. The drawing page size is reflected by the white page you see on the screen with a grid overlaid on it. The printer paper size matches the actual page size in your printer.

You set the printer page size, and that's what Visio uses as the default drawing page size. That's why the default drawing surface represents a 8 1/2×11-inch page. However, page size varies by printer—you can have 8 1/2×14 inches, or even 11×17 "tabloid" size. In architectural firms, engineering firms, and others, printers can produce drawings 60 inches wide and more.

We're going to jump into this topic now by preparing to print.

SETTING UP THE PRINTING PROCESS

If you're going to print your drawing, you should set up Visio for printing, which means checking whether the printing paper size and the drawing page size match. When you select a template in Visio, the drawing page size is set to match the printing paper size, but because a number of things can happen to alter that unintentionally, it's a good idea to check whether the drawing size and paper size match.

The way you do this is to select the File > Page Setup menu item to bring up the Page Setup dialog, shown in Figure 2.41.

Figure 2.41
The Page Setup dialog.

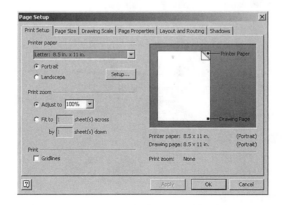

You use the Print Setup tab to check on the printing paper size, and the Page Size tab to check on the drawing surface.

Both of these tabs show the same illustration—the Printer Paper and Drawing Page overlapped on top of each other. That's fine—your printing and drawing pages are set up well. When you print, you'll get the results you expect.

However, take a look at Figure 2.42. There, the drawing page is at right angles to the printer paper.

Figure 2.42
Noncoordinated pages.

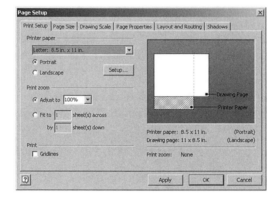

If you've checked this before printing, good catch. How do you fix this problem? The issue is that the drawing page is in landscape orientation, which means it's wider than it is tall, and the printer paper is in portrait orientation, meaning the paper is taller than it is wide.

Fixing this problem is simple—just make the paper and page orientations match. That means selecting the right orientation for your drawing—portrait or landscape—and setting printer paper and drawing page to match. Let's say you want to use portrait orientation in this case. As shown in Figure 2.42, the printer paper is already in Portrait orientation, so click the Page Size tab, as shown in Figure 2.43.

Figure 2.43
The Page Size tab.

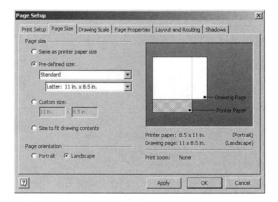

As you can see in Figure 2.43, the drawing page is set up in Landscape orientation. Change that by clicking the Portrait orientation radio button, and the printer paper and drawing page will line up.

In fact, even when the printer paper and drawing page match up, they're not really necessarily matched—printer paper has margins. If a shape falls outside a margin, Visio won't print that shape.

You can find the margin settings (and change them) for your printer in the Print Setup dialog, which you access by selecting File > Page Setup, clicking the Print Setup tab, and clicking the Setup button. That opens the Print Setup dialog shown in Figure 2.44.

Figure 2.44
The Print Setup
dialog.

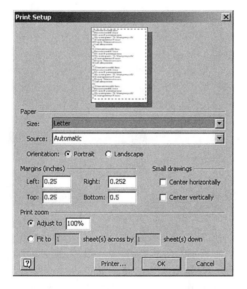

You can see the margin settings in Figure 2.44, and you can change them. Most modern printers allow you to set margin settings to very small mounts, so if you are not getting your full drawing printed, try changing the margin settings. Bear in mind that you can't change those settings to zero and have a printer print your drawing edge to edge, so you must allow for nonzero margins in your drawing.

PREVIEWING YOUR DRAWING

Before printing a drawing, it's worthwhile to check what it will look like when it comes out of the printer with the Print Preview dialog, which you access with the File > Print Preview menu item.

Although the Page Setup dialog shows you the relative alignment of printer paper and drawing page, it doesn't show you what the actual page that will be printed looks like—where the shapes will go, whether they overlap the margins, and so on. The Print Preview dialog will do all that.

Take a look at the Print Preview dialog shown in Figure 2.45. The margins of the printer paper appear as light grey (nearly invisible, in case you can't make them out in the book) margins around the perimeter of the paper. As you can see, all the shapes fall well inside the margins except for the triangle. The triangle's lower-left corner falls outside the printing space, into a margin, and accordingly, Visio has truncated it to match.

Figure 2.45
The Print Preview dialog.

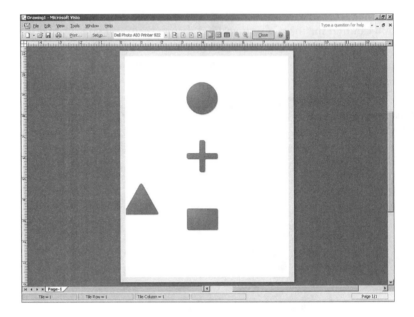

If you have this problem—if a shape is cut off by a margin—there are several things you can try. You can rearrange the shapes in the drawing so that no shape is cut off by the margin. That's probably the easiest solution. You can also reduce the drawing to fit the printer paper, as you'll see later in this chapter. And, of course, you can try adjusting the margins to make them smaller.

Note that the Print Preview dialog has its own toolbar, as shown in Figure 2.45. Here are the buttons in that toolbar, left to right:

- **New**—This drop-down menu lets you create a new drawing, showing all the template categories.
- **Open**—Lets you open another drawing.
- **Save**—Lets you save the current drawing.
- **Print Page**—Lets you print the current page.
- **Print**—Opens the Visio Print dialog.
- **Setup**—Opens the Page Setup dialog.
- **Printer Select drop-down box**—Lets you select the printer to print on.
- **First Tile**—Displays the first tile (as discussed later).

- **Previous Tile**—Displays the previous tile (as discussed later).
- **Next Tile**—Displays the next tile (as discussed later).
- **Last Tile**—Displays the last tile (as discussed later).
- **Single Tile**—Displays a single tile in a tiled drawing (as discussed later).
- **Whole Page**—Displays all the tiles in a tiled drawing (as discussed later).
- **Current View**—Displays only the region of the drawing that was visible before you opened Print Preview.
- **Zoom Out**—Zooms out.
- **Zoom In**—Zooms in.
- **Close**—Closes the Print Preview window.
- **Help**—Opens the Help system.

PRINTING

When you've checked page alignment and page setup, as well as the print preview, it's time to print. You do that with the File > Print menu item, which opens the Print dialog shown in Figure 2.46.

Figure 2.46
The Print dialog.

Choose the printer you want to print on from the drop-down list of printers in this dialog.

Select the number of copies you want to print.

If you want to check on your printer, click the Properties button to open your printer's properties dialog, and configure it as you like; then click OK to get back to the Visio Print dialog.

Select the page range in the Print dialog—all pages or just the ones you select.

When you're ready to print, click OK in the Print dialog.

That's it—your drawing is printed!

That covers many printing operations, but there's a lot more coming up—such as adding headers and footers to your drawings.

USING HEADERS AND FOOTERS

Headers are made up of text that appears at the top of every page in your drawing, and footers are the text that appears at the bottom of every page in your drawing. You need to set the header and footer only once in a drawing—after you've set them, they're set for every page.

You can use headers and footers for dates, page numbers, copyright notices, titles, and so forth. To see how the header and/or footer is going to appear in your printer pages, use Print Preview.

Besides plain text, here are the items you can place in your headers and footers:

- Page number
- Page name
- Current time
- Total number of printed pages
- Current date in short format
- Current date in long format
- Filename
- File extension
- Filename and extension

When you select one or more of these items, Visio inserts a code, beginning with "&," into the text for the header or footer. When the page prints, the actual value is substituted for the code.

To set a header and/or a footer for your drawing, select the View > Header and Footer menu item, which opens the Header and Footer dialog shown in Figure 2.47.

Headers and footers a divided up into left, center, and right parts. You set them in the corresponding text boxes shown in Figure 2.47. For example, as you see in the figure, the left header part is set to "Confidential," the center to "SuperDuperBig Co.," and the right part to the current page number.

If you want to change the font used for the header and footer, click the Choose Font button, which opens the Choose Font dialog shown in Figure 2.48.

Figure 2.47
The Header and
Footer dialog.

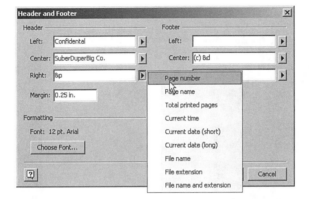

Figure 2.48
The Choose Font
dialog.

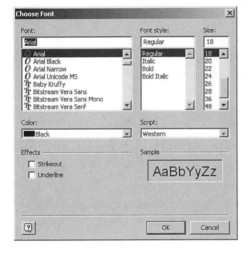

Select the font and font size you want in the Choose Font dialog and click the OK button.

How do you get Visio to insert codes for the special items such as page numbers? You click the arrow at the edge of each part text box, as shown in Figure 2.47. That gives you a list of codes that Visio will insert in your header and/or footer text, at the location you choose. As you can see in Figure 2.47, the code for page number has been inserted in the right part of the header.

You can see how the header and footer will look on the printed page in Print Preview, so select File > Print Preview to get to that preview, as shown in Figure 2.49.

TIP

In tiled drawings—drawings that Visio prints over several pages of printer paper—Visio will, unfortunately, print a header and footer for every printed page, if you're using headers and footers. One way out of that is to add your header and footer to a background page for the drawing instead. More on tiled drawings and background pages is coming up in this chapter.

Figure 2.49
The header and footer in Print Preview.

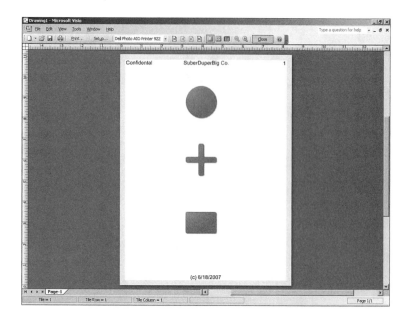

PRINTING A DRAWING'S GRIDLINES

Sometimes, you might want to print a drawing's gridlines, as they appear on the screen. But you'll notice that when you print a drawing, the gridlines disappear. How can you get them to print?

When you're designing an office layout, for example, it can be very useful to display the gridlines to make actually placing office furniture easier.

To make Visio print the gridlines for a drawing, follow these steps:

1. Select File > Page Setup. This opens the Page Setup dialog.
2. Click the Print Setup tab. This displays the Print Setup options.
3. Click the Gridlines check box. This makes sure that the drawing's gridlines will be printed.

When you follow these steps, the gridlines are printed as part of the drawing, as shown in Print Preview in Figure 2.50.

Figure 2.50
Printing gridlines in
Print Preview.

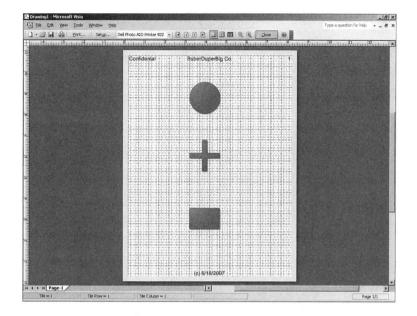

PRINTING A PORTION OF A DRAWING

What if you want to print only part of a drawing? It turns out that you can print just the shapes you select.

To print part of a drawing, follow these steps:

1. Select the shapes you want to print. You can select them by clicking them, using the Area Select tool, or using the Lasso Select tool. You can even select shapes with the keyboard—press the Tab key until the shape you want has a rectangle around it, and press Enter to select the shape. Then Tab to the other shapes you want to add and press Shift+Enter.

2. Select File > Page Setup. Check your page alignment with the printer page.

3. Select File > Print Preview. Check the Print Preview.

4. Select File > Print. This opens the Print dialog.

5. Select printer options. Select the printer options you want to use.

6. In the Page Range area, click Selection. This tells Visio you want to print only the selection. You can see this operation at work in Figure 2.51.

7. Click OK. This prints the selected shapes.

Now you can print only the shapes you've selected, if you want to.

Figure 2.51
Printing selected
shapes.

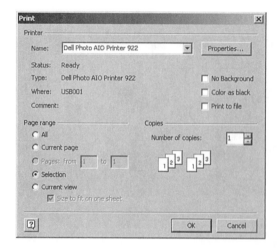

ALTERING PRINTED DRAWING SIZE

In Visio, the printer page size and the drawing page size can be different, and relating them is an object worthy of study as you gain more control over Visio. This section begins that exploration by discussing how to handle oversize drawings and how to change the print scale.

Changing the print scale of a drawing can let you fit more onto a printed page than you'd be able to fit otherwise. For example, if you have a drawing that's a lot bigger than your printed page, you can reduce the scale of the drawing on the printed page to compensate.

CREATING OVERSIZE DRAWINGS

Here's an example, showing how to create oversize drawings. It's easy enough—by default, when you create a drawing, the drawing size is set to the printer paper size, and that's usually 8 1/2×11 inches. But what if you want to create a drawing that's double that size, 17×22 inches?

You can do that by changing the drawing page size, which you do by following these steps:

1. Select File > Page Setup. This opens the Page Setup dialog.
2. Click the Page Size tab. The page size refers to the drawing page size.
3. Click the Custom Size radio button. This lets you enter a custom size for the drawing.
4. To change the drawing size, enter new dimensions. This example uses 17×22 inches, as shown in Figure 2.52.

Note that now the drawing page fits over four printer pages, because we've doubled the drawing page's size in both dimensions, as shown in Figure 2.52. So if you print this drawing now, it will print over four different printer pages.

How can you fix that, short of changing the paper in the printer to be 11×22 inches?

Figure 2.52
Changing the
drawing size.

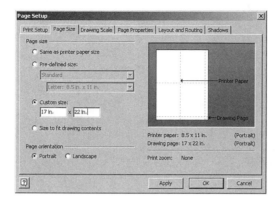

CHANGING A DRAWING'S PRINT SCALE

You can change a drawing's print scale in order to print oversize drawings. Now that we have an oversize drawing that fits over four printer pages, how can you change things so that the drawing comes out on just one printer page?

You can do that by changing the drawing's *print scale*. The print scale is just a comparison between drawing size and printing size, and so here, we want to reduce the print scale to fit the whole drawing on one sheet of printer paper.

Currently, our drawing fits onto four printed pages, 2×2 pages. To fit the same content on a single page, you want to reduce that drawing using what factor when it comes to printing?

You want to set the print scale to 50%. That's because 50% reduces the drawing size by 50% in both the x and y directions, which means that the printed output will now be 1×1 pages—or one page.

That's how the print scale works—it takes an oversize drawing and lets you reduce it to print it. Or you can take a small drawing and enlarge it, all by using the print scale.

Okay, so how do we reduce the print scale of our oversize drawing to 50%? Doing so won't affect the drawing page size of 11×22 inches, but it will let us reduce that size to the printed page for output.

Just follow these steps to change the print scale:

1. Select File > Page Setup. This opens the Page Setup dialog.
2. Click the Print Setup tab. This lets you select the printing options.
3. Click the Adjust To radio button in the Print Zoom region. This lets you enter a custom print scale for the drawing to be printed with.
4. Enter your new print scale. You can see a print scale of 50% entered in Figure 2.53.
5. Click OK to close the Page Setup dialog.

Figure 2.53
Changing the print scale.

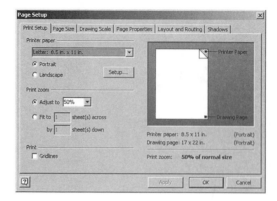

Note that in Figure 2.53, the Printer Paper and the Drawing Page exactly overlap—that's because we expanded our drawing by 200%, and then reduced it to 50% for printing. Perfect.

Great—now you can create oversize (or undersize) drawings, and reduce (or enlarge) the printed version.

PRINTING TILED DRAWINGS

Now you know how to fit oversize drawings onto a single piece of paper. But there are times when you actually want oversize drawings to come out on separate pieces of paper, as when you're designing a presentation for many people, or printing office layout plans that need to show some detail, and so on.

You can print drawings as "tiled," which lets you print them on multiple pages. Then you can tape or assemble the printed pages to show the final, enlarged drawing.

Here's how to tile a drawing page over several printed pages:

1. Select the File > Page Setup menu item. This opens the Page Setup dialog.
2. Click the Print Setup tab. This lets you select the printing options.
3. Click the Fit To radio button in the Print Zoom region. This lets you enter the number of pages to tile your drawing.
4. Enter the number of horizontal and vertical tiles you want. In Figure 2.54, we're creating three tiles across and three tiles down.
5. Click OK to close the Page Setup dialog.

Note that in Figure 2.54 the figure shows 3×3 pages for the printer output.

After you've tiled a drawing, you can take a look at it in Print Preview, as shown in Figure 2.55, by selecting File > Print Preview.

Figure 2.54
Tiling a drawing.

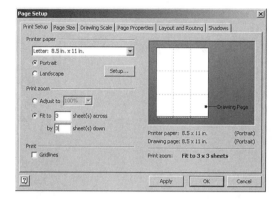

Figure 2.55
A tiled drawing in
Print Preview.

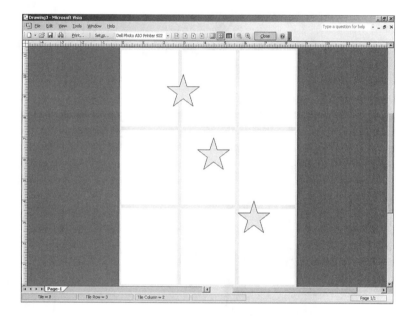

Note how the three stars in this figure look—as you can see, two of the stars overlap margins. That means that when you print, those shapes will be affected. To avoid that problem, you can reduce the margin size, and move the stars.

You can also select one of the tiles in the Print Preview view to examine individually—just move the mouse pointer over the tile you want to see, and a red rectangle will appear, outlining it, as shown in Figure 2.56.

Selecting a tile by clicking it brings that tile up in Print Preview, as shown in Figure 2.57.

Figure 2.56
Selecting a tile.

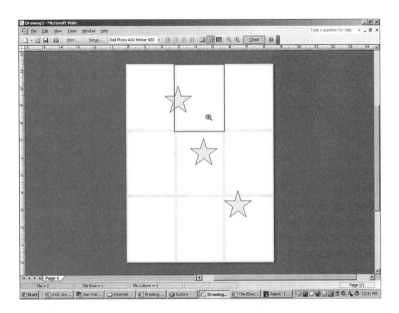

Figure 2.57
An individual tile.

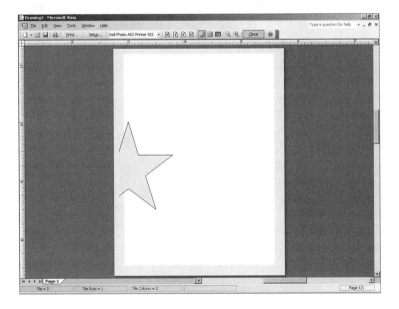

Note also the four buttons to the right of the printer name in the toolbar. These let you navigate from tile to tile:

- **First Tile**—Displays the first tile.
- **Previous Tile**—Displays the previous tile.
- **Next Tile**—Displays the next tile.
- **Last Tile**—Displays the last tile.

The next two buttons, to the right of the four buttons, also let you work with tiles:

- **Single Tile**—Displays a single tile in a tiled drawing.
- **Whole Page**—Displays all the tiles in a tiled drawing.

How can you get back from viewing individual tiles to viewing the whole page at once? Just click the Whole Page button, or click the Zoom Out button (the magnifying icon with the minus sign in it).

Does this mean that you must alternate between your drawing and the Print Preview screen to align your shapes to avoid margins?

Not at all—you can add the page breaks to your drawing surface. To do that, just select View > Page Breaks. You can see the page breaks in a drawing, as shown in Figure 2.58.

Cool.

Figure 2.58
Showing page breaks.

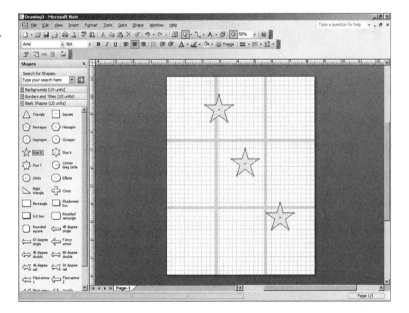

PRINTING TO SCALE

Visio is not a professional CAD program, but you can use it to print to scale. That is, you can set up Visio to draw diagrams in which 1 inch corresponds to 1 foot, or 1/2 inch corresponds to 2 feet, and so on.

That's useful if you're drawing someone a map—in which case, don't forget to indicate the scale using some text in the drawing. It's also useful when you have some physical layout you're drawing, such as an office layout.

Note once again that Visio is not a CAD program—which means that you shouldn't use it for projects in which scale is absolutely critical. Don't use it to design printed circuits, for example—printer resolution isn't good enough for that. However, if absolute scale isn't a big issue, Visio can get the job done for you.

Here's how to set the scale for a drawing:

1. Select the File > Page Setup menu item. This opens the Page Setup dialog.

2. Click the Drawing Scale tab. This lets you select the drawing scale.

3. Click the Pre-defined Scale or Custom Scale radio buttons. These are the two types of scales you can use.

4. Specify the scale you want. If you've selected a predefined scale, select the scale you want. If you've selected a custom scale, fill in the two text boxes, as shown in Figure 2.59.

5. Click OK to close the Page Setup dialog.

Figure 2.59
Setting a custom scale.

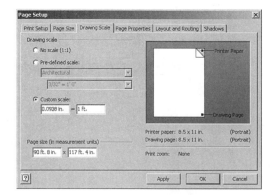

That sets the scale for your drawing. It doesn't affect the printing properties of your drawing—if your drawing fits on one page before you set the drawing scale, it will still fit on one page after you've set the drawing scale. Now, however, your drawing is set up to mirror real life at a certain scale, such as 1/2 inch to the mile. Make sure that you note the scale in the drawing so that people using your drawing know what's going on. This is a good item to be placed on a background page.

NOT PRINTING SELECTED SHAPES

Sometimes, it's convenient to avoid printing some part of a drawing. For example, employees wouldn't be interested in the plumbing details of an office layout. You might want to omit the plumbing details from printing when you print the drawing. Or you might have part of your drawing that's top-secret, and you want to keep it hush-hush. Avoiding printing out that part of the drawing could be important.

Say, for example, that you have the drawing shown in Figure 2.60, and that you don't want to print the hexagon in the middle when the page is printed. How could you do that?

Figure 2.60
A drawing.

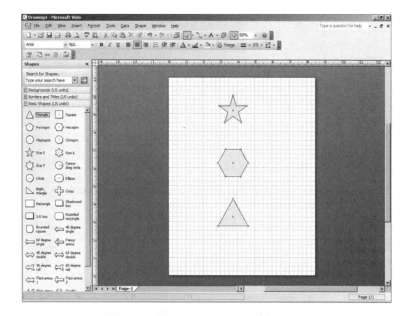

To make sure that a shape doesn't print with the rest of the drawing, follow these steps:

1. Right-click the shape not to draw and select Format > Behavior. This opens the Behavior dialog.

2. Select the Behavior tab. This lets you select the behavior options.

3. Select the Non-printing Shape check box. When you select this check box, shown in Figure 2.61, this makes the shape nonprintable.

4. Click OK to close the Behavior dialog.

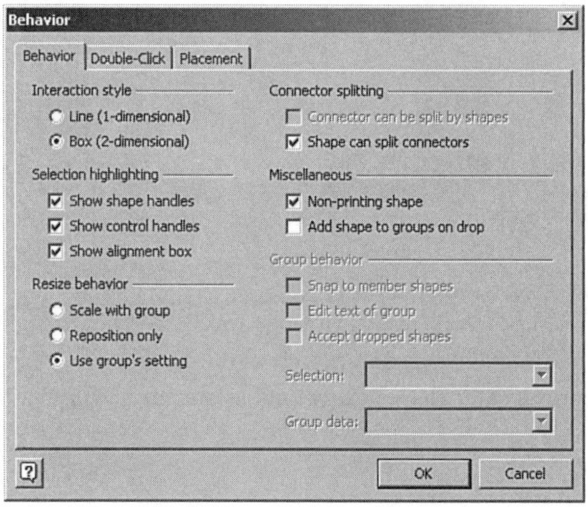

Figure 2.61
Setting nonprinting behavior.

Now take a look at the drawing in Print Preview.

As you can see in Print Preview, the shape that's been marked as nonprinting doesn't appear in Print Preview. Cool—now you've told Visio what shapes it shouldn't print.

If you change your mind and want to print the shape again, follow the same steps as listed previously and deselect the Non-printing Shape check box. That will make the shape printable once again.

PRINTING BACKGROUNDS

Drawings can have backgrounds in Visio. A background is an image that all pages in the drawing share. And you can print backgrounds separately in Visio. More on backgrounds is coming up in this book, but we'll get a sneak peek now by seeing how to print backgrounds.

To create a drawing with a background, start by creating your drawing, as shown in Figure 2.62. Here, we're using the Basic Drawing template of the General template category, and drawing a few shapes, as you can see in the figure.

Figure 2.62
A drawing with three shapes.

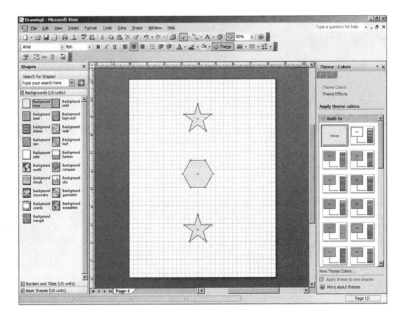

Now, to add a background the easy way, just open the Backgrounds stencil in the Basic Drawing template, and drag a background, such as the Background Stripes background, to the drawing. This action installs that background, as shown in Figure 2.63 (the background is very faint).

Figure 2.63
Adding a background
to a drawing.

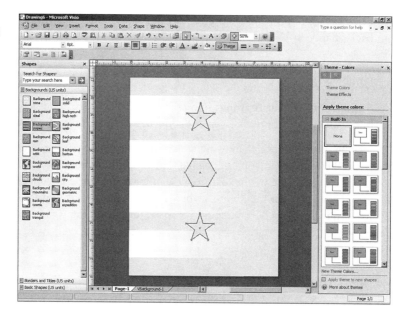

That gives a background to your drawing—but now how can you print just that background?

Take a look at Figure 2.63, and you'll see a new tab at the bottom of the drawing surface, corresponding to the background (next to the Page-1 tab).

When you click that tab, the background appears by itself, as shown in Figure 2.64.

Figure 2.64
A background.

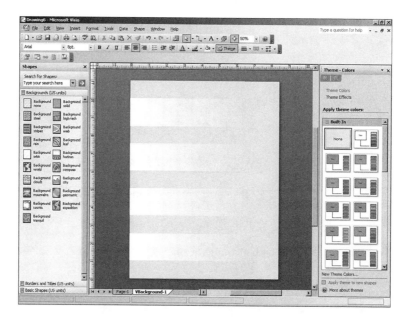

Now you're free to print that background—just select File > Print. And that's how you print out backgrounds in Visio.

PRINTING LAYERS

Visio also lets you divide drawings into *layers*. You'll see more about layers later, but it's worth discussing how to print layers individually now that we're discussing printing.

By default, all the layers in a drawing appear in that drawing at the same time, and they all print together. However, you can change that behavior, handling the different layers differently. For example, you might want to view only the electrical circuits, in their own layer, in an office layout. Or, for the plumber's benefit, you might want to print only the piping layer. As your drawings become more complex, layers are going to become more and more important.

How do you create layers? Follow these steps:

1. Select View > Layer Properties. This opens the Layer Properties dialog.

2. Click the New button, enter the name of a new layer, and click OK. This example creates the layers Layer 1 and Layer 2, which involves clicking the New button twice.

3. In the Layer Properties dialog, deselect Layer 2's Print check box. As shown in Figure 2.65, this makes Layer 2 nonprintable.

Figure 2.65
Making a layer nonprintable.

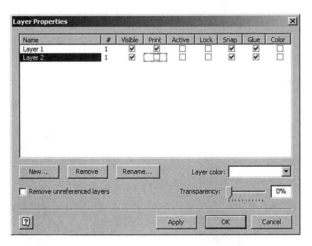

4. Click OK in the Layer Properties dialog. This closes the Layer Properties dialog.

This creates two layers, and makes Layer 2 nonprintable.

Now create a drawing with a couple of shapes, as shown in Figure 2.66.

Figure 2.66
Drawing a few shapes.

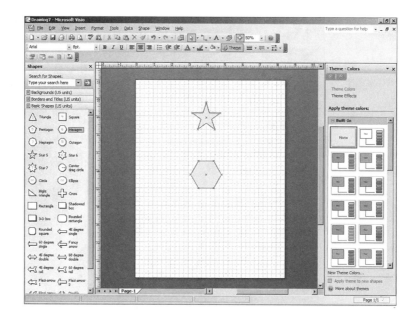

Now right-click a shape and select Format > Layer, opening the Layer dialog shown in Figure 2.67.

Figure 2.67
Selecting layers.

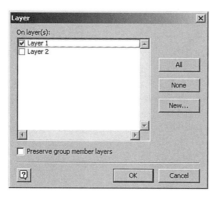

Select Layer 1 for the top shape, and Layer 2 for the bottom shape in the Layer dialog. That assigns the top shape to Layer 1, and the bottom shape to Layer 2.

Layer 2 was, however, made nonprintable, as you recall. So when you take a look at this drawing in Print Preview, as shown in Figure 2.68, the second shape—which is in the non-printing layer, doesn't appear.

Figure 2.68
Printing layers.

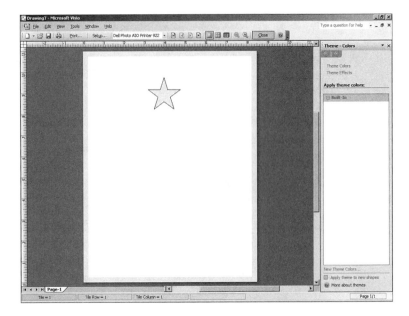

Cool. Now you can divide your drawings into layers, and then print selective layers at will.

CHAPTER 3

CONNECTING SHAPES AND ADDING TEXT

In this chapter

WORKING WITH CONNECTORS AND TEXT

In this chapter, we're going to examine two central topics in Visio: connectors and text. You'll get the full Visio story here on both topics, and there's a lot to discuss.

We're going to start with the technology available to you in Visio to connect shapes.

ALL ABOUT CONNECTORS

Connectors in Visio are those lines that connect shapes. In fact, connectors are actually shapes in Visio. They're one-dimensional shapes that are used most frequently to connect two-dimensional shapes. You can tell the difference between one- and two-dimensional shapes in Visio by the behavior of the shape when you select it. One-dimensional shapes will display endpoints, whereas two-dimensional shapes will display a selection frame with green sizing and rotation handles.

Because they're shapes themselves, connectors also have properties you can use to customize them. So far, you've seen only line connectors, but there are other types as well, such as arrows.

Connectors are fundamental to many types of Visio diagrams. You might not need them in, say, office layouts, but you do when you're creating an organization chart. Or a software flowchart. Or an electrical circuit.

For example, take a look at Figure 3.1—an organization chart. The connectors there make the relationships between people clear.

Figure 3.1
An organization chart.

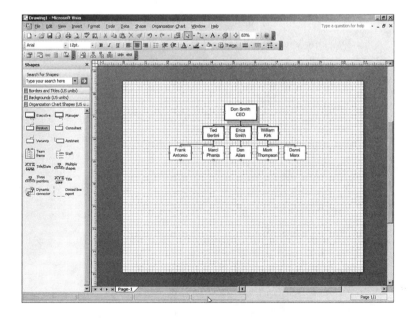

There are all kinds of ways of connecting shapes in Visio, such as these:

- **Select the Connector tool in the toolbar**—This tool is in the Standard toolbar.

- **Drag a connector from the Shapes window to the drawing surface**—Many types of connectors appear in stencils.

- **Click the Connect Shapes button in the toolbar**—This tool is in the Action toolbar.

- **Use automatic connection points**—They're those light-blue triangles that appear around shapes.

In Visio, connectors are not just simple lines. You can have dynamic connectors, which will reconnect themselves to other connection points as you move a shape in order to not make the drawing look tortuous. And there are smart connectors that change their shape or form to avoid other shapes as you adjust your drawing. You're going to see this kind of behavior in this chapter.

There are many different ways of adding connectors to a drawing. For example, you can use automatic connections. To do that, make sure that the AutoConnect tool has been selected (it appears in the toolbar with a border around it). The AutoConnect tool appears in Figure 3.1 just to the left of the Zoom box at the right end of the top toolbar.

When you use AutoConnect, Visio connects shapes for you. You can use it with the two shapes shown in Figure 3.2—just let the mouse rest on a selected shape, and the automatic connection points will appear, as light blue triangles. Roll the mouse over one of those automatic connection points, and it will darken to dark blue—and a neighboring shape will get a red rectangle around it, indicating that it's the target of the automatic connector. You can see this at work in Figure 3.2.

Figure 3.2
Automatic
connectors.

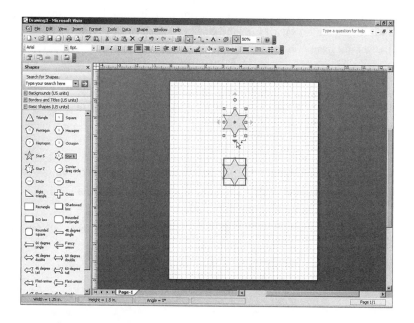

If you click the darkened automatic connector, the connector will be drawn between the shapes, as shown in Figure 3.3.

Figure 3.3
An automatic connection.

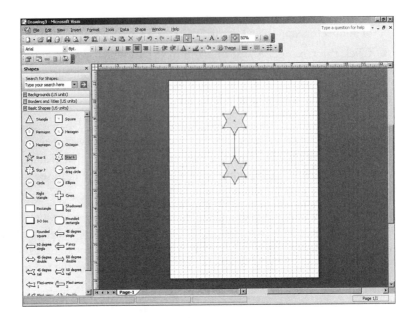

CREATING CONNECTION POINTS

That's fine as far as it goes, but sometimes shapes don't have connection points where you want them. Connection points appear in shapes as small blue ×s, and you can see them at the vertices of the stars in Figure 3.3. But what if there is no connection point where you want it? You end up with the kind of situation shown in Figure 3.4, in which the connector that should have gone to the middle of the upper edge of the square instead went to one corner of the square.

In Visio, you can create your own connection points on a shape! Visio provides connection points at the vertices of most shapes. However, that's often not enough, so it's handy to be able to add connection points yourself.

Here's how you do it:

1. Select a shape. This is the shape you want to add connection points to.
2. Click the drop-down arrow in the Connector tool in the toolbar. This tool is to the left of the Text tool (showing the letter *A*).
3. Select the Connection Point tool. This tool is the one that lets you create connection points.
4. Hold down the Ctrl key and click the shape where you want a new connection point. That creates the new connection point. Impressive.

Figure 3.4
Connecting a star and a square.

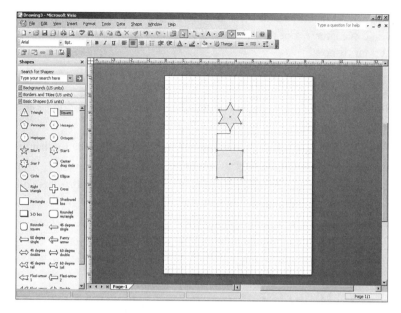

That lets you add a new connection point to a shape. Now you can change the connector shown in Figure 3.4 to the one shown in Figure 3.5, which looks a lot better.

Figure 3.5
Using a new connection point.

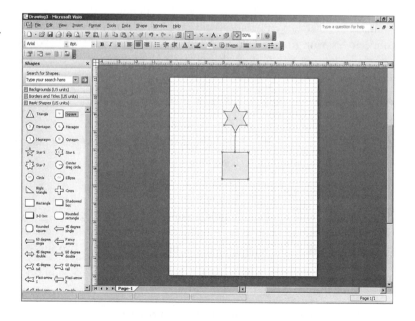

Being able to add your own connection points is a powerful part of Visio, and lets you customize what's going on with your drawing. It's a simple skill, but it's a strong one.

You can even add your newly configured shape to a new stencil in Visio, using techniques you'll see later. From then on, you'll have the new shape—with the new connection point—at your disposal.

DELETING CONNECTION POINTS

You can also delete connection points from a shape that you don't want to use. To do so, follow these steps:

1. Click the drop-down arrow in the Connector tool in the toolbar. This tool is to the left of the Text tool (showing the letter *A*).

2. Select the Connection Point tool. This tool is the one that lets you create connection points.

3. Click the connection point you want to remove. The connection point turns magenta.

4. Press the Delete key. That deletes the connection point.

ALL ABOUT GLUE

There's a concept you have to understand about connectors, and that concept is *glue*. In Visio, this is the concept that sticks connectors to connection points.

If there were no glue, you'd have to reshape connectors every time you moved a connected shape. You'd have to reconnect the connection points on the moved shape, and modify the connector to match. With glue, all of that is taken care of—the shapes you move still stay connected, saving you the bother of having to reconnect them. As you go on in Visio, this is a big help, because you'll move shapes around frequently until you get things the way you want them.

Without glue, adjusting a drawing would be a lot more work than you'd want to put up with.

There are two types of glue: point-to-point glue (also called static glue) and shape-to-shape glue (also called dynamic glue).

POINT-TO-POINT GLUE

Point-to-point glue is all about gluing connection points together. This kind of glue is also called static glue, and it sticks two connection points together. Those connection points are stuck with the same connector no matter how you move the two shapes around.

In other words, point-to-point glue is just what it sounds like—a means of making a connector stick from one point to another one.

That means that when you move shapes, you risk having a contorted connector if you use point-to-point glue. For example, take a look at Figure 3.6, in which the two shapes are connected by point-to-point static glue. When you move the shapes with respect to each other, as shown in the bottom of the figure, the same two points stay connected, which gives you the result shown in the figure.

Figure 3.6
Using a point-to-point glue.

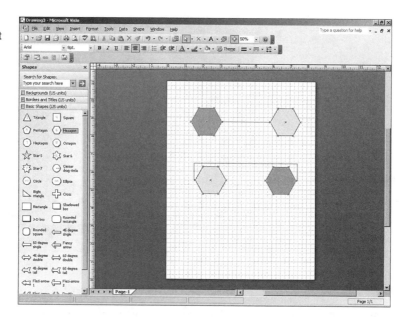

That's what it means to use point-to-point glue: The connection points you connect this way are always connected.

SHAPE-TO-SHAPE GLUE

The other method of connecting connection points is with shape-to-shape glue. With this kind of glue, the two shapes are glued together, not just two points. That means the connector between two shapes will switch between connection points as you move the shapes. The connector will connect the two shapes using the most convenient connection points.

Because, when you use this type of glue, connectors can connect to any connection points on shapes, this type of glue is also called dynamic.

You can see shape-to-shape glue behavior in Figure 3.7, in which the two shapes are connected using shape-to-shape glue. When you move the two shapes with respect to each other, as shown in the bottom part of the figure, the connector reconnects to the most convenient connection points.

That's what shape-to-shape glue means—the connectors will be able to switch from connection point to connection point, as is the most convenient, and they make that switch automatically.

Because this is the type of glue that gets used most often in Visio, it's the default type of glue.

Figure 3.7
Using a shape-to-shape glue.

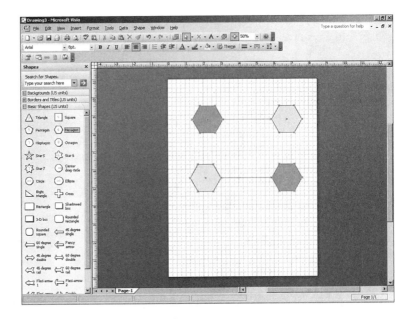

HOW DO YOU KNOW WHICH TYPE OF GLUE YOU'VE GOT?

How can you tell what kind of glue a connector uses? Some connectors use shape-to-shape glue, and others point-to-point.

One way of making that determination, of course, is to see how shapes act as you move them around—point-to-point glue keeps two points connected no matter what; shape-to-shape glue lets the connector switch from connection point to connection point.

But there's a quicker way to check. Just select the connector, as shown in Figure 3.8. If the connector uses point-to-point glue, the endpoints will appear in dark red, and a tiny × and + will appear in them.

On the other hand, if the connector uses shape-to-shape glue, the endpoints will be larger, colored a lighter red, as shown (in glorious black-and-white) in Figure 3.9. And there is no × or + in either endpoint.

So that's the easy way to check which kind of glue you have—just select the connector, and the endpoints will tell you. Small dark red endpoints mean you have point-to-point glue; large lighter red endpoints mean you have shape-to-shape glue.

Figure 3.8
Point-to-point glue.

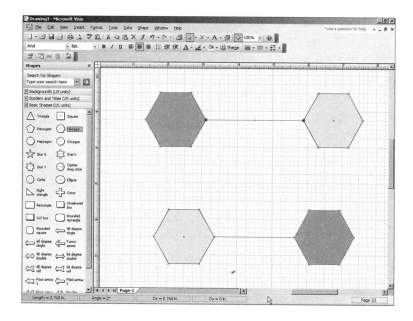

Figure 3.9
Shape-to-shape glue.

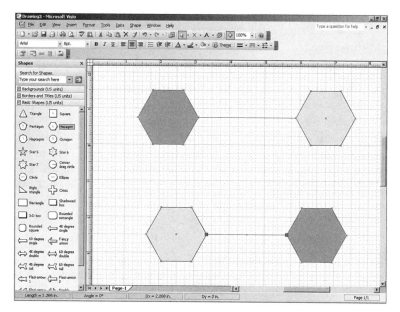

GETTING FROM ONE GLUE TYPE TO ANOTHER

Depending on your drawing requirements, you might want to switch from one type of glue to another. For example, if you've created your own connection points and always want to use them in particular shapes, you might want to switch away from the shape-to-shape glue that Visio uses as the default. On the other hand, you may want to switch to shape-to-shape glue if you're using point-to-point glue in drawings that change a lot, forcing you to move shapes around.

It turns out to be possible to switch from glue type to glue type, but it takes a little fancy work with the mouse. After you're familiar with the process, it goes faster.

Let's take a look at the process of switching between glue types now.

GOING FROM POINT-TO-POINT TO SHAPE-TO-SHAPE GLUE

Your connectors might be set up to use point-to-point glue, and you would prefer shape-to-shape glue. How do you change from the one to the other?

You can switch connectors from using point-to-point glue to using shape-to-shape glue easily enough. Just follow these steps:

1. Select the pointer tool in the Standard toolbar. This tool is the standard arrow mouse pointer.
2. Select the connector you want to change. The connector's endpoints—small dark red boxes—appear.
3. Drag an endpoint away from a shape and then drag the endpoint back toward the shape until a red box appears around the entire shape. This is how you select shape-to-shape glue.
4. Release the mouse button. This changes the connector to shape-to-shape.
5. Repeat the preceding steps for the other endpoint of the connector. Doing so converts the connector to using shape-to-shape glue.

It's also worth noting that shape-to-shape connections work only with dynamic connectors, because those connectors have "elbow" joints that allow the connector to bend as you move connected shapes. If you don't see elbow joints on a connector when you move shapes—if you're just dealing with a straight connector—you can't use shape-to-shape glue. More on dynamic connectors is coming up in this chapter.

GOING FROM SHAPE-TO-SHAPE TO POINT-TO-POINT GLUE

Bear in mind that when you're using shape-to-shape glue, you don't get to choose which connection points Visio will connect—it automatically connects the nearest two on the two shapes you're connecting. If you want to maintain control over which connection points to connect, go with point-to-point glue instead.

How can you convert a connector from being shape-to-shape to being point-to-point? Follow these steps:

1. Select the pointer tool in the Standard toolbar. This tool is the standard arrow mouse pointer.
2. Select the connector you want to change. The connector's endpoints—small dark red boxes—appear.

3. Drag an endpoint away from a shape and then drag the endpoint back toward the connection point you want to connect to. This is how you select point-to-point glue. A red box appears around the connection point only—not the whole shape.

4. Release the mouse button. This changes the connector to point-to-point.

5. Repeat the preceding steps for the other endpoint of the connector. Doing so converts the connector to using point-to-point glue.

So that's how you change the glue used by connectors. You just drag an endpoint away from the shape, and then drag it back. When a single connector is highlighted and you release the mouse button, the connector is converted to point-to-point. When the whole shape is surrounded by a red box and you release the mouse button, the connector is converted to shape-to-shape.

As you can see, heavy use of the mouse is indicated here—you have to drag connector endpoints away from shapes and then back to them. After you get used to this process, however, it's easy to do.

SETTING OPTIONS FOR GLUE

You can also set various glue options, such as where connectors can attach to shapes. Connectors can attach to shapes in places other than simply connection points—they can also attach to guides (guides are lines you can add to the drawing to help you position shapes where you want them—more on guides later), vertices of shapes, and even shape handles. You can even attach connectors, using glue, to a shape's very geometry—that is, the lines that make up the shape.

There are five options for glue that you can set.

To set glue options, you use the Snap & Glue dialog. What's the Snap part of Snap & Glue? That's coming up later, but the idea is that when you move shapes, they can "snap" to various positions, such as points on the drawing grid.

Here's how you use the Snap & Glue dialog to set glue options:

1. Select Tools > Snap & Glue. This opens the Snap & Glue dialog, shown in Figure 3.10.

Figure 3.10
The Snap & Glue dialog.

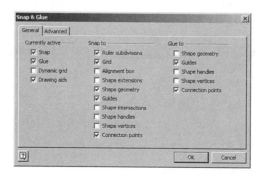

2. Select the check boxes in the Glue To area of the dialog. That lets you select the glue options you want.

3. Click OK. This closes the Snap & Glue dialog.

Using the Snap & Glue dialog, you can connect connectors using glue to these items:

- Shape geometry
- Guides
- Shape handles
- Shape vertices
- Connection points

GLUING CONNECTORS

There are many ways to connect connectors between shapes, and we'll go over them here, now that we've covered the basics of handling glue. The way you create connections is up to you—you can select from among all the following techniques.

DRAGGING SHAPES

This first technique is a rapid one that helps you create drawings rapidly. It allows you to drag as many shapes as you want from the Shapes window to the drawing surface, and connections are made automatically. The connectors used are shape-to-shape.

Here's how to make this work:

1. Select the Connector tool. This tool is just to the left of the Text tool (which displays a large *A*).

2. Select the shape to connect to in the drawing surface. You need to select the shape to connect to this way to make this technique work.

3. Drag the shape you want to connect to the drawing surface. Visio draws a shape-to-shape connector between the two shapes.

4. Repeat the preceding steps until all the connected shapes you want are displayed. Don't forget to change the mouse pointer back to the standard one by clicking the mouse pointer tool in the toolbar.

This is one of the easiest ways of creating connectors—using the Connector tool and letting Visio do the work for you.

DRAWING CONNECTORS WITH THE CONNECTOR TOOL

You can also use the Connector tool to draw connections between existing shapes. And depending on how you draw the connector, you'll get either a point-to-point connector or a shape-to-shape connector.

Here's how to create a point-to-point connector:

1. Select the Connector tool. This tool is just to the left of the Text tool (which displays a large *A*).

2. Move the mouse pointer over a connection point on a shape on the drawing surface. The connection point becomes outlined in red.

3. Press the mouse button. This starts the connection process.

4. Drag the mouse pointer to another's shape connection point. This draws the point-to-point connector.

5. Release the mouse button. This draws the point-to-point connector.

That creates a point-to-point connector between any two shapes using the Connector tool.

Here's how to create a shape-to-shape connector using the Connector tool in Visio:

1. Select the Connector tool. This tool is just to the left of the Text tool (which displays a large *A*).

2. Move the mouse pointer to a shape (not connection point). The shape becomes outlined in red.

3. Press the mouse button. This starts the connection process.

4. Drag the mouse pointer to another's shape connection point. This draws the shape-to-shape connector.

5. Release the mouse button. This draws the point-to-point connector.

And that's it—drawing shape-to-shape connectors is easy with the Connection tool.

As you can see, drawing connectors using the Connector tool is easy and convenient.

USING THE CONNECT SHAPES FEATURE

Here's an easy way to connect multiple shapes at once—you can use the Connect Shapes tool, which appears in the Action toolbar. Using this tool, you can connect multiple shapes at once, as shown in Figure 3.11.

The Connect Shapes tool shows two boxes separated vertically, with a red line connecting them. It's the third tool from the left in the Action toolbar, and it appears at the location of the mouse pointer in Figure 3.11.

Here's how you connect multiple shapes using the Connect Shapes tool in Visio:

1. Select the Pointer tool on the Standard toolbar. This tool is the standard mouse arrow pointer.

2. Holding down the Shift key, click the first shape to connect. The shape becomes selected.

3. Then, still holding down the Shift key, click the other shapes you want to connect. Make sure you click them in the order you want the connections to follow.

4. Click the Connect Shapes tool in the Action toolbar. This makes the connectors appear.

And that's it—an easy way to connect multiple shapes. If you don't like the way that Visio has connected your shapes, just drag the endpoints of connectors to where you want them.

Figure 3.11
The Connect Shapes tool.

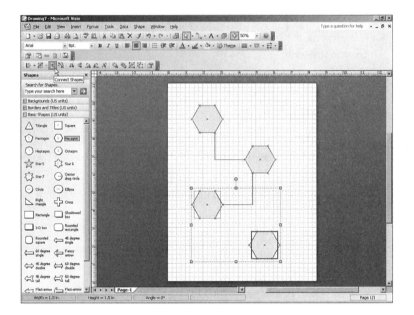

USING AUTOMATIC CONNECTORS

As of Visio 2007, you can also use automatic connectors to create connections between shapes. You've already see automatic connectors at work, and we'll review the ways to use them here.

The first method lets you create connectors as you add shapes to a diagram. Here's how it works:

1. Place a shape on the drawing surface. This is the shape that you're going to connect to.

2. Drag the shape you want to connect to the first shape. You'll see four light blue triangles; these are automatic connection points.

3. Move the second shape around until one of the automatic connection points on the original shape turns dark. This is the connection point that the second shape will connect to.

4. Drop the second shape. Visio connects the shapes using the automatic connection point you've selected.

Here's the second method—this is a good technique if you already have existing shapes that you want to connect:

1. Select the shape you want to connect from. Visio displays automatic connection points.

2. Hover over the automatic connection point you want to use. Visio darkens the connection point.

3. Make sure that the target shape appears with a red box around it. Visio selects the target shape it thinks you want to connect to automatically by surrounding it in a red box.

4. Click the dark blue automatic connection point. Visio draws the connector between the shapes.

And here's the third method. Say you have a shape already on the drawing surface, and want to draw a shape connected to that original shape. Here's how you can do it:

1. Make sure that the original shape is on the drawing surface. This is the shape that Visio will connect to.

2. Select the second shape, the one you want a connection to. Do this by highlighting the second shape in the Shapes window.

3. Hover the mouse over the original shape until the automatic connection points appear. These automatic connection points are light blue.

4. Move the mouse until one of the automatic connection points turns dark blue. That's how you select where the second shape will connect to.

5. Release the mouse button. Visio draws the shape selected in the Shapes window, and connects it to the original shape automatically, using the automatic connection point you've selected.

USING THE CONNECTOR STENCIL

Visio comes with a special connector stencil, which you can display in your own templates. Just select File > Shapes > Visio Extras > Connectors to display the Connector stencil.

You can see the Connector stencil at the left in Figure 3.12.

You can drag a connector from the Connectors stencil to the drawing surface, then connect the endpoints to connection points on the shapes. You can see this at work in Figure 3.12, in which heptagons are connected.

You can also use the Connect Shapes tool:

1. Select the Pointer tool on the Standard toolbar. This tool is the standard mouse arrow pointer.

2. Select File > Shapes > Visio Extras > Connectors to display the Connector stencil. The custom connector stencil appears.

3. Click the connector you want to use. The connector becomes selected.

4. Holding down the Shift key, click the first shape to connect. The shape becomes selected.

5. Then, still holding down the Shift key, click the other shapes you want to connect. Make sure you click them in the order you want the connections to follow.

6. Click the Connect Shapes tool in the Action toolbar. This makes the connectors appear.

Figure 3.12
Special connectors.

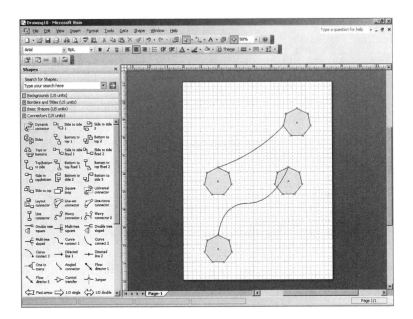

DRAGGING CONNECTORS FROM STENCILS

Some standard stencils also contain connectors. For example, the Basic Shapes stencil of the Basic Diagram template contains a Dynamic connector and a Line-Curve connector. You can drag the connectors you find in stencils to the drawing surface and then connect the endpoints of the connector to connection points on shapes.

Most of the connectors you'll find in the various standard stencils also appear in the special connector stencil, which you can open with File > Shapes > Visio Extras > Connectors.

Here's how to use the connectors you'll find in various standard stencils:

1. Select the Pointer tool on the Standard toolbar. This tool is the standard mouse arrow pointer.

2. Select the connector you want and drag it onto the drawing surface. The connector appears on the drawing surface.

3. To create a point-to-point connector, drag an endpoint of the connector to a connection point until the connection point appears inside a small red box.

   Drop the endpoint on the connection point. A small dark red box should appear at the join of the connector and the connection point.

4. To create a shape-to-shape connector, drag an endpoint of the connector to a shape until the shape appears inside a red box. Drop the endpoint on the shape. A bright red box should appear at the join of the connector and the connection point.

5. Repeat the process for all endpoints of your new connectors.

You can also use the Connect Shapes tool:

1. Select the Pointer tool on the Standard toolbar. This tool is the standard mouse arrow pointer.

2. Select File > Shapes > Visio Extras > Connectors to display the connector stencil. The custom connector stencil appears.

3. Click the connector you want to use. The connector becomes selected.

4. Holding down the Shift key, click the first shape to connect. The shape becomes selected.

5. Then, still holding down the Shift key, click the other shapes you want to connect. Make sure you click them in the order you want the connections to follow.

6. Click the Connect Shapes tool in the Action toolbar. This makes the connectors appear.

MOVING CONNECTORS AROUND

Connectors are by no means simply stuck in place—you can move them around as you want. That's good to know, because when you're creating drawings, things change and move around. In other words, if you decide that a connector would be better in another place, it's easy to move it.

Here's how to move a connector:

1. Select the Pointer tool on the Standard toolbar. This tool is the standard mouse arrow pointer.

2. Select the connector you want to move. The connector's endpoints appear.

3. Drag the connector's endpoint to its new location. The connector moves to your new location.

4. To create a point-to-point connector, drag the endpoint of the connector to a connection point until the connection point appears inside a small red box. Drop the endpoint on the connection point. A small dark red box should appear at the join of the connector and the connection point.

5. To create a shape-to-shape connector, drag an endpoint of the connector to a shape until the shape appears inside a red box. Drop the endpoint on the shape. A bright red box should appear at the join of the connector and the connection point.

6. Repeat the process for all endpoints of the connector you want to move.

In other words, to move a connector, just reconnect its endpoints. That's all it takes—Visio will do the rest.

WHEN CONNECTORS CROSS

You can specify the behavior of connectors that cross in Visio. For example, take a look at Figure 3.13, in which two wires cross in an electrical circuit drawing.

Figure 3.13
Crossing connectors.

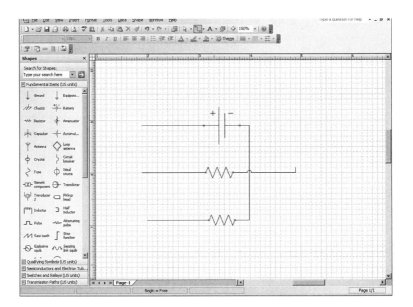

As you see, the connector that crosses another connector "jumps" over the other connector using an arc, which is standard for electrical circuits.

How do you specify the crossing behavior of connectors in Visio? Here's what you do:

1. Select File > Page Setup. The Page Setup dialog appears.

2. Click the Layout and Routing tab. That's shown in Figure 3.14.

3. Select the types of lines that you want to create line jumps for in the Add Line Jumps To box. We're adding line jumps to horizontal lines here.

4. Select a style in the Line Jump Style box. Arcs are the default; you can also choose gaps, squares, and other options, from a two-sided to a seven-sided polygon.

5. Change the height of the jump. Drag the Vertical Size bar.

6. Change the width of the jump. Drag the Horizontal Size bar.

7. Click OK. The Page Setup dialog closes.

Figure 3.14
Specifying connectors' crossing behavior.

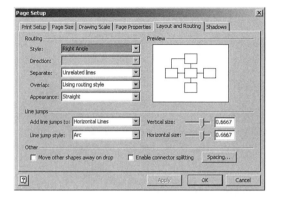

You can also use the Layout & Routing toolbar, shown in Figure 3.15, to specify line-jump behavior. As you see in the figure, we're making line jumps into arcs.

Figure 3.15
The Layout & Routing toolbar.

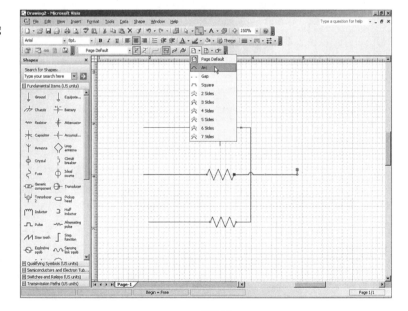

AUTOMATICALLY LAYING OUT SHAPES

After you've connected up your shapes, you can let Visio lay out your shapes automatically. This option is available if you want to see whether Visio can untangle drawings and make them clearer. It saves you the trouble of arranging your shapes yourself, and provides several different layout types:

- Radial
- Flowchart
- Circular
- Compact Tree
- Hierarchy

After you've placed the shapes you want on the drawing, and connected them, you can use this option to have Visio lay out the shapes. After Visio does its thing, you can fine-tune the arrangement by dragging shapes around yourself. And bear in mind that if you don't like what you see, you can always use Edit > Undo.

Here's how to use the automatic layout option:

1. Drag the shapes you want to the drawing.
2. Add the connectors you want to use.
3. Choose the shapes to arrange. Hold down the Shift key and click the shapes to arrange. If you want to arrange all shapes, select either all or none of the shapes—if no shapes are selected, Visio arranges all the shapes in the drawing.
4. Select Shape > Configure Layout. This opens the Configure Layout dialog, shown in Figure 3.16.

Figure 3.16
The Configure Layout dialog.

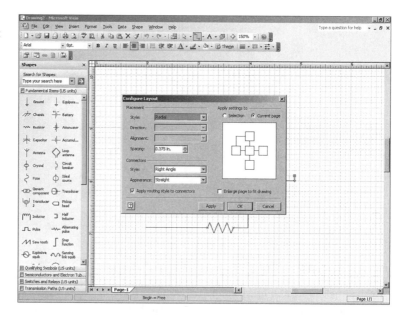

5. Select a layout style, such as Radial or Circular. The sample layout in the dialog box changes to match.

6. Select a direction, such as Top to Bottom or Left to Right. The sample layout in the dialog box changes to match. You usually use Top to Bottom for organization charts, for example.

7. Select an alignment: left, center, or right. The sample layout in the dialog box changes to match. You usually use Center for organization charts, for example.

8. Select the style of the connector you want to use in the Connectors area. The drop-down box has options for organization chart, flowcharts, trees, and so on. The sample layout in the dialog box changes to match.

9. Select the appearance of the connector you want to use in the Connectors area. You can choose between straight and curved. The sample layout in the dialog box changes to match.

10. Click OK. Visio arranges your shapes and connectors automatically.

Give this a try—you may be happy with the result, you may not. Just keep in mind that you can undo it if you don't like it.

DRAWING CURVED CONNECTORS

The default connector type in Visio is the right-angle connector, which can be moved and twisted as shapes move. But there are two other connector types as well—straight connectors and curved connectors.

Straight connectors just draw straight lines between connection points. As you move the shapes around, this connector stays straight.

Curved connectors are very much like straight connectors, but, of course, they're curved. You can bend their arc any way you like.

To make a connector right-angled, straight, or curved, right-click the connector and select from these options:

- Right-Angle Connector
- Straight Connector
- Curved Connector

For example, you can see a curved connector in Figure 3.17—including the control points you use to make curved connectors bend just the way you want them.

You can also use the File menu to set the default shape for connectors. To make the default connector straight or curved, select File > Page Setup, and click the Layout and Routing tab. Next, in the Appearance list, click Straight or Curved. New connectors that you add to your drawing will now be straight or curved.

Figure 3.17
A curved connector.

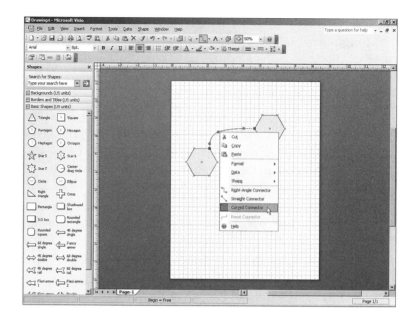

ADDING ARROWS, POINTS, OR OTHER LINE ENDS TO A CONNECTOR

You can also add arrows, points, or other line ends to a connector. Here's what you do:

1. Select a connector.
2. Select Format > Line.
3. In the Line Ends area, choose the type and size of line end that you want.
4. Click OK.

You can also use the Line Ends tool on the Formatting toolbar for the same purpose.

WORKING WITH TEXT

Text in Visio usually goes into *text blocks*. Text blocks are associated with shapes, and wherever the shape goes, the text block goes as well. Text blocks show frames in which you can insert text; the text is all that shows unless the text block is specifically selected.

Sometimes, you may want to add text to a drawing that's not connected to a shape, such as a title. For that, you use a *text shape*. Note that Visio usually provides alternatives for having to use freestanding text shapes—the Borders and Titles stencil, part of many templates, lets you enter titles for your drawing directly.

So how do you add text to a shape? Start by simply double-clicking the shape (or select the shape and press F2). That makes the text block for the shape appear, as shown in Figure 3.18.

Figure 3.18
A text block.

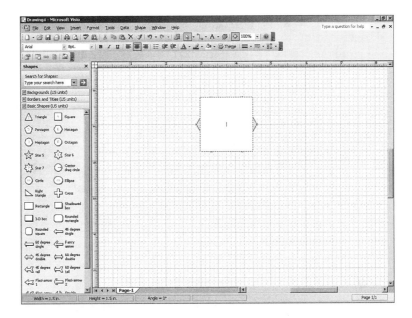

If your Visio zoom factor is set to anything under 100%, Visio zooms the shape to 100% to display the text block.

Enter your text, as shown in Figure 3.19. If your text is too long, Visio automatically wraps that text. You can press Enter to type multiple lines of text as well.

Figure 3.19
Entering text.

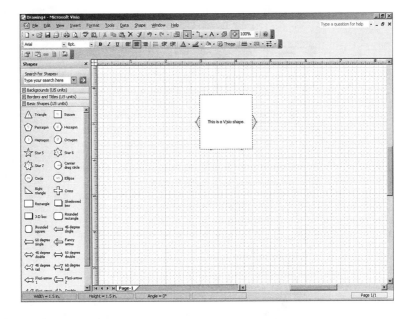

By default, Visio enters text in 8-point Arial font, which can be hard to see. To format the text, right-click the text block and select Format Text, opening the Text dialog shown in Figure 3.20. Adjust the font and font size there, then click OK.

Figure 3.20
Formatting text.

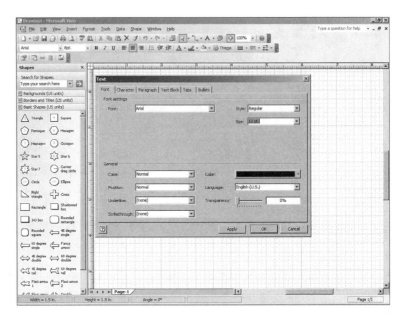

After you've entered and formatted your text, click outside the shape, which deselects the text block. The text in the block now appears inside the shape, as shown in Figure 3.21.

Figure 3.21
Text inside a shape.

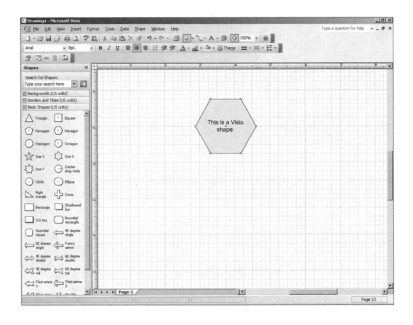

Want to create text not associated with any shape? Just use the Text tool in the Standard toolbar (the Text tool shows a capital letter *A*).

Then just drag the mouse to create a freestanding text block, not associated with a shape, or click your drawing to have Visio display a text block.

You can see a new freestanding text block in Figure 3.22.

Figure 3.22
A freestanding text block.

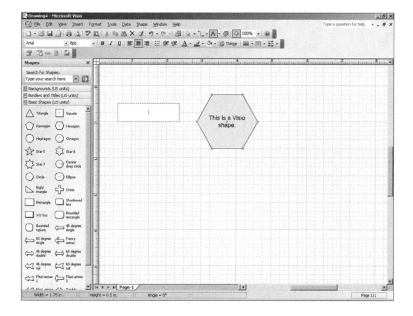

Enter the text you want in the text block, and right-click the text block, selecting Format Text to format that text. After formatting, click outside the text block to remove the text block frame and make the text itself appear, as shown in Figure 3.23.

That creates freestanding text in a drawing. Not bad.

In fact, Visio created a text shape for you here—text is never actually truly freestanding in Visio. The text shape exists just to hold text—it has no lines to its geometry.

Figure 3.23
Freestanding text.

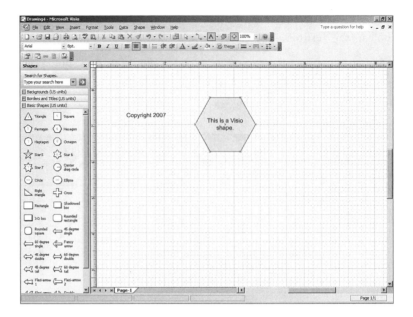

MOVING TEXT BLOCKS

You can move text blocks associated with shapes using the Text Block tool. This tool appears when you click the arrow next to the Text tool (the capital *A* in the Standard toolbar). When you click that arrow, two entries appear in a drop-down list: Text Tool and Text Block Tool.

To move a text block, select Text Block Tool. Click the shape that encloses the text you want to move. The green dotted text block frame becomes visible.

Drag the text block to its new position. That new position can be outside the shape entirely.

Drop the text block by releasing the mouse button. Format the text as you want it by right-clicking the text block and selecting Format Text.

Finally, click the arrow pointer tool in the Standard toolbar to get you back to the standard mouse pointer.

You can see an example in Figure 3.24, in which the text associated with the shape has been moved outside the shape.

However, the text block is still associated with the shape—if you select the shape and move it around, the text block will follow. Nice.

Figure 3.24
Moving a text block.

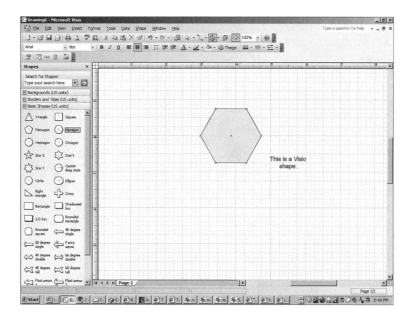

RESIZING TEXT BLOCKS

You can also resize text blocks as you like. For example, you might not like the way Visio has broken your text at the ends of lines, and you can change that by giving the text block a new size.

Here's how to resize a text block:

1. Select the Text Block tool from the drop-down arrow next to the Text tool.
2. Click the shape that contains the text block. Visio selects the text block by making its green dotted frame appear.
3. By dragging the text block frame's sizing handles, resize the text block. The mouse cursor changes to a double-headed arrow during this operation.
4. Click the Pointer tool in the Standard toolbar. This deselects the text block.

ALIGNING TEXT

You can also align the text you enter into text blocks horizontally or vertically.

To align text, follow these steps:

1. Select the Text Tool button in the Standard toolbar.
2. Select the Shape whose text you want to align. Visio selects and displays the text block, surrounded by a green dotted frame.
3. Select the text you want to align. If you want to align all the text, you don't need to specifically select any of it.

4. Right-click the text and select Format Text. The Text dialog appears.

5. To align the text horizontally, click the Paragraph tab. You can see this tab in Figure 3.25.

Figure 3.25
The Paragraph tab.

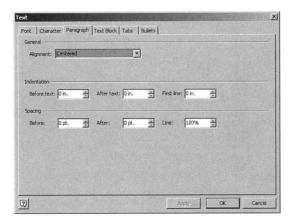

Select the alignment—Left, Centered, or Right—from the Alignment box shown in Figure 3.25.

6. To align the text vertically, click the Text Block tab.

Select the alignment—Top, Middle, or Bottom—from the Alignment box.

7. Click OK to close the Text dialog. Visio aligns the text for you.

You can see the text alignment options in Figure 3.26.

Figure 3.26
The text alignment options.

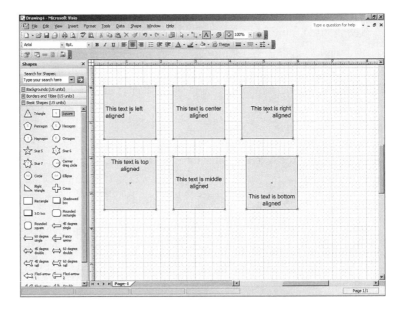

SETTING TAB STOPS

You can also use tabs in text blocks, as shown in Figure 3.27.

Figure 3.27
Using tabs.

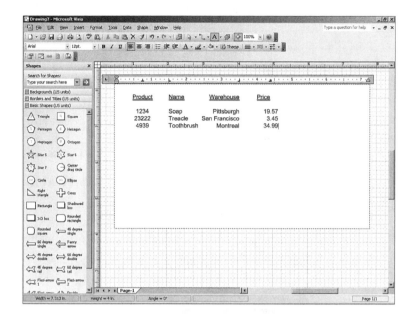

You can see the various types of tabs available in Visio in Figure 3.27. These tabs appear as icons in the tab toolbar, shown at the top of the text block.

Moving from left to right, the first tab stop, which looks like an upside-down *T*, is a center tab. As you can see, the text in the Product column, below the text ruler, is indeed centered.

The next tab stop, looking like an *L*, is a left-aligned tab—and you can see that the text in the column below this tab, the Name column, is indeed left-aligned.

The next tab stop, which looks like a backward *L*, is a right-aligned tab stop, and you can see that the text in the column below the tab stop is right-aligned.

The final tab stop in the text ruler, which looks like an upside-down *T* with a dot, is a decimal-point alignment tab stop. The text in the column below it is aligned on the decimal point.

How do you create these tab stops? Follow these steps:

1. Click the Text tool on the Standard toolbar.
2. Click the shape whose text you want to edit. Visio displays the text block as selected.
3. Right-click the text block and select the Text Ruler item. Visio displays the text ruler at the top of the text block.

4. Click the button that displays the tab type at the left in the Text Ruler until the type of tab you want appears. Visio cycles through the various tab types as you click the button, whose caption changes to match.

5. Click the text ruler at the location where you want the new tab. Visio displays the new tab in the text ruler.

6. Repeat the preceding steps to add other tabs to the text ruler.

And that's it—you've created the tabs you want. To delete them, simply drag them off the ruler.

Want more precise control over your tab stops, such as their exact position? Use the Tabs tab in the Text dialog. Here's how:

1. Click the Text tool on the Standard toolbar.

2. Click the shape whose text you want to edit. Visio displays the text block as selected.

3. Select Format > Text or right-click the text block and select Format Text. Visio displays the Text dialog, shown in Figure 3.28.

Figure 3.28
Using the Tabs tab of the Text dialog.

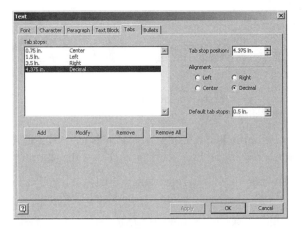

4. Click the Tabs tab. Visio displays the Tabs tab, shown in Figure 3.28.

5. To add a tab precisely, click Add. Visio creates a new tab stop.

6. Enter a measurement in the Tab Stop Position box.

7. Select an alignment in the Alignment area. Select from Left, Right, Center, and Decimal.

8. Repeat the preceding steps to add more tabs.

9. Click OK to close the Text dialog.

That lets you set your tabs with great precision.

CREATING BULLETED LISTS

You can also format your text into bulleted lists using Visio. Bulleted lists are commonly displayed in Visio drawings, because they can sum up data and information handily.

You can create a bulleted list format for a blank text block, or for text that already exists. Either way, Visio lets you create bulleted lists easily.

Here are the steps to follow:

1. Click the Text tool on the Standard toolbar.

2. Click the shape whose text you want to edit. Visio displays the text block as selected.

3. Select Format > Text or right-click the text block and select Format Text. Visio displays the Text dialog.

4. Click the Bullets tab. Visio displays the Bullets tab, shown in Figure 3.29.

Figure 3.29
Using the Bullets tab.

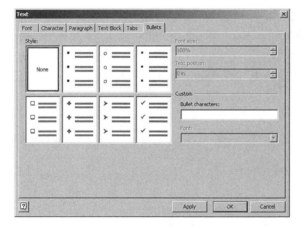

5. Click the Bullet style you want in the Style box.

6. Click OK—Visio applies the bullet style and closes the Text dialog.

You can see what the results look like in Figure 3.30.

Figure 3.30
Creating a bulleted list.

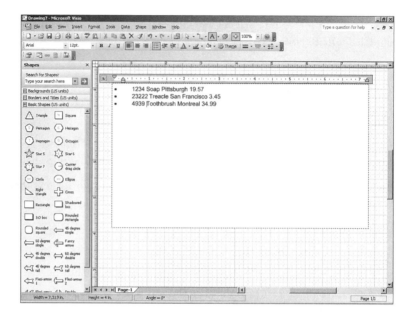

CREATING NUMBERED LISTS

Creating numbered lists is a little more difficult than simply creating bulleted lists in Visio. That's because Visio has no actual built-in support for numbered lists—but you can format and create them anyway.

Here are the steps to follow—first format the text that will go into a text block, giving it a list format:

1. Select a text block.

2. Select Format > Text or right-click the text block and select Format Text. Visio displays the Text dialog.

3. Click the Text Block tab. Visio displays the Text Block tab, as shown in Figure 3.31.

Figure 3.31
Using the Text Block tab.

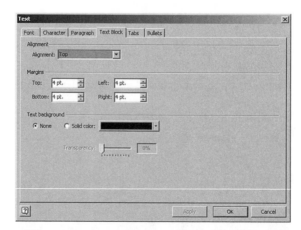

4. Select Top in the Alignment box.

5. Click the Paragraph tab. Visio displays the Paragraph tab, as shown in Figure 3.32.

Figure 3.32
Using the Paragraph tab.

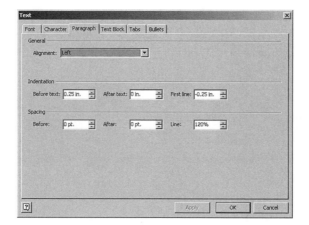

6. Select Left in the Alignment box.

7. Enter a value, such as 0.25, in the Indentation Before Text box. This sets the left indent.

8. Enter a value, such as -.25, in the Indentation First Line box. This gives you space to type the number before every item in the list.

9. Click OK. Visio closes the Text dialog.

That sets up the formatting for the list.

Now you can create items in the list like this:

1. Type the item's number, starting with 1.

2. Press Tab.

3. Enter the text for the item.

4. Press Enter.

5. Repeat the process for the other items in the list.

You can see a sample numbered list in Figure 3.33.

Figure 3.33
A numbered list.

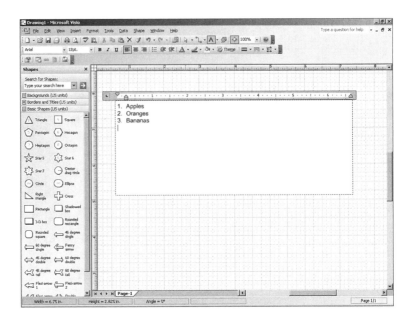

FORMATTING PARAGRAPHS

Visio lets you format paragraphs extensively. At first, you wouldn't think that Visio supports such advanced text formatting, but in fact, it's as good as a word processor such as Microsoft Word.

You can indent the first line of paragraph text, for example, specifying that indentation in inches. That gives an automatic paragraph indentation to your text.

You can also specify the amount of space before and after paragraphs in Visio. This space is measured in points (1/72nds of an inch).

Here's how to format paragraphs in Visio:

1. Select the Text tool in the Standard toolbar.

2. In a text block or text shape, select the text you want to format. If you want to format all the text in the text block or text shape, just select the text block or shape.

3. Select Format > Text or right-click the text block and select Format Text. Visio displays the Text dialog.

4. Click the Paragraph tab. Visio displays the Paragraph tab.

5. Enter a value (in inches) in the Before Text, After Text, and First Line boxes to specify the paragraph's indentation. The Before Text and After Text boxes set the indentation of the paragraph as a whole, and the First Line box sets the indentation of the first line of the paragraph.

6. Enter a value (in points) in the Before, After, and Line boxes to set the line and paragraph spacing. The Before and After boxes set the amount of space before and after the paragraph, and the Line box sets the vertical spacing of the lines in the paragraph.

7. Click OK. Visio closes the Text dialog.

You can see a formatted paragraph in Figure 3.34.

Figure 3.34
A formatted paragraph.

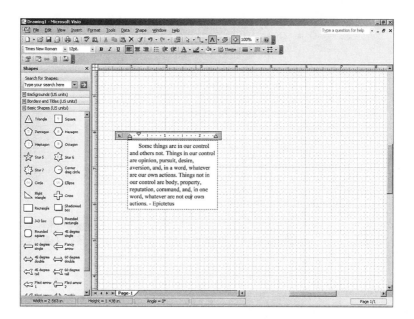

SPELL-CHECKING YOUR TEXT

Visio's support for text is so strong that it even includes a (good) spell-checker. In fact, that spell-checker is enabled by default, as you can see if you make a spelling mistake.

Take a look at Figure 3.35, in which we've spelled "desire" as "desere" by mistake. Visio catches the error and underlines the offending word with a wavy red underline.

That's fine as far as it goes, but what if you type a legitimate word that's not in Visio's spell-checker? How can you turn automatic spell-checking off?

To turn automatic spell-checking off, follow these steps:

1. Select Tools > Spelling Options. Visio opens the Spelling Options dialog shown in Figure 3.36.

2. Deselect the Check Spelling as You Type check box.

That's it—Visio will no longer check your spelling automatically.

Figure 3.35
Catching a spelling error.

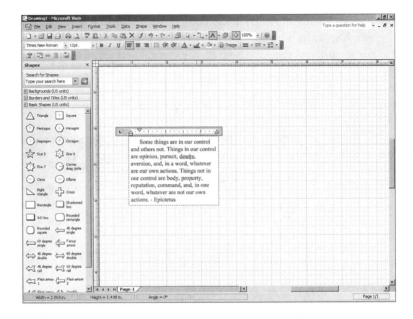

Figure 3.36
Setting spelling options.

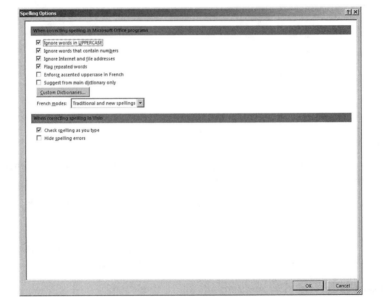

After you've turned off spell-checking, how do you actually spell-check text? Just follow these steps:

1. Select the Text tool in the Standard toolbar.

2. In a text block or text shape, select the text you want to spell-check. If you want to check all the text in the text block or text shape, just select the text block or shape.

3. Select Tools > Spelling > Spelling or click the Spelling button in the Standard toolbar (the one with the letters ABC and a check mark). If there are spelling errors, Visio opens the Spelling dialog shown in Figure 3.37. If there are no errors, you'll see a dialog box with the message "The spelling check is complete."

Figure 3.37
Catching a spelling error.

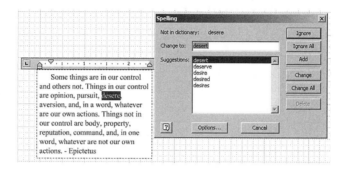

4. Use the buttons in the Spelling dialog. Here are the buttons and what they do:

Ignore—Ignores what Visio thinks is a spelling error.

Ignore All—Ignores all occurrences of what Visio is flagging as an error.

Add—Adds the word to the Visio dictionary.

Change—Changes the misspelled word to the Visio suggestion—you can select the new word from a list if Visio finds several possible words.

Change All—Changes all occurrences of the misspelled word.

Delete—This button is enabled when Visio finds two of the same word next to each other; Visio flags the second word for deletion, and you can delete it by clicking this button.

5. Continue the preceding steps until the spell-check is complete. When the spell-check is done, you'll see a dialog box with the message "The spelling check is complete."

6. Click OK. Visio closes the Spelling dialog.

FORMATTING TEXT

Visio lets you format your text, changing your text's color, font, and style (such as italic). Formatting text lets you escape the defaults Visio has picked out for your text.

FORMATTING TEXT USING THE TEXT DIALOG

Formatting text is easy in Visio—just follow these steps:

1. Select the Text tool in the Standard toolbar.

2. In a text block or text shape, select the text you want to format. If you want to format all the text in the text block or text shape, just select the text block or shape.

3. Select Format > Text or right-click and select Format Text. Visio opens the Text dialog with the Font tab selected, as shown in Figure 3.38.

Figure 3.38
The Text dialog.

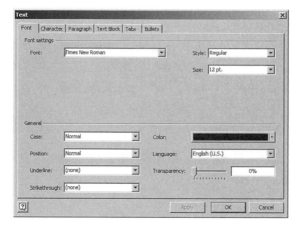

4. Make the changes you want to make:

To alter the text style: Click the Style drop-down box and select from Regular, Italic, Bold, and Bold Italic.

To alter the text's font: Click the Font drop-down box and select a font, such as Times New Roman. All the fonts registered on your system are available.

To alter the text size: Click the Size drop-down box and select a point size for your font.

To alter the case of your text: Click the Case drop-down box and select from Normal, All Caps, Initial Caps, and Small Caps.

To alter the text position: Click the Position drop-down box and select from Normal, Superscript, and Subscript.

To underline the text: Click the Underline drop-down box and select from (none), Single, and Double.

To strike through your text: Click the Strikethrough drop-down box and select from (none), Single, and Double.

To alter your text's color: Click the Color drop-down box and select one of the displayed colors.

To alter the spell-checker's language: Click the Language drop-down box and select one of the displayed languages.

To alter your text's transparency: Drag the Transparency slider to your desired setting. Modifying text transparency and overlaying that text can make for some striking effects.

5. Click OK. Visio closes the Text dialog.

As you can see, you can format your text in many ways using the Text dialog. You can see some sample text formatted in Figure 3.39, in which the text appears in a large red (black-and-white in the figure) font.

Figure 3.39
Formatted text.

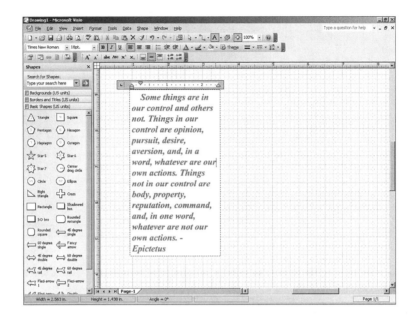

FORMATTING TEXT USING THE FORMAT PAINTER

You can also use the Format Painter tool to copy formatting from one section of text to another, or from one text block to another. For example, take a look at Figure 3.40, which shows two text blocks—the block on the left contains specially formatted text, and the text block on the right uses default text settings.

How can you copy the format of the text block on the left to the one on the right? You can use the Format Painter tool. Here's how:

1. Select the Text tool in the Standard toolbar.
2. In a text block or text shape, select the text you want to copy the format from.
3. Click the Format Painter tool in the Standard toolbar. This tool shows a paintbrush icon. The mouse pointer shows an arrow and a paintbrush.
4. Click the target text to be formatted. Visio formats the target text the same as the source text.

You can see the results in Figure 3.41, in which each text block has the same formatting.

Figure 3.40
A formatted text block.

Figure 3.41
Two formatted text blocks.

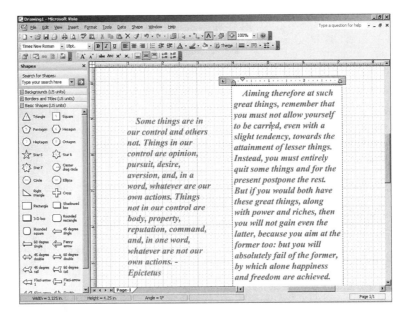

After you click the target text, the cursor reverts to the Text Tool cursor, and the Format Painter becomes inactive. To make the Format Painter "sticky"—which means making it remain active after you've used it, so that you can use it on further text blocks—just double-click the Format Painter tool in the Standard toolbar instead of single-clicking it when you start using the Format Painter.

The Format Painter tool is one of the few that have only a toolbar button, without any corresponding menu item.

SELECTING BACKGROUND COLORS

You can also select the background color of text blocks in Visio. For example, the text in Figure 3.42 is light green (as displayed in black-and-white in the figure, of course).

Figure 3.42
A text block with a background color.

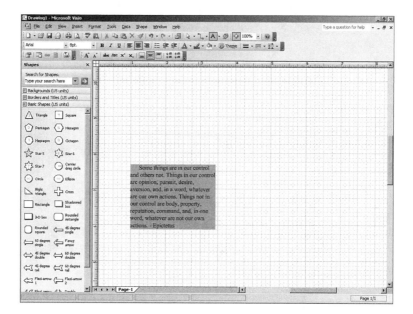

How can you set a text block's background color? Follow these steps:

1. Click the Text tool in the Standard toolbar.
2. Select the text block you want to format.
3. Select Format > Text or right-click the text and select Format Text. Visio shows the Text dialog.
4. Click the Text Block tab. Visio displays the Text Block tab, as shown in Figure 3.43.
5. Select the Solid Color radio button in the Text Background area.
6. Select a color from the Solid Color drop-down box. Visio shows the color selected.
7. Slide the transparency slider, if desired, to set the color's transparency.
8. Click OK. Visio closes the Text dialog.

Figure 3.43
The Text Block tab.

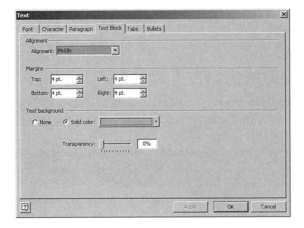

ROTATING YOUR TEXT

By default, Visio's text is drawn horizontally—but that doesn't stop you from rotating it to fit your shapes, as shown in Figure 3.44.

Figure 3.44
Rotating text.

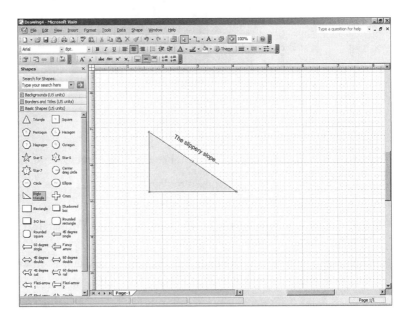

You also can rotate text to label the vertical axis in a graph, or whatever you want.

Rotating text is not difficult in Visio, if you follow these steps:

1. Select the Text Block or Standard Pointer tool in the toolbar.

2. Select the text block you want to rotate. Visio selects the text block and shows its selection frame.

3. Drag the rotation handle of the selection frame, rotating the text as you want it. Visio rotates the text to match.

4. Release the mouse button.

By default, Visio lets you rotate text only in 15° increments. However, you can rotate text at any angle you want if you follow these steps:

1. Select the Text Block or Standard Pointer tool in the toolbar.

2. Select the text block you want to rotate. Visio selects the text block and shows its selection frame.

3. Select View > Size & Position Window. Visio displays the Size & Position window, shown in Figure 3.45.

4. Enter the angle for the text. 0° is horizontal.

Figure 3.45
Using the Size &
Position window.

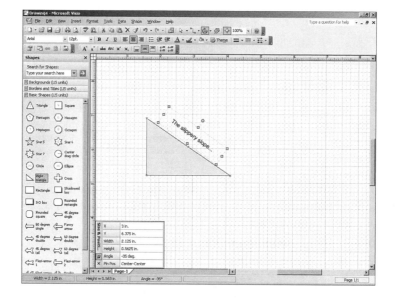

RESIZING TEXT BLOCKS

As you're typing in a text block or text shape, you might want to resize the text block or shape—but there are no sizing handles available. That's awkward, because as you type the text, it is broken depending on the bounding rectangle.

So how do you resize a text block or text shape? You just follow these steps:

1. Select the Text Block or Standard Pointer tool in the toolbar.

2. Select the text block you want to resize. Visio selects the text block and shows its selection frame.

3. Drag a sizing handle of the selection frame, resizing the selection frame as you want it. Visio realigns the text to match.

4. Release the mouse button.

GIVING TEXT SHAPES BORDERS

When you use text shapes for captions or titles in your drawing, you might want to surround that text with a border, as shown in Figure 3.46.

Figure 3.46
A text shape with a border.

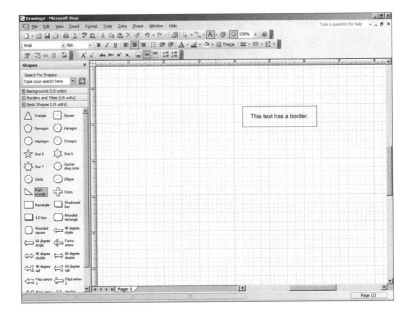

You can easily format borders for text shapes. Just right-click the text shape with the Pointer tool and select Format > Line, opening the Line dialog box shown in Figure 3.47.

Figure 3.47
Formatting lines.

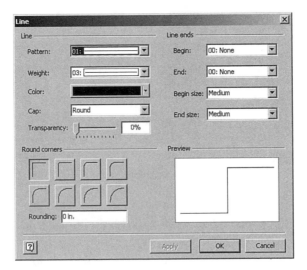

In the Line dialog, you can set these items concerning a text shape's border:

- **Pattern**—Select from a straight line or various dotted ones.
- **Weight**—Specify how thick you want the line.
- **Color**—Set the color of the line.
- **Cap**—Choose the line's cap: Round, Square, or Extended.
- **Transparency**—Specify how transparent you want the line.

3

GUIDES, RULERS, AND CUSTOM SHAPES

In this chapter

VISIO AND PLACEMENT TOOLS

A big part of Visio is placing shapes just as you want them, and Visio has plenty of tools to assist in that. For example, you can snap shapes to the grid in Visio, or use the rulers to align shapes as you need them.

Here's a list of the concepts coming up in this chapter:

- **Alignment**—Alignment means aligning shapes with respect to each other. Shapes that are vertically aligned will look even in the vertical sense—even if they're not the same size. Visio has several tools that help you align your shapes.

- **Distribution**—Distribution refers to how shapes are spaced. If you distribute shapes, they're evenly spaced in the drawing. Visio also supports various ways of helping you distribute your shapes in a drawing.

- **Gridlines**—Gridlines are those horizontal and vertical lines on the drawing surface that let you place shapes. You can "snap" shapes to the grid if you want to.

- **Guides**—Guides act as lines and points of reference in Visio. For example, guides would be helpful if you wanted to restrict part of a drawing to a specific region. Guide lines and guide points let you outline regions, such as those bounded by walls, for example, so that you can arrange the contents of an office. Guide lines and points are used to provide locations for shapes to snap to or glue to.

- **Rulers**—Rulers appear at the top and left of a drawing to give you a sense of scale, and to help you to place your shapes in a drawing.

- **Scale**—Scale relates the measurements in your drawing to measurements in real life. You don't use scale for drawings such as organization charts, but you do for drawings that correspond to physical layouts, such as office layouts. The scale of a drawing is given as the ratio of *drawing measurement* : *real-life measurement*. For example, if 1 inch corresponded to 1 foot in an office layout, you'd have a scale of 1 inch : 1 foot.

- **Size & Position window**—This window lets you place shapes with great accuracy, setting a shape's upper-left point, as well as its width and height.

- **Snap**—Snap is a tool that pulls shapes into alignment. You can snap shapes to other shapes, gridlines, or guide lines and guide points in Visio. This is a great feature that allows you to align shapes to some reference point automatically.

You can access many of the alignment options in Visio using the View menu. Here are some of the items in this menu that are important in this chapter:

- **View > Connection Points**—Lets you toggle connection point visibility on or off.

- **View > Grid**—Lets you toggle the gridlines on and off in a drawing.

- **View > Guides**—Lets you toggle the guides in a drawing on and off.

- **View > Rulers**—Lets you toggle rulers on and off.

There's also a toolbar that specializes in alignments: the Snap & Glue toolbar, which you can display by right-clicking the toolbar and selecting Snap & Glue. This toolbar appears in Figure 4.1.

Figure 4.1
The Snap & Glue toolbar.

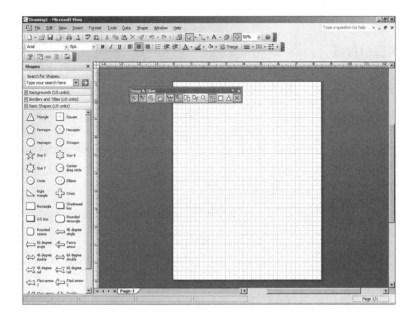

Here are the buttons in this toolbar, from left to right (there is no Snap & Glue menu that these buttons correspond to):

- **Toggle Snap**—Lets you toggle snapping on and off.
- **Toggle Glue**—Lets you attach shapes to the items you specify in the Snap & Glue dialog.
- **Snap to Dynamic Grid**—Makes shapes snap to the dynamic grid, which is a set of dotted lines that appears as you drag shapes into a drawing.
- **Snap to Drawing Aids**—Lets you draw shapes such as lines and squares at a particular angle.
- **Snap to Rule Subdivisions**—Makes shapes snap to the nearest ruler subdivision.
- **Snap to Grid**—Makes shapes snap to the nearest gridline.
- **Snap to Alignment Box**—Makes shapes snap to other shapes' alignment boxes.
- **Snap to Shape Intersections**—Snaps shapes to points on other shapes, such as their midpoint.
- **Glue to Shape Geometry**—Glues shapes to the edges of other shapes.
- **Glue to Guides**—Glues shapes to guide lines and guide points.
- **Glue to Shape Handles**—Glues shapes to the shape handles of other shapes.

- **Glue to Shape Vertices**—Glues shapes to the vertices of other shapes.
- **Glue to Connection Points**—Glues shapes to the connection points of other shapes.

Okay, that's given us some overview. Time to get started.

HANDLING THE DRAWING GRID

If you create a new drawing, Visio displays a drawing grid on the drawing surface, as shown in Figure 4.1. By default, the drawing grid has lines spaced every 1/4 inch.

The idea behind the grid is to let you place shapes accurately. The gridline spacing isn't set in stone—you can alter it easily. And Visio will alter the spacing for you as well. For example, if you zoom in on a drawing (set the Zoom factor in the Zoom box to 200%, or hold down the Ctrl key and roll the mouse wheel), the grid changes as you zoom, as shown in Figure 4.2, in which the gridlines are 1/16 inch apart.

Figure 4.2
Zooming in.

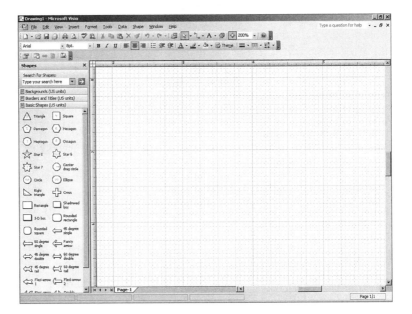

In other words, the drawing grid is variable by default. When you zoom in, more lines appear, and when you zoom out, fewer lines appear. You can also make the gridlines fixed— that's coming up in a minute.

SETTING GRID DENSITY

You can set the *density* of the lines in a drawing grid. There are four possible settings:

- Fine
- Normal
- Coarse
- Fixed

You set gridline density with the Ruler & Grid dialog that opens when you select the Tools > Ruler & Grid menu item. This dialog appears in Figure 4.3, in which the Normal grid density has been selected both horizontally and vertically.

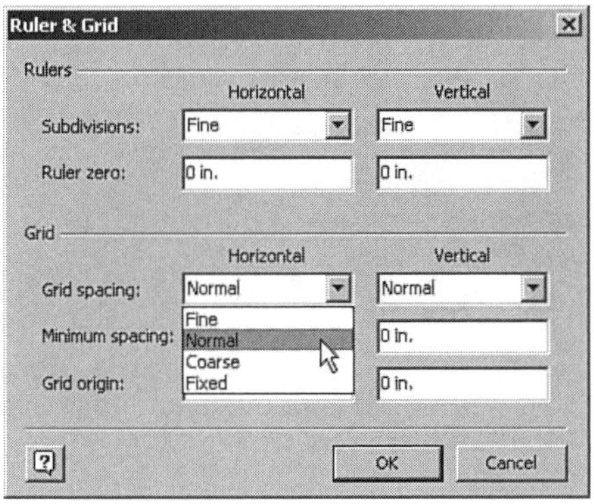

Figure 4.3
The Ruler & Grid dialog.

Despite the name, the Normal grid density (which displays gridlines every 1/2 inch) is not the default for drawings; Fine (which displays gridlines every 1/4 inch) is the default.

As shown in Figure 4.3, the Normal grid density does indeed display gridlines every 1/2 inch in the default view (which shows the drawing with a zoom setting of 50%).

This is an important fact to remember—by default, the grid is *variable* in Visio. Don't assume that the lines are always 1/4 inch apart, for example—the gridlines depend on a lot of factors.

TIP

> Want to turn off the grid? Just click the Grid button on the View toolbar, or select View > Grid. Without the grid, you'll see how the drawing will look when you print it.

SETTING THE GRID'S ORIGIN

You can also set the grid's origin to a new location. The origin of the grid is the lower-left point in a drawing, but you can reset that as you like.

For example, say that you have 1/2-inch margins on your printed page—you can set the origin of the drawing grid to (1/2 inch, 1/2 inch), as shown in the Ruler & Grid dialog in Figure 4.4.

SETTING A FIXED GRID

You can also make the grid *fixed*. That can be very useful if you're working to scale, such as 1/4 inch : 1 foot, and you want constant 1/4-inch lines to appear in the drawing.

In this case, the 1/4-inch lines will appear and stay 1/4 inch apart, no matter how much you zoom in or zoom out.

Figure 4.4
Setting the grid origin.

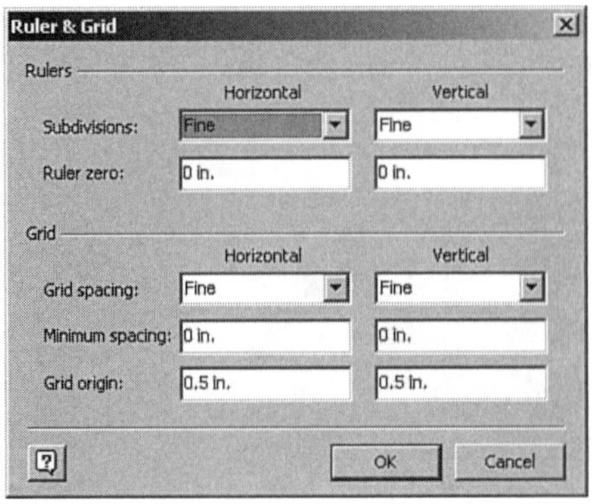

To make the grid fixed, select Fixed in the Grid Spacing drop-down list box, as shown in Figure 4.5.

Figure 4.5
Setting a fixed grid.

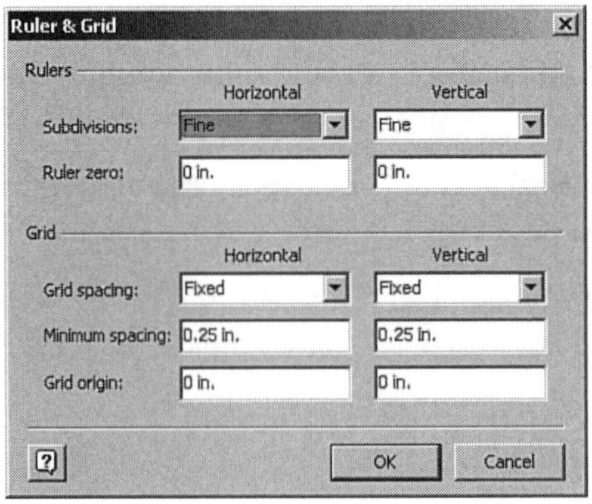

How can you set the spacing for the fixed gridlines? You set that in the Minimum Spacing box, as shown in Figure 4.5, in which the fixed gridlines are being set to 1/4 inch apart.

WORKING WITH THE DYNAMIC GRID

There's another way of aligning shapes—you can align them to each other. One way of doing this in Visio is to use the *dynamic grid* feature.

To enable the dynamic grid feature, select Tools > Snap & Glue, select the Dynamic Glue check box in the Currently Active region of the dialog, and then click OK to close the dialog. Or you can click the Snap to Dynamic Grid button on the Snap & Glue toolbar.

The dynamic grid is automatically enabled when you create a flowchart, but not in other drawing types.

When you've enabled the dynamic grid, dotted lines appear when the shape you're dragging is aligned either vertically or horizontally, or both, with another shape, as shown in Figure 4.6.

Figure 4.6
Using the dynamic grid.

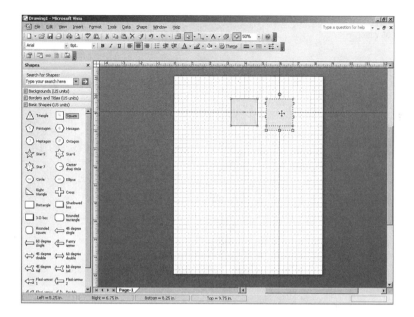

That's how it works—you drag a shape onto a drawing, and dynamic gridlines appear as the shape is aligned with other shapes already on the drawing. When those dynamic gridlines appear, you can drop the shape you're dragging, and the shape will be in alignment with the previous shape(s).

GETTING A SENSE OF SCALE

Many Visio drawings don't need to be done to scale—organization charts, for example. What difference does it make if an Executive box is 1 inch or 1 1/4 inches? Nothing depends on the actual measurement.

However, sometimes scale is important, as when you're creating an office layout or drawing a map. Then the people who refer to your drawing will make use of that scale when it comes time to put your drawing to work.

Usually, when you create a drawing, Visio sets the default scale to 1 : 1. That makes the drawing actual size compared to the printed page.

But Visio can use different scales as well, as you see when you use the Maps and Floor Plans template category's Office Layout template, shown in Figure 4.7.

Notice the ruler measurements in Figure 4.7—they're in feet, not inches. That's because office layouts are created by default using the Visio Architectural scale, as you see in the Print > Page Setup dialog's Drawing Scale tab, shown in Figure 4.8.

As shown in Figure 4.8, the office layout drawing uses a predefined Visio scale, the Architectural scale, where one drawing page corresponds to a space of 22 feet×17 feet.

Figure 4.7
Creating an office layout.

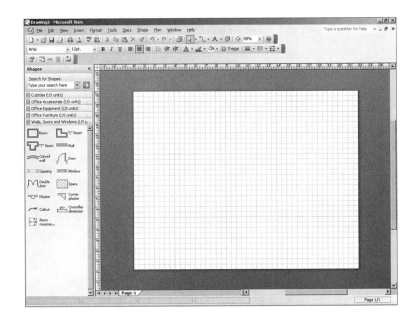

Figure 4.8
An office layout's scale.

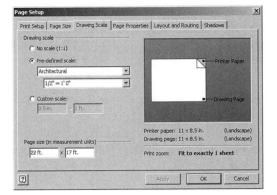

The Architectural scale is one of four predefined scales in Visio:

- Architectural
- Civil Engineering
- Metric
- Mechanical Engineering

In the Architectural scale, 1/2 inch = 1 foot.

You can also set a custom scale yourself. To do so, follow these steps:

1. Select File > Page Setup. Visio opens the Page Setup dialog box to let you set your custom scale.

2. Click the Drawing Scale tab. Visio displays the Drawing Scale tab, shown in Figure 4.9.

Figure 4.9
Setting a custom scale.

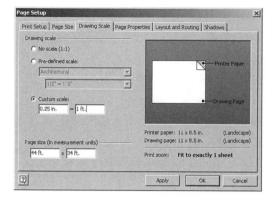

3. Select the Custom Scale radio button.

4. Set your scale. In the figure, 1/4 inch = 1 foot. Visio displays the real-world size corresponding to one page, as shown in the figure, where the page corresponds to 44 feet×34 feet.

5. Click OK. Visio closes the Page Setup dialog.

That's how it works—you enter the scale you want, such as 1/4 inch = 1 foot, and Visio shows you the area corresponding to one page, as shown in Figure 4.9, where the page corresponds to 44 feet×34 feet.

When you're designing a space that has some real physical dimensions, setting the drawing scale so that one page just fills your real space can be invaluable. Being able to cover the whole space with one drawing makes the design process much easier—you can see where the edges are for the space right there as you're designing the shapes that will fill it.

SNAPPING SHAPES

Say that you want to set up two shapes so that they're exactly 1 inch apart. You could fiddle with the individual placements to no end—or you could simply rely on Visio's default Snap feature, which snaps shapes to various guides and boundaries like a magnet.

Using the Snap feature, setting two shapes 1 inch apart is no problem at all—just move the second shape to approximately the right position, and it will snap to various gridlines, 1/4 inch apart, or the space halfway between such lines—in other words, shapes will snap to 1/8-inch positions automatically.

Visio turns on the Snap feature automatically for rulers, gridlines, connection points, and guides. There are other elements you can turn Snap on for; here is the list of the possible elements:

- **Alignment box**—A shape's selection frame, visible when the shape is selected.
- **Connection points**—The points on a shape where you can add connectors.
- **Grid**—Vertical and horizontal gridlines, and the space exactly halfway between them.
- **Guides**—Lines or points that your shapes can be assigned to help you align them.
- **Ruler divisions**—The tick marks that appear in rulers.
- **Shape extensions**—Dotted lines that extend from a shape.
- **Shape geometry**—The edges of a shape.
- **Shape handles**—The handles that appear when a shape is selected.
- **Shape intersections**—The locations at which shapes intersect.
- **Shape vertices**—The points on a shape where lines meet.

You can configure the Snap feature with the Tools > Snap & Glue dialog, which you see in Figure 4.10. You can make Visio snap shapes to any of the previous elements using this dialog, as shown in the Snap To region in the figure.

Figure 4.10
Setting the Snap feature.

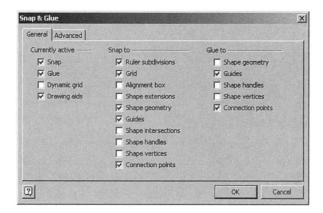

You can also set the Snap strength, which is the number of pixels away from an element a shape can be before snapping to that element. To set the snap strength for various elements, select the Advanced tab in the Snap & Glue dialog, as shown in Figure 4.11.

Simply set the number of pixels that you want the Snap feature to be active for from each element in the Snap & Glue dialog. For example, setting the Snap strength for gridlines to 5 pixels means that when you move a shape, it will snap to gridlines when it's within 5 pixels.

TIP

> Want to turn off Snap altogether? Just click the Toggle Snap button on the Snap & Glue toolbar, or select Tools > Snap & Glue, and deselect the Snap check box in the Currently Active area of the General tab.

Figure 4.11
Setting the Snap
feature.

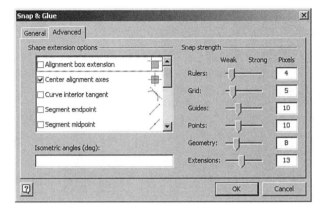

USING RULERS

Rulers appear at the top and to the left of the drawing space in Visio. You can set the scale used in those rulers yourself—but note that this is a drawing-space-only thing—it doesn't affect the way the drawing is printed.

The units of the rulers depend on a number of factors; for example, they're usually in inches if you ask Visio to use a US units template, but centimeters if you ask it to use metric units.

Setting rulers to the units you select can be very useful if you've set a custom scale and the tick marks on the rulers become too close to be read well. You can also set the origin of the rulers, which is useful if you don't want to measure everything from the edges of the drawing surface. For example, in an office layout, you might want to measure distances from the actual walls, and you can do that by resetting the rulers' origin.

Want to change the rulers' units? Here's what you do:

1. Select File > Page Setup. Visio opens the Page Setup dialog box.
2. Click the Page Properties tab. Visio displays the Page Properties tab.
3. Click the down arrow on the Measurement Units box. Visio displays the available units, as shown in Figure 4.12.
4. Select a set of units.
5. Click OK. Visio closes the Page Setup dialog.

Note the wide range of units available in Figure 4.12—everything from inches to miles.

You can also set the rulers' origin in Visio.

You might want to do that, for example, when designing an office layout, as shown in Figure 4.13.

Figure 4.12
Setting the rulers'
units.

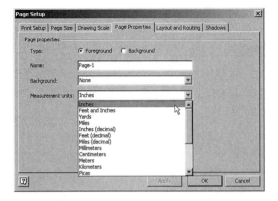

Figure 4.13
Resetting the rulers'
origin.

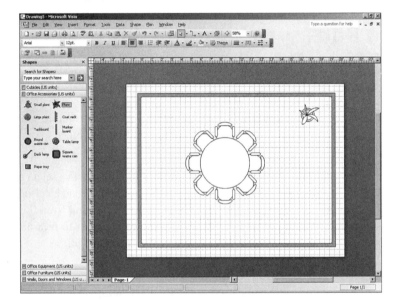

Here, the origin has been set to the inner upper-left corner of the room's walls, so all measurements are with respect to that corner—not with respect to the drawing.

Want to set the origin of the rulers in a drawing? Here's how you do it:

1. Move the mouse to where the two rulers intersect. Visio changes the mouse pointer to a four-headed arrow.

2. Hold down the Ctrl key and drag the mouse pointer to the new origin in your drawing. Visio draws vertical and horizontal dotted lines that follow the mouse as you drag it.

3. Release the mouse button. Visio adjusts the origin of the rulers to match the location you moved it to.

That resets the origin of both rulers.

HANDLING GUIDE LINES AND GUIDE POINTS

Guide lines and guide points are special lines and points you can use to align shapes as you draw them. Guide lines are good for aligning shapes, and guide points are good when you want to fix the exact location of a shape.

There are two ways of aligning shapes to guides: snap or glue. Snapping is best when you want to use guide lines; gluing is better when you want to use guide points.

To enable guides for snapping and gluing, follow these steps:

1. Select Tools > Snap & Glue. Visio opens the Snap & Glue dialog.
2. Select the General tab. Visio shows the General tab.
3. Select the Guides check box in the Snap To and/or Glue To areas.
4. Click the Advanced tab. Visio shows the Advanced tab.
5. Set the Guides Snap Strength value to a higher setting. Use a setting of 25 or more.
6. Click OK. Visio closes the Snap & Glue dialog.

So what's glue all about? When you glue a shape to a guide line or guide point, that shape—or shapes, if you've glued multiple shapes—moves when you move that guide line or guide point. That's what glue is all about: connecting things together. In this case, you can line up multiple shapes along a guide line, for example, and move them together.

How do you create guide lines? That's coming up next.

CREATING GUIDE LINES

Guide lines appear as single lines on the drawing surface, and you can use them to align shapes. They're custom lines you draw yourself.

To create a guide line, follow these steps:

1. To create a vertical guide, move the mouse over the vertical ruler; to create a horizontal guide, move the mouse over the horizontal ruler. Visio changes the mouse pointer into a double-headed arrow.
2. Drag the mouse. Visio displays the new guide line as a blue line while you drag.
3. Release the mouse button when the guide line is where you want it. Visio draws the new guide line.

You can see a horizontal guide line and a vertical guide line in Figure 4.14. Guide lines like these help you adjust the alignment of shapes as you drag new shapes onto a drawing, or as you drag existing shapes around.

Figure 4.14
Horizontal and vertical guide lines.

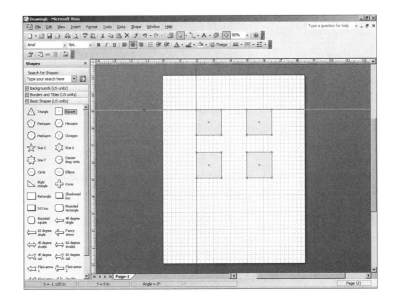

Now you can make shapes snap to or glue to the new guide lines.

Want to rotate a guide line? That's easy enough—just draw the guide line and follow these steps:

1. Select the guide line. Visio colors the new guide line green.
2. Select View > Size & Position Window. Visio displays the Size & Position window.
3. Enter the angle for the guide line. The angle is 45° for the guide line in Figure 4.15.

Figure 4.15
A rotated guide line.

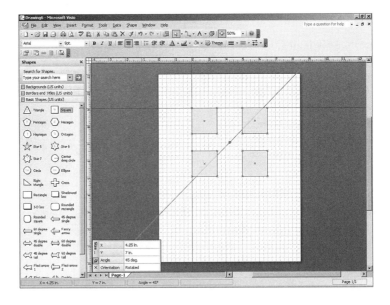

As you can see, rotating guide lines is no problem at all.

CREATING GUIDE POINTS

If you want to pin a shape—or a number of shapes—to a particular location in a drawing, use a guide point.

How do you create a guide point? Follow these steps:

1. Move the mouse to the intersection of the rulers. The mouse pointer changes to a four-headed arrow.

2. Drag the mouse to the new location of the guide point. Do not hold down the Ctrl key (which would move the rulers' origin). A vertical and horizontal blue line appear as you drag the mouse.

3. Release the mouse button when the mouse pointer is where you want the guide point. The new guide point—a circle with a cross in it—appears.

You can see a guide point in Figure 4.16, at the center of the drawing.

Figure 4.16
A guide point.

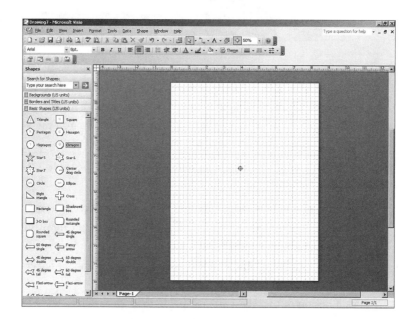

Now you can glue various shapes to that guide point, as shown in Figure 4.17.

Figure 4.17
Gluing to a guide
point.

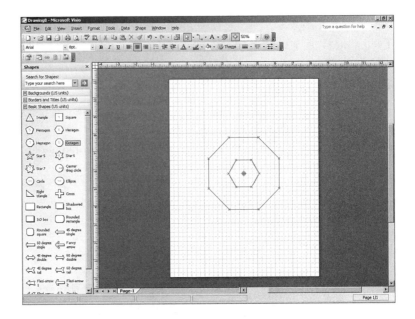

ALIGNING SHAPES AND DISTRIBUTING SHAPES

Visio also provides tools for aligning and distributing shapes besides guides. For example, you can align a whole set of shapes vertically or horizontally. You can also distribute shapes automatically, making their arrangement more pleasing to the eye.

To align shapes, you first select the shape to align to, and then select from among various options. Here's how it works:

1. Select the shape you want to align to. The shape's selection frame appears.
2. Holding down the Ctrl key, select the shapes you want to align. The result looks something like what's shown in Figure 4.18.
3. Select Shapes > Align Shapes. Visio displays the Align Shapes dialog shown in Figure 4.19.
4. Click a button in the Align Shapes dialog to align the shapes.
5. Click OK. Visio closes the Align Shapes.

Figure 4.18
Selecting shapes.

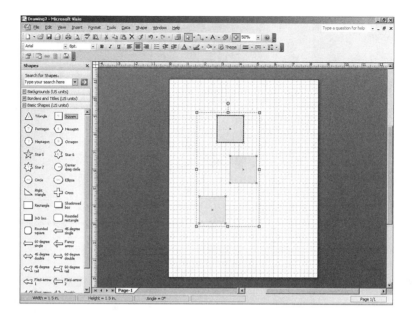

Figure 4.19
The Align Shapes
dialog.

And the result appears in Figure 4.20, in which the shapes are aligned horizontally.

Visio lets you right-align, center-align, and left-align shapes both vertically and horizontally.

You can also distribute shapes using Visio. Distribution is the process of positioning shapes evenly in a drawing, and you can distribute shapes automatically using the Shape menu's Distribute item.

For example, take a look at the shapes in Figure 4.21. How would you distribute the shapes so that they're equidistant vertically?

Figure 4.20
Aligning shapes.

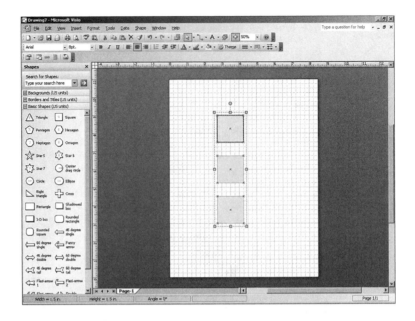

Figure 4.21
Shapes to distribute.

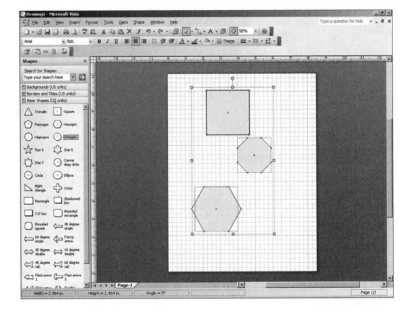

To distribute these shapes, follow these steps:

1. Select the shapes you want to distribute. You must select at least three shapes.

2. Select Shape > Distribute or click the drop-down arrow in the Distribute Shapes button on the Action toolbar. This opens the Distribute Shapes dialog shown in Figure 4.22.

Figure 4.22
The Distribute Shapes dialog.

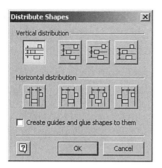

3. Click a button in the Distribute Shapes dialog corresponding to the distribution you want. Select from vertical or horizontal distribution.

4. Click OK. Visio closes the Distribute Shapes dialog, and distributes the shapes, as shown in Figure 4.23.

Figure 4.23
Distributed shapes.

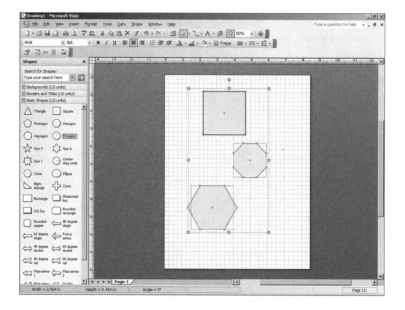

If you want to create guides when distributing shapes, select the Create Guides and Glue Shapes to Them check box in the Distribute Shapes dialog.

CREATING CUSTOM SHAPES

Now we're entering new territory: how to create your own shapes in Visio.

Visio contains thousands of shapes, and many people get along without ever having to create their own shapes. They're fine with all the electrical circuits, organization layouts, basic shapes, flowcharts, and more that Visio can create for them.

But you might have a specialized need. You might need to plan a warehouse full of L-shaped computer components, and you might not be satisfied with the shapes Visio has to offer you. In other words, you might want to create your own shape.

You can do that in Visio, and that works mostly by modifying existing shapes or creating them from scratch. You can add the new shapes to drawings or stencils. In other words, Visio is extensible, and you're going to see how to extend it here.

Here are some of the toolbar buttons you can use when modifying or creating shapes yourself:

- **Arc Tool**—On the Drawing toolbar. Draws arcs.
- **Bring to Front**—On the Action toolbar. Brings a shape to the front of a stack of shapes.
- **Ellipse Tool**—On the Drawing toolbar. Draws ellipses.
- **Flip Horizontal**—On the Action toolbar. Flips a shape horizontally.
- **Flip Vertical**—On the Action toolbar. Flips a shape vertically.
- **Format Painter**—On the Standard toolbar. Lets you copy the format of a shape to another shape, including themes.
- **Freeform Tool**—On the Drawing toolbar. Lets you draw freeform, using the mouse.
- **Line Tool**—On the Drawing toolbar. Draws straight lines.
- **Pencil Tool**—On the Drawing toolbar. Draws arcs, lines, or circles, based on how you use the mouse.
- **Rectangle Tool**—On the Drawing toolbar. Draws rectangles.
- **Rotate Left**—On the Action toolbar. Rotates a shape 90° to the left.
- **Rotate Right**—On the Action toolbar. Rotates a shape 90° to the right.
- **Send to Back**—On the Action toolbar. Sends a shape to the back of a stack of shapes.

DRAWING SHAPES

You can use the drawing tools as a start when drawing shapes—and the shapes you draw are treated as full-fledged shapes by Visio.

We'll take a look at how to draw your own shapes here, starting with using the Line tool.

CREATING SHAPES WITH THE LINE TOOL

To display the Drawing toolbar, right-click any toolbar and select the Drawing item, which brings up the Drawing toolbar, shown in Figure 4.24.

Figure 4.24
The Drawing toolbar.

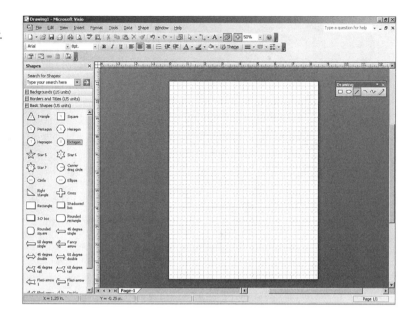

You can click the Line tool in the Drawing toolbar, and draw a line like this:

1. Click the drawing at the point where you want the line to start.

2. Drag the mouse to the end of the line you want to draw. Visio draws a dotted guide line connecting the mouse location to the starting point of the line.

   At every 45° interval as you rotate the mouse around the start point, Visio lengthens the guide line into a ray that extends to the edge of the drawing—this feature helps you align your line along 45°-angle increments.

3. Release the mouse button. Visio draws the line from the start to the endpoint you've specified.

Visio selects the line you've created and highlights its endpoints. To also highlight its control point in the middle (which is used to bend the line), select the Pencil tool in the Drawing toolbar, as shown in Figure 4.25.

You can manipulate the line as discussed in Chapter 2, "Working with Shapes," to display all kinds of additional handles, as shown in Figure 4.26.

Although you can draw lines using the Drawing toolbar, Visio doesn't actually treat simple lines as shapes. Instead, you have to draw a closed shape for that to work.

Figure 4.25
Selecting a line.

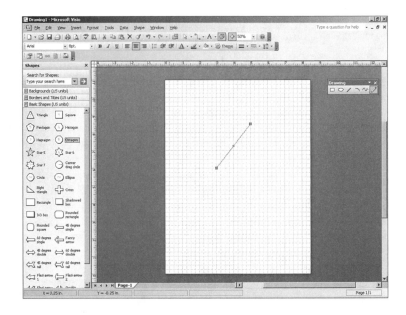

Figure 4.26
A line's handles.

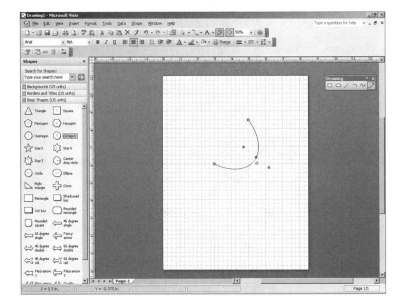

DRAWING CLOSED SHAPES

Want to create your own custom shape? Probably the easiest way of doing that is to simply draw a closed shape with the Line tool.

Here's the trick: To draw a closed shape, you have to draw each side of the shape consecutively, one after the other. If you don't, if you start working with some other part of the drawing before completing the shape, Visio won't treat your new closed figure as a shape.

So how can you create a closed shape that Visio will recognize as a shape by using the Line tool? Follow these steps:

1. Draw a line using the Line tool and the mouse. Visio draws the line from the start to the endpoint you've specified.

2. Release the mouse button. Visio draws the line's endpoints, as shown in Figure 4.27.

Figure 4.27
A line's endpoints.

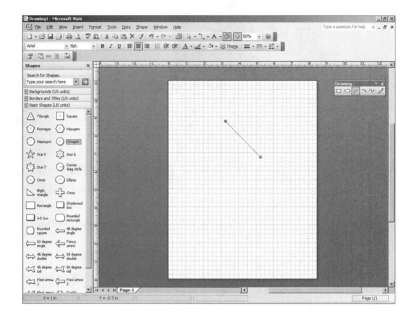

3. Press the mouse button over an endpoint of the line, and drag the mouse to create a new line.

4. Release the mouse button. Visio draws the new line, as well as control points and a selection frame around the new shape under development, as shown in Figure 4.28.

5. Repeat the preceding two steps for all the other lines in the new shape. Visio draws the new lines.

6. Finally, draw a line from the last line's endpoint to the first line's starting point, closing the shape. Visio fills the new shape with the current color, as shown in Figure 4.29. The shape is surrounded with a selection frame, and the control points on the lines that make up the shape are highlighted.

If you're using a theme, the new shape is filled using the theme's colors.

It's advisable to have Snap turned on (select Tools > Snap & Glue, then select the General tab, and make sure that the Snap check box is selected in the Currently Active area) when you create new shapes this way. Having Snap turned on makes it much easier to connect the final line to the first line's starting point.

Figure 4.28
Two-thirds of a new shape.

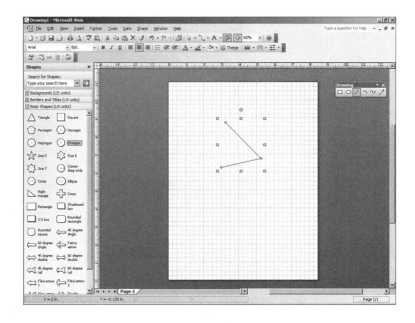

Figure 4.29
A completed shape.

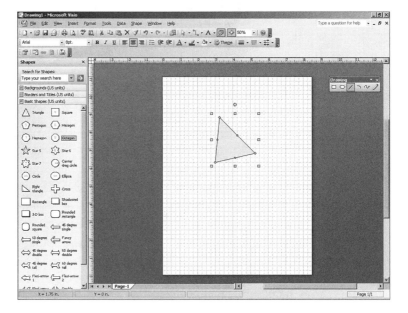

And that's it—you've created a new, basic shape, as shown in Figure 4.29. Very cool.

As you can see if you select the Pointer tool, the new shape is even enabled with automatic connection points, as shown in Figure 4.30.

Figure 4.30
A completed shape's automatic connection points.

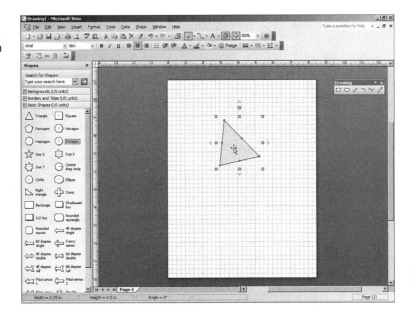

CREATING SHAPES WITH THE ARC TOOL

You can use the Arc tool in the Drawing toolbar to draw sections of ellipses—and the figures you draw using this tool are also treated as shapes by Visio if they're closed.

Here's an example, showing how to use the Arc tool:

1. Draw an arc using the Line tool and the mouse. Visio draws the arc from the start to the endpoint you've specified.

2. Release the mouse button. Visio draws the arc's endpoints, as shown in Figure 4.31.

3. Press the mouse button over an endpoint of the arc, and drag the mouse to create a new arc.

4. Release the mouse button. Visio draws the new arc, as well as control points and a selection frame around the new shape under development.

5. Repeat the preceding two steps for all the other arcs and other lines in the new shape. Visio draws the new arcs and lines.

6. Finally, draw a line from the last arc's endpoint to the first arc's starting point, closing the shape. Visio fills the new shape with the current color, as shown in Figure 4.32. The shape is surrounded by a selection frame, and the control points on the lines that make up the shape are highlighted.

You don't need to make your shape out of arcs, of course—you can use lines or freeform drawing, or whatever drawing tool you want.

Figure 4.31
An arc's endpoints.

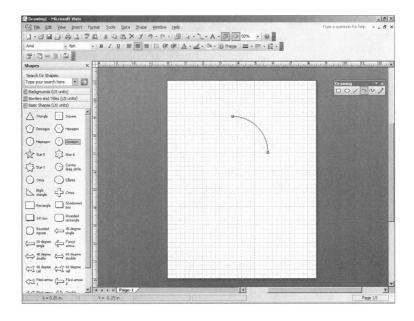

Figure 4.32
A completed shape
based on arcs.

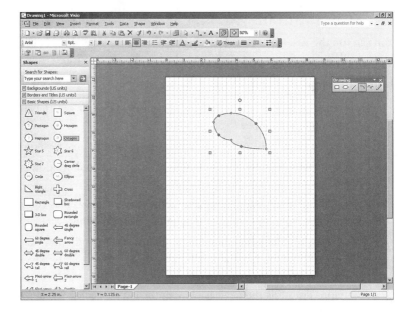

CREATING SHAPES WITH THE PENCIL TOOL

You can use the Pencil tool in the Drawing toolbar to draw curves or lines (the curves are
sections of a circle). Here's an example, showing how to use the Pencil tool to draw a closed
shape:

1. Draw a segment using the Pencil tool and the mouse. Drag the mouse in a straight line to draw a line, and in a circular path to draw part of a circle.

2. Release the mouse button. Visio draws the figure's endpoints.

3. Press the mouse button over an endpoint of the first segment, and drag the mouse to create a new segment.

4. Release the mouse button. Visio draws the new segment, as well as control points and a selection frame around the new shape under development.

5. Repeat the preceding two steps for all the other segments in the new shape. Visio draws the new segments.

6. Finally, draw a segment from the last segment's endpoint to the first segment's starting point, closing the shape. Visio fills the new shape with the current color, as shown in Figure 4.33.

Figure 4.33
A completed shape based on the Pencil tool.

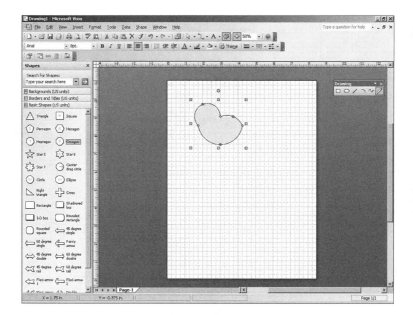

CREATING SHAPES WITH THE ELLIPSE AND RECTANGLE TOOLS

You can use the Ellipse and Rectangle tools to draw shapes as well. Because the ellipses and rectangles you draw are already closed, they are full-fledged closed shapes as soon as you draw them.

Here's how to draw ellipses (or rectangles) as completed shapes:

1. Select the Ellipse (Rectangle) tool.

2. Press the mouse button at one corner of the bounding rectangle of the ellipse (rectangle) you want to draw.

3. Drag the mouse to the opposite corner of the bounding rectangle of the ellipse (rectangle) you want to draw.

4. Release the mouse button. Visio draws the new ellipse (rectangle), as well as control points and a selection frame around the new shape, as shown in Figure 4.34.

Figure 4.34
An ellipse shape.

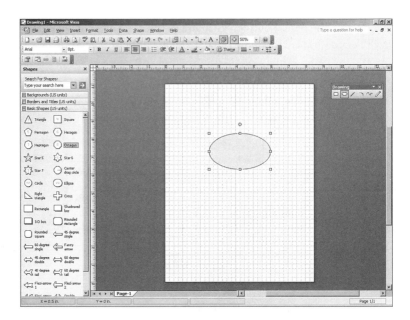

CREATING SHAPES WITH THE FREEFORM TOOL

You can use the Freeform tool in the Drawing toolbar to draw freeform figures—and if you close those figures, Visio treats the figures as 2D shapes. Here's an example, showing how to use the Freeform tool to draw a closed shape:

1. Select the Freeform drawing tool in the Drawing toolbar.

2. Press the mouse button at the position you want to start the freeform figure.

3. Drag the mouse to draw the freeform figure.

4. Close the figure. You close the figure by dragging the mouse back to the starting point of the figure.

5. Release the mouse button. Visio completes the figure and closes the shape, filling it with color, as shown in Figure 4.35.

Figure 4.35
A completed shape
based on the
Freeform tool.

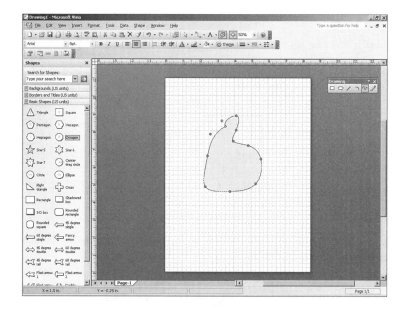

JOINING AND COMBINING SHAPES

When it comes to making your own shapes, Visio also supports various actions: Union, Combine, Fragment, Intersect, and Subtract. For example, taking the union of two shapes adds them together, and unites them to create the resulting shape.

We'll take a look at these operations next, using the two shapes—an octagon and a star—shown in Figure 4.36.

Figure 4.36
Two shapes.

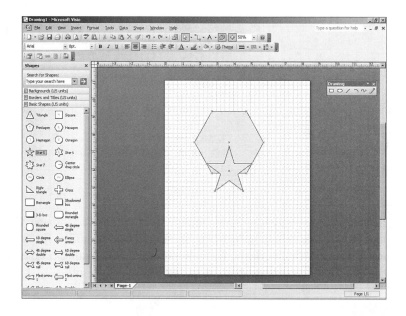

CREATING A UNION OF SHAPES

The Union operation unites shapes. The Union command creates a new shape with the shared perimeters of the selected shapes.

To use the Union operation, do this:

1. Draw your shapes.

2. Arrange your shapes.

3. Select the shapes you want to operate on. Visio encloses the shapes in a combined selection frame.

4. Select Shape > Operations > Union. Visio creates a new shape, which is the union of the shapes you've selected, as shown in Figure 4.37.

Figure 4.37
A union of shapes.

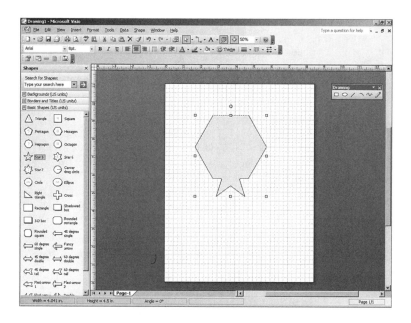

And that's it. As you can see, Visio created a new shape—the union of the two earlier shapes.

Creating unions of shapes is a great idea when you have shapes you want to build from others.

COMBINING SHAPES

The Combine operation combines multiple shapes into a single shape. Combining shapes will create a cutout where two of those shapes overlap. If another shape overlaps that cutout, the part that overlaps is retained. Visio keeps alternating cutting out and retaining shape parts until it's processed all the shapes you're combining.

To use the Combine operation, do this:

1. Draw your shapes.

2. Arrange your shapes.

3. Select the shapes you want to operate on. Visio encloses the shapes in a combined selection frame.

4. Select Shape > Operations > Combine. Visio creates a new shape, which is the combination of the shapes you've selected, as shown in Figure 4.38.

Figure 4.38
Combining shapes.

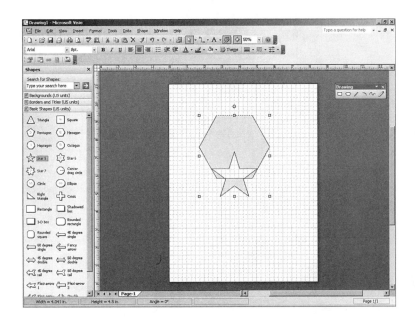

In other words, combining shapes works a little differently than the word "combining" would indicate—Visio alternates cutting out and retaining overlapping parts.

FRAGMENTING SHAPES

The Fragment operation splits shapes into fragments. The overlapping parts of multiple selected shapes are cut out, and can be treated as their own new shapes.

To use the Fragment operation, do this:

1. Draw your shapes.

2. Arrange your shapes.

3. Select the shapes you want to operate on. Visio encloses the shapes in a combined selection frame.

4. Select Shape > Operations > Fragment. Visio creates new shapes, made up of the fragments of the shapes you've selected, as shown in Figure 4.39.

Figure 4.39
Fragmenting shapes.

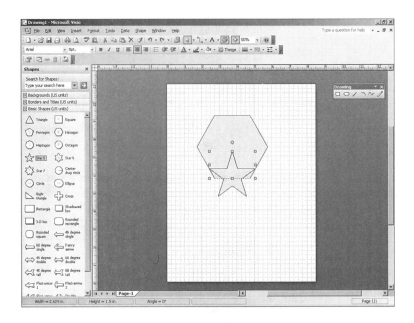

Now each of the pieces in Figure 4.39, cut where the original shapes overlapped, is a new shape. You can drag those new shapes as you like, as shown in Figure 4.40.

Figure 4.40
Shape fragments.

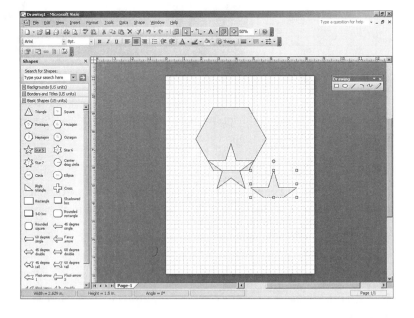

Think about it—being able to fragment shapes like this can be very useful, and amounts to cutting up shapes as you want them.

For example, say you wanted to cut an existing shape into three parts—you could simply overlap a rectangle with the shape and then fragment the combined shapes.

INTERSECTING SHAPES

The Intersect operation gives you the intersection of multiple shapes. In other words, Visio retains only the part that is common to all your selected shapes.

To use the Intersect operation, do this:

1. Draw your shapes.

2. Arrange your shapes.

3. Select the shapes you want to operate on. Visio encloses the shapes in a combined selection frame.

4. Select Shape > Operations > Intersect. Visio creates a new shape, which is the intersection of the shapes you've selected, as shown in Figure 4.41.

Figure 4.41
Intersecting shapes.

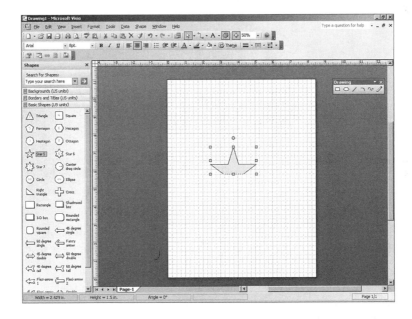

That is to say, Visio retains only the parts of the selected shapes that all the shapes have in common.

SUBTRACTING SHAPES

The Subtract operation subtracts, or removes, the second shape you select from the first. The first shape is the shape that remains—after the second shape is subtracted.

To use the Subtract operation, do this:

1. Draw your shapes.

2. Arrange your shapes.

3. Select the shapes you want to operate on. Visio encloses the shapes in a combined selection frame.

4. Select Shape > Operations > Subtract. Visio creates a new shape, which is the subtraction of the shapes you've selected, as shown in Figure 4.42.

Figure 4.42
Subtracting shapes.

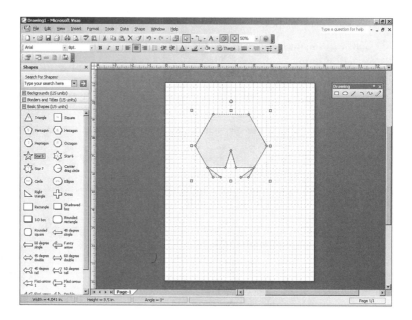

Subtraction is the only shape operation in which the actual order in which you select the shapes matters, because the second shape is subtracted from the first shape.

STACKING SHAPES

When you have a number of overlapping shapes, they have a *stacking order*, and you can restack them as you like using commands in the Shape menu.

For example, take a look at the black shape in Figure 4.43, which is in the middle of a stack of five squares.

There are four options in the Shape menu for stacking:

- Bring to Front
- Send to Back

- Bring Forward
- Send Backward

We'll take a look at these options next.

Figure 4.43
A stack of shapes.

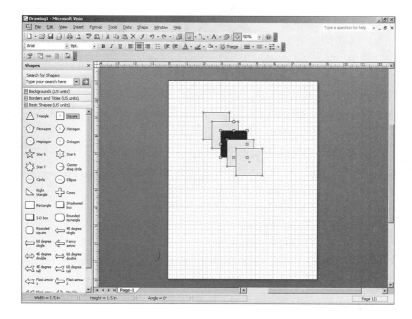

BRINGING SHAPES TO THE FRONT

When you bring a shape to the front in the stacking order, that shape appears on top of all the other shapes in the stack.

Here's how to bring a shape to the front of a stack:

1. Draw your shapes.
2. Arrange your shapes in a stack.
3. Select the shape you want to move. Visio encloses the shape in a combined selection frame.
4. Select Shape > Order > Bring to Front. Visio brings the selected shape to the front, as shown in Figure 4.44.

Bringing shapes to the front of the stacking order is a good idea if you want to uncover them and make them stand out.

Figure 4.44
Bringing a shape to
the front.

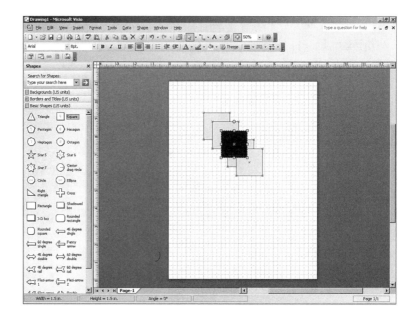

SENDING SHAPES TO THE BACK

When you send a shape to the back in the stacking order, that shape appears on the bottom of all the other shapes in the stack.

Here's how to send a shape to the back of a stack:

1. Draw your shapes.
2. Arrange your shapes in a stack.
3. Select the shape you want to move. Visio encloses the shape in a combined selection frame.
4. Select Shape > Order > Send to Back. Visio sends the selected shape to the back of the stacking order, as shown in Figure 4.45.

Sending shapes to the back of the stacking order can be a good idea if you want to establish a selected shape as the foundation of a stack of shapes.

BRINGING SHAPES FORWARD

When you bring a shape forward, it advances one place in the stacking order.

Here's how to bring a shape forward:

1. Draw your shapes.
2. Arrange your shapes in a stack.
3. Select the shape you want to move. Visio encloses the shape in a combined selection frame.

4. Select Shape > Order > Bring Forward. Visio brings the shape one step forward in the stacking order, as shown in Figure 4.46.

Figure 4.45
Sending a shape to the back.

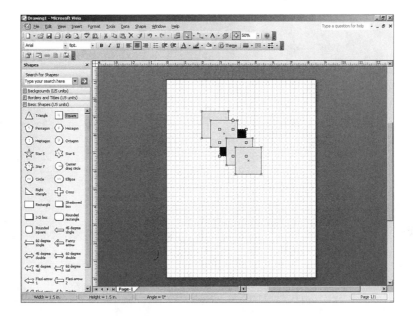

Figure 4.46
Bringing a shape forward.

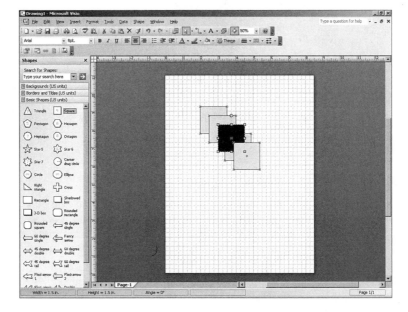

SENDING SHAPES BACKWARD

When you send a shape backward, it goes back one place in the stacking order.

Here's how to send a shape backward:

1. Draw your shapes.
2. Arrange your shapes in a stack.
3. Select the shape you want to move. Visio encloses the shape in a combined selection frame.
4. Select Shape > Order > Send Backward. Visio sends the shape one step backward in the stacking order, as shown in Figure 4.47.

Figure 4.47
Sending a shape backward.

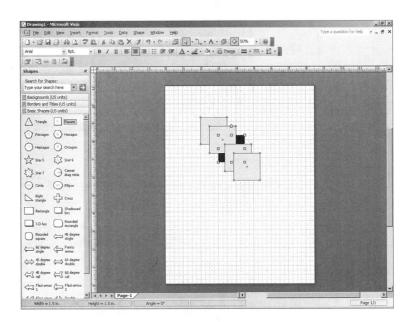

WORKING WITH SHAPES

Visio supports thousands of shapes—but maybe it doesn't have just the perfect shape for you. Maybe the office chairs are pointing the wrong direction, for example. Or maybe that triangle doesn't have a flat side pointing up.

Well, you can manipulate the shapes in Visio—turning them, flipping them, reshaping them, moving control points, and more. That's what this section is all about—working with Visio shapes.

DRAGGING VERTICES

Say you've drawn the star shown in Figure 4.48. But it's not quite right, you feel—the top point should be taller. What can you do?

Figure 4.48
A star shape.

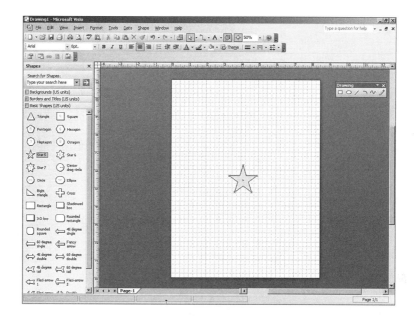

You can drag a vertex of the star to where you want it, that's what you can do. But if you select the star with the Pointer tool and then resize the star, the whole star will be resized.

That's not what you want at all—you want to just resize the top point.

You can do that if you drag the appropriate *vertex*. You already know what vertices are—they're those green diamonds that appear where two lines meet.

To view a shape's vertices, you can use one of these tools from the Drawing toolbar:

- Arc tool
- Freeform tool
- Line tool
- Pencil tool

Those are the tools—not the Standard Pointer tool—that you can use to move vertices. When you select one of these tools and click a shape, its vertices (and if you select the Pencil too, its control points—small green circles) appear. You can drag those vertices as you like, including lengthening just the top point, as shown in Figure 4.49.

Here's how to move a vertex of a shape in general:

1. Draw a shape.
2. Display the Drawing toolbar. Right-click the toolbar and select the Drawing item.
3. Select the Arc, Freeform, Line, or Pencil tool.
4. Select the Shape. Visio displays the shape's vertices.

5. Drag the vertex to its new position. Visio reshapes the shape to match (and the dragged vertex is recolored magenta).

6. Release the mouse button.

Figure 4.49
Lengthening the top point of a star shape.

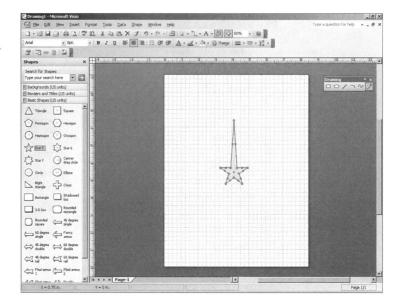

It's worth mentioning that if you select the Pencil tool (but not the Standard Pointer, Arc, Freeform, or Line tools), the selected shape's control points also appear, as shown in Figure 4.49. You can drag those control points—usually at the halfway mark on a line that connects two vertices—to reshape it, using the Pencil tool, as shown in Figure 4.50.

Figure 4.50
Reshaping a star shape using control points.

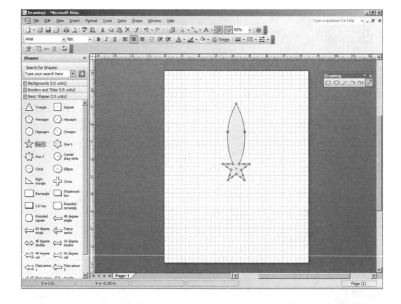

That's fine—but what if a shape doesn't have a vertex where you want to reshape it? You can add one yourself—that's coming up next.

ADDING VERTICES TO A SHAPE

What if you wanted to create the reclining chair shape shown in Figure 4.51?

Figure 4.51
A reclining chair shape.

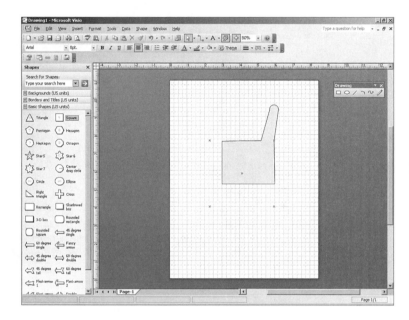

You could draw it yourself from scratch—or you could alter, say, a square to create that shape, if you add some vertices to a square so that you can use the Pencil tool to alter the square as shown in Figure 4.51.

Visio provides vertices on all its shapes, but there may not be enough for your purposes. It turns out that you can add your own vertices if you follow these steps:

1. Draw a shape.
2. Display the Drawing toolbar. Right-click the toolbar and select the Drawing item.
3. Select the Pencil tool.
4. Select the Shape. Visio displays the shape's current vertices and control points.
5. Hold down the Ctrl key and click a line segment where you want to add a new vertex. Visio adds a new vertex and a control point between this vertex and the previous vertex.
6. Repeat the preceding step to add vertices.

Now that you have your own vertices, you can alter any shape the way you want it, such as the reclining chair shown in Figure 4.51.

ROTATING A SHAPE

Take a look at Figure 4.52, in which you see an office layout under design. There's a chair in the upper-left corner of the office, and it's at an angle.

Figure 4.52
Adding a chair at an angle.

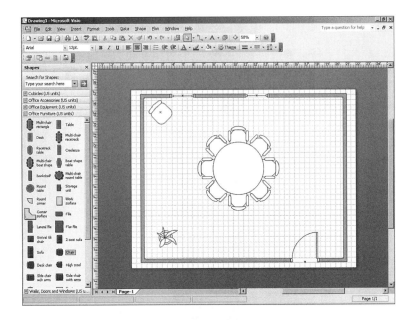

When you drag a chair onto the drawing surface, it appears horizontally, and to have it appear as it does in Figure 4.52, you need to rotate it.

So how do you rotate shapes? There are three primary techniques:

- **Use the rotation handles**—The rotation handles let you rotate a shape without a lot of work, but the resulting angle is not very precise.

- **Use the Rotate Right and Rotate Left buttons on the Action toolbar**—This is a quick method, but it's limited to 90° rotations.

- **Use the Size & Position window**—The most precise of the rotation methods, this lets you specify an exact angle of rotation.

We'll take a look at these techniques here.

USING ROTATION HANDLES

The quickest method of rotating a shape is to use rotation handles—those green circles that appear at the top of a selection frame when you select a shape with the Pointer tool.

Here's how to use rotation handles:

1. Select the Pointer tool in the Standard toolbar. The mouse cursor becomes an arrow.

2. Select the shape to rotate. The shape's rotation handle, a green circle, appears at the top of the selection frame.

3. Drag the rotation handle clockwise or counterclockwise. The shape rotates and the mouse cursor changes to a circular arrow.

4. Release the mouse button.

Here's the important point: By default, Visio snaps the rotation angle to 15°, which is not very precise—that means you can rotate the shape only by 15° increments. You can reduce that snap angle by moving the mouse away from the shape after selecting the rotation handle. For example, as you can see in the status bar at the bottom of Figure 4.53, the snap angle is now only 5°. That means you can rotate the shape in 5° increments.

Figure 4.53
Reducing the snap angle of rotation.

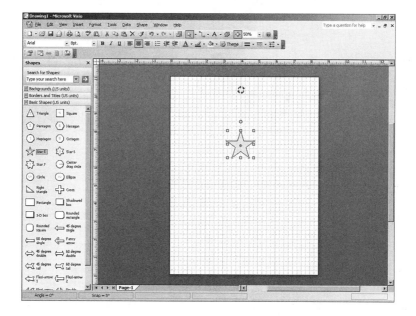

USING THE ROTATE RIGHT AND ROTATE LEFT BUTTONS

The Action toolbar has Rotate Right and Rotate Left buttons that you can use to rotate a shape 90° at a time. Here's how to rotate shapes using this technique:

1. Select the Pointer tool in the Standard toolbar. The mouse cursor becomes an arrow.

2. Select the shape to rotate.

3. Display the Action toolbar. Right-click the toolbar and select the Action item.

4. Click the Rotate Right or Rotate Left button in the Action toolbar. The selected shape rotates 90° to match. The Rotate Right button is the seventh from the left in the Action toolbar; the Rotate Left button is the eighth from the left.

5. Keep clicking the button for 180°, 270°, and so on.

You can see an example in Figure 4.54. There, a chair has been added at the upper right—but the default angle of this shape has it facing the wall.

Figure 4.54
An added chair.

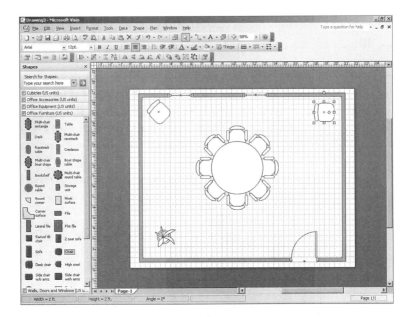

A single click of the Rotate Right button in the Action toolbar rotates the chair so that it points into the room, as shown in Figure 4.55.

Figure 4.55
Rotating the added chair.

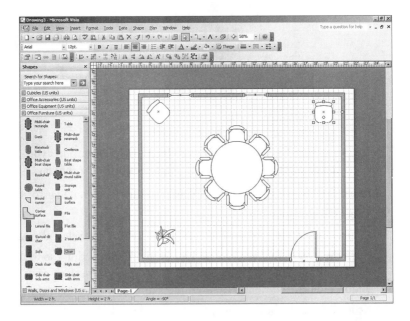

USING THE SIZE & POSITION WINDOW

You can also use the Size & Position window to rotate shapes. Here's how it works:

1. Select the Pointer tool in the Standard toolbar. The mouse cursor becomes an arrow.
2. Select the shape to rotate.
3. Display the Size & Position window. Select View > Size & Position Window.
4. Enter the rotation angle in the Size & Position window. Visio rotates the shape to match.

For example, you can see the chair at the upper right has been rotated 245° in Figure 4.56.

Figure 4.56
Rotating a chair using the Size & Position window.

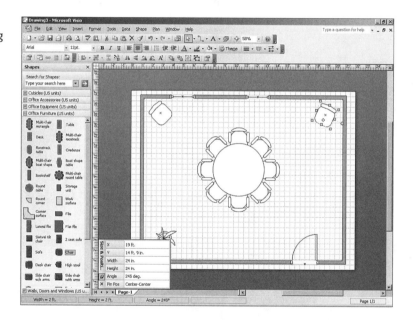

While we're discussing rotation, it's worth noting that Visio rotations take place around a rotation pin, which is a small circle with a cross in it, as shown in Figure 4.53.

FLIPPING A SHAPE

You can also use the buttons in the Action toolbar to flip shapes horizontally or vertically. Here's how that works:

1. Select the Pointer tool in the Standard toolbar. The mouse cursor becomes an arrow.
2. Select the shape to flip.
3. Display the Action toolbar. Right-click the toolbar and select the Action item.

4. Click the Flip Horizontal or Flip Vertical button in the Action toolbar. The selected shape flips to match. The Flip Horizontal button is the fifth from the left in the Action toolbar; the Flip Vertical button is the sixth from the left.

STYLING SHAPES

The shapes Visio offers take many forms, but they're all pretty generic in appearance. A couch is a couch—with none of the fabric styling you might want to see. A star is a star—not colored the way you might want it to be colored.

You can change all that yourself. In this section, you'll see how to style shapes in various ways. Coming up in the next chapter, you'll see how to use themes to augment the styling process.

ALTERING LINE STYLE

By default, the lines Visio uses for most shapes are simply thin black lines, but you can change that. Want a blue dash-dot-dash line? You can do it. Want to thicken a line? No problem. Want to add arrowheads to a line? You can do that too.

Here's how to do it:

1. Select the shape whose line style you want to alter.
2. Select Format > Line, or right-click the shape and select Format > Line. The Line dialog appears, as shown in Figure 4.57.

Figure 4.57
The Line dialog.

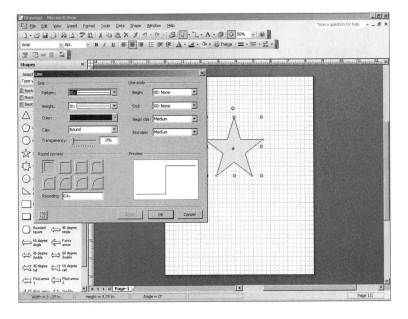

3. Select a pattern in the Pattern box. Visio shows you what the pattern looks like in the Preview box.

4. Select a thickness in the Weight box. Visio shows you what the thickness looks like in the Preview box.

5. Select a color in the Color box. Visio shows you what the color looks like in the Preview box.

6. Select a bluntness for the lines in the Cap box. Select from Square, Round, or Extended.

7. Select the transparency of the lines by sliding the Transparency slider. Visio shows you what the transparency looks like in the Preview box.

8. Select the roundness of the corners of your shape by clicking a roundness button. Visio shows you what the roundness looks like in the Preview box. If you have an exact roundness size in mind, type it into the Rounding box.

9. For 1D shapes, select the line ends in the Begin, End, Begin Size, and End Size boxes.

10. Click OK. Visio closes the Line dialog and applies the new style.

You can see an example in Figure 4.58, which shows a star with styled lines.

Figure 4.58
Styled lines in a shape.

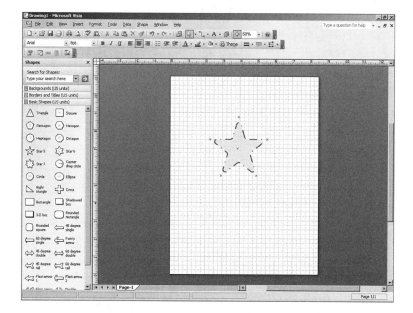

SETTING FILLS, PATTERNS, AND SHADOWS

Besides line styles, Visio also lets you style the fill colors, patterns, and shadows of shapes. You can do all that with the Fill dialog, coming up next.

Here's how it works:

1. Select the shape whose fill style you want to alter.

2. Select Format > Fill, or right-click the shape and select Format > Fill. The Fill dialog appears, as shown in Figure 4.59.

Figure 4.59
The Fill dialog.

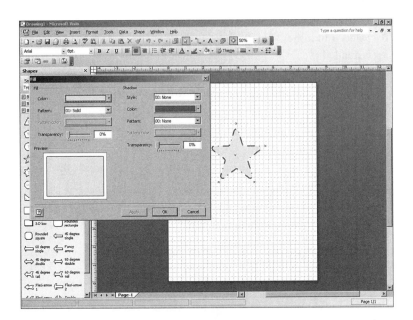

3. Select a color in the Color box. Visio shows you what the color looks like in the Preview box.

4. Select a pattern in the Pattern box. Visio shows you what the pattern looks like in the Preview box.

5. Select a pattern color in the Pattern Color box. Visio shows you what the pattern color looks like in the Preview box.

6. Select the transparency of the fill by sliding the Transparency slider. Visio shows you what the transparency looks like in the Preview box.

7. Select a shadow style in the Shadow Style box. Visio shows you what the shadow looks like in the Preview box.

8. Select a shadow color in the Shadow Color box. Visio shows you what the shadow looks like in the Preview box.

9. Select a shadow pattern in the Shadow Pattern box. Visio shows you what the shadow pattern looks like in the Preview box.

10. Select a shadow pattern color in the Shadow Pattern Color box. Visio shows you what the shadow pattern color looks like in the Preview box.

11. Select the shadow transparency by sliding the Shadow Transparency slider. Visio shows you what the shadow looks like in the Preview box.

12. Click OK. Visio closes the Fill dialog and applies the new style.

You can see an example in Figure 4.60, in which the star from Figure 4.58 has been given a gradient fill and a shadow.

Figure 4.60
Styling the fill in a shape.

GROUPS, PAGES, AND LAYERS

GETTING INTO VISIO

There's a heck of a lot of Visio coming up in this chapter—themes, groups, layers, and pages. All these topics are central to Visio, and you're going to get a good introduction to them here.

These are all topics you have to master to consider yourself experienced with Visio—especially the topic of layers, which gets you into some serious drawing.

We're going to start off with some work on customizing themes, then get into creating groups of shapes.

CUSTOMIZING THEMES

The fastest way to change colors in a drawing is to use themes. Themes provide you with collections of colors and effects, and when you make a theme active, you enable those colors and effects.

Want to create new theme colors? Here's how to do it:

1. Click the Theme button in the Formatting toolbar. This is the button with the word "Theme" on it.

2. Click the Theme Colors link. Visio shows the built-in theme colors, as shown in Figure 5.1.

Figure 5.1
The Theme Colors pane.

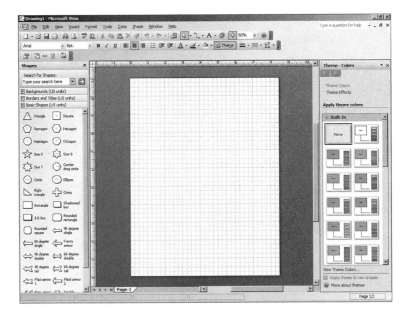

3. Click the New Theme Colors link. Visio displays the New Theme Colors dialog, shown in Figure 5.2.

Figure 5.2
The New Theme
Colors dialog.

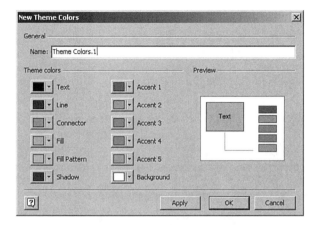

4. Enter a name for the new theme colors in the Name field.

5. Choose the colors for the Text, Line, Connector, Fill, Fill Pattern, and Shadow elements.

6. Choose the five accents and the background, if you want to.

7. Click OK. Visio displays your new theme colors in the Custom Themes box, as shown in Figure 5.3.

Figure 5.3
New theme colors.

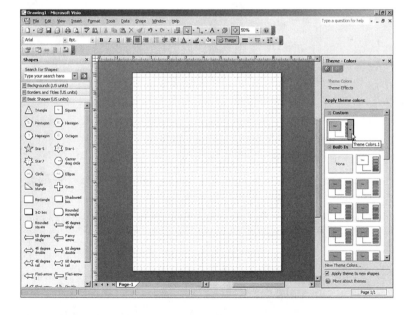

Now you've got a new theme—and you can use this theme at any time. Just select Format > Theme, select your new theme (or any theme), and you're set. Any new shapes you drag to the drawing surface will use the newly selected theme.

How about creating new theme effects? So far, you've set the new colors for elements in drawings, but not the effects, such as the font and line thickness.

Here's how you can set the effects for a theme:

1. Click the Theme button in the Formatting toolbar. This is the button with the word "Theme" on it.

2. Click the Theme Effects link. Visio shows the built-in theme effects, as shown in Figure 5.4.

Figure 5.4
The Theme Effects pane.

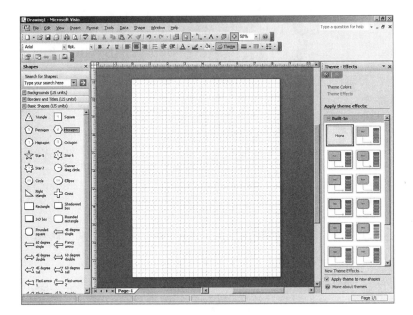

3. Click the New Theme Effects link. Visio displays the New Theme Effects dialog, shown in Figure 5.5.

4. Enter a name for the new theme effects in the Name field of the General tab.

5. Click the Text tab. You can select the text effects, such as the font. Visio displays the changes you've made in the Preview box.

6. Click the Line tab. Select the line formatting features, such as line weight, line pattern, transparency, and corner rounding.

7. Click the Fill tab. Select fill effects, such as pattern and transparency.

8. Click the Shadow tab. Select shadow effects, such as style, transparency, X and Y offset, magnification, and direction.

9. Click the Connector tab. Select connector effects, such as pattern, weight, transparency, corner rounding, and so on.

10. Click OK. Visio displays your new theme effects in the Custom Themes box, as shown in Figure 5.6.

Figure 5.5
The New Theme
Effects dialog.

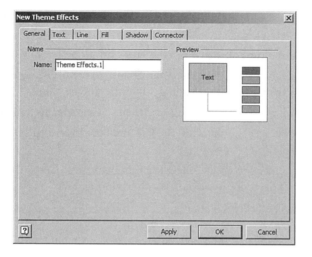

Figure 5.6
New theme effects.

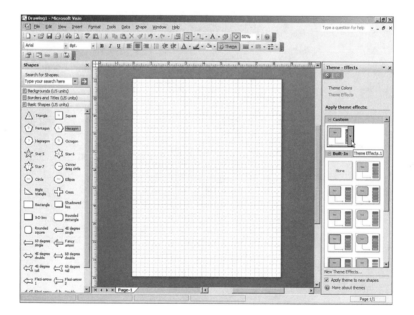

COPYING THEMES

If you don't want to create new themes from scratch every time, but instead want to simply modify an existing theme, you can do that. One good way of modifying an existing theme is to copy it first, then make your modifications.

Here's how to make a copy of an existing theme:

1. Click the Theme button in the Formatting toolbar. This is the button with the word "Theme" on it.

2. Click the Theme Colors link or the Theme Effects link as appropriate. Visio displays the matching task pane.

3. Hover the mouse over a theme. Visio displays a drop-down arrow next to the theme.

4. Click the drop-down arrow and select the Duplicate item. Visio copies the theme and duplicates it in the Custom box, adding ".1" to the theme name.

For example, when you copy the Subdued theme, Visio creates Subdued.1.

5. Hover the mouse over the theme in the Custom box. Visio displays a drop-down arrow next to the theme.

6. Click the drop-down arrow and select the Edit item. Visio opens the Edit Theme Colors or Edit Theme Effects dialog, as shown in Figure 5.7.

7. Make your edits and click OK.

Okay, that covers customizing themes. Coming up next: grouping shapes together.

Figure 5.7
Editing theme effects.

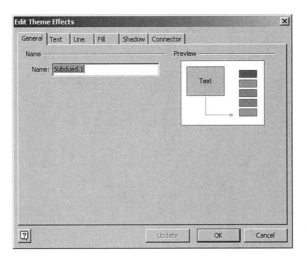

GROUPING SHAPES

Suppose you have a bunch of shapes that you've arranged just as you like them. It's taken some time, but now you've got them where you want them. Then you decide you need to move the whole assembly of shapes a little to the right—and you try dragging it with the mouse.

Immediately, everything comes apart. Rats!

You could remember to select all the shapes when you want to move them—or you could *group* the shapes together.

When you group shapes together, they stay together, and you can move them as a whole, or flip them, or rotate them, and so on. We'll start this discussion with creating groups.

CREATING A GROUP

You can group shapes together no matter how close or how far apart they are in a drawing (but they do have to be on the same page). In other words, groups don't have to consist solely of overlapping shapes.

How do you create a group of shapes from multiple individual shapes? Follow these steps:

1. Select the shapes you want to group.

2. Select Shape > Grouping > Group, or click the Group button in the Action toolbar. Visio creates the group and surrounds it with a selection frame.

You can see an example in Figure 5.8, in which you start with three star shapes.

Figure 5.8
Three star shapes.

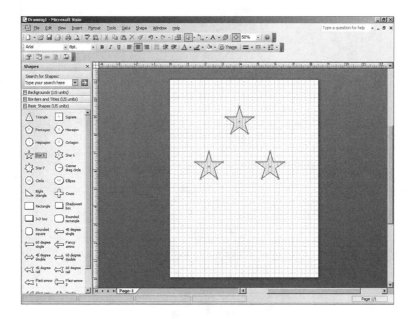

Now select the stars, as shown in Figure 5.9.

Next, select Shape > Grouping > Group, or click the Group button in the Action toolbar. Visio puts the star shapes into the same group and creates a selection frame around the group, as shown in Figure 5.10.

Figure 5.9
Three selected star shapes.

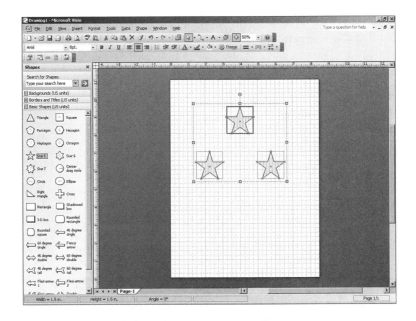

Figure 5.10
A group of star shapes.

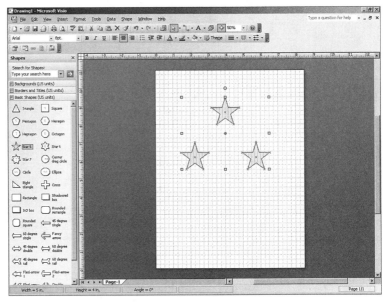

Now you can move, flip, or rotate the new group, and all the shapes in it will act together. For example, you can see the new group being rotated in Figure 5.11.

Figure 5.11
Rotating a group of star shapes.

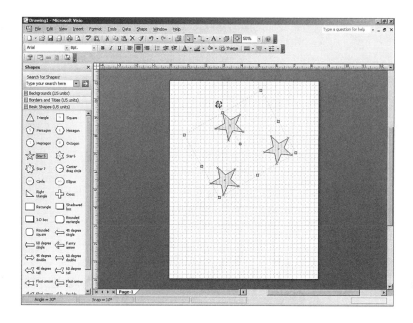

UNGROUPING A GROUP

Okay, that looks fine. But what if you wanted to change the contents of that group? What if, for example, you wanted to add a fourth star? Can you ungroup the shapes?

Yes, you can. Follow these steps to ungroup the shapes in a group:

1. Select the group. Visio surrounds the group with a selection frame.
2. Select Shape > Grouping > Ungroup, or click the Ungroup button in the Action toolbar. Visio ungroups the shapes in the group.

Here's an example. You can see a group in Figure 5.10, in which the three stars are in a Visio group. Now select Shape > Grouping > Ungroup or click the Ungroup button in the Action toolbar, and you'll see the shapes ungrouped, as shown in Figure 5.12.

Now you can add other shapes to the group, as shown in Figure 5.13, in which another star has been added and the four stars have been put together into a single group.

That's one way to add new shapes to a group—ungrouping, adding the shape, and then grouping again. But actually, there's a shortcut.

5

Figure 5.12
Ungrouping shapes.

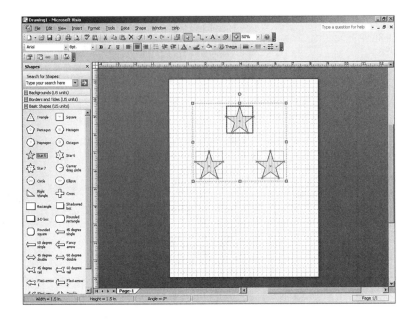

Figure 5.13
Creating a new group.

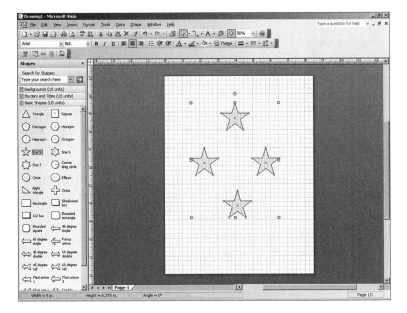

ADDING SHAPES TO A GROUP

You can add shapes to groups easily. For example, say that you wanted to add two more stars to the group shown in Figure 5.13. Here's how you could do it:

1. Select the group you want to add shapes to. Visio surrounds the group with a selection frame.

2. Select the shape(s) to add. Visio selects the shapes, as shown in Figure 5.14.

Figure 5.14
Selecting shapes to add to the group.

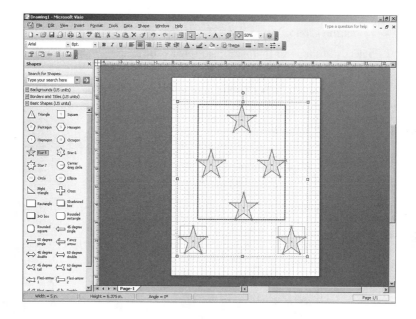

3. Select Shape > Grouping > Add to Group. Visio adds the new shapes to the group, as shown in Figure 5.15.

You can remove shapes from groups as well.

Figure 5.15
Creating a new group with six stars.

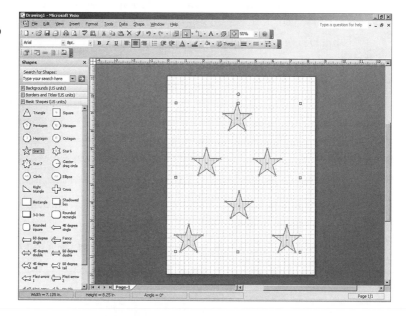

REMOVING SHAPES FROM A GROUP

Want to remove shapes from a group? Just follow these steps:

1. Select the group. Visio selects the group.
2. Select the shape to remove. Visio selects the shape, as shown in Figure 5.16.

Figure 5.16
Selecting shapes to remove from the group.

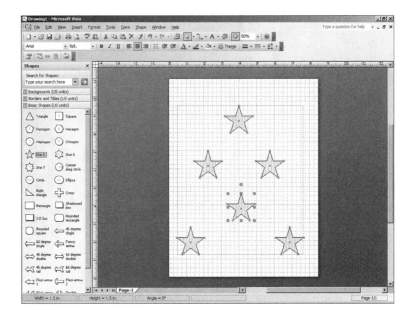

3. Select Shape > Grouping > Remove from Group. Visio removes the shape from the group, and selects it.
4. Press the Delete key to delete the removed shape. Visio removes the shape, as shown in Figure 5.17.

ADDING TEXT TO A GROUP

Usually, when you double-click a shape, Visio opens a text box for you to add text to the shape. That doesn't work with a group—double-clicking doesn't do anything unless you double-click a shape in a group, in which case that shape is selected.

Want to add text to a group? Simple enough—just follow these steps:

1. Select the group. Visio displays the selection frame for the group.
2. Select Edit > Open Group. Visio zooms in on the group.
3. Double-click the shape you want to add text to. Visio opens a text box for the shape, as shown in Figure 5.18.

Figure 5.17
Removing a shape
from a group.

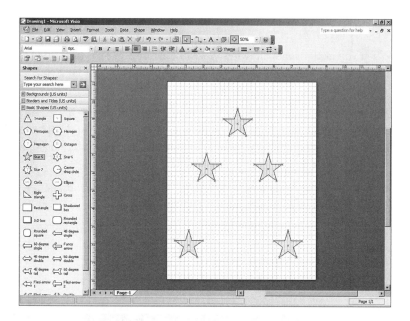

Figure 5.18
Adding text to a
shape in a group.

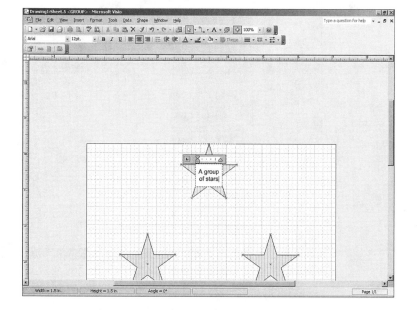

4. Enter your text. Type some text, as shown in Figure 5.18.

5. Click the zoom window's close button (the × at the upper right). Visio closes the zoom window, and your text appears in the shape you selected.

Okay, that covers what you can do with groups.

Now it's time to start digging into working with multiple pages.

HANDLING PAGES

When you create a new drawing in Visio, that drawing has only one page. But you might have many pages in your drawing—for example, you might be laying out multiple offices in an office building.

Pages in Visio are not like pages in a word processor, in which text moves fluidly between pages as you add or remove text. Each page contains its own shapes, and they don't move between pages—unless you specifically move them yourself. Each page can have its own printing orientation and its own page setup.

To make multiple-page drawings, you need to know how to add (and remove) pages. You need to know how to view multiple pages at once, and how to move between pages.

There's a lot coming up on pages next, starting with reorienting pages.

REORIENTING PAGES ON-THE-FLY

Suppose you have the situation shown in Figure 5.19.

Figure 5.19
Shapes overlapping the drawing page.

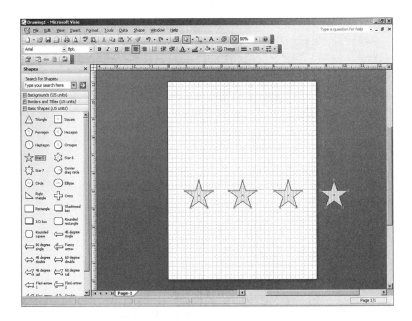

In the figure, you've drawn a set of stars—but the page isn't wide enough to fit all your stars on it (it's interesting to note that Visio lets you draw off the page).

What can you do? In this case, you can reorient the page from portrait to landscape, as shown in Figure 5.20.

Figure 5.20
Reorienting a page.

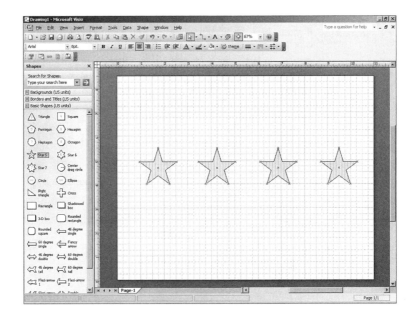

How do you reorient the page? Follow these steps:

1. Select File > Page Setup. Visio displays the Page Setup dialog.
2. Select the Print Setup tab. Visio displays the Print Setup tab, as shown in Figure 5.21.

Figure 5.21
The Print Setup tab
of the Page Setup
dialog.

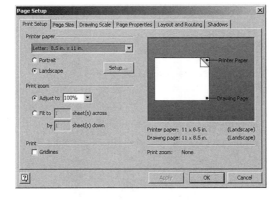

3. Click Portrait or Landscape in the Printer Paper area. Visio changes the paper orientation to match.
4. Click the Page Size tab. Note that Visio has changed the drawing page's orientation to match the orientation you set in the Print Setup tab.
5. Click OK. Visio closes the Page Setup dialog.

TIP

If you do have the situation shown in Figure 5.19, in which your drawing is off to one side, you can first try to center the drawing. Select Shape > Center Drawing to center the drawing. In fact, some kinds of drawings support special commands for rearranging drawing elements—for example, when you're creating an organization chart, you can use Organization Chart > Re-layout or Organization Chart > Best Fit to Page menu items.

SETTING THE PAGE SIZE

When you have multiple pages in a drawing, you can resize each page as you like. Bear in mind that drawing page size has nothing to do with the paper size in your printer—you can scale the two to match, as already covered.

Visio lets you set the drawing page size in various ways:

- Predefined sizes
- Custom measurements
- Drawing content sets drawing page size

The predefined page size option has all kinds of sizes you can use: 148×210 millimeters, 22×34 inches, 24×36 inches, and so on.

You use the Page Size tab in the Page Setup dialog to set drawing page size. Here's how it works:

1. Select File > Page Setup. Visio opens the Page Setup dialog.
2. Click the Page Size tab. Visio displays the Page Size tab shown in Figure 5.22.

Figure 5.22
The Page Size tab.

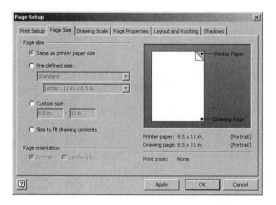

3. Select an option for the page size:

   Same as Printer Paper Size—This is the default, and it sets your drawing page size to the printer paper size.

   Pre-defined Size—Select from four categories: Standard, Metric, ANSI Engineering, and ANSI Architectural.

Custom Size—Enter your own custom size—the height in the first box, the width in the second box. Optionally, you can use "in" for inches, and "mm" for millimeters. Use this way of setting the page size if you have some nonstandard size in mind.

Size to Fit Drawing Contents—Select this option if you want the page size to fit the contents of the drawing. This option makes sure that the drawing fills the page, without too much whitespace around the edges. It's a good option for drawings without a specific scale, such as a flowchart or an organization chart.

4. Click OK. Visio closes the Page Setup dialog.

In fact, there's another way to change the drawing size—on-the-fly. Follow these steps:

1. Select the Pointer tool. Visio changes the mouse cursor to an arrow.

2. Press and hold the Ctrl key.

3. Move the mouse over the edge of the drawing that you want to move. Visio changes the mouse pointer to a two-headed arrow.

4. Drag the edge of the drawing surface to the new size you want it to be. You can see the drawing page's new dimensions in the Visio status bar.

This technique is a fast and easy one if you're setting your own custom size for the drawing page.

ADDING PAGES TO A DRAWING

Many times when you're creating a drawing, you'll need multiple pages. You might have a drawing with many associated pages, such as rooms in a house. Or you might be doing organization charts for every department in a large corporation.

You can also use multiple pages to create overview drawings and detail drawings, as you would for architectural drawings.

In addition, you might use multiple pages to keep track of the history of your project. When multiple people are working on the same project, you might want to keep their edits separate to maintain a history of what's going on with the project.

Or you might just want to create a slideshow of pages, as you might see in Microsoft PowerPoint.

When you add a page to a drawing, that page is added at the end of the current foreground pages—so technically, you're not inserting pages at all, even though that's what Visio says you're doing. You're simply adding pages to the whole page count, and the new page becomes the new last page.

TIP

You can, however, reorder pages, and you'll see how to do that in this chapter.

Here's how you add more pages to a drawing:

1. Select the page whose properties you want to copy. Visio always copies the properties of the current page when inserting a new page. That means, for example, that the current template is copied to the new page.

2. Right-click the Page tab at the bottom of the drawing surface and select Insert Page, or select Insert > New Page. Visio displays the Page Setup dialog, with the Page Properties tab displayed, as shown in Figure 5.23.

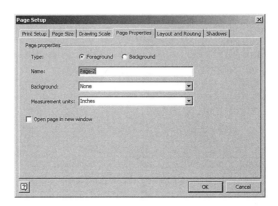

3. Select the Foreground type. This creates a regular Visio page. Background pages are coming up later in this chapter.

4. Accept the suggested name or enter a new one. For example, you can see that Visio suggests "Page-2" in Figure 5.23.

5. Select a background page if so desired.

6. Select new measurement units if so desired.

7. Select the Open Page in New Window check box when you want to display the new page in a new window, rather than the current window. By default, this check box is not checked, which means you access new pages using the page tabs at the bottom of the drawing surface. But if you check this check box, Visio creates the new page in a new window. More on this right after this list of bullets.

8. Click OK. Visio displays a new page tab at the bottom of the drawing surface, which you can see in Figure 5.24. You can alternate between pages by clicking that tab.

By default, the new page is inserted at the end of the current drawing, and you access it by clicking the page tabs at the bottom of the drawing surface.

However, you can instruct Visio to give the new page its own window if you select the Open Page in New Window check box. When you do that, the new page has its own page tab, as in Figure 5.24, but it also has its own window, which is accessible from the Window menu (unless you create the new page in its own window, it's not going to be separately accessible in the Window menu).

Figure 5.24
A new page tab.

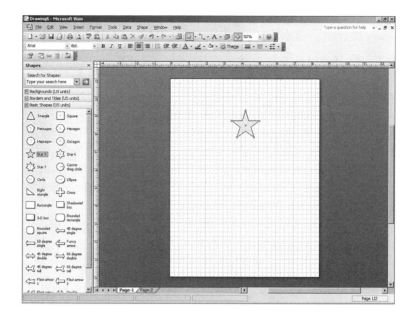

That means you can use the Window menu's items to handle the new page. For example, if you select Window > Tile, you'll see the new page tiled next to the original page, as shown in Figure 5.25.

Figure 5.25
Tiling pages.

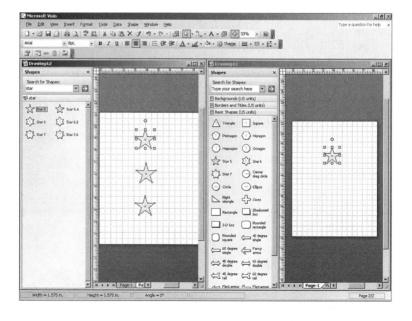

You don't have to tile the new pages—you can also cascade them by using the Window > Cascade option.

Note that the name given to the new pages is appended with a colon followed by the page number—for example, in Figure 5.25, you can see Drawing4:1 and Drawing4:2.

Note also that when you put a page in a new window, there's no template for it (the star shapes were added to the second page's template pane as a result of a search). When you don't use a new window, the template for the currently visible page is used in the new page, but that's not the case when you create a page in a new window—it's up to you to install a new template for it. You can do that by selecting a template from the File > Shapes submenus.

You can also create new windows at any time with Window > New Window. That opens the current drawing in an additional window, without any templates. You choose the templates you want with the File > Shapes submenu items.

That's how you add new pages to a drawing—by right-clicking the Page tab and selecting Insert Page, or selecting Insert > New Page. When you do that, you've got a multipage drawing, and you can move from page to page using the page tabs.

Now you're able to create drawings that overview and detail pages, or history pages, or slideshows. Very cool.

DELETING PAGES

Want to delete a new page? You can do that very simply by right-clicking a page tab and selecting the Delete Page item. That deletes the page whose tab you've selected.

You can even delete multiple pages at once in Visio. Here's how that works, step by step:

1. Select Edit > Delete Pages. Visio displays the Delete Pages dialog, listing the current pages in your drawing, as shown in Figure 5.26.

Figure 5.26
The Delete Pages dialog.

2. Select the page(s) you want to delete in the Delete Pages dialog.
3. Select the Update Page Names check box. If you select this check box, Visio will renumber the remaining pages for you. Note that this option works only when the page names have a number at the end.

4. Click OK. Visio removes the pages you've selected and closes the Delete Pages dialog.

TIP

> The page deletion you performed becomes permanent when you save the drawing to disk. After you've saved the file, you can't use the Undo menu item to undo page deletions—up to that point, you can use the Edit > Undo Delete Pages menu item to undo a delete operation. Another way of undoing a delete page operation is to simply close the drawing without saving any changes—when you open the drawing again, the deleted page will be back (assuming you haven't saved the changes to the drawing after deleting the page).

HANDLING MULTIPLE PAGES

Now that you're working with multiple page drawings, it's worth going through the techniques Visio includes for multiple-page drawings—how to navigate between pages, how to reorder pages, and so on.

We'll start by discussing navigating from page to page.

NAVIGATING BETWEEN PAGES

One way to navigate between pages in a drawing is to use the tabs that appear at the bottom of the drawing surface.

That's the way you move from page to page—you click the page tabs at the bottom of the drawing surface. There are no buttons in toolbars for this purpose—which is a little odd, because you'd think that there would be some buttons for this in the Action toolbar or the View toolbar. But, apparently, Microsoft didn't consider multipage drawings a common enough occurrence to add any toolbar buttons for navigation.

There is a menu item you can use for navigation—you select Edit > Go To, and then the individual page. You can see this menu item in Figure 5.27, in which it's listing the three pages in the drawing. It's also a little odd that this menu item appears in the Edit menu and not the View menu.

Clicking the page tabs at the bottom of the drawing surface is convenient enough—it's when you're working on the drawing that you want to move from page to page, and the page tabs are right there for you to use.

If you have only a few pages in your drawing, Visio displays a tab for each page at the bottom of the drawing surface. However, if you have multiple pages, it's possible that Visio won't be able to display a tab for each page at the bottom of the drawing surface. In that case, it will display arrows that you can use to scroll among the page tabs.

5

Figure 5.27
Navigating between pages.

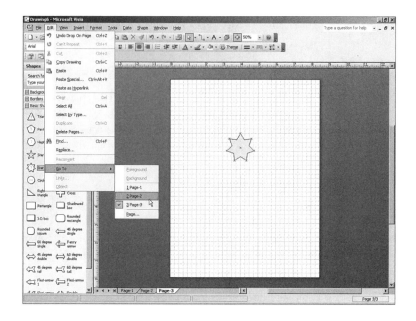

VIEWING MULTIPLE PAGES AT ONCE

You already know that you can put a page in its own window (which makes it accessible for viewing along with other pages concurrently) when you insert a new page by selecting the Open Page in New Window check box.

However, you can also put existing pages into their own windows so that you can view multiple pages concurrently—you don't have to put those pages into separate windows when you insert them.

Here's how to put existing pages into their own windows:

1. Select the Edit > Go To > Page menu item. The Page menu item is at the bottom of the list of pages in the Edit > Go To submenu. This opens the Page dialog.

2. Select the page you want to display in its own window.

3. Select the Open Page in New Window check box. This check box in the Page dialog is shown in Figure 5.28.

4. Click OK. Visio opens the selected page in its own window.

5. Repeat the preceding steps for any additional pages you want to open in their own windows.

When you open a page in a new window, it becomes the current page in your drawing.

Figure 5.28
The Page dialog.

Here's an alternative method for opening pages in new windows:

1. Select the page you want to display in its own window.
2. Select the Window > New Window menu item. Visio opens the page in a new window.
3. Repeat the preceding steps for any additional pages you want to open in their own windows.

After you've opened pages in their own windows, you're ready to view multiple pages at once. You can use the Window > Tile or Window > Cascade menu items for that.

To view multiple pages side by side, select the Window > Tile menu item. When you do, the pages in the current drawing appear tiled on the screen, including their template panes.

To view pages in overlapping windows, select the Window > Cascade menu item. That displays each of the pages you've put into their own windows in an overlapping window, cascading from upper left to lower right.

RESETTING PAGE ORDER

When you add pages to a drawing, you can't specify the page order. You can't say to Visio, for example, "Insert this new page between the current pages 15 and 16." And that's a shame, because when you start a drawing, you might have little sense of the order of drawings to come.

You might be working on an architectural plan, for example, and suddenly find that the overview of a specific area is getting very complex in unforeseen ways. And you'd like to add a detail page for that part of the plan.

You might not want to add that new detail page at the end of the plans—you might want to add it directly after the page showing the overview it's a part of. But Visio lets you insert pages only at the end of a drawing.

The way out of this problem is to reorder the pages you've inserted into a drawing. And doing that is easy enough—just drag the page tabs into the new order you want. For example, look at the page tabs in Figure 5.29, and you'll see that Page-3 has been dragged to the number-two spot.

Figure 5.29
Reordering pages.

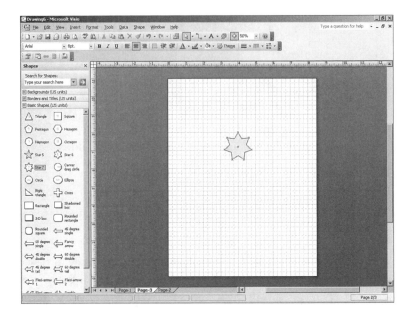

That's fine, but now your page order, as indicated by the page tabs, reads: Page-1, Page-3, Page-2. That doesn't look particularly good—however, you can change it. See the next section.

RENAMING PAGES

If you've reordered pages, you might want to rename them, because Visio doesn't handle that task automatically.

There are two ways to rename pages in Visio: the short way, and the more involved way.

The short way is indeed short—all you have to do is right-click the page tab of the page you want to rename, and select the Rename Page item. Doing so highlights the name of the page in the page tab, as shown in Figure 5.30.

Now all you have to do is click the tab and enter the new name of the page. Simple.

You can also do this in a more involved way:

1. Display the page you want to rename.

2. Select File > Page Setup to display the Page Setup dialog. Visio opens the Page Setup dialog.

Figure 5.30
Renaming pages.

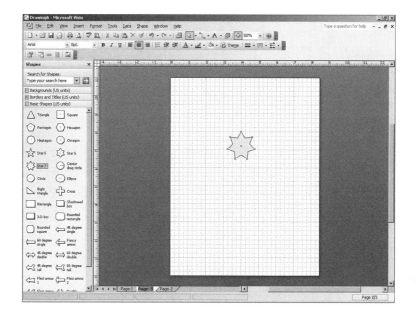

3. Click the Page Properties tab. Visio opens the Page Properties tab, shown in Figure 5.31.

Figure 5.31
The Page Properties tab.

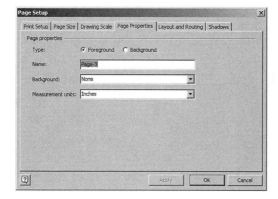

4. Enter the page's new name in the Name box. You can see this box in Figure 5.31.
5. Click OK. Visio closes the Page Setup dialog.

When you do this, the page's name in the associated page tab is changed. Nice.

TIP

Here's a trick I sometimes use to renumber pages automatically. I insert a bogus page at the end of a drawing using Insert > New Page. Then I select Edit > Delete Pages menu item. In the Delete Pages dialog, I select the last-added bogus page, and click the Update Page Names check box. Visio then does the work of renumbering the pages for me while it removes the bogus end page.

DISPLAYING PAGES AS A SLIDESHOW

Now that you're working with multiple pages in your drawings, you can arrange them in full-screen slideshows. That's great if you want to present your drawings, à la Microsoft PowerPoint, to a meeting, for example. All you'd need is an overhead projector interfaced to your computer, and violà, you're on the big screen.

Displaying pages on the full screen is also a good way of getting details you might miss otherwise.

Here's how to display your pages on the full screen, and move between pages:

1. Select the first page of your drawing. Click the page tab corresponding to the first page.

2. Select View > Full Screen or press F5. Visio displays the page on the full screen, as shown in Figure 5.32.

Figure 5.32
A page seen in full-screen view.

3. To navigate between pages, take these actions:

To move to the next page, press N, the Page Down key, the right-arrow key, or the left mouse button.

To move to the previous page, press P, the Page Up key, or the left-arrow key.

4. To restore the normal Visio screen, press F5 or Esc.

If you want to, you can also right-click the full-screen display and select Next Page or Previous Page from the context menu that appears, as shown in Figure 5.33.

Figure 5.33
The full-screen
context menu.

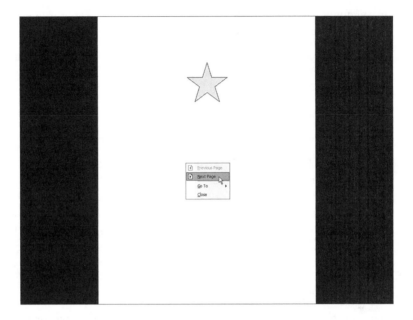

You can also use the context menu's Go To item to specify the page to go to, and the Close menu item to restore the Visio window.

TIP

> Speaking of navigation from page to page, you can also use hyperlinks in Visio drawings. If you use hyperlinks, you can click the hyperlink shape to go to a new page. Hyperlinks are coming up later in the book.

INTRODUCING BACKGROUNDS

Now it's time to start talking about backgrounds in Visio drawings.

Backgrounds provide underlays for pages. The normal page is called a foreground page, and the background is the background page.

There are many uses for background pages. You might want a sense of consistency across all the pages in a drawing, and a background, which appears behind every foreground page, gives you that. A consistent background gives drawings a nice effect.

Or you might want to include a company logo behind every page in your drawing. You might want to add a "watermark" to every page for added professionalism.

Or you might have a set of common elements that you want to appear in every page, and putting them in the background of every page can be useful. For example, room walls might be a common background element for every page in an office layout drawing.

Or you might have a copyright, or a date, that you want to appear in every page of your drawing. The uses of backgrounds in Visio are unlimited.

You can assign background pages to foreground pages, and although you can assign only one background page to a foreground page, you can assign background pages to background pages—allowing you to add as many background pages as you want.

Here are the kind of background pages you can create:

- A single background page for multiple foreground pages
- Individual background pages for individual foreground pages
- A background page for another background page

Note that when you're working with a foreground page and a background page, they're independent when it comes to selecting shapes and working with them. If you're working with the foreground page, you can't edit or delete shapes on the background page. This, of course, makes it a good idea to place items you want to protect on the background.

CREATING A BACKGROUND PAGE

To use a background page in Visio, you have to create it and then assign it to another page (foreground or background page). About the only thing you can do with an unassigned background page is to print it, and that's not very thrilling.

Here's how you create a background page:

1. Select a page in your drawing.
2. Select Insert > New Page. Visio displays the Page Setup dialog with the Page Properties tab selected, as shown in Figure 5.34.

Figure 5.34
The Page Setup dialog, Page Properties tab.

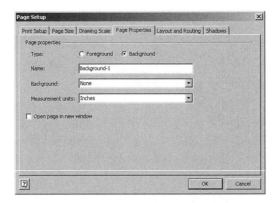

3. Select the Background radio button. That's the option that makes this page a background page.

4. Optionally, enter a new name in the Name box. By default, Visio calls your first background page for the current drawing Background-1.

5. Select None or an existing background in the Background box.

6. Select the units by which you want to measure in the background page, in the Measurement Units box.

7. Click OK. Visio closes the Page Setup dialog and displays the new background page on the drawing surface—note that its tab reads "Background-1."

You can see the new background page in Figure 5.35.

Figure 5.35
A new background page.

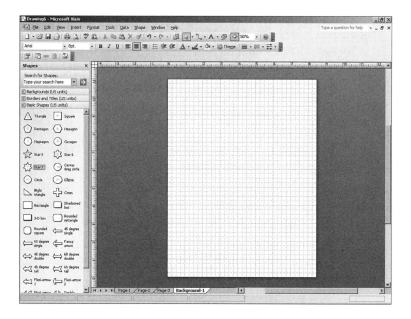

So far, so good.

Now you have to assign the background page to another page, whether that other page is a foreground page or another background page.

To assign the new background page, Background-1, to another page, follow these steps:

1. Select the page that you want to assign the background to.

2. Select File > Page Setup. Visio displays the Page Setup dialog with the Print Setup tab selected.

3. Select the Page Properties tab. Visio displays the Page Properties tab, shown in Figure 5.36.

Figure 5.36
The Page Setup
dialog, Page
Properties tab.

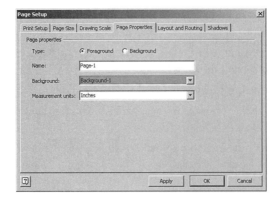

4. Click the Background drop-down arrow. Visio displays a list of existing backgrounds—in this case, that's only the Background-1 page, which is displayed by name (as well as an option for no background page: None).

5. Select the background page you want to assign to the current page. You can see how this looks in this example in Figure 5.36, in which Background-1 is selected.

6. Select the units by which you want to measure in the background page, in the Measurement Units box.

7. Click OK. Visio closes the Page Setup dialog and connects Background-1 as the background page of the current page.

That's how you connect a background page to the any page.

How would you *un*assign a background page? That's easy as well—just follow these steps:

1. Select the page that you want to assign the background to.

2. Select File > Page Setup. Visio displays the Page Setup dialog with the Print Setup tab selected.

3. Select the Page Properties tab. Visio displays the Page Properties tab.

4. Click the Background drop-down arrow. Visio displays a list of existing backgrounds.

5. Select None in the Background drop-down list. This unassigns any background page assigned to the current page. Optionally, you can select any other background page to assign to the current page.

6. Click OK. Visio closes the Page Setup dialog and unassigns the current background from this page.

ALTERING A BACKGROUND PAGE

How do you add shapes and text to your background page? Because the background page is a page like any other—it's just marked as a background page—you add shapes to it as you would any other page.

In other words, all you have to do is select the background page's tab, make the changes you want to the background page, and you're set. The changes made to the background page will now appear automatically under the foreground page for whatever foreground page you've associated the background page with.

For example, take a look at Figure 5.37, in which a copyright notice in a text shape has been added to a background, Background-1.

Figure 5.37
Editing a background by adding text.

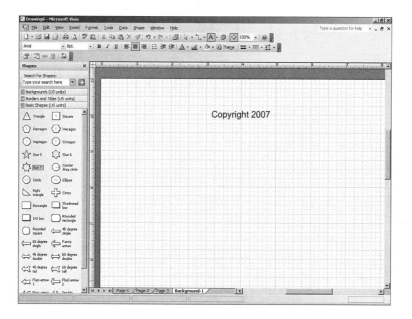

When you're done with the background, your changes will appear in any page that has that background, as shown in Figure 5.38.

> **TIP**
>
> Want to make your background appear light so that it doesn't contrast with what's in the foreground? Set your background's transparency to high.

Figure 5.38
Using a background and a foreground.

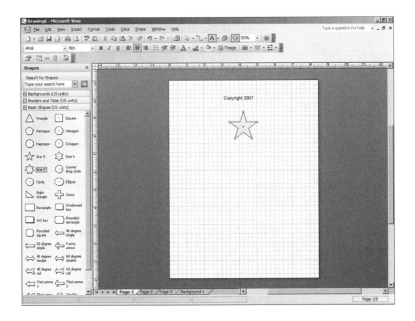

HANDLING SPECIAL BACKGROUND SHAPES

Visio has its own set of background shapes, ready for you to use. Most of those backgrounds are simply abstract images, but you'll also find mountains, cityscapes, and maps.

Plenty of such prebuilt backgrounds are available. How do you find them? Just select File > Shapes > Visio Extras > Backgrounds, opening the stencil shown in Figure 5.39.

Figure 5.39
The Background stencil.

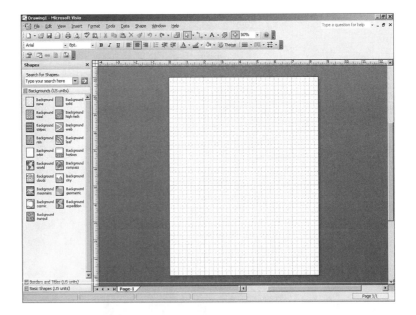

You can see the background shapes by name in the stencil: Background Steel, Background Mountains, Background World, and so on.

Want to use one of those prebuilt backgrounds? Just drag it onto the current drawing surface, as shown in Figure 5.40, in which Background Expedition was dragged to the drawing surface.

Figure 5.40
Using a prebuilt background.

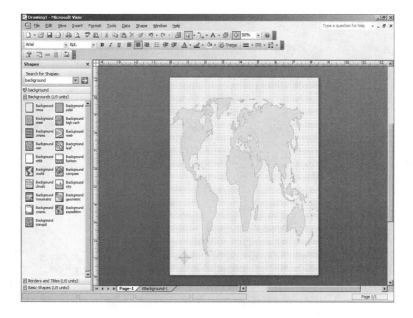

Notice what happens—after you drag a background shape onto the drawing surface, it's treated like a background page. As you can see, there's a new tab at the bottom of the drawing surface: VBackground-1.

If you select that page and then select File > Page Setup, and click the Page Properties tab, you'll see that the new page is indeed a background page—the Background radio button is clicked.

Background shapes represent an easy way to add a background to a drawing—how much easier could it get? All you have to do is display the Backgrounds stencil and drag a background shape onto the drawing surface. Visio itself creates a new background page, using that shape.

In fact, there are even more backgrounds available than the 19 you see in Figure 5.40. Just enter "background" into the Search for Shapes box in the template pane and you'll get 37 matches.

5

TURNING PAGES

"Turning pages" doesn't mean turning them as in turning a book's pages—but rather, turning them at an angle.

For example, take a look at Figure 5.41. There, an office is at an angle, and is built that way in the building. But the user has added furniture along a horizontal floor plan, and turning the page makes it easier to work with that floor plan.

Figure 5.41
Using a pre-built background.

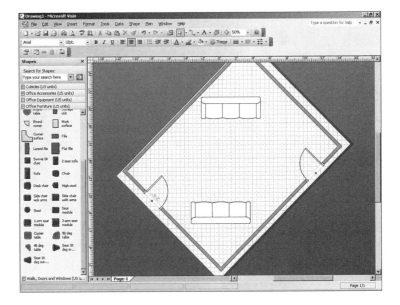

Sometimes, when you're working on a drawing, it's easiest to turn the page at an angle, because that helps when you drag shapes onto the drawing page.

So how do you do that? How do you turn pages at angles?

It's easier than you might think—just follow these steps:

1. Display the page you want to turn.

2. Select the Pointer tool.

3. Press Ctrl and move the mouse pointer to any corner of the page. Visio changes the mouse cursor to a circular arrow mouse cursor.

4. Drag the mouse to rotate the page. Visio rotates the page.

   Look at the status bar as you rotate the page if you want to keep track of the angle you're rotating to.

   Move the mouse pointer farther out from the center of the page to make the step in the angle finer. That is, the "Snap" in the angle might be 10° if the mouse cursor is close to the page corner, but only 1° if the mouse cursor is some distance away from the page corner. You can make the angle you turn the page as precise as you want.

5. Release the mouse button and the Ctrl button when the rotation is done.

That's it—it's as easy as that to rotate a page.

HANDLING LAYERS

Now it's time to introduce layers in Visio. This is a big topic, and an important one. As you go on in Visio and create more detailed drawings, layers will become increasingly useful.

Using layers lets you break up your drawings into stacked sheets. You can think of a layered drawing as one that's composed of multiple surfaces, each of which can contain shapes.

Imagine, for example, that you're designing architectural plans. Your plans may have elements that are important to various specialists, such as electrical circuits and plumbing, and they may also show where the furniture is meant to go. When it comes time to work with the electrical contractor, you might want to print out only the electrical circuits part of the drawing; when you work with the plumber, you might want to print out only the specialized plumbing part of the diagram.

You can do that with layers. Using layers, you can break up your drawing so that the circuits are on one layer, the plumbing is on another, and the furniture is on yet another. By default, all the elements will appear to be on the same drawing, but in fact, they're in layers. And that means you can access just the circuits layer, which has only the circuits on it, or the plumbing layer, which has only the pipes of interest to the plumber.

In other words, using layers lets you break up complex-multielement drawings according to whatever organization makes the most sense. Layers are a powerful tool.

You can think of layers as transparent sheets that you can place elements on, which, taken together, form a drawing.

How do layers differ from backgrounds? Backgrounds are designed to give common elements to all the pages in a drawing; layers are not. Layers are just a means of breaking up your drawing into stacked sheets. Actually, background pages can themselves have layers.

In fact, some templates create layered drawings automatically. For example, the Business category's Office Layout template creates a drawing that has these built-in layers:

- Building Envelope
- Computer
- Dimensions
- Door
- Electrical Appliance
- Equipment

- Furniture
- Power/Comm.
- Movable Furnishings
- Nonmovable Furnishings
- Wall
- Window

5

And various shapes can be on any of these different layers. Actually, shapes can be assigned to multiple layers in a drawing—they're not restricted to a single layer.

Using layers, then, you can separate the information a drawing displays, hiding information when needed. In other words, layers let you deal with complex drawings in an easy manner.

DETERMINING WHICH LAYERS A SHAPE IS ASSIGNED TO

When you create a new drawing based on a template that has multiple layers built in, and drag a shape onto the drawing, which layer(s) is that shape assigned to?

For example, when you create a new office layout, which has the previous 12 layers built into it, and drag a shape like a PC onto that drawing, Visio assigns the PC to some of the layers, but not others. How can you tell which layers the PC has been assigned to? (You'll see later how to change the layers a shape has been assigned to.)

For example, take a look at Figure 5.42, which illustrates this scenario—a PC shape has been dragged onto the drawing surface in an Office Layout template.

Figure 5.42
A PC on an Office Layout template.

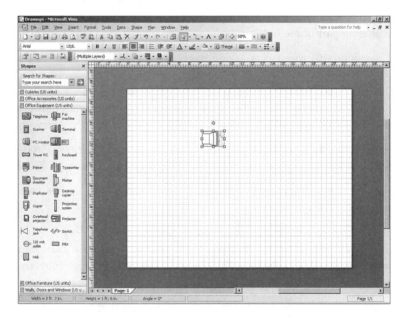

How can you determine which layers the PC has been assigned to? Select the PC and then select View > Layer Properties, or click the Layer Properties button in the View toolbar, which displays the Layer Properties dialog, shown in Figure 5.43.

As you can see in Figure 5.43, the PC shape belongs to these layers in the office layout drawing:

- Computer
- Electrical Appliance
- Equipment
- Power/Comm.

Figure 5.43
The layer properties
of a PC shape.

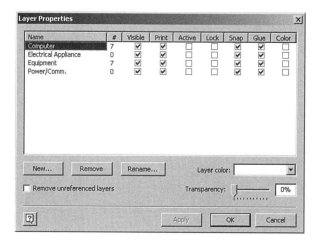

Take a look at the columns in the Layer Properties dialog, which gives an indication of what's to come with layers—you can individually configure these properties for shapes on layers:

- Visible
- Print
- Active
- Lock

- Snap
- Glue
- Color

Okay, that lets you know which layers a shape belongs to, and gives you an overview of which properties are available.

Now what if you want to create your own layers? That's coming up next.

CREATING YOUR OWN LAYERS

Not all templates create layered drawings—for example, the General template category's Basic Shapes template doesn't. How can you create your own layers in such a case?

You can use the Layer Properties dialog to create new layers. (Note that just because this dialog doesn't show any layers doesn't mean that there aren't any in the drawing. This dialog is intended to show the layers for a selected shape—if no shape is selected, no layers are shown.)

Here's how creating a new layer works:

1. Select View > Layer Properties, or click the Layer Properties button on the View toolbar. Visio displays the Layer Properties dialog, shown in Figure 5.44.
2. Click New. Visio displays the New Layer dialog, shown in Figure 5.45.

Figure 5.44
The Layer Properties dialog.

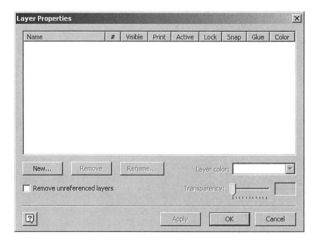

Figure 5.45
The New Layer dialog.

3. Enter the name you want to give the new layer and click OK. You can see the new name, Layer 1, used in Figure 5.46.

Want to remove a layer? No problem.

Figure 5.46
A new layer in the Layer Properties dialog.

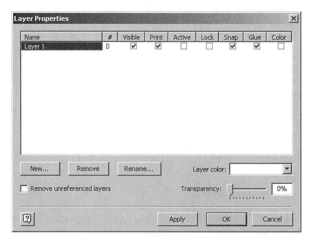

DELETING LAYERS

You can also delete layers as easily as creating new ones.

Follow these steps to delete a layer:

1. Select a shape that appears on the layer you want to delete.
2. Select View > Layer Properties, or click the Layer Properties button on the View toolbar. Visio displays the Layer Properties dialog, shown in Figure 5.46.
3. Select the layer you want to remove.
4. Click Remove. Visio displays the warning dialog shown in Figure 5.47.

Figure 5.47
A warning dialog.

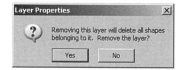

5. Click Yes to remove the layer.
6. Click OK.

That deletes a layer.

For that matter, you can also rename layers.

RENAMING LAYERS

Want to rename a layer? Just follow these steps:

1. Select a shape that appears on the layer you want to rename.
2. Select View > Layer Properties, or click the Layer Properties button on the View toolbar. Visio displays the Layer Properties dialog, shown in Figure 5.46.
3. Select the layer you want to rename.
4. Click Rename. Visio displays the Rename Layer dialog, shown in Figure 5.48.

Figure 5.48
The Rename Layer dialog.

5. Enter the new name for the layer.
6. Click OK to rename the layer.
7. Click OK.

And there you have it—it's easy enough to rename a layer.

And now it's time to assign shapes to layers.

ASSIGNING SHAPES TO LAYERS

When you drag a generic shape to a drawing, the shape is not assigned to any particular layer (that's not true of templates that have prebuilt layers, because each shape in the template is already assigned to various layers). So how can you assign a shape to a layer or layers?

Just follow these steps:

1. Select a shape that you want to assign. If the shape is in a group, click the group and then click the shape itself to select that shape.
2. Select Format > Layer. Visio displays the Layer dialog, shown in Figure 5.49.

Figure 5.49
The Layer dialog.

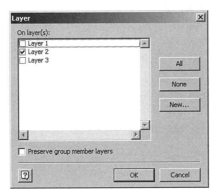

3. Select the layer(s) you want to assign the shape to. Note that you can select multiple layers to assign the shape to—as many as you want. In Figure 5.49, the shape is being assigned to Layer 2.
4. Click OK.

You can also remove a shape from a layer if you want to. Just follow these steps:

1. Select a shape that you want to deassign. If the shape is in a group, click the group and then click the shape itself to select that shape.
2. Select Format > Layer. Visio displays the Layer dialog, shown in Figure 5.49.
3. Deselect the layer(s) you want the shape to be assigned to.
4. Click OK.

Okay, what about hiding a layer? After all, that's one of the big plusses of layers—being able to selectively display information.

HIDING LAYERS

When you want to dissect your drawing into its various layers, hiding layers is a good idea.

Take a look at Figure 5.50, for example. That figure shows two star shapes in different layers, as labeled—Layer 1 and Layer 2.

Figure 5.50
Two star shapes in different layers.

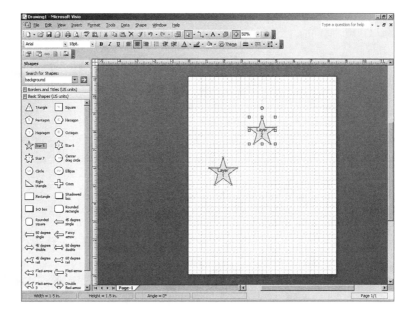

If you hide Layer 1, the star from Layer 1 disappears, leaving the star from Layer 2 only, as shown in Figure 5.51.

Figure 5.51
Hiding Layer 1.

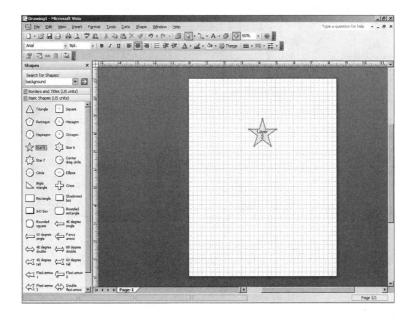

Conversely, if you hide Layer 2, you're left with only the shapes on Layer 1, as shown in Figure 5.52.

Figure 5.52
Hiding Layer 2.

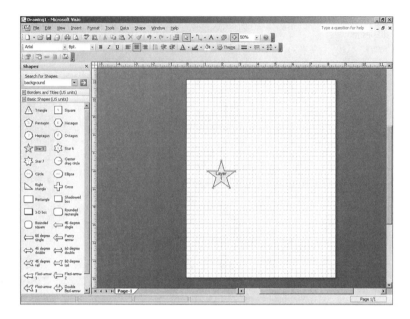

So how do you go about hiding a layer? Follow these steps:

1. Select View > Layer Properties, or select Layer Properties in the View toolbar. Visio displays the Layer Properties dialog, shown in Figure 5.53.

Figure 5.53
The Layer Properties dialog.

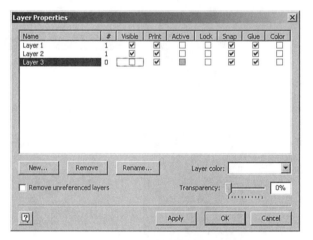

2. Deselect the check box in the Visible column for the layer you want to hide. If you want to toggle all the layers to be visible or invisible, click the Visible button at the top of the column.

3. Click OK.

That hides the layer you want to hide—on your computer, anyway. If you want to stop the layer from being printed out, follow these steps:

1. Select View > Layer Properties, or select Layer Properties in the View toolbar. Visio displays the Layer Properties dialog.

2. Deselect the check box in the Print column for the layer you want not to print. If you want to toggle all the layers to be printable or not printable, click the Print button at the top of the column.

3. Click OK.

ASSIGNING SHAPES TO ACTIVATED LAYERS

When you "activate" a layer, Visio assigns all newly dragged unassigned shapes to that layer. "Activation" might seem a funny name for this process, but it's the name that Visio uses.

When you activate multiple layers, Visio assigns all newly dragged shapes that have not been explicitly assigned to other layers to all the layers you activate.

How do you activate a layer? Here's how:

1. Select View > Layer Properties, or select Layer Properties in the View toolbar. Visio displays the Layer Properties dialog, shown in Figure 5.54.

Figure 5.54
Activating a layer in the Layer Properties dialog.

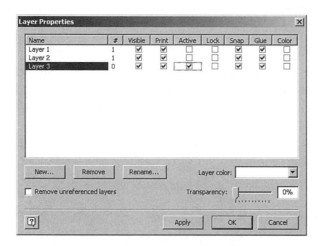

The user is about to make Layer 3 active in Figure 5.54.

2. Select the check box in the Active column for the layer you want to activate. If you want to toggle all the layers to be active, click the Active button at the top of the column.

3. Click OK.

Now all unassigned shapes will be assigned to Layer 3 when you drag shapes onto the drawing surface. For example, dragging a new star shape to the drawing surface assigns that shape to Layer 3, as you can see in Figure 5.55, in which Layer 3 is checked.

And that's how active layers work.

Figure 5.55
A shape assigned to an active layer.

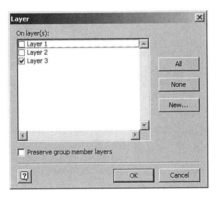

HANDLING BACKGROUND PAGES AND LAYERS

As you know, you can assign layers to foreground pages—how about background pages?

Yes, you can use layers in background pages as well. Here's how to add layers to a background page:

1. Display your background page. Select the appropriate tab at the bottom of the drawing surface, or use the Edit > Go To submenu to access the background page.

2. Select View > Layer Properties, or click the Layer Properties button on the View toolbar. Visio displays the Layer Properties dialog.

3. Click New. Visio displays the New Layer dialog.

4. Enter the name you want to give the new layer and click OK. You can see the new name, Background Layer 1, used in Figure 5.56.

Figure 5.56
A new background layer in the Layer Properties dialog.

LOCKING LAYERS

When you lock a layer, you can't add, move, or delete shapes on that layer. In fact, you can't even select them. Locking a layer is a good way to preserve it from accidental change.

How do you lock a layer? Here's how:

1. Select View > Layer Properties, or select Layer Properties in the View toolbar. Visio displays the Layer Properties dialog, shown in Figure 5.57.

Figure 5.57
Locking a layer in the Layer Properties dialog.

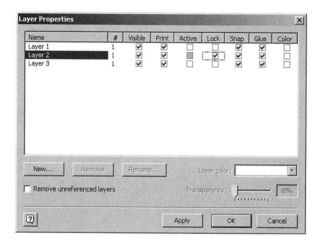

The user is about to lock Layer 2 in Figure 5.57.

2. Select the check box in the Lock column for the layer you want to lock. If you want to toggle all the layers to be locked, click the Lock button at the top of the column.
3. Click OK.

And that locks a layer. Note that you can't lock active layers.

USING SNAP AND GLUE WITH LAYERS

You can also see Snap and Glue columns in Figure 5.57—what are they about?

If you select Snap for a particular layer, shapes in that layer can snap to shapes in other layers, and the other way around as well. If you deselect Snap for a layer, shapes on that layer can still snap to shapes on other layers, but not the other way around.

How about the Glue option? If you select the Glue option, shapes on the layer can glue to shapes on other layers, and the other way around. If you deselect the Glue option, shapes on that layer can glue to shapes on other layers, but not the other way around.

CHAPTER 6

BUILDING YOUR OWN STENCILS, TEMPLATES, AND REPORTS

In this chapter

HANDLING STENCILS

You can use an application like Visio "out of the box" forever and get great value. There are thousands of shapes to choose from, and dozens of stencils. In fact, some people will never feel the need to customize Visio at all, and will simply work with what's already there.

On the other hand, if you persist with Visio, you'll find that customizing Visio in some ways will save you a great deal of work. Visio includes good facilities for customizing itself, and we're going to start taking a look at that process in this chapter.

In fact, you might actually look at the topics in this chapter—custom stencils, custom templates, and custom master shapes—as extensions of Visio, not just personalizations. In other words, that's what we're going to start doing in this chapter: extending Visio.

Visio has good support for this process, as you're going to see in this chapter.

You've been seeing how to work with stencils ever since Chapter 1, and this chapter takes you beyond the basics.

USING THE STENCIL TOOLBAR

There's a special toolbar for dealing with stencils—including creating new stencils—and that's the Stencil toolbar, shown in Figure 6.1.

Figure 6.1
The Stencil toolbar.

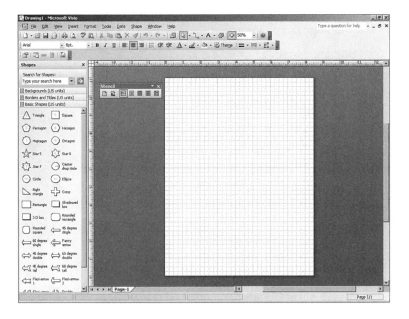

To display the Stencil toolbar, right-click the toolbar and select Stencil, or select View > Toolbars > Stencil.

Here's what the buttons in the Stencil toolbar do, from left to right:

- **New Stencil**—Lets you create a new stencil.
- **Show Document Stencil**—Lets you display the Document stencil for your drawing (Document stencils are coming up).
- **Icons and Names**—Lets you customize a stencil's appearance by having it display only the shapes' icons and names.
- **Names Under Icons**—Lets you customize a stencil's appearance by having it display shapes' names under their icons.
- **Icons Only**—Lets you customize a stencil's appearance by having it display only shapes' icons. This is a good option if you know the icons of the shapes you want to work with by sight, because it allows you to cram more shapes into a stencil.
- **Names Only**—Lets you customize a stencil's appearance by having it display only the shapes' names.
- **Icons and Details**—Lets you customize a stencil's appearance by having it display shapes' icons and details. This isn't usually a great option, because most icons' "details" simply tell you to drag the icon to the drawing surface to use it. And that's not something you need to be told over and over.

For example, take a look at Figure 6.2, in which you see a stencil displayed with the Icons and Names option.

Figure 6.2
The Icons and Names option.

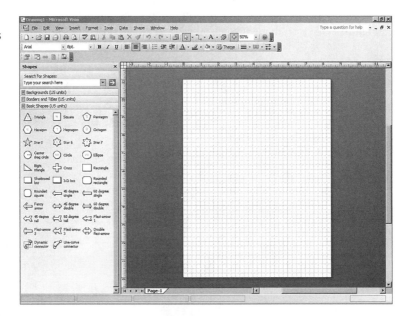

In Figure 6.3, you can see the Names Under Icons option in use.

Figure 6.3
The Names Under Icons option.

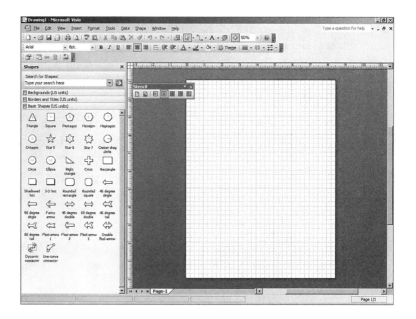

You can see the Icons Only option used in Figure 6.4—note how much space you save with this option. That makes it a good option if you have a stencil with a lot of shapes in it—enough to make scrolling a pain—and can get along with only the shapes' icons.

Figure 6.4
The Icons Only option.

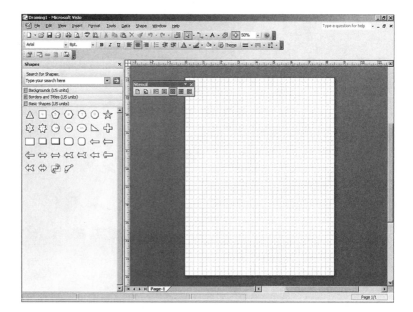

The Names Only option appears in Figure 6.5. This is another good space-saving option.

Figure 6.5
The Names Only
option.

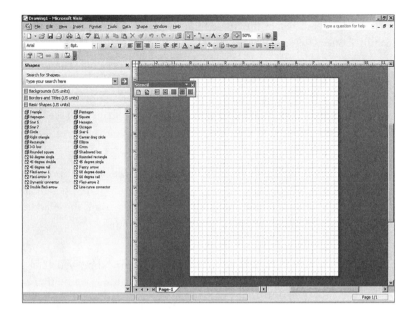

And the Icons and Details option appears in Figure 6.6.

Figure 6.6
The Icons and Details
option.

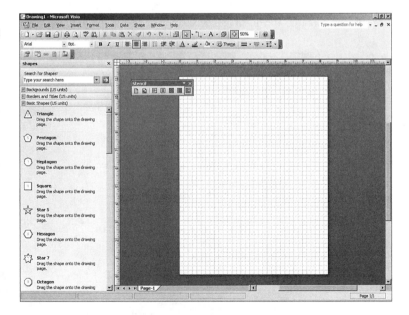

6

Note that all the shapes in the Icons and Details option simply display the text "Drag the shape onto the drawing page"—which is not very helpful.

So what about another of the Stencil toolbar's buttons, Show Document Stencil? What's that all about?

HANDLING DOCUMENT STENCILS

Visio creates a Document stencil when you start working on a drawing. What's a Document stencil? It's a special stencil in which Visio stores the shapes you've already used. In other words, a Document stencil is a repository of shapes you've put to work, stored in this stencil for easy repeat access.

Document stencils can be more useful than you might think—for example, say that you've made use of stencils not part of your template (you may have opened additional stencils with the File > Shapes menu item, for example). After using those additional stencils, you might have closed them. But what if you needed another copy of a shape from one of those closed stencils?

Do you need to search for and open the stencil again? Nope—you can just take a look in the Document stencil, and the shapes you've already used will be there ready for reuse.

How do you open the Document stencil? You can use the Show Document Stencil button in the Stencil toolbar, or you can select the File > Shapes > Show Document Stencil menu item.

For example, take a look at Figure 6.7, in which you see the Document stencil at the left. Note that it contains all the shapes already used in the drawing.

Figure 6.7
The Document stencil.

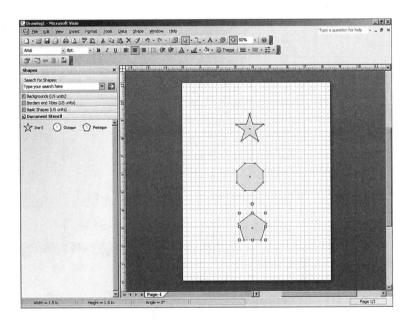

When you drag another shape onto the drawing surface, that shape appears in the Document stencil, as shown in Figure 6.8.

Figure 6.8
Using the Document stencil.

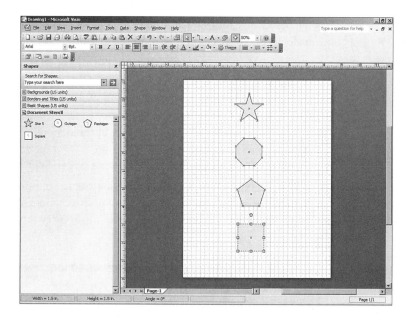

That's the Document stencil—one is created for each drawing, whether or not you use it. It's always there; just open it to use it. The Document stencil provides a good, handy way to organize the shapes you're using in a drawing as you draw.

Want to close the Document stencil? Just close it as you would any stencil: Right-click the stencil's title bar and select Close. That closes the Document stencil, but it's still there in case you need it; to access it again, just open it again.

BUILDING CUSTOM STENCILS

Often when you work with drawings, you'll find yourself using the same shapes over and over. For example, you might be laying out an entire office building, and as you design each office, you'll be using many of the same furniture icons.

If you are using the same shapes over and over, consider putting them into a custom stencil. Custom stencils let you organize your shapes just like Document stencils do, except that you have complete control over what goes into a custom stencil.

How do you create a custom stencil? One way of creating a custom stencil is by basing it on an existing stencil or drawing:

1. Access the shapes you want to put in the custom stencil. You can do that in any one of these three ways:

   - Open a drawing that uses the shapes you want. Doing so makes it easy to drag those shapes to a custom stencil. If you don't have such a drawing, you can create one, made up of the shapes you want in the custom stencil.

   - Open the stencil you want to base your custom stencil on. Or open the Document stencil, if it contains the shapes you want in the custom stencil. Be sure to scroll so that you can see all the shapes you want, to make dragging them easier.

   - Create the custom shapes you want to place in the custom stencil. You can use any custom shape in a custom stencil, and in fact, this is one of the biggest uses for custom stencils—to store the custom shapes you've built.

2. Select File > Shapes > New Stencil, or click the New Stencil button in the Stencil toolbar. The new stencil, named Stencil*n*, where *n* is a positive whole number, appears at the left in Visio, as shown in Figure 6.9. Visio adds 1 to *n* every time you create a brand-new stencil.

Figure 6.9
Creating a new stencil.

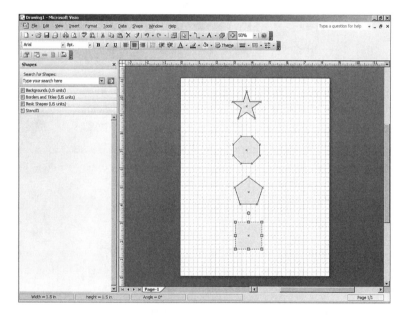

You have the option of using US units or Metric units—just select the New Stencil (US Units) or New Stencil (Metric) items when you create the new stencil.

3. Drag the shapes you want onto the custom stencil. You can drag those shapes using one of these two methods:

   - Drag shapes from the drawing page. When you do, be sure to hold down the Ctrl key, which makes sure that Visio knows you want to copy the shape, not just move it (if you don't do this, Visio moves the shape off the drawing when you drag it, and drops it into the new stencil). Visio names the first dragged shape Master.0, the next one Master.1, and so on (you'll see how to rename these in a minute), as shown in Figure 6.10.

Figure 6.10
Dragging shapes to a new stencil.

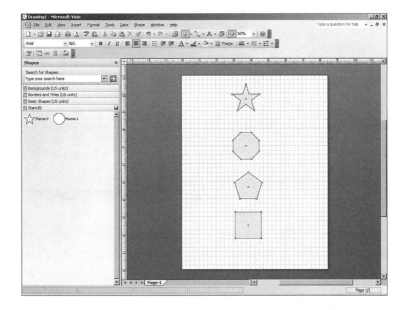

- Drag shapes from another stencil or the Document stencil. Do that by clicking the source stencil's title bar, opening that stencil. Then drag the shape you want (no need for the Ctrl key here—Visio doesn't move shapes off stencils, it copies them instead) to the title bar of the new, custom stencil. That makes Visio open the custom stencil, and you can drop the shape onto it. If you drag shapes from other stencils, they retain their name (Star 5, Square, and so on) in the custom stencil, unlike when you drag them from drawings.

4. Right-click the custom stencil's title bar and select Save As. Visio opens the Save As dialog, shown in Figure 6.11.

   Note that Visio has already created a stencil named Favorites for you—you can use this stencil to save your favorite shapes to.

5. Enter a name for the stencil in the File Name box of the Save As dialog. The name for this stencil is Stencil3, as shown in Figure 6.11.

6. Click Save. Visio saves the new stencil, and the new, custom stencil is now open for you in the template pane, as shown in Figure 6.10.

Now you can use the shapes in your new stencil. Note that the Document stencil appears only on a drawing-by-drawing basis, so although that's okay for organizing your shapes in a single drawing, it's better to create a custom stencil if you have multiple shapes that you want to bring to drawing after drawing.

Figure 6.11
Saving a new stencil.

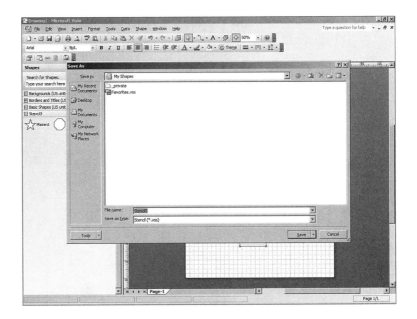

How do you open your new stencil from another drawing? You can select the File > Shapes > My Shapes > *Stencil Name* menu item. In this example, that's File > Shapes > My Shapes > Stencil3, as shown in Figure 6.12—selecting that menu item opens the new, custom stencil, ready for you to use.

Figure 6.12
Accessing your new stencil.

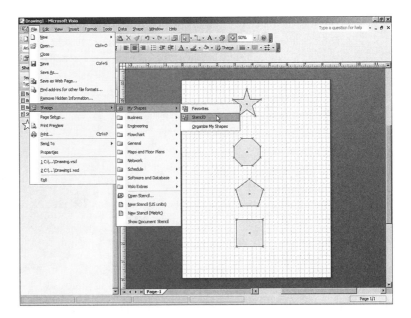

That's the way to create a new stencil and add shapes to it. Note that you don't, in fact, have to add new shapes to a custom stencil before saving it—you can create and save an empty custom stencil.

For that matter, you can drag new shapes onto a custom stencil at any time. Or you can even delete shapes from custom stencils. So you don't have to get everything just right on the first try—you can always come back later and modify a custom stencil.

But what about the names Master.0 and Master.1? We want to change the names of those shapes in our custom stencil to something more explanatory. How do you do that?

RENAMING MASTER SHAPES

You've already seen that when you drag shapes from a drawing to a custom stencil, Visio gives names to the new master shapes in the custom stencil—Master.0, Master.1, and so on. Not the most descriptive of names.

You can change those names easily in Visio, and this section discusses how.

In fact, you can also provide text for tool tips to display when the mouse hovers over the shape, and this section discusses that subject as well.

And you can even provide keywords for each shape that Visio can match when you perform keyword searches. This allows you to add your own custom shapes to the kind of searches you perform in Visio to find shapes interactively.

So how do you rename shapes? Follow these steps:

1. Access the stencil that holds the shapes you want to rename. For example, click the stencil's title bar, or open it using the File > Shapes menu item.

2. Right-click the stencil and select the Edit Stencil menu item. This displays a red asterisk in the stencil's title bar. You can see this asterisk (in black and white) at the left in Stencil3's title bar in Figure 6.10.

   This asterisk indicates that the stencil is in edit mode, and you can do things like edit the master shapes in it.

3. Right-click a shape and select Edit Master > Master Properties. This causes Visio to open the Master Properties dialog shown in Figure 6.13.

4. Enter a name for the shape in the Name box. This is your chance to change names like Master.0 to Star, for example.

5. Enter a description in the Prompt box. You might include information on what the particular shape is intended to be used for, for example. This is the description that will pop up in a tool tip when you hover the mouse over the shape.

6. Select a size in the Icon Size box. The standard size for icons is 32×32 pixels, but the other options are Tall (32×64), Wide (64×32), and Double (64×64). Unless you have a good reason, stick with the default 32×32 size.

7. Select the alignment for the shape's name. You can select from Left, Right, or Center (the default).

6

Figure 6.13
The Master Properties dialog.

8. Enter the words you want to be able to search for the shape with in the Keywords box. In addition to descriptive keywords, you can use special terms to find your custom shapes rapidly, such as including the word "Custom" in your list of search terms for the shape.

9. Click OK. Visio closes the Master Properties dialog.

10. Right-click the stencil and select the Edit Stencil menu item. This causes Visio to ask whether it should save your changes; click Yes. This takes the stencil out of edit mode, and removes the red asterisk from the stencil's title bar.

Now you can see the new name for the shape, as shown in Figure 6.14.

Figure 6.14
A renamed shape.

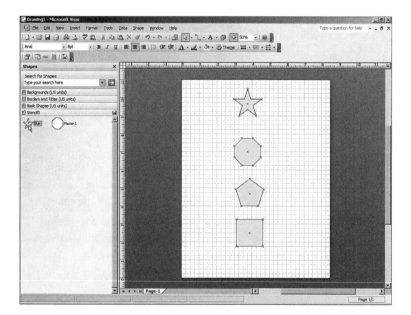

And the new tool tips you've created are in place as well.

Can you add shapes to the stencils that come built into Visio? Actually, you can. Select File>Shapes>Open Stencil, and navigate to Program Files/Microsoft Office/Office 12/1033. When opening the stencil you want to edit, select the down arrow on the Open button and select Open Original.

ADDING SHAPES TO STENCILS THE EASY WAY

Want a quick way to add shapes from existing Visio stencils to custom stencils—no dragging needed? You can do it all with context menus.

Sometimes, you might see a shape in a stencil that you feel should be in a custom stencil of yours. For example, the Triangle shape in the Basic Shapes stencil is an attractive one—what if you want to add that to a custom stencil?

You can add such shapes to your custom stencils simply. Just follow these steps:

1. Open the stencil you want to copy the shape from in the template pane.

2. Right-click the shape you want to copy to the custom stencil, and select the Add to My Shapes item. That displays the custom stencils' names, as shown in Figure 6.15.

Figure 6.15
Adding a shape to a custom stencil.

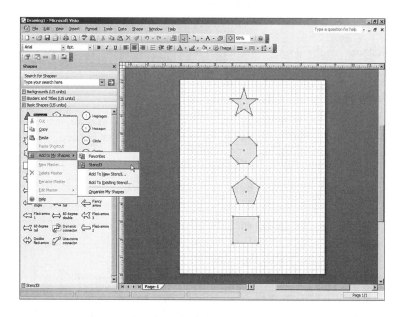

3. Select the name of the stencil that you want to copy the shape to. Visio copies the shape to the custom stencil you've selected.

In other words, you can save shapes—with their original names—to a custom stencil easily. Just right-click the shape, select Add to My Shapes, and select the stencil to save the shape to. Easy.

Visio will ask you before you close the stencil whether you want to save the changes to the stencil.

DELETING MASTER SHAPES FROM CUSTOM STENCILS

Want to delete a shape from a custom stencil?

Things change, and your custom stencils are no exception. Say, for example, that you've created a new and better version of a shape. Or that you just no longer need a particular shape. It's time to delete.

Here's how you can delete a shape from custom stencils:

1. Open the stencil you want to delete the shape from in the template pane.
2. Right-click the stencil and select the Edit Stencil menu item. This displays a red asterisk in the stencil's title bar. You can see this asterisk (in black and white) at the left in Stencil3's title bar in Figure 6.10.
3. Right-click the shape you want to delete, and select the Delete item. Visio deletes the shape from the custom stencil.
4. Right-click the stencil and select the Edit Stencil menu item. This causes Visio to ask whether it should save your changes; click Yes. This takes the stencil out of edit mode, and removes the red asterisk from the stencil's title bar.

That's it—you're done.

CREATING CUSTOM ICONS

Sometimes, you might want to create your own icons for your shapes, and you can do it using Visio. That's worthwhile for custom shapes you've created yourself, for example.

Want to create a custom icon? Here's how to do it:

1. Access the stencil that holds the shapes you want to work on. For example, click the stencil's title bar, or open it using the File > Shapes menu item.
2. Right-click the stencil and select the Edit Stencil menu item. This displays a red asterisk in the stencil's title bar. You can see this asterisk (in black and white) at the left in Stencil3's title bar in Figure 6.10.

   This asterisk indicates that the stencil is in edit mode, and you can do things like edit the master shapes in it.
3. Right-click a shape and select Edit Master > Edit Icon Image. This causes Visio to open the Icon Edit dialog, shown in Figure 6.16.
4. Edit the icon image the way you want. The mouse cursor changes to a pencil shape that you can edit the icon with.
5. Close the Icon Edit window. You can use the × button at the upper right in the window.

Figure 6.16
Editing an icon.

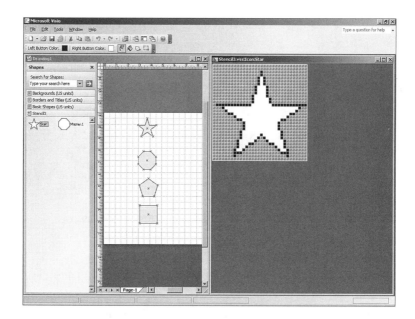

6. Right-click the stencil and select the Edit Stencil menu item. This causes Visio to ask whether it should save your changes; click Yes. This takes the stencil out of edit mode, and removes the red asterisk from the stencil's title bar.

BUILDING CUSTOM TEMPLATES

Templates set a great deal of information about a drawing—the colors used, the page orientation, and the page size, as well as the text style used. And it opens specific stencils for you to use.

Some corporations create their own custom templates, using, for example, corporate colors and page size, as well as corporate backgrounds. Doing so makes sure that all the drawings you create with Visio have a consistent look, no matter how many drawings you create.

You might also want to build custom templates to customize some aspect of drawings. Doing so can lend some professionalism to your Visio use.

Here are the steps to follow to create your own custom template:

1. Base your template on an existing template or drawing. Select File > New and then select a drawing type to create a new Visio drawing. Or, to base your template on an existing Visio drawing, open that drawing with File > Open.

2. Select File > Shapes to open stencils you want to add to your template. This causes Visio to add those stencils to your template when you save it as a template.

3. Close any stencils you don't want in your template. Right-click a stencil's title bar and select Close to close it.

6

4. Select File > Page Setup. Visio opens the Page Setup dialog, shown in Figure 6.17.

Figure 6.17
The Page Setup dialog, Print Setup tab.

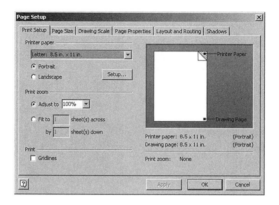

5. Select the Print Setup tab in the Page Setup dialog and select the Print options, such as Portrait or Landscape.

6. Select the Page Size tab in the Page Setup dialog and select the Page Size options, such as using a custom page size. You can see this tab in Figure 6.18.

Figure 6.18
The Page Setup dialog, Page Size tab.

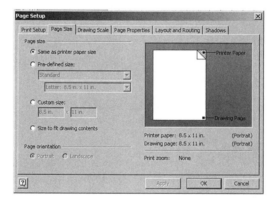

7. Select the Drawing Scale tab in the Page Setup dialog and select the Drawing Scale options, such as using a predefined scale. You can see this tab in Figure 6.19.

8. Create a background page, if you want one. Do that by right-clicking a page tab at the bottom of the drawing surface and selecting Insert Page, which opens the Page Setup dialog to the Page Properties tab, as shown in Figure 6.20.

Select the Background radio button in the Page Properties tab to make the new page a background page, then customize the page as you want.

9. Select File > Save As. This opens the Save As dialog, shown in Figure 6.21.

Figure 6.19
The Page Setup dialog, Drawing Scale tab.

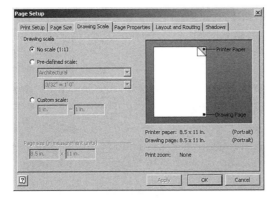

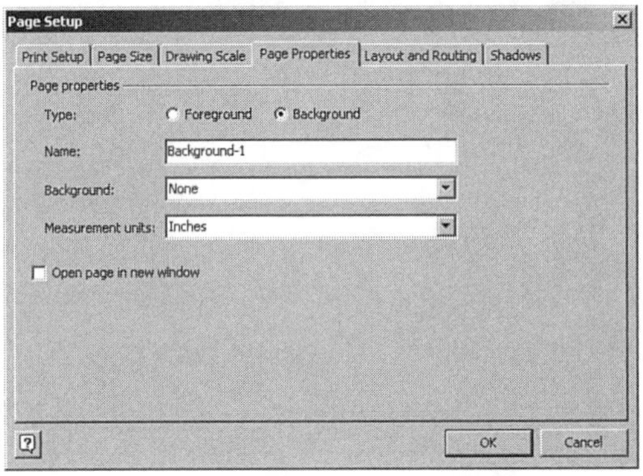

Figure 6.20
The Page Setup dialog, Page Properties tab.

Figure 6.21
The Save As dialog.

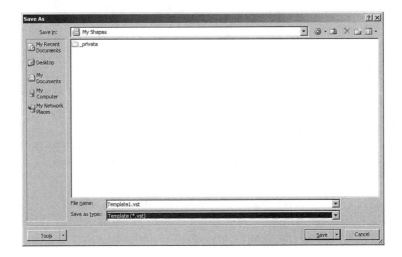

10. Select the folder where you want to save your new template in the Save As dialog. Select the Visio Solutions folder if you want to make this template an "official" choice, visible when you start Visio or when you select File > New and select a template.

11. Enter a name for the new template in the File Name box.

12. Select Template (*.vst) in the Save as Type box. You can see this in Figure 6.21.

13. Click Save. Visio saves your new template.

If you've stored the new template in the Visio Solutions folder, it will be accessible when Visio displays the Getting Started page as it starts up, or you can select your new template with File > New.

You can also create a new drawing from a custom template with the File > New Drawing from Template menu item. That opens the New Drawing from Template dialog, shown in Figure 6.22.

Figure 6.22
The New Drawing from Template dialog.

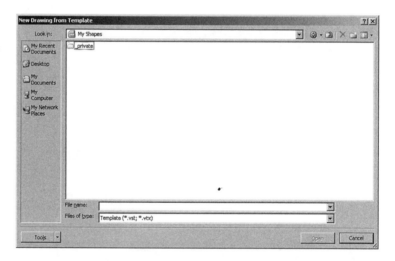

ADDING DATA TO VISIO SHAPES

The shapes you use in Visio can get fairly advanced, and that includes associating data with them.

In fact, all Visio shapes can store data. For example, you might have a flowchart drawing with various shapes in the flowchart, all of which have captions. But if that flowchart is for any kind of complex process—such as an ordering and procurement system—there's going to be more to the process than you can fit into the shape captions.

For example, you might want to store the actual address of your suppliers. Or you might want to store the suppliers' restrictions, or their phone number—you might even want to store comments on their reliability, or special deals they offer.

Or you might have an electrical circuit drawing, and need to store more information about particular components—specifying, for example, whether a specific resistor is a 1% or a 5% precision resistor. Or the possible load properties of a battery. Or the response time of a relay.

Or you might want to store inventory numbers for the furniture in an office layout, or for computer parts. Or part numbers. Or the cost of each item. Or any of a thousand pieces of information.

Visio lets you store that kind of information in shapes, and it calls such data *shape data*. Every data item is considered a custom property of the shape, and is stored along with the shape itself.

Some shapes, such as office furniture, already have a list of shape data items that Visio associates with the shape. You can access that data by right-clicking a shape and selecting Data > Shape Data, thereby opening the Shape Data dialog—if the shape has data properties already associated with it—as shown in Figure 6.23.

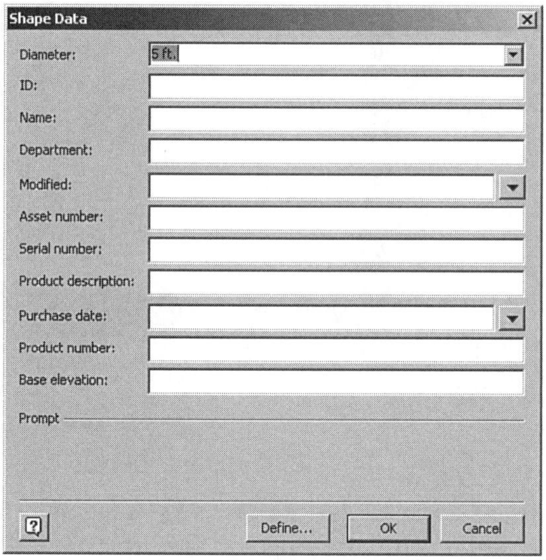

Figure 6.23
Visio shape data.

You can also access shape data another way: by using the Shape Data window. Just select View > Shape Data Window, and that window appears, as shown in Figure 6.24.

The Shape Data window is convenient, because you only need to click a shape to display its data in the Shape Data window automatically, which is very handy.

If there's no data and no data properties associated with a shape, Visio tells you so when you right-click the shape and select Data > Shape Data. And in that case, Visio asks whether you want to add data to the shape.

We're going to take a look at the shape data possibilities now.

One thing that's important to know from the outset is that shape data is stored in shape data *properties*. For example, take a look at Figure 6.23. The office table there has all the data properties you see listed in the Shape Data dialog—Diameter, ID, Name, and so on.

Those properties exist to be filled with data, and you can see that the Diameter property does indeed have data associated with it—"5 ft."

In other words, shape data properties are labeled placeholders, ready to store data. And the actual shape data is the data—text, numeric, whatever—that is stored in those properties.

Figure 6.24
The Shape Data window.

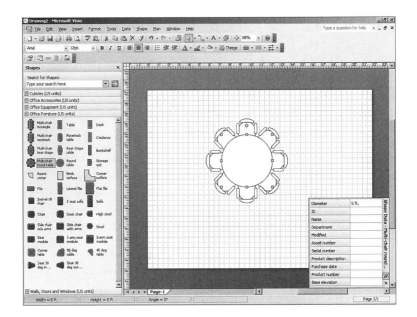

ADDING SHAPE DATA

The data in Visio shapes is customizable—which means you can add your own custom data to shapes, as well as customize which data properties the shape has.

Want to add custom data to a shape?

No problem.

Want to remove shape data properties?

No problem. For example, you might not want a Purchase Date data property for a particular shape, and you can get rid of it.

We'll start with the basics. Want to add data to a Visio shape? Here's how to do it:

1. Open the drawing containing the shape whose data you want to store or edit.
2. Right-click the shape and select Data > Shape Data. Visio opens the Shape Data dialog, shown in Figure 6.23.
3. Enter the data you want to store in each shape data property. As example appears in Figure 6.25.
4. Click OK. Visio closes the Shape Data dialog.

Figure 6.25
Entering shape data.

That's it—Visio stores the data you've entered with the shape, as you can see by opening the Shape Data dialog again, or by saving the drawing, reopening it, and then opening the Shape Data dialog for the round table again.

You can also enter shape data into the Shape Data window. That is, the Shape Data window isn't read-only; you can enter data in it as well. Just click the property whose data you want to edit, and type your new data.

That's a handy way to enter data for multiple shapes—just click them, enter the appropriate data into the Shape Data window, and then move on to the next shape. Make sure you save your drawing after updating shape data like that.

CREATING CUSTOM SHAPE DATA PROPERTIES

As good as Visio is, it can't anticipate every data item that you may want to associate with shapes. For example, you may want to assign an Employee Name property to office furniture in order to connect every piece of office furniture with the person responsible for it.

But the office furniture shapes have no Employee Name shape data property, as yet.

However, you can add that kind of shape data property to shapes, and we're going to see how next.

In fact, you can add custom shape data properties to shapes on the drawing surface, or a shape in a stencil (that is, a master shape)—even shapes in the Document stencil.

We'll take a look at this now, starting with how to add custom shape data properties to shapes on the drawing surface.

6

ADDING SHAPE DATA PROPERTIES TO SHAPES ON THE DRAWING SURFACE

How do you add custom shape data properties to an instance of a shape—that is, to a shape as drawn on the drawing surface?

Just follow these steps:

1. Open the drawing containing the shape whose data properties you want to edit.

2. Right-click the shape and select Data > Shape Data. Visio opens the Shape Data dialog, shown in Figure 6.23.

    Visio opens the Shape Data dialog if the shape has data associated with it.

    If the shape doesn't have any shape data associated with it, Visio tells you that and asks whether you want to add some data to the shape. Click Yes.

3. Click the Define button. Visio opens the Define Shape Data dialog, shown in Figure 6.26.

Figure 6.26
The Define Shape Data dialog.

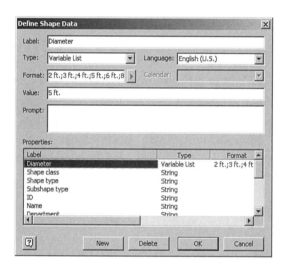

As you can see, there's a lot going on in this dialog.

4. Click New. Visio creates a new shape data property, as shown in Figure 6.27.

    The new property is given a name like Property16, as you see in Figure 6.27—because, in this case, the round table you're adding this new property to has 15 properties to start.

5. Enter a name for the new property in the Label box if you want to use a more descriptive name.

6. Select a type for the new property in the Type Box. For example, select the String type for text string properties, Number for numeric properties, and so on.

7. Select a format style in the Format box. The options available will depend on how you set the Type. For example, if you selected Number for the type, the Format box will contain the options Whole Number, Fraction, Floating Point, and so on.

Figure 6.27
Creating a new property in the Define Shape Data dialog.

8. Enter a description of the kind of data you expect in this property in the Prompt box. The prompt text appears in the bottom of the Shape Data dialog when you select this property. It also appears as a tool tip when you hover the mouse over the property's label in the Shape Data dialog.

9. Optionally, enter a value for the property in the Value box if you want to give the property a default value. The new property, Employee Name in this case, appears in the Define Shape Data dialog, as shown in Figure 6.28.

Figure 6.28
A new property in the Define Shape Data dialog.

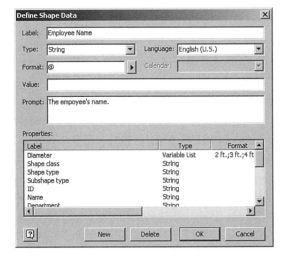

10. Click New and repeat the process for other new properties you want to create.

11. Click OK. Visio closes the Define Shape Data dialog.

Visio displays the new property, Employee Name in this case, in the Shape Data dialog, as shown in Figure 6.29.

Figure 6.29
A new property in the
Shape Data dialog.

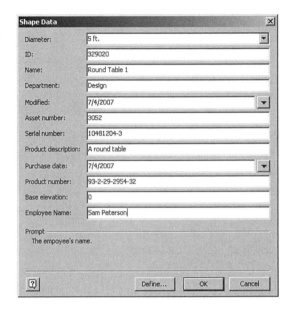

12. Enter any data for the new property. You can see the name Sam Peterson entered in Figure 6.29.

13. Click OK. Visio closes the Shape Data dialog.

Okay, that's how to create a custom shape data property for an instance of a shape.

You can also create properties that are lists. Here's how to do that:

1. Open the drawing containing the shape whose data properties you want to edit.

2. Right-click the shape and select Data > Shape Data. Visio opens the Shape Data dialog, shown earlier in Figure 6.23.

   Visio opens the Shape Data dialog if the shape has data associated with it.

   If the shape doesn't have any shape data associated with it, Visio tells you that and asks whether you want to add some data to the shape. Click Yes.

3. Click the Define button. Visio opens the Define Shape Data dialog.

4. Click New if an existing property is highlighted. Visio creates a new shape data property (there's no need to click New if the shape doesn't have any data associated with it—Visio will create a new property automatically).

   The new property will be given a name like Property16, as shown earlier in Figure 6.27—because, in this case, the round table you're adding this new property to has 15 properties to start.

5. Enter a name for the new property in the Label box if you want something more descriptive.

6. Select Fixed List or Variable List for the new property in the Type Box.

7. Enter the list items separated by semicolons in the Format box. The options you enter in this box will be the items in the new list. You can see this in Figure 6.30.

Figure 6.30
Creating a list in the Define Shape Data dialog.

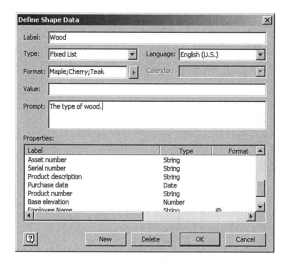

8. Enter a description of the kind of data you expect in this property in the Prompt box. The prompt text appears in the bottom of the Shape Data dialog when you select this property. It also appears as a tool tip when you hover the mouse over the property's label in the Shape Data dialog.

9. Click New and repeat the process for other new properties you want to create.

10. Click OK. Visio closes the Define Shape Data dialog.

    Visio displays the new property—Wood in this case—in the Shape Data dialog, as shown in Figure 6.31.

11. Select a value for the new property from the drop-down list that appears. You can see the new property's drop-down list in Figure 6.31.

12. Click OK. Visio closes the Shape Data dialog.

Okay, you've added a new shape data property to a shape—now how about deleting that property when you need to?

6

Figure 6.31
A new property in the
Shape Data dialog.

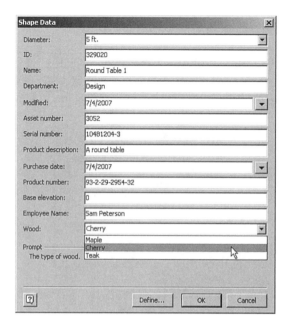

REMOVING SHAPE DATA PROPERTIES FROM SHAPES ON THE DRAWING SURFACE

Want to delete a custom shape data property for an instance of a shape? Follow these steps:

1. Open the drawing containing the shape whose data properties you want to edit.
2. Right-click the shape and select Data > Shape Data. Visio opens the Shape Data dialog, shown earlier in Figure 6.23.
3. Click the Define button. Visio opens the Define Shape Data dialog, shown earlier in Figure 6.26.
4. Select the property to delete and click Delete. Visio deletes the property. For example, the Employee Name property is about to be deleted from the round table shape in Figure 6.32.
5. Select any other properties to delete, and repeat the process until finished.
6. Click OK. Visio closes the Define Shape Data dialog.
7. Click OK. Visio closes the Shape Data dialog.

That covers how to add and delete shape data properties for shapes on the drawing surface.

Now how about doing the same for master shapes in stencils?

Figure 6.32
Deleting a property in the Shape Data dialog.

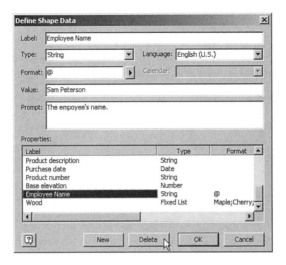

ADDING SHAPE DATA PROPERTIES TO SHAPES IN STENCILS

You can also add custom shape data properties to the shapes in custom stencils or the Document stencil. Doing so is a great idea if you want to assign data to properties every time you create a shape using a master shape in a stencil.

For example, if you know you're going to want an employee name every time you draw a piece of office furniture, it makes sense to add an Employee Name shape data property to the furniture shapes in the custom stencil they appear in.

Want to add shape data properties to a shape in a stencil? Just follow these steps:

1. Open the custom stencil or Document stencil containing the shape whose data properties you want to edit.

2. Right-click the stencil's title bar and select Edit Stencil If the Stencil Is a Custom Stencil. A red asterisk appears at the left in the title bars of custom stencils, as shown in Figure 6.33, in which Stencil3 is being edited.

3. Drag the shape you want to alter to the drawing surface. You can see this step in Figure 6.34.

4. Right-click the shape and select Data > Shape Data. Visio opens the Shape Data dialog, shown earlier in Figure 6.23.

   Visio opens the Shape Data dialog if the shape has data associated with it.

   If the shape doesn't have any shape data associated with it, Visio tells you that and asks whether you want to add some data to the shape. Click Yes.

5. Click the Define button. Visio opens the Define Shape Data dialog.

6. Click New if an existing property is highlighted. Visio creates a new shape data property (there's no need to click New if the shape doesn't have any data associated with it—Visio will create a new property automatically).

Figure 6.33
Editing a custom stencil.

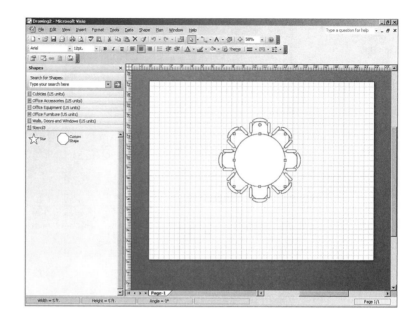

Figure 6.34
Dragging a shape to the drawing surface.

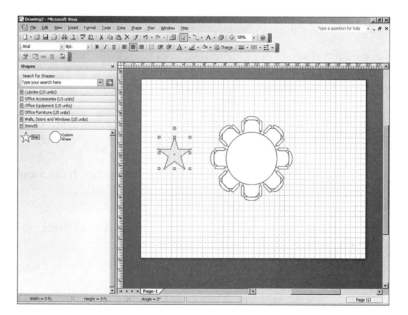

7. Enter a name for the new property in the Label box.

8. Select a type for the new property in the Type Box. For example, select the String type for text string properties, Number for numeric properties, and so on.

9. Select a format style in the Format box. The options available will depend on how you set the Type. For example, if you selected Number for the type, the Format box will contain the options Whole Number, Fraction, Floating Point, and so on.

10. Enter a description of the kind of data you expect in this property in the Prompt box. The prompt text appears in the bottom of the Shape Data dialog when you select this property. It also appears as a tool tip when you hover the mouse over the property's label in the Shape Data dialog.

11. Optionally, enter a value for the property in the Value box if you want to give the property a default value.

12. Click New and repeat the process for other new properties you want to create.

13. Click OK. Visio closes the Define Shape Data dialog.

14. Enter any data you want for the new property.

15. Click OK. Visio closes the Shape Data dialog.

16. Right-click the shape in the custom stencil or Document stencil and select Delete to delete it. Visio deletes the master shape from the stencil.

17. Press Ctrl and drag the modified shape to the custom stencil or Document stencil. Visio copies the modified shape to the custom stencil or Document stencil.

18. Right-click the stencil's title bar and select Save. Visio saves the new version of the stencil.

19. Right-click the stencil's title bar and select Edit Stencil if the stencil is a custom stencil. The red asterisk disappears from the title bars of custom stencils.

All right, how about removing shape data from shapes in stencils?

REMOVING SHAPE DATA PROPERTIES FROM SHAPES IN STENCILS

Need to remove a property for a master shape in a custom stencil or a Document stencil? Here's how to go about it:

1. Open the custom stencil or Document stencil containing the shape whose data properties you want to edit.

2. Right-click the stencil's title bar and select Edit Stencil If the Stencil Is a Custom Stencil. A red asterisk appears at the left in the title bars of custom stencils.

3. Drag the shape whose properties you want to alter to the drawing surface.

4. Right-click the shape and select Data > Shape Data. Visio opens the Shape Data dialog.

5. Click the Define button. Visio opens the Define Shape Data dialog.

6. Select the property to delete and click Delete. Visio deletes the property.

7. Select any other properties to delete, and repeat the process until finished.

8. Click OK. Visio closes the Define Shape Data dialog.

9. Click OK. Visio closes the Shape Data dialog.

10. Right-click the shape in the custom stencil or Document stencil and select Delete to delete it. Visio deletes the master shape from the stencil.

6

11. Press Ctrl and drag the modified shape to the custom stencil or Document stencil. Visio copies the modified shape to the custom stencil or Document stencil.

12. Right-click the stencil's title bar and select Save. Visio saves the new version of the stencil.

13. Right-click the stencil's title bar and select Edit Stencil If the Stencil Is a Custom Stencil. The red asterisk disappears in the title bars of custom stencils.

MODIFYING SHAPE DATA FOR MULTIPLE SHAPES

You can also modify the shape data for multiple shapes at once. All you have to do is select the multiple steps and make the modifications you want to make.

Just follow these steps:

1. Open the drawing containing the shapes whose data properties you want to edit.

2. Select the shapes whose properties you want to modify. You can see an example in Figure 6.35.

Figure 6.35
Selecting shapes.

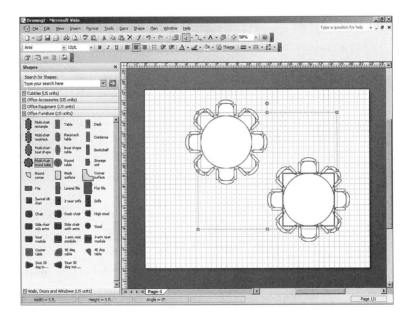

3. Right-click the selected shapes and select Data > Shape Data. Visio opens the Shape Data dialog, as you see in Figure 6.36.

4. Enter the changes you'd like to make for all the shapes at once. For example, the Department property is being changed to Facilities in Figure 6.36.

5. Click OK. Visio closes the Shape Data dialog.

Figure 6.36
Opening the Shape
Data dialog.

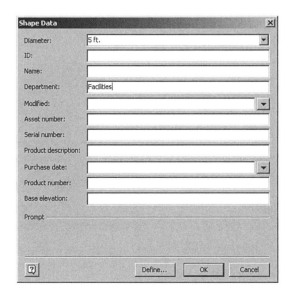

Now you can check the properties of either shape shown in Figure 6.35, and you'll find that the Department property is set to Facilities for both. Not bad.

There's one thing to note here, however: If you select shapes that are different types, Visio displays only the properties that the shapes have in common. For example, if one shape has a Department property and another selected shape doesn't, you won't see Department in the Shape Data dialog. Only properties common to all the selected shapes will appear in the Shape Data dialog.

CREATING REPORTS

You can also report on data stored in shapes, which makes that data more visible. Visio gives you the tools to create all kinds of predefined reports. In fact, there are 23 varieties of predefined reports in Visio, ready for you to use.

To create a report, you need to give Visio a definition of the report you want. A report definition indicates the following:

- The shapes you want the report to report on
- The shape data you want to report
- The title of the report
- Sorting guidelines

It's easiest to create reports using Visio's predefined report types, because you don't have to create your own report definitions from scratch. And you're not locked into a rigid format using the predefined reports, either—Visio lets you modify them as needed.

So how do you create a predefined report?

That's coming up next.

CREATING A PREDEFINED REPORT

There are 22 predefined report types in Visio, but not all of them apply for every drawing. Some drawings might have only three report types that apply, for example. And some might have six.

The predefined reports fall into categories; for instance:

- **Asset reports**—List information about asset type, name, manufacturer, and so on.
- **Count reports**—Count the items in a drawing.
- **Numeric reports**—Can perform various operations, such as summing values and finding averages.

Here are all 22 report types in Visio:

Asset Reports	Move
Calendar Event	Network Device
Count Positions	Network Equipment
Door Schedule	Organization Chart Report
Equipment List	PC Report
Flowchart	Pipeline List
Gantt Chart	Space Report
HVAC Diffuser	Valve List
HVAC Duct	Web Site Map All Links
Instrument List	Web Site Map with Errors
Inventory	Window Schedule

Here's how to create a predefined report:

1. Open the drawing containing the shapes whose data properties you want to report on.
2. Select Data > Reports. Visio opens the Reports dialog, shown in Figure 6.37.

   The Reports dialog you see in Figure 6.37 lists all the predefined reports. To narrow that list down to the ones that make sense for the current drawing, see the next step.
3. Select the Show Only Drawing-Specific Reports check box if it's not already selected. Visio narrows the list of predefined reports to those pertinent to your drawing, as shown in Figure 6.38.

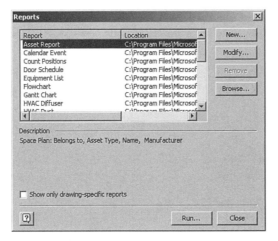

Figure 6.37
Opening the Reports dialog.

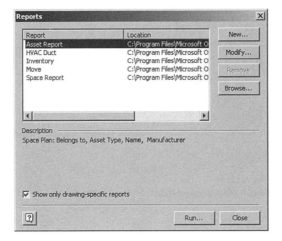

Figure 6.38
The Reports dialog showing drawing-specific choices.

4. Select the report type you want to create. For example, the Inventory report type is selected in Figure 6.39.

5. Click Run. Visio displays the Run Report dialog, shown in Figure 6.40.

6. Select the type of report you want to generate:

- **HTML**—Creates a report in HTML format. Visio gives the report the name Report_x.html, where x is a number starting with 1, which Visio uses for your first report. You can also set the name of the report yourself, as well as its location. After the report is created, Visio opens it in your default browser.

- **Visio Shape**—Creates a Visio shape that displays the report in table form. Visio not only creates this shape, but also displays it in your drawing immediately. Very handy when you want to add the report to a drawing.

6

- **Excel**—Creates a report in Microsoft Excel format. The report will be an Excel spreadsheet, and Visio launches Excel to display that report as soon as it's generated.

- **XML**—Creates a report in XML format. This option causes Visio to store its report in an XML document, and to open that document in your default XML reader (usually Microsoft Internet Explorer). Reports in XML format can often be read by other applications.

Figure 6.39
Selecting a report.

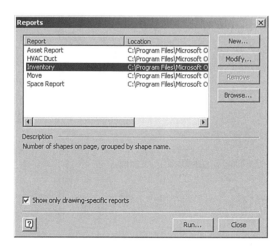

Figure 6.40
The Run Report dialog.

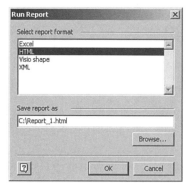

7. Click OK. Visio creates the report and launches it in the application appropriate to the report format.

You can see an HTML report, reporting on the inventory in an office layout drawing, in Figure 6.41.

You can see a Visio shape–based report in Figure 6.42.

Figure 6.41
An HTML report.

Figure 6.42
A shape report.

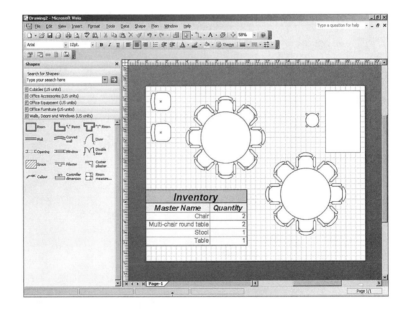

You can see an Excel-based report in Figure 6.43.

And you can see an XML-based report in Figure 6.44.

And that's how to create a report using the predefined report types that come with Visio.

However, Visio can't anticipate all the kinds of reports you might want—for that, you're going to have to create custom reports.

Figure 6.43
An Excel report.

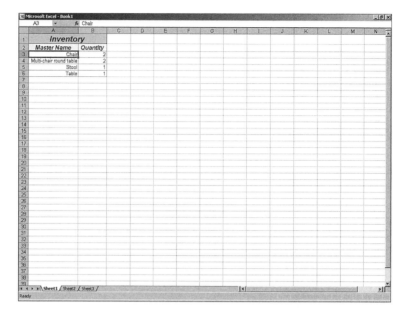

Figure 6.44
An XML report.

CREATING CUSTOM REPORTS

You can also create custom reports in Visio, in which you tailor what's reported on.

You can specify what conditions various property settings must match in custom reports—for example, you might specify that all shapes included in your custom report must have a

Department property set to "Facilities"; then, to be included in your report, a shape's Department property must be set that way.

To create a custom report, you must do the following:

- Select the shapes you want to report on
- Select the properties and, optionally, the values of those properties that you want to report on
- Select how you want the report organized

Here are the steps to follow to create a new custom report:

1. Open the drawing you want to work with.
2. Select Data > Reports. Visio opens the Reports dialog, shown in Figure 6.45.

Figure 6.45
Opening the Reports dialog.

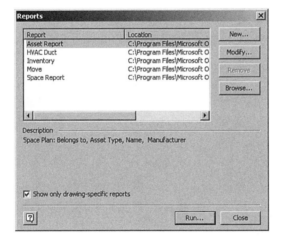

3. Click New. Visio opens the Report Definition Wizard dialog, shown in Figure 6.46.

Figure 6.46
Opening the Report Definition Wizard dialog.

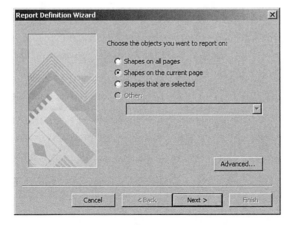

The Shapes on All Pages option lets you generate a custom report for all shapes on all the pages in your drawing.

The Shapes on the Current Page option lets you generate a report for the shapes on the current page, and it's the default option.

The Shapes That Are Selected option lets you generate your new custom report for only the shapes that are selected in the current drawing.

The fourth option, Other, is enabled only for specific drawing types, such as Organization Chart drawings.

4. Select a shape selection option. For example, you can see the Shapes on the Current Page option selected in Figure 6.46.

5. If you have specific property criteria (such as Purchase Date = 2007) to select, click the Advanced button. Visio opens the Advanced dialog, shown in Figure 6.47.

Figure 6.47
Entering advanced report criteria.

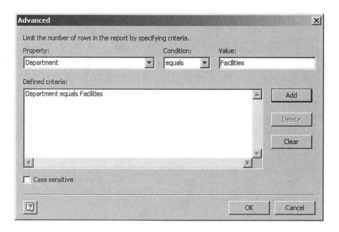

Select the property you want to specify a match criteria for. For example, you might select the Department property, as shown in Figure 6.47.

Select a comparison operation, such as Equals, Does Not Equal, or Exists. This operation specifies how you want to compare property values to fixed values. For example, you might select Equals, as shown in Figure 6.47.

Enter a value in the Value box, specifying the value you want to compare to the property value. For example, you can see in Figure 6.47 that the Department property is being compared to the value Facilities.

Select the Case Sensitive check box when you want to make the comparison case-sensitive.

Click Add—Visio adds the new comparison to the Defined criteria box, as you can see in Figure 6.47.

Repeat the preceding steps for any additional criteria you want property values to match.

Click OK to close the Advanced dialog.

6. Click Next. In this pane of the Report Wizard, Visio gives you the chance of specifying which properties you want displayed in columns in your custom report, as shown in Figure 6.48.

Figure 6.48
Selecting property columns.

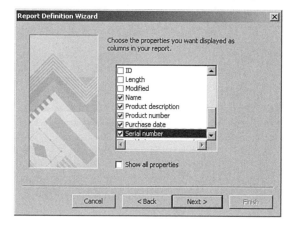

7. Select the Show All Properties check box if you want to select from among all available properties, not just the ones Visio selects. This option lets you select properties that appear in other drawings, not just the current drawing. If you want to select other properties from other drawings, select this check box.

8. Select each property you want to display as its own column in the final report.

9. Click Next. This opens the new pane shown in Figure 6.49.

Figure 6.49
Selecting a report title.

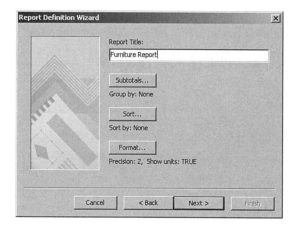

6

10. Enter a title for your report in the Report Title box. For example, you can see the title Furniture Report in Figure 6.49.

11. Click the Subtotals button if you want to group your results. You can see the Subtotals dialog in Figure 6.50.

Figure 6.50
The Subtotals dialog.

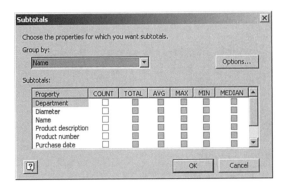

Select a property in the Group By box to group your reports items using that property. You can see the Name property selected in Figure 6.50.

Click the Options button to display the grouping options. The grouping options let you get rid of duplicate items in report groups. Groups can also include overall totals so that you can see statistics for the whole report, and other items.

Select the Subtotals options you want. You can add averages, maximums, minimums, and so on to your report for the properties you selected to appear in your report.

Click OK. Visio closes the Subtotals dialog and the Report Definition Wizard reappears.

12. Click the Sort button to indicate how your results should be sorted. You can see the Sort dialog in Figure 6.51.

Figure 6.51
The Sort dialog.

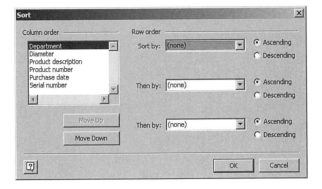

Set up the column order for your custom report by altering the order of the properties in the Column Order list. Select a column and use the Move Up and Move Down buttons.

Choose property names in the Row Order drop-down boxes. Select Ascending or Descending order as appropriate.

Click OK. Visio closes the Sort dialog and the Report Definition Wizard reappears.

13. Click the Format button to indicate how your results should be formatted. You can see the Format dialog in Figure 6.52.

Figure 6.52
The Format dialog.

Select the number of places you want for decimal precision; the default is 2, as shown in Figure 6.52.

Select the Show Units check box when you want Visio to display the units for each value.

Click OK. Visio closes the Format dialog and the Report Definition Wizard reappears.

14. Click Next. You can see the final pane of the Report Definition Wizard in Figure 6.53.

Figure 6.53
The final pane of the Report Definition Wizard.

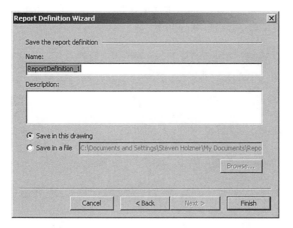

6

15. Enter a name for your report definition in the Name box. You can see the name ReportDefinition_1 in Figure 6.53. This is the name that will appear in the Run Report dialog when it's time to run your report and create your custom report.

16. Enter a description for your report definition in the Description box.

17. Select a save location for your report definition. You can save your report definition in the current drawing or in a file, as indicated by the radio buttons in Figure 6.53.

If you save the custom report definition to the current drawing, make sure you save the drawing before closing it, or the report definition will be lost.

18. Click Finish. Visio closes the Report Definition Wizard and you see the Reports dialog, shown in Figure 6.54.

Figure 6.54
ReportDefinition_1 in the Reports dialog.

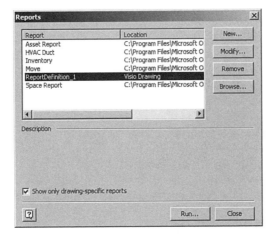

Note that your new report definition, ReportDefinition_1, appears in the Reports dialog in Figure 6.54.

That's your new, custom report definition, ready for use.

19. Click Run. If you select Visio Shape in the Select Report Format box, you'll end up with the custom report shown in Figure 6.55.

Figure 6.55
A new custom report.

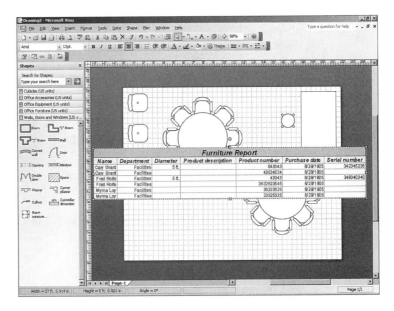

Congratulations, you've created a new custom report definition and created a report using that definition.

CHAPTER **7**

Controlling Shape Behavior and Marking Up Drawings

In this chapter

MODIFYING SHAPE BEHAVIOR

There are hundreds of Visio shapes, and they all behave in pretty standard ways. However, some shapes work in different ways. For example, double-clicking an organization chart opens that chart's text for modification—but double-clicking a report linked to an Excel spreadsheet makes Visio display that spreadsheet for modification.

Just how your shapes handle double-clicking is at least partly up to you in Visio. For example, if you double-click a chair in an office layout, nothing happens by default. But you can change that so that Visio displays custom shape data that you added to the chair.

There's other shape behavior you can change in Visio as well—for example, you can convert 2D shapes (which show selection frames when selected) to 1D shapes (which show endpoints when selected). You can convert 2D shapes into connectors this way, for example.

We'll start by seeing how to convert 2D shapes into 1D shapes.

CONVERTING 2D SHAPES INTO 1D SHAPES— AND BACK AGAIN

Sometime, you might want to convert a 2D shape into a 1D shape when you want to make your own connector. Or you might want to convert a 1D shape into a 2D shape to rotate it easily. How can you do that?

For example, take a look at Figure 7.1, in which you see a special 2D arrow drawn as a connector.

Figure 7.1
A special 2D arrow drawn as a connector.

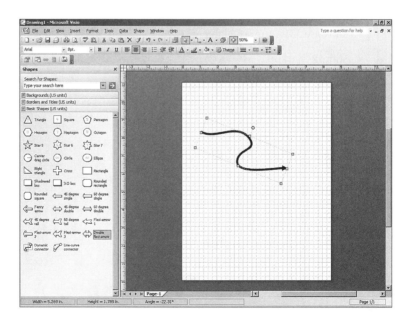

However, that arrow is a 2D arrow, which means that it displays a selection frame when selected. How would you change that arrow to a 1D shape, as connectors are? To use that arrow as a connector, you have to convert it to a 1D shape.

Here's how to convert a 2D shape into a 1D shape:

1. Create the 2D shape that you want to convert to 1D.

2. Right-click the shape and select Format > Behavior. That opens the Behavior dialog, shown in Figure 7.2.

Figure 7.2
The Behavior dialog.

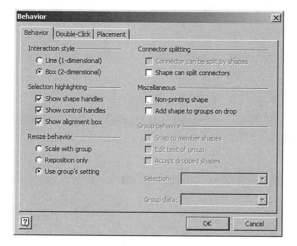

3. Select the Line (1-Dimensional) radio button in the Interaction Style region of the Behavior dialog. You can see this radio button in Figure 7.2.

4. Click OK. That converts the 2D arrow into a 1D arrow, as shown in Figure 7.3, in which you can see that when the arrow is selected, you now see endpoints, not a selection frame.

That converts a 2D shape into a 1D shape—and now you can use it as a connector, connecting to connection points on other shapes.

How about going the other way and converting a 1D shape into a 2D shape? Follow these steps:

1. Create the 1D shape that you want to convert to 2D.

2. Right-click the shape and select Format > Behavior. That opens the Behavior dialog, shown in Figure 7.4.

3. Select the Box (2-Dimensional) radio button in the Interaction Style region of the Behavior dialog. You can see this radio button in Figure 7.4.

7

Figure 7.3
A 1D shape.

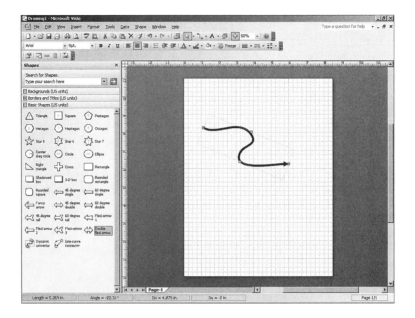

Figure 7.4
Using the Behavior
dialog.

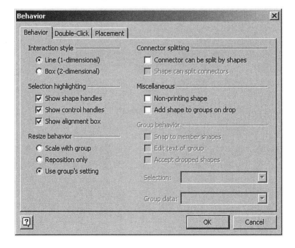

4. Click OK. That converts the 1D shape into a 2D shape, as shown in Figure 7.5, where you can see that when the shape is selected, you see a selection frame, not endpoints.

That converts a 1D shape into a 2D shape.

Figure 7.5
A 2D shape.

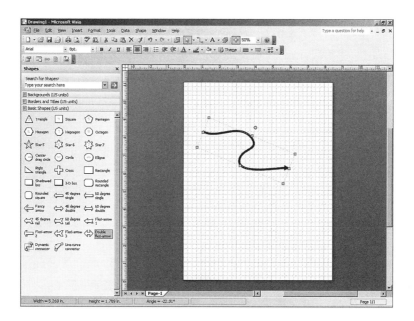

SPECIFYING SHAPES' GROUP BEHAVIOR

When you group shapes together, they behave as a group. When you click a group, that group is selected; when you double-click a shape in a group, that shape is selected.

However, you can switch this behavior around—that is, you can have a shape selected when you click the group, and the whole group selected when you double-click the group.

Here's how to set this group behavior:

1. Open the drawing that contains the group you want to work with. You can see an example in Figure 7.6.

2. Right-click one of the group's shapes and select Format > Behavior. That opens the Behavior dialog, shown in Figure 7.7. (Note that the Behavior menu item won't be available unless you specifically right-click a shape in the group.)

3. Select one of the following options from the drop-down Selection list:

    - **Group Only**—Selects the group as a whole when clicked, but not the shapes in the group.

    - **Group First**—Selects the group when clicked, then the shapes inside the group when double-clicked. This is the default in Visio.

    - **Members First**—Selects a shape in the group when clicked, then the group as a whole when double-clicked.

4. Click OK. Visio closes the Behavior dialog.

7

Figure 7.6
A group.

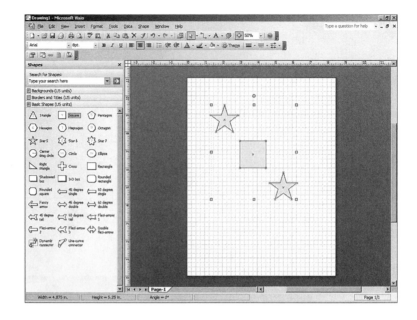

Figure 7.7
Displaying the
Behavior dialog.

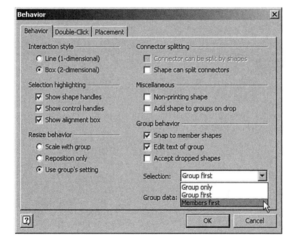

SPECIFYING DOUBLE-CLICK BEHAVIOR FOR SHAPES

You can also customize the behavior of shapes when they're double-clicked. For example, you can make Visio jump to another page when you double-click a shape, or open a help page, or run a macro.

Jumping to a new page is especially useful in Visio drawings when you want to create master/detail drawings. For example, you might have a map of the world in a drawing, and when you double-click a continent, that continent opens. Say you double-click

North America—a new page might open that shows the states in North America. And double-clicking a state might allow you to go down another level in detail, showing the cities in that state that your company has outlet stores in, for example.

If you want to modify the double-click behavior of shapes, just follow these steps:

1. Open the drawing that contains the shape whose double-click behavior you want to modify.
2. Right-click the shape and select Format > Behavior. This opens the Behavior dialog.
3. Click the Double-Click tab. This opens the Behavior dialog's Double-Click tab, shown in Figure 7.8.

Figure 7.8
Displaying the Behavior dialog's Double-Click tab.

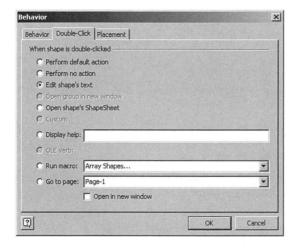

4. Select one of the following options:
   - **Perform Default Action**—Performs the default action for the shape.
   - **Perform No Action**—Disables double-clicking.
   - **Edit Shape's Text**—Opens the shape's text in a text box for editing. This is the default action.
   - **Open Group in New Window**—Opens a double-clicked group in a new Visio window.
   - **Custom**—Lets you specify a custom action.
   - **Display help**—Lets you display help.
   - **OLE Verb**—Lets you specify an OLE (object linking and embedding) verb to connect to another application when the shape is double-clicked.
   - **Run Macro**—Lets you specify a macro to run. There are many predefined macros available in the drop-down list box, such as one that launches the Database Export Wizard.

7

- **Go to Page**—Lets you specify a page to open when the shape is double-clicked. Select the page from the drop-down list box. Select the Open in New Window check box if you want the page to be opened in a new window.

5. Click OK. Visio closes the Behavior dialog.

That gives you the options you can select from for a shape's double-click behavior.

LOCKING YOUR DRAWINGS WHEN NEEDED

Visio drawings are often shared, and that means exposing your precious work to the dangerous hands of others. How can you protect your shapes, groups, and drawings from being modified, even inadvertently?

That's what this section is all about.

LOCKING SHAPES

Say that you have a shape loaded with shape data and you want to protect that shape against being altered. How can you do that?

Just follow these steps:

1. Open the drawing in which the shape you want to lock is contained.

2. Right-click the shape and select the Format > Protection menu item. Visio opens the Protection dialog, shown in Figure 7.9.

Figure 7.9
The Protection dialog.

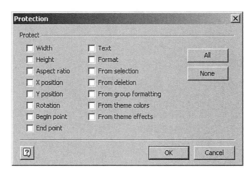

3. Select from among the following options:
   - **Width**—Lock the width of the shape.
   - **Height**—Lock the height of the shape.
   - **Aspect Ratio**—Lock the ratio between the shape's width and height.
   - **X Position**—Lock the shape's X position.
   - **Y Position**—Lock the shape's Y position.
   - **Rotation**—Lock the shape from being rotated.

- **Begin Point**—Lock a 1D shape's begin point.
- **End Point**—Lock a 1D shape's end point.
- **Text**—Lock a shape's text.
- **Format**—Lock any changes to the shape's format.
- **From Selection**—Lock a shape from being selected. You need to do more to get this to work, however. In addition to selecting this option, select View > Drawing Explorer. Then right-click the name of the drawing (at the top of the Drawing Explorer window) and select Protect Document. In the Protect Document dialog, select the Shapes check box and click OK.
- **From Deletion**—Lock a shape from being deleted.
- **From Group Formatting**—Lock a shape from being formatted as part of a group.
- **From Theme Colors**—Lock a shape from reflecting changes in theme colors.
- **From Theme Effects**—Lock a shape from reflecting changes in theme effects.

4. Click OK. Visio closes the Protection dialog.

TIP

> Want to set these protection levels permanently for a shape? Add the shape to a custom stencil, and set its protection there.

LOCKING LAYERS

Visio also lets you lock layers against change. That's useful if, for example, you're designing architectural plans for a building and are done with the plumbing layer. You can lock that layer and continue with the rest of your drawing, safe in the knowledge that the plumbing layer won't be inadvertently affected by other changes.

How do you lock a layer? Follow these steps:

1. Open the drawing in which the layers you want to lock are contained.
2. Select View > Layer Properties or click the Layer Properties button on the View toolbar. Visio opens the Layer Properties dialog, shown in Figure 7.10.
3. Click the Lock check box for all the layers you want to lock. For example, layer 2 is being locked in Figure 7.10.
4. Click OK. Visio closes the Layer Properties dialog.

Being able to protect layers like this is another argument for dividing your drawing into layers in the first place.

7

Figure 7.10
The Layer Properties dialog.

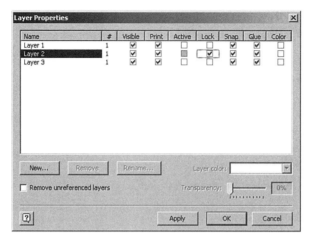

LOCKING DRAWINGS

You can even lock a complete drawing, using the Drawing Explorer window. How does that work?

Just follow these steps:

1. Open the drawing you want to lock.

2. Select View > Drawing Explorer Window or click the Drawing Explorer button in the View toolbar. Visio opens the Drawing Explorer window, shown in Figure 7.11.

Figure 7.11
The Drawing Explorer window.

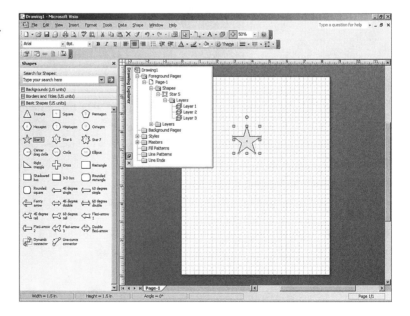

3. Right-click the drawing's name in the Drawing Explorer window and select Protect Document. Visio opens the Protect Document dialog, shown in Figure 7.12.

Figure 7.12
The Protect
Document dialog.

4. Select from among the following options:
   - **Styles**—Locks creating, editing, or deleting of styles. However, users can still apply styles.
   - **Shapes**—Stops selection of shapes when selection protection is set for individual shapes.
   - **Preview**—Makes the preview window inaccessible.
   - **Backgrounds**—Stops changes to a drawing's background page.
   - **Master Shapes**—Stops any changes to the master shapes.

5. Click OK. Visio closes the Protect Document dialog.

And that's it—you've your whole drawing from changes.

LOCKING FILES

Visio also lets you mark whole files as read-only, which means they're not for editing.

This is the safest way to protect a file—nothing about a drawing protected this way can be changed. You can make your drawings read-only this way in Visio.

Want to save a drawing (or other file) as read-only? Do this:

1. Open the drawing (or other file) you want to save as read-only.
2. Select File > Save As. Visio opens the Save As dialog, shown in Figure 7.13.
3. Select the folder you want to save the file in.
4. Enter the name of your file in the File Name box. You can see the name Drawing1 in Figure 7.13.
5. Select the down arrow in the Save button, and select Read Only. You can see this option being selected in the Save As dialog in Figure 7.13.

   After you've selected the Read Only item and released the mouse button, Visio saves the file and closes the Save As dialog.

   If a user wants to create a writable version of your file, the user can select File > Save As and create a writable copy of your file.

Figure 7.13
The Save As dialog.

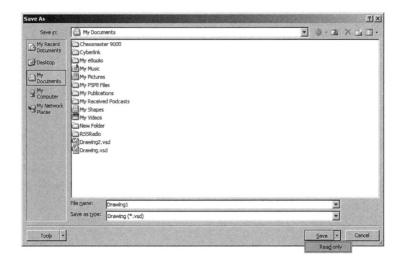

Okay, that completes our discussion on locking various aspects of a Visio drawing—from shapes through layers, up to drawings and whole files, you have many options here.

Next, we're going to take a look at marking up drawings for fun and profit.

MARKING UP YOUR DRAWINGS

Visio lets you mark up your drawings by adding comments to them. There are plenty of reasons to add markup to your drawings—for example, you might suddenly think of something you wanted to add to a drawing, something you don't have time for right now but that you don't want to forget. Marking up your drawings by adding such notes is one reason to use markup.

Another reason is that Visio drawings are often passed around in groups. People in the group may want to comment on your drawing (whether you want those comments or not!). Your boss may want to write you notes on your work. And your colleagues might want to add markup giving you their feedback.

There are many reasons to use markup in Visio drawings, and Visio has a lot of support for markup. That's coming up next.

There are two main ways to add markup to drawings in Visio: as comments and as digital ink.

Comments are just what they sound like—text annotations or notes that you add to drawings. You can add comments to suggest changes to the author of a drawing, or to remind you to complete some addition or change, or just to add information to a drawing.

Digital ink, on the other hand, mimics handwriting or drawing by hand. You can circle shapes, "write" by hand, and more. You might use digital ink to underline elements in a drawing, circle shapes, or write "handwritten" notes on a drawing.

USING COMMENTS

How do you add comments to a drawing? You can create comments in small shapes that you can move around in a drawing. And you can also open or close comments as you like.

Here's how to add a comment to a drawing:

1. Open the drawing you want to add a comment to.
2. Select Insert > Comment. You can see the comment box that opens in Figure 7.14.

Figure 7.14
Creating a comment.

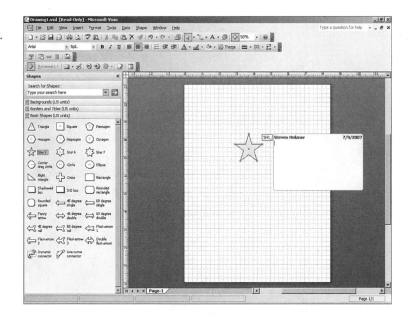

3. Enter your comment. You can see a comment that's been typed in Figure 7.15.
4. Click outside the comment box. Visio closes the comment box, leaving the small shape with your initials in it, as shown in Figure 7.16.
5. Move the collapsed comment box to an appropriate place in your drawing. After creating the comment, you can move it where you want it.

7

Figure 7.15
Adding text to a comment.

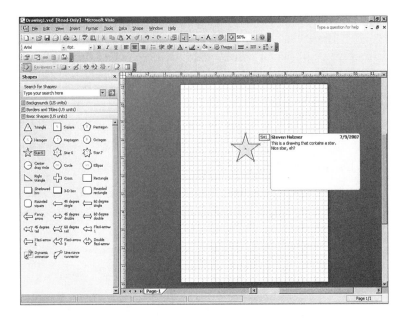

Figure 7.16
A collapsed comment.

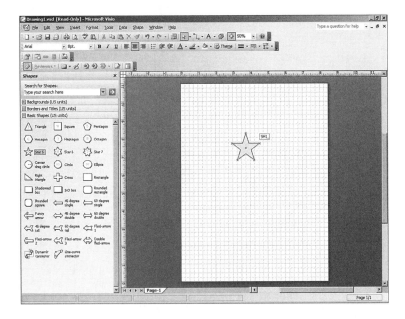

6. To view the comment, click the collapsed comment box. You can see the results in Figure 7.17.

Want to edit a comment? Don't just click it—double-click it. That opens the comment for editing, as shown in Figure 7.18.

Figure 7.17
A comment.

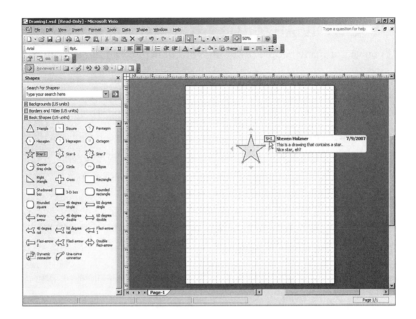

Figure 7.18
Editing a comment.

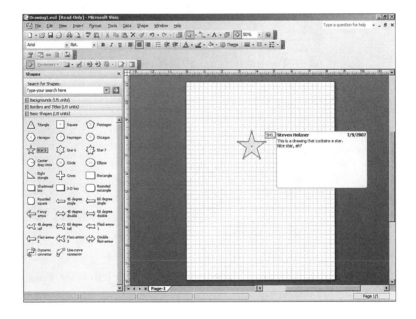

As with other Office products, Visio automatically assigns a different color to each commenter, and their comments will appear in that color in a drawing. That's not visible in Figure 7.18, but it's something you should know about in Visio.

7

ALL ABOUT MARKUP TRACKING

If you've got many people reviewing your drawing, you might want to use markup tracking.

When you use markup tracking, each reviewer's comments are kept separate and distinct, so you know who wrote what. As you're going to see, reviewers' comments are placed on *overlays* on a drawing.

Working with markup starts by setting up some onscreen tools. With that as a starting point, you can continue on to viewing, adding, and deleting markup. We'll start with the Reviewing toolbar.

THE REVIEWING TOOLBAR

The Reviewing toolbar shows all the tracking tools, and if you're going to use tracking, it's a good one to know about. You can see the Reviewing toolbar in Figure 7.19.

Figure 7.19
The Reviewing toolbar.

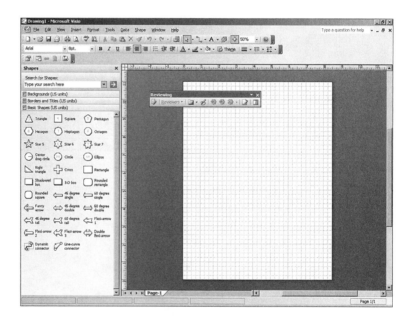

The Reviewing toolbar also has a drop-down list built into it for working with comments, and that list appears in Figure 7.20.

Here's what the buttons in the Reviewing toolbar are, from left to right (including the items in the Comment drop-down list):

- **Show/Hide Markup**—Makes markup overlays visible or invisible in Visio.
- **Reviewers**—Lists the names of the reviewers of a drawing.
- **Insert Comment**—Creates a new comment.

Figure 7.20
The Reviewing toolbar's drop-down list.

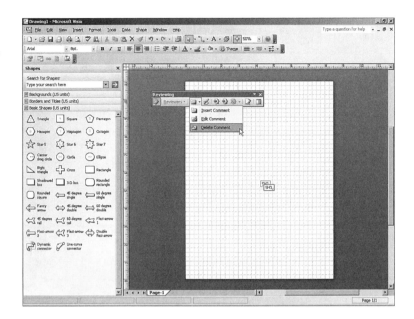

- **Edit Comment**—Lets you edit a new comment by putting the comment into edit mode.
- **Delete Comment**—Deletes the selected comment.
- **Ink Tool**—Displays the Ink toolbar.
- **Previous Markup**—Selects the markup previous to the current markup.
- **Next Markup**—Selects the markup after the current markup.
- **Delete Markup**—Deletes the current markup.
- **Delete Comment**—Deletes the selected comment.
- **Track Markup**—Turns markup tracking on or off.
- **Reviewing Pane**—Displays or hides the Reviewing pane.

Okay, how about putting all this to work by adding some markup to a drawing?

ADDING MARKUP

It's not difficult to add markup to a drawing. When you're adding markup, the drawing is surrounded with a colored border, and Visio shows the Reviewing pane, which lists your name and the changes made to the drawing.

Here's how to add markup to a drawing:

1. Open the drawing you want to add markup to.
2. Click the Track Markup button on the Reviewing toolbar, or select Tools > Track Markup. Visio adds a colored border around the drawing and displays the Reviewing task pane, shown in Figure 7.21.

Figure 7.21
Tracking markup.

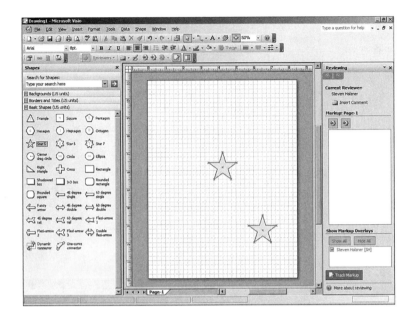

3. Make changes to the drawing. Visio displays every change you made to the drawing, as shown in Figure 7.22.

Figure 7.22
Adding markup.

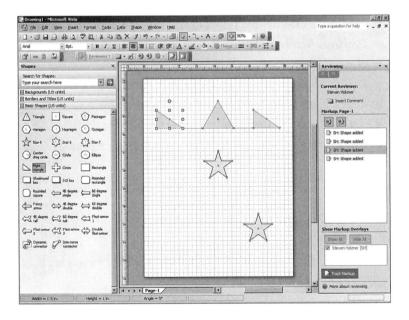

Note that when you're in track markup mode, you can't select any of the elements of the original drawing, so you can't actually edit it.

4. Click the Track Markup button on the Reviewing toolbar, or select Tools > Track Markup to turn off markup tracking. Visio removes the colored border around the drawing and displays the added markup in the Reviewing task pane, as shown in Figure 7.23.

5. Save the drawing. That saves the markup connected in the drawing as well.

Figure 7.23
Added markup.

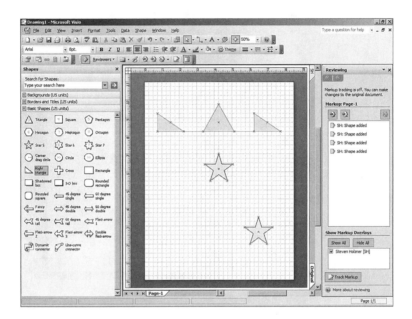

The shapes you added to the drawing while tracking markup are displayed in a different color than the original shapes, although that's hard to see in Figure 7.23.

You can close the Reviewing pane by clicking the Reviewing Pane button in the Reviewing toolbar, or by selecting View > Task Pane.

VIEWING MARKUP

Tracking markup turns on a markup overlay for the current reviewer, which the reviewer can add shapes to and use to perform other work. That's how markup works—by giving reviewers their own overlay and letting them do work in it.

On the other hand, simply viewing markup just displays the overlays, and lets you select from among them.

When you add markup, you can make changes to your reviewing overlay; when you view markup, you can't make changes to any overlay.

So perhaps you've circulated a drawing among your colleagues, and want to view the markup they've added. How do you do that?

7

Just follow these steps:

1. Open the drawing you want to view the markup in.

2. Select View > Task Pane, or click the Reviewing Pane button in the Reviewing toolbar. Visio displays the Reviewing pane, shown in Figure 7.24.

Figure 7.24
The Reviewing pane.

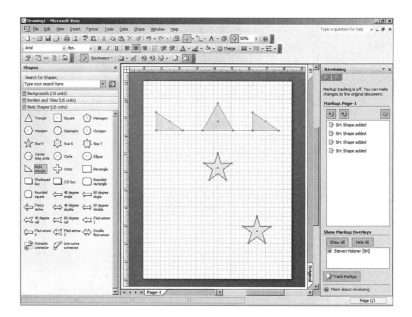

3. If you don't see markup in the Reviewing pane, click the Show/Hide Markup button in the Reviewing toolbar. If you still don't see any markup in the box labeled Markup: Page-1 (or whatever the name of the current page is), there is no markup associated with the page.

4. Select the overlay you want by clicking the tab with the reviewer's initials at the right in the drawing surface. Visio displays overlays using tabs that display the initials of each reviewer.

You can select the overlay you want by clicking the correct tab.

You can also select overlays with the Reviewers drop-down list in the Reviewing toolbar, as shown in Figure 7.25.

Here are the overlay options in the Reviewing toolbar—they're also visible at the bottom of the Reviewing pane:

Select Show All to view all overlays at once.

Select Hide All to hide all overlays.

Select a reviewer by name to see his or her overlay.

Note also that the original drawing appears when you click the Original tab (see Figure 7.25) at the bottom of the tab stack.

Figure 7.25
The Reviewers drop-down list.

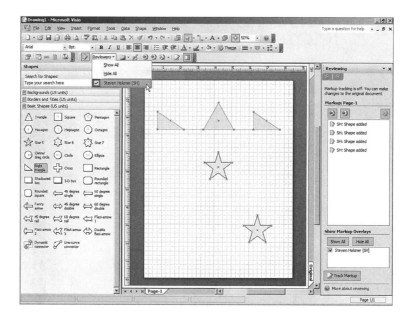

5. Select a reviewer's markup item in the Markup: Page-*x* box. Visio selects the shape associated with the markup, and you can read the action the reviewer took (such as "Shape added") in the Markup: Page-*x* box.

6. Click the Next Markup or Previous Markup buttons in the Reviewing toolbar. Alternatively, you can click the Next Markup or Previous Markup buttons in the Reviewing pane (these buttons appear under Markup: Page-1 in Figure 7.25), or click a markup entry in the Markup: Page-*x* box to navigate to other markup entries.

All right, now you're able to view the markup added by reviewers of your drawing.

DELETING MARKUP

Say that you disagree with the markup a reviewer has added to your drawing. How can you get rid of it?

You can delete that markup. Here's how to do that by deleting individual markup:

1. Open the drawing you want to delete markup in.

2. Select View > Task Pane, or click the Reviewing Pane button in the Reviewing toolbar. Visio displays the Reviewing pane.

3. If you don't see markup in the Reviewing pane, click the Show/Hide Markup button in the Reviewing toolbar.

4. Select the markup you want to delete in the Markup: Page-*x* box.

7

5. Click the down arrow next to the Delete Markup button on the Reviewing toolbar and select Delete Markup. You can see this in Figure 7.26.

Figure 7.26
Deleting individual markup.

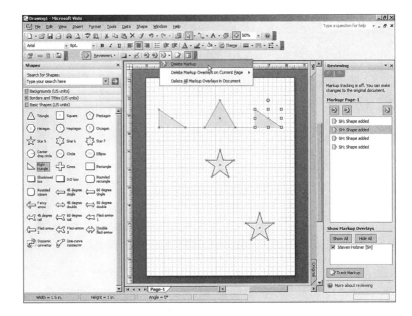

The markup is deleted, as shown in Figure 7.27.

Figure 7.27
Individual markup deleted.

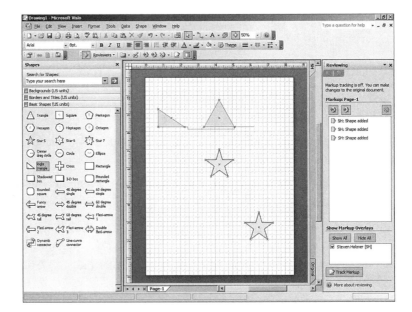

Want to delete all markup overlays on the current page? Follow these steps:

1. Open the drawing you want to delete markup in.
2. Select View > Task Pane, or click the Reviewing Pane button in the Reviewing toolbar. Visio displays the Reviewing pane.
3. If you don't see markup in the Reviewing pane, click the Show/Hide Markup button in the Reviewing toolbar.
4. Click the down arrow next to the Delete Markup button on the Reviewing toolbar and select Delete Markup Overlays on Current Page. A new menu opens, as shown in Figure 7.28.

Figure 7.28
Deleting markup.

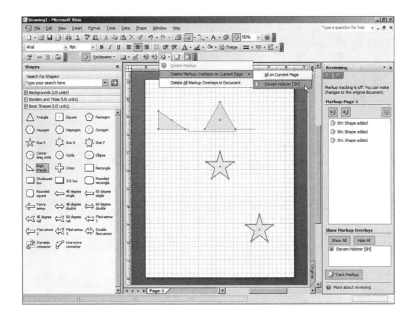

Select from the submenu items shown in Figure 7.28:

- **All on Current Page**—Deletes all markup on the current page.
- *Reviewer's name*—Deletes markup on the current page by the specified reviewer.

Visio deletes the markup you specified.

Want to get rid of all markup overlays in a drawing? Follow these steps:

1. Open the drawing you want to delete markup in.
2. Select View > Task Pane, or click the Reviewing Pane button in the Reviewing toolbar. Visio displays the Reviewing pane.
3. If you don't see markup in the Reviewing pane, click the Show/Hide Markup button in the Reviewing toolbar.

4. Click the down arrow next to the Delete Markup button on the Reviewing toolbar and select Delete All Markup Overlays in Document. Visio deletes all the markup in your drawing.

That's how to delete the markup in a drawing.

But what if you don't want to delete the markup in a drawing, but want to incorporate it into the original instead?

INCORPORATING MARKUP

Reviewers might make many suggestions in your drawings: new shapes, changes to shapes, format changes, changed text, and other changes. If you decide that the reviewer is right, how can you incorporate such a change into your drawing?

This is an interesting question, because the markup that reviewers add to your drawing stays in the color that Visio selected for them, even if you turn off Track Markup, and even if you remove the Reviewing pane.

Unlike other Office products like Microsoft Word, however, Visio does not provide a mechanism for incorporating the changes suggested by other reviewers into your drawing. In other words, there's no Accept Change option as there is in Microsoft Word, so there's no easy way to incorporate reviewers' changes into your drawing.

Visio suggests that, if you want to do this, if you want to incorporate a change made by a reviewer into your original drawing, you reconstruct what the reviewer did from scratch in the original drawing. But that's not a great solution—you might miss something, such as shape data added to a custom shape.

Nor is it a great solution to just leave the markup as it is—it will be printed along with the rest of your drawing, but the reviewer's shapes will be printed in the reviewer's colors. And when you view the drawing in Visio, you'll always have to deal with markup overlays.

So how can you incorporate a reviewer's markup into the original drawing? What's the best way?

Here's one method, which copies the markup from the reviewer's overlay to the original drawing:

1. Open the drawing you want to delete markup in.

2. Select View > Task Pane, or click the Reviewing Pane button in the Reviewing toolbar. Visio displays the Reviewing pane.

3. If you don't see markup in the Reviewing pane, click the Show/Hide Markup button in the Reviewing toolbar.

4. Turn off Markup Tracking by clicking the Track Markup button on the Reviewing toolbar, or by selecting Tools > Track Markup. Visio displays the message "Markup tracking is off. You can make changes to the original document" in the Reviewing pane.

5. Select the markup item you want to incorporate into the original drawing. Visio highlights the selected markup item and selects it on its markup overlay.

6. Select Edit > Copy. Visio copies the markup.

7. Click the Original tab.

8. Select Edit > Paste. Visio pastes a copy of the markup.

9. Drag the copy of the markup over the reviewer's markup. The copy of the markup now covers the reviewer's original markup.

10. Click the reviewer's tab. Visio now displays the reviewer's markup, not the Original tab.

11. Select the reviewer's markup.

12. Click Delete Markup in the Reviewing pane, or select Delete Markup with the drop-down arrow next to the Delete Markup button in the Reviewing toolbar. Visio deletes the reviewer's markup.

   The reviewer's markup (in the reviewer's color) disappears, and you can see the copied version of the markup on the original drawing (in the original drawing's color).

13. Repeat the preceding steps for any other markup you want to incorporate from this author.

14. To remove the rest of the markup from this author, select the down arrow next to the Delete Markup button on the Reviewing toolbar and select Delete Markup Overlays on Current Page > *Reviewer's Name* [*Initials*].

15. Repeat the preceding steps for any other markup you want to incorporate from other authors.

That's one way of incorporating markup into your drawing. It's odd that Visio doesn't offer a quicker solution here, such as an Accept Markup option or something similar, as in other Office products.

That's how markup works—using it, people can add changes and suggestions to your drawing. And you can add markup to their drawings—just don't forget to turn on the Track Markup option.

WORKING WITH DIGITAL INK

There's another way of creating markup in Visio: digital ink. Using digital ink, you can draw on a drawing—writing notes, circling shapes, and so on.

Digital ink is perhaps best used with a tablet PC or a graphics tablet, but even if you just have a mouse, you can still use digital ink.

You use digital ink with the Digital Ink tool, which looks like a toolbar, and which you can see in Figure 7.29.

7

Figure 7.29
The Digital Ink tool.

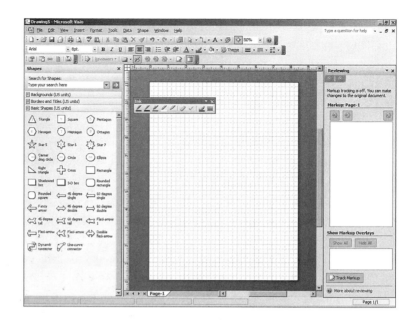

How do you display the Digital Ink tool? You can click the Ink Tool button in the Reviewing toolbar, or you can right-click the toolbar and select the Ink item.

Here are what the buttons in the Ink tool mean, from left to right:

- **1 Ballpoint Pen**—Lets you draw using a "ballpoint pen" whose color is blue.
- **2 Ballpoint Pen**—Lets you draw using a "ballpoint pen" whose color is black.
- **3 Felt-Tip Pen**—Lets you draw using a "felt-tip pen."
- **4 Highlighter**—Lets you draw using a "highlighter" whose color is yellow.
- **5 Highlighter**—Lets you draw using a "highlighter" whose color is green.
- **Eraser**—Lets you erase markup you've drawn.
- **Close Ink Shape**—Closes an ink shape.
- **Ink Color**—Lets you select an ink color.
- **Ink Thickness**—Lets you select the drawing thickness.

Those are the ink tools—let's put them to work.

CHOOSING AN INK TOOL

You have your choice of ink tools in Visio—two ballpoint pens, a felt-tip pen, and two highlighters.

To choose an ink tool to draw with, just click it in the Ink toolbar. The mouse cursor changes to a pen-shaped pointer, as shown in Figure 7.30.

Figure 7.30
Selecting a pen.

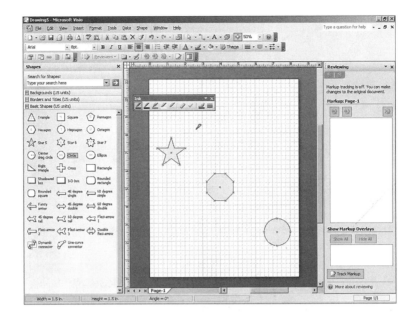

What's the difference between the drawing tools? The ballpoint pens draw in 1-point thickness (a point is 1/72 of an inch); the felt-tip pen in 1 3/4 points (which is still pretty thin). The highlighters draw in a 10-point thickness, but because they're highlighters, they draw transparently—you can see what's underneath.

Okay, that lets you select a drawing tool. Now how about drawing something with it?

DRAWING WITH INK TOOLS

It's time to draw with the ink tools. Want to write a note? Circle a shape? Cross something out? You can do it with the ink tools.

Just follow these steps:

1. Open the drawing that you want to draw in.
2. Open the Ink tool. Right-click the toolbar and select Ink or click the Ink Tool button in the Reviewing toolbar.

   The Ink tool appears.
3. Select an Ink tool. For example, select the Ballpoint Pen tool.
4. Draw using the Ink tool. You can see an example in Figure 7.31.

   A second or so after you finish drawing, Visio draws a blue rectangle surrounding what you've drawn.

   Visio treats what you've drawn as a shape—you can resize it at will.
5. Select the Pointer tool. That ends your session with the ink tools.

7

Figure 7.31
Drawing using ink tools.

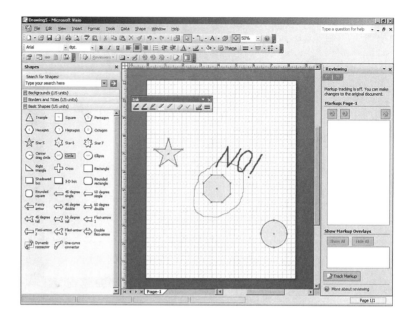

CHANGING DRAWING THICKNESS

Want to change the drawing thickness from the default? Just follow these steps:

1. Open the drawing that you want to draw in.

2. Open the Ink tool. Right-click the toolbar and select Ink or click the Ink Tool button in the Reviewing toolbar.

   The Ink tool appears.

3. Select an Ink tool. For example, select the Ballpoint Pen Tool.

4. Change the thickness by selecting a thickness from the Ink Thickness drop-down box. You can see this drop-down box in Figure 7.32.

5. Draw using the Ink tool.

6. Select the Pointer tool. That ends your session with the ink tools.

Figure 7.32
Selecting ink
thickness.

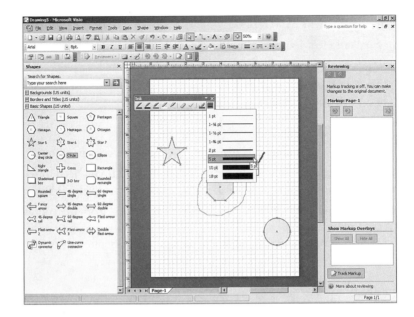

CHANGING INK SHAPES TO GEOMETRY

You can also change ink shapes to geometry, which upgrades them to full shape status. That means you can alter the ink drawing's line color, line style, transparency, shadow, and fill color.

How do you change an ink shape to geometry? Follow these steps:

1. Open the drawing that you want to convert ink shapes to true Visio shapes in.

2. Right-click the digital ink shape and select Convert Ink to Geometry. This causes Visio to change the ink shape into a full-fledged Visio shape.

Note that sometimes you'll get a 1D shape instead of a 2D shape this way—that happens when the shape isn't a closed shape. If you want the shape to be 2D, right-click it and select Format > Behavior to open the Behavior dialog. Select the Behavior tab, select the Box (2-Dimensional) option, and then click OK.

CHANGING INK SHAPES TO TEXT

In fact, Visio lets you convert ink shapes into text—that is, you can draw words and, under some circumstances, Visio can convert those words into text.

This works best with words you've drawn using a tablet PC or graphics tablet, but sometimes it will also work with the mouse.

Here's how to convert ink words into text in Visio:

1. Open the drawing that contains the ink shapes to convert to text.
2. Select the ink words you want to convert to text. If you need to select a number of pieces of text to create a word, the conversion most likely isn't going to work.
3. Right-click the text and select Convert Ink to Text from the context menu that opens.

Note that converting ink shapes to text is a very finicky business in Visio.

CHAPTER 8

LINKING AND EMBEDDING OBJECTS AND PUBLISHING TO THE WEB

In this chapter

DEALING WITH OBJECTS

The computer environment has become a whirl of information, and Visio drawings are just one part of that. In fact, the support for connecting Visio to other applications is very good.

For example, you can create, as you're going to see, hyperlinks to Visio drawings from Microsoft Word documents, Excel workbooks, PowerPoint presentations, and other applications as well. When you click the link, the Visio drawing is launched.

And you can go the other way as well. Hyperlinks can link from Visio to other applications' documents. For example, you can link from Visio to Word, Excel, PowerPoint, and other applications.

And there's more. Besides creating hyperlinks, you can link drawings from Visio to other applications so that those other applications can display Visio drawings—and since they're linked, they'll stay up-to-date with what you do to the drawing in Visio.

You can also embed Visio objects in other applications, and vice versa. This way, you can insert copies of Visio objects in other applications, and the other way around as well. When you want to edit those objects, you can do it in their host application—editing a Visio object in Word, for example.

We'll take a look at all this in this chapter, starting with hyperlinks.

USING HYPERLINKS

Hyperlinks can take all kinds of forms today—underlined text, icons, graphic objects that change the mouse cursor, and others. You can create hyperlinks in Visio to other applications, and you can create hyperlinks in other applications to Visio.

You can create hyperlinks in Visio that link page to page as well. That's a very common form of using hyperlinks, and you're going to see how to create them here.

Hyperlinks in Visio work a little differently depending on whether you're in full-screen mode or normal mode.

To access full-screen mode, press F5 in Visio, or select View > Full Screen. When you're in full-screen mode—or if you use Visio drawings as web pages—the mouse cursor changes to a hand pointer (if you're using Internet Explorer to view the Visio drawing as a web page, or if you're in full-screen mode in Visio). If you have a shape that acts as a hyperlink, click the shape when the cursor changes.

In normal (not full-screen) mode in Visio, the cursor changes to an arrow icon that shows a globe. Click the hyperlinked shape to follow the hyperlink in Visio.

So how do you actually create a hyperlink? That's coming up next.

CREATING A HYPERLINK BETWEEN PAGES

The most common type of hyperlink in Visio is a link between Visio pages. These types of hyperlinks are typically connected with Visio shapes.

Want to create a hyperlink between pages? Follow these steps:

1. Open the multipage drawing that you want to add hyperlinks to.

2. Add a shape that you want to act as a hyperlink to the drawing. You can see an example in Figure 8.1.

Figure 8.1
Creating a hyper-linked shape.

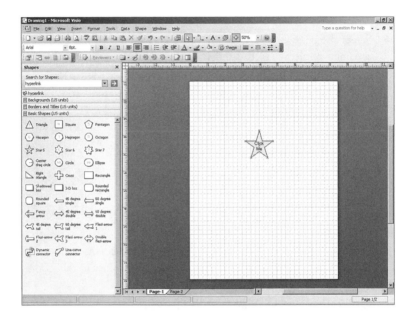

3. Select the shape. Visio displays a selection frame around the shape.

4. Select Insert > Hyperlinks. That opens the Hyperlinks dialog, shown in Figure 8.2.

Figure 8.2
The Hyperlinks dialog.

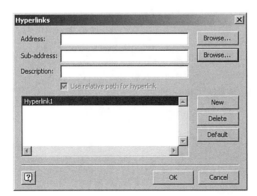

8

5. Click the Browse button next to the Sub-address box. That opens the Hyperlink dialog (as distinct from the Hyperlinks dialog), shown in Figure 8.3.

Figure 8.3
The Hyperlink dialog.

6. Select the page you want to link to in the Page drop-down box. For example, you can see Page-2 selected in this box in Figure 8.3.

7. To link to a specific shape, enter the name of the shape in the Shape text box. How do you find the name of a shape (such as Star.1)? You have to run Visio in developer mode.

   To do so, follow these steps:

   Select Tools > Options.

   Click the Advanced tab.

   Select the Run in Developer Mode check box.

   Click OK.

   Right-click the shape and select Format > Special in the context menu.

   Read the shape's name from the Name box.

8. Select a zoom factor. You can select the zoom with which the target of the hyperlink is shown, such as 400% or 50%. Select the zoom factor in the Zoom drop-down box, shown in Figure 8.3.

9. Click OK in the Hyperlink dialog. That closes the Hyperlink dialog, and you then see the Hyperlinks dialog.

10. Enter text in the Description box of the Hyperlinks dialog to be displayed when the mouse hovers over the linked shape. You can see the text "Go to Page-2" in Figure 8.4.

Figure 8.4
Adding a description to a hyperlink.

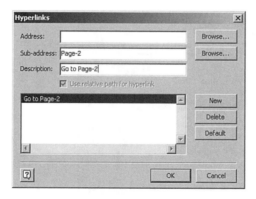

11. Click OK in the Hyperlinks dialog. That closes the Hyperlinks dialog.

12. Repeat as needed to add other hyperlinks to the shape. Visio shapes can have multiple hyperlinks.

Now there's a hyperlink connected with the shape—and the mouse cursor changes to a hyperlink cursor when the mouse hovers over the shape, as shown in Figure 8.5.

Figure 8.5
A hyperlinked shape.

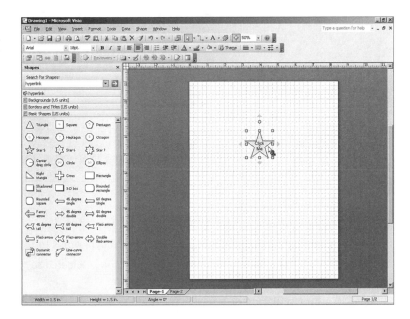

Now you've created a hyperlink—how do you actually use it to navigate to the hyperlink's target?

Right-clicking the hyperlinked shape opens a context menu listing its hyperlinks. Selecting the Go to Page-2 item (note that that's the description you entered for the hyperlink) takes you to Page-2, as shown in Figure 8.6 (note that the Page-2 tab is selected at the bottom of the drawing surface).

How about hyperlinking a whole drawing? You can do that—and doing so will make the mouse cursor appear as a hyperlink cursor for the whole page. This is a good option if you want to display a Visio drawing as a presentation, using hyperlinks to navigate from page to page.

Figure 8.6
Jumping to a new page.

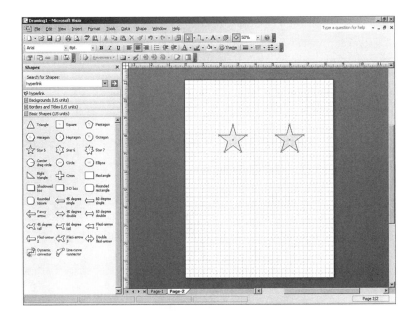

Follow these steps to hyperlink a whole page:

1. Open the multipage drawing that you want to add hyperlinks to.

2. Select Insert > Hyperlinks. Make sure that no shape is selected so that the hyperlink will be added to the page as a whole.

3. Click the Browse button next to the Sub-address box. That opens the Hyperlink dialog.

4. Select the page you want to link to in the Page drop-down box.

5. To link to a specific shape, enter the name of the shape in the Shape text box. How do you find the name of a shape (such as Star.1)? You have to run Visio in developer mode.

   To do so, follow these steps:

   Select Tools > Options.

   Click the Advanced tab.

   Select the Run in Developer Mode check box.

   Click OK.

   Right-click the shape and select Format > Special in the context menu.

   Read the shape's name from the Name box.

6. Select a zoom factor. You can select the zoom with which the target of the hyperlink is shown, such as 400% or 50%. Select the zoom factor in the Zoom drop-down box, shown earlier in Figure 8.3.

7. Click OK in the Hyperlink dialog. That closes the Hyperlink dialog, and you then see the Hyperlinks dialog.

8. Enter text in the Description box of the Hyperlinks dialog to be displayed when the mouse hovers over the page.

9. Click OK in the Hyperlinks dialog. That closes the Hyperlinks dialog.

Now the entire page is a hyperlink, as shown in Figure 8.7, in which the mouse cursor is the hyperlink cursor.

Figure 8.7
A hyperlinked page.

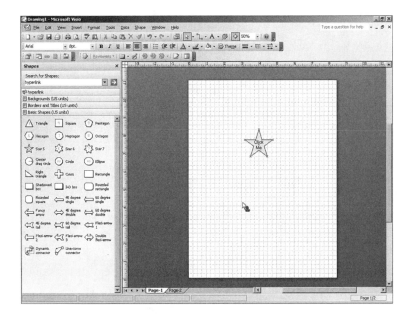

USING HYPERLINK SHAPES

Visio comes complete with special shapes that are meant to be used as hyperlinks, and you can find those shapes by searching for "hyperlink" in the Shapes pane's search box.

Here's how to use the hyperlink shapes to create a link between pages in Visio:

1. Open the multipage drawing that you want to add hyperlinks to.

2. Search for "hyperlink" in the Shapes pane. You can see the resulting shape matches in Figure 8.8.

3. Drag a hyperlink shape to the drawing. That opens the Hyperlinks dialog automatically, as shown in Figure 8.9.

Figure 8.8
Hyperlink shapes.

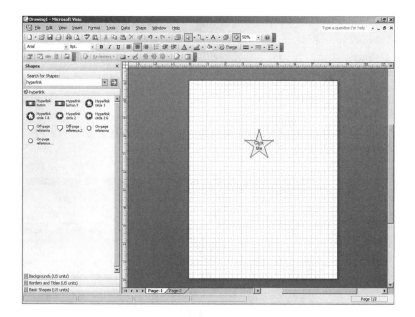

Figure 8.9
The Hyperlinks dialog.

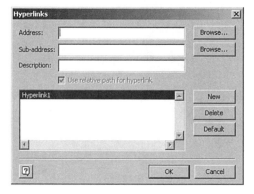

4. Click the Browse button next to the Sub-address box. That opens the Hyperlink dialog, shown in Figure 8.10.

5. Select the page you want to link to in the Page drop-down box. For example, you can see Page-2 selected in this box in Figure 8.10.

6. To link to a specific shape, enter the name of the shape in the Shape text box. How do you find the name of a shape (such as Star.1)? You have to run Visio in developer mode.

Figure 8.10
The Hyperlink dialog.

To do so, follow these steps:

> Select Tools > Options.
>
> Click the Advanced tab.
>
> Select the Run in Developer Mode check box.
>
> Click OK.
>
> Right-click the shape and select Format > Special in the context menu.
>
> Read the shape's name from the Name box.

7. Select a zoom factor. You can select the zoom with which the target of the hyperlink is shown, such as 400% or 50%. Select the zoom factor in the Zoom drop-down box, shown earlier in Figure 8.3.

8. Click OK in the Hyperlink dialog. That closes the Hyperlink dialog, and you then see the Hyperlinks dialog.

9. Enter text in the Description box of the Hyperlinks dialog to be displayed when the mouse hovers over the linked shape.

10. Click OK in the Hyperlinks dialog. That closes the Hyperlinks dialog, and you can see the hyperlink shape in Figure 8.11.

Figure 8.11
A hyperlink shape.

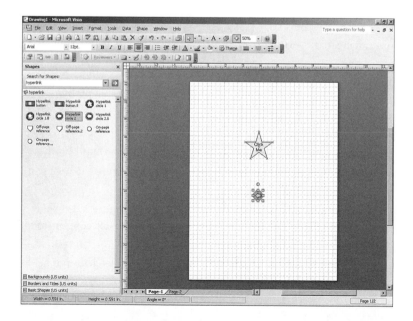

11. Adjust the hyperlink shape as you want, rotating it or resizing it. For example, you can see the hyperlink shape rotated by 180° in Figure 8.12.

Figure 8.12
A rotated hyperlink shape.

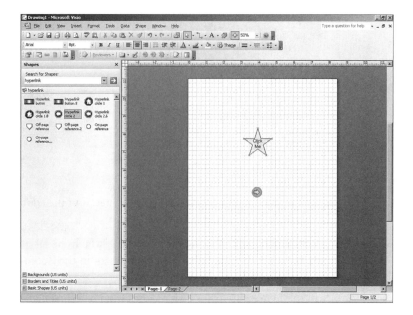

12. Repeat as needed to add other hyperlink shapes to the drawing.

That shows you the possibilities when it comes to linking to different pages in Visio. How about linking to web pages or other files?

CREATING HYPERLINKS TO WEB PAGES

You can create hyperlinks to web pages in Visio just as easily as linking from page to page.

Here's how to do it:

1. Open the drawing that you want to add web-based hyperlinks to.
2. Add a shape that you want to act as a hyperlink to the drawing. You can see an example in Figure 8.13.
3. Select the shape. Visio displays a selection frame around the shape.
4. Select Insert > Hyperlinks. That opens the Hyperlinks dialog, shown in Figure 8.14.
5. Enter the URL of the web page you want to link to in the Address box. Alternatively, click the Browse button and select the Internet Address drop-down option. You can see the home page for Visio 2007, http://office.microsoft.com/en-us/visio/default.aspx, entered in the Address box in Figure 8.14.
6. Enter text in the Description box of the Hyperlinks dialog to be displayed when the mouse hovers over the linked shape. You can see the text "Go to Visio 2007 home page" in Figure 8.14.

Figure 8.13
Creating a hyper-
linked shape.

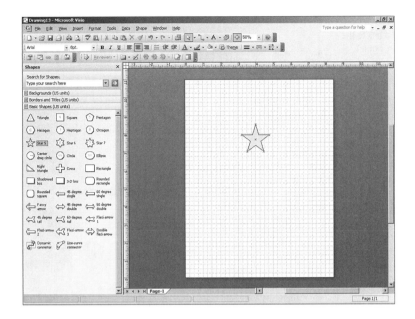

Figure 8.14
The Hyperlinks
dialog.

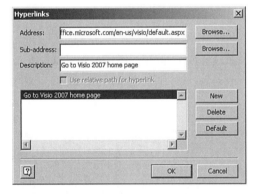

7. Click OK in the Hyperlinks dialog. That closes the Hyperlinks dialog.

8. Repeat as needed to add other hyperlinks to the shape. Visio shapes can have multiple hyperlinks.

That's all it takes. Now when the user opens the hyperlink connected with the shape, the Visio 2007 home page opens in your default browser, as shown in Figure 8.15.

In addition, you can link to various files on your machine.

Figure 8.15
Opening a link to the Visio 2007 home page.

CREATING HYPERLINKS TO FILES

You can create hyperlinks to files in Visio as well as to web pages. Here's how to do it:

1. Open the drawing that you want to add file-based hyperlinks to.
2. Add a shape that you want to act as a hyperlink to the drawing. You can see an example in Figure 8.16.

Figure 8.16
Creating a shape that is hyperlinked.

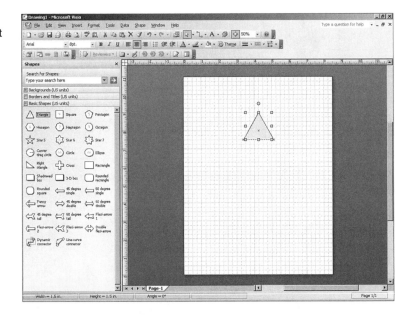

3. Select the shape. Visio displays a selection frame around the shape.

4. Select Insert > Hyperlinks. That opens the Hyperlinks dialog, shown in Figure 8.17.

Figure 8.17
Using the Hyperlinks dialog.

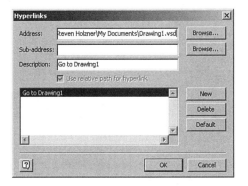

5. Enter the path of the file you want to link to in the Address box. You can see the path to a Visio drawing, Drawing1.vsd, entered in the Address box in Figure 8.17.

   Of course, you don't need to open a Visio drawing—you can open any kind of file.

6. Enter text in the Description box of the Hyperlinks dialog to be displayed when the mouse hovers over the linked shape. You can see the text "Go to Drawing1" in Figure 8.17.

7. Click OK in the Hyperlinks dialog. That closes the Hyperlinks dialog.

8. Repeat as needed to add other hyperlinks to the shape. Visio shapes can have multiple hyperlinks.

That's all it takes. Now when the user opens the hyperlink connected with the shape, Drawing 1 opens, as shown in Figure 8.18.

Figure 8.18
Opening a file using a hyperlink.

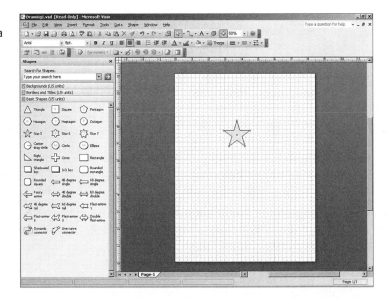

8

And there you have it—creating hyperlinks in Visio. Cool.

Next up: Visio and object linking and embedding.

Introducing Visio and OLE

Object linking and embedding (OLE) is a technique supported by many Windows applications, and it's designed to let you share data, and to present that data in host applications much as that data would appear in its home application.

For example, using OLE, you can embed a section of a Microsoft Excel worksheet in other applications, such as Microsoft Word, as shown in Figure 8.19.

Figure 8.19
A Microsoft Excel worksheet in Microsoft Word.

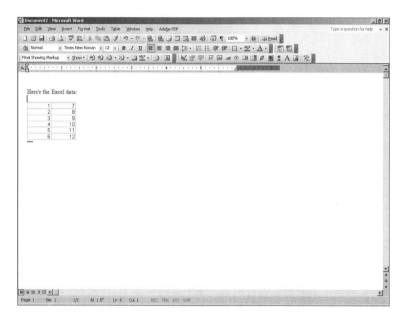

Note that OLE has nothing to do with the hyperlinks you just saw. Hyperlinks let you navigate from document to document, whereas OLE is a technique that lets you access data in various objects.

What's the difference between linking and embedding?

When you *link* to an object, you're actually connecting to a file. That file exists on disk, and you can update it using the home application. When you display that linked object in a host application like Visio, you're actually opening the file and displaying the data in it.

When you *embed* an object, on the other hand, you're embedding a copy of a file in the host application. You can edit the object in the host application, but you can't edit the object directly, as a file on disk, using the home application.

Linking works best when you have a file that changes frequently and that you want to keep updated while displaying that file's data in other applications. Embedding works better when you want to distribute host application documents and you don't want to have to also distribute source files.

We'll take a look at OLE in Visio now, starting with linking.

LINKING OBJECTS IN VISIO

We're going to take a look at how to link objects to and from Visio now, starting with linking Visio objects into other applications. Then we'll take a look at how to link objects from other applications into Visio.

LINKING VISIO OBJECTS INTO OTHER APPLICATIONS

To link an object into a host application document, make sure you've first saved that object in a (home-application) file. Here's how you can link to Visio drawings from other applications:

1. Open the drawing you want to link to. This drawing should be in a file, such as
    Drawing3.vsd, which is shown in Figure 8.20.

Figure 8.20
A source drawing.

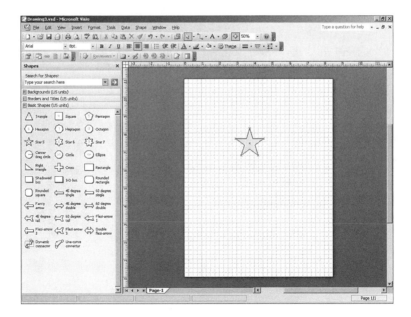

2. Select the page you want to link.
3. Select Edit > Copy Drawing. This copies the link information into the clipboard. Make sure that nothing in the drawing is selected to make this work.

4. Open the host application's document that you want to paste the link into. For example, you might want to paste the link into a Microsoft Word document, as shown in Figure 8.21.

Figure 8.21
A Microsoft Word document.

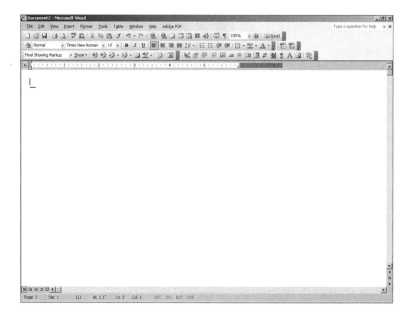

5. Select Edit > Paste Special in the host application. The actual menu item you use may vary by application, but in Office applications, it's Edit > Paste Special.

Selecting that menu item opens the Paste Special dialog, shown in Figure 8.22.

Figure 8.22
The Paste Special dialog.

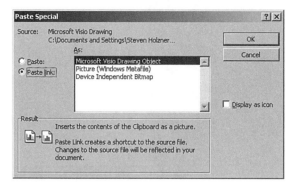

6. Select Microsoft Visio Drawing Object in the As box. This tells the host application which format the linked file is in.

7. Select the Paste Link radio button. This creates a link to the Visio file. You can see this radio button selected in Figure 8.22.

8. Click OK. The host application pastes the link and closes the Paste Special dialog. The host application displays the linked-to Visio data, as shown in Figure 8.23.

Figure 8.23
Linked-to Visio data in Word.

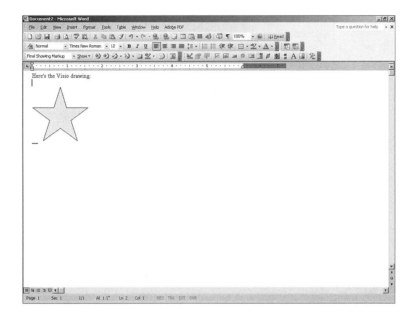

And that's it—congratulations, you've linked to a Visio file's data using Microsoft Word.

LINKING OBJECTS INTO VISIO

On the other hand, you can also link objects from other applications into Visio. Here's an example that links a Microsoft Word document stored in a file into Visio.

Just follow these steps:

1. Open the Visio drawing you want to link to the other application's file.
2. Select Insert > Object. Visio opens the Insert Object dialog, shown in Figure 8.24.
3. Select the Create from File radio button.
4. Select the Link to File check box.
5. Click the Browse button, and browse to the file you want to link to. Visio opens the Browse dialog. Browse to the file you want to link to and click Open.

   Visio displays the file you are linking to in the File Name box of the Insert Object dialog, as shown in Figure 8.24, where we're linking to a Word file named Sample.doc.
6. If you want to display the linked-to file as an icon, select the Display as Icon check box. Visio displays the file's data by default, but you can also display the linked-to file as an icon.

Figure 8.24
The Insert Object dialog.

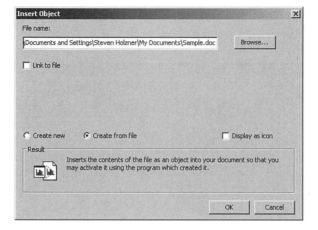

7. Click OK in the Insert Object dialog. Visio closes the Insert Object dialog and displays the data in the file you've linked to, as shown in Figure 8.25, in which the contents of the Word document `Sample.doc` are being displayed. Cool.

Figure 8.25
Linking to a Word document in Visio.

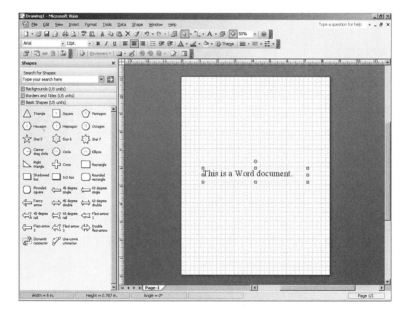

RESIZING AND MOVING LINKED OBJECTS

Want to resize or move linked objects in Visio?

No problem, just follow these steps:

1. Select a linked object. Just click the object, and Visio displays a selection frame around the linked-to object.

2. Resize the object. Drag the resizing handles as needed to resize the object.

3. Rotate the object. Drag a rotation handle as needed.

4. Move the object. Drag the selection frame containing the object to a new location in the drawing.

That is to say, you can use the selection frame of a linked-to object just as you can the selection frame of a normal shape.

EDITING LINKED OBJECTS

You can edit linked-to data in the data's home application, of course. For instance, you can edit the sample file `Sample.doc`, and the changes will be reflected in Visio after you save the Word document.

However, you can edit the linked object's data in Visio as well. To do that, follow these steps:

1. Open the Visio drawing that contains the linked-to object.

2. To edit the data in the host application, Visio, double-click the displayed data in the linked-to object. Visio surrounds the linked-to data with a thick border, as shown in Figure 8.26.

Figure 8.26
Linking to a Word document in Visio.

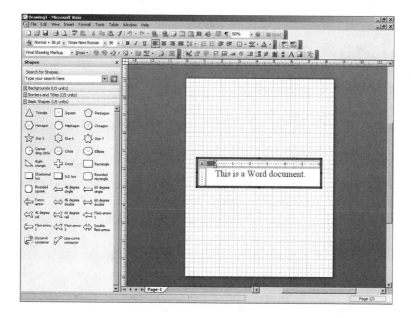

That border you see in Figure 8.26 means you're now editing the data in Microsoft Word—which has temporarily taken over Visio. You can see, for example, that the menu bar now shows the menu items that appear in Word, not Visio.

Alternatively, you can right-click the linked-to data and select Document Object > Edit, or select the linked-to data and select Edit > Document Object > Edit to open the linked-to data for editing.

3. Make your edits and save the file. You can see edited Word text in Figure 8.27 in Visio.

Figure 8.27
Edited Word text.

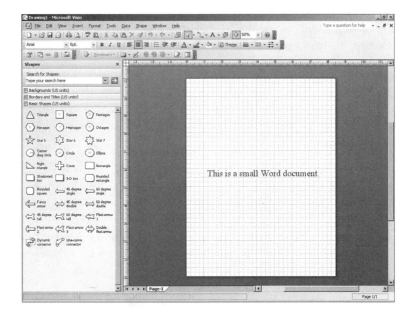

That's how to edit linked-to data.

Want to open linked-to data in its home application, instead of Visio? Just follow these steps:

1. Open the Visio drawing that contains the linked-to object.

2. To open the data in its home application, Word, right-click the data and select Document Object > Open. Alternatively, select the linked-to data and select Edit > Document Object > Open to open the linked-to data. Visio launches the linked-to data in its home application, which is Word in this case, as shown in Figure 8.28.

3. Make your edits and save the file in the home application.

That enables you to edit the object in the full version of the object's home application, not just the small windowed version you get when you edit linked-to data in situ in Visio.

Keep in mind that you're responsible for maintaining the link—if the source file moves, for example, the link is broken. And if you send the Visio file to another user, on another machine, the link will be broken too—unless you also send the linked-to file, which has to be put into the same path location as it is on your machine.

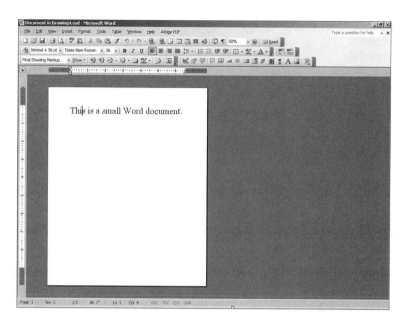

Figure 8.28
Opening a Word document from Visio.

EMBEDDING OBJECTS IN VISIO

Besides linking to objects in Visio, you can also embed objects. An embedded object lives in a Visio drawing—it's not dependent on an external file.

That means you don't have to worry about breaking the link inadvertently, as can happen with linked objects. You also have more discretion about what you embed—you can embed a whole Excel worksheet into a Visio drawing, or just part of that worksheet.

We'll start by embedding a whole file in Visio.

EMBEDDING WHOLE FILES INTO VISIO

Want to embed a whole file's data into Visio? Here's how to do it:

1. Open the Visio drawing you want to embed the other application's file in.
2. Select Insert > Object. Visio opens the Insert Object dialog, shown in Figure 8.29.
3. Select the Create from File radio button.
4. Make sure that the Link to File check box is *not* selected.
5. Click the Browse button, and browse to the file you want to embed. Visio opens the Browse dialog. Browse to the file you want to embed and click Open.

   Visio displays the file you are linking to in the File Name box of the Insert Object dialog, as shown in Figure 8.29, in which we're linking to the Word file named Sample.doc.

Figure 8.29
Using the Insert Object dialog.

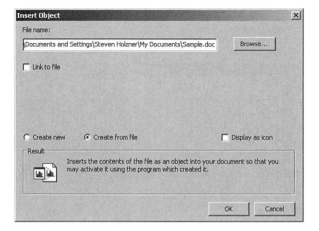

6. If you want to display the embedded object as an icon, select the Display as Icon check box. Visio displays the file's data by default, but you can also display the embedded file as an icon.

7. Click OK in the Insert Object dialog. Visio closes the Insert Object dialog and displays the data in the file you've embedded, as shown in Figure 8.30, in which the contents of the Word document `Sample.doc` are being displayed.

Figure 8.30
Embedding a Word document in Visio.

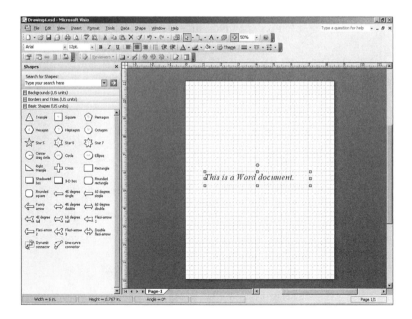

That embeds the entire contents of a file in Visio. Want to embed just a part of a file? That's coming up next.

EMBEDDING SECTIONS OF FILES INTO VISIO

Want to embed only a section of a file's data into Visio? Here's how to do it:

1. Open the application whose data you want to embed in a Visio drawing.
2. Select the data you want to embed in Visio. For example, you can see part of an Excel worksheet selected in Figure 8.31.

Figure 8.31
Selecting Excel data.

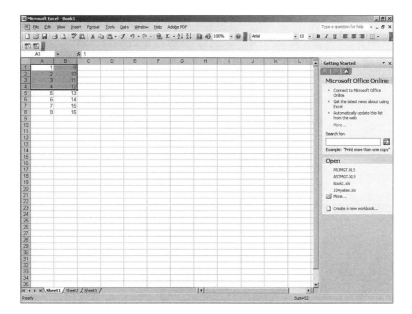

3. Press Ctrl + C or Edit > Copy to copy the data you want to embed in Visio.
4. Open the Visio drawing you want to embed part of the other application's file in.
5. Select Edit > Paste Special. This opens the Paste Special dialog, shown in Figure 8.32.

Figure 8.32
Using the Paste
Special dialog.

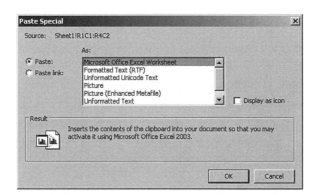

8

6. Make sure that the Paste radio button is selected.

7. If you want to display the embedded object as an icon, select the Display as Icon check box. Visio displays the file's data by default, but you can also display the embedded file as an icon.

8. Click OK in the Paste Special dialog. Visio closes the Paste Special dialog and displays the data in the file you've embedded, as shown in Figure 8.33, in which the selected part of the Excel worksheet is being displayed.

Figure 8.33
Embedding part of an Excel worksheet in Visio.

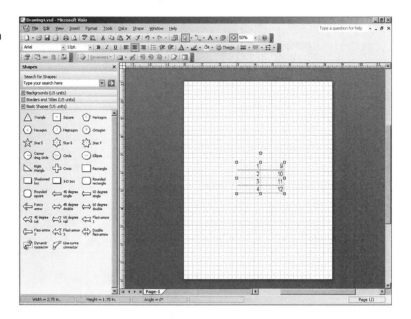

What about embedding Visio objects into other applications?

EMBEDDING VISIO OBJECTS INTO OTHER APPLICATIONS

Here's how you can embed Visio objects into other applications:

1. Open the drawing you want to embed in another application. You can see an example in Figure 8.34.

2. Select the section of the drawing you want to embed in the other application. You can see the selection in Figure 8.34.

3. Select Edit > Copy or Edit > Copy Drawing. This copies the data you want to embed.

4. Open the host application's document that you want to embed the Visio drawing into. For example, you might want to embed a Visio object into a Microsoft Word document.

Figure 8.34
A source drawing.

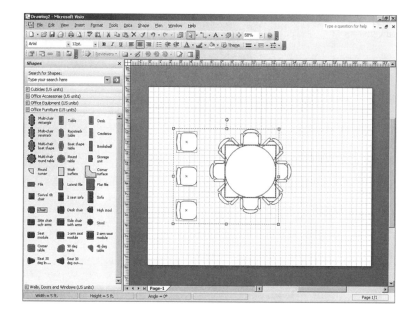

5. Select Edit > Paste Special in the host application. The actual menu item you use may vary by application, but in Office applications, it's Edit > Paste Special.

   Selecting that menu item opens the Paste Special dialog, as shown in Figure 8.35.

Figure 8.35
The Microsoft Word
Paste Special dialog.

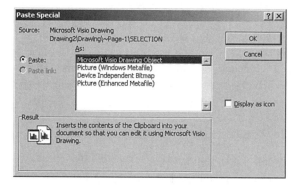

6. Select Microsoft Visio Drawing Object in the As box. This tells the host application which format the linked file is in.

7. Select the Paste radio button. This embeds the Visio object. You can see this radio button selected in Figure 8.35.

8. Click OK. The host application embeds the Visio object and closes the Paste Special dialog.

   The host application displays the embedded Visio data, as shown in Figure 8.36.

8

Figure 8.36
Embedded Visio data
in Word.

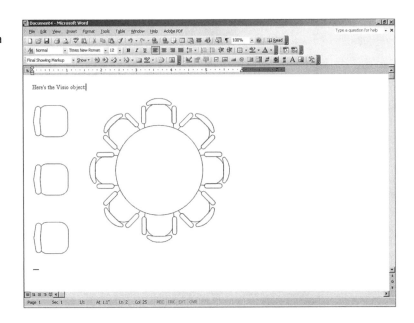

And that's it—you've embedded a Visio object in Microsoft Word.

EDITING EMBEDDED OBJECTS

Just as you can with linked-to objects, you can edit embedded objects in Visio as well. However, there are some differences here—unlike with linked-to objects, you're not editing the data in a file here, you're editing the data in the embedded object.

Among other things, that means you can't edit the data in a file and expect to see the data in an embedded object change—it won't. When you edit an embedded object, you're editing the data in that object, not in a file.

If you want to edit the data in an embedded object, follow these steps:

1. Open the Visio drawing that contains the embedded object.

2. To edit the data in Visio, double-click the displayed data in the embedded object. Visio surrounds the embedded data with a thick border, as you saw with linked-to objects.

   That border means you're now editing the data in the home application, which has temporarily taken over Visio. The Visio menu bar now shows the menu items that appear in the home application, not Visio.

   Alternatively, you can right-click the embedded data and select Document Object > Edit, or select the embedded data and select Edit > Document Object > Edit to open the embedded data for editing.

3. Make your edits to the embedded data.

4. Click outside the selected embedded data. Visio removes the thick border around the embedded data.

5. Save the Visio drawing. Doing so causes Visio to save the edits to the embedded data.

Want to open embedded data in its home application, instead of Visio? Just follow these steps:

1. Open the Visio drawing that contains the embedded object.

2. To open the data in the data's home application, right-click the data and select Document Object > Open. Alternatively, select the embedded data and select Edit > Document Object > Open. Visio launches the embedded data in its home application.

3. Make your edits in the home application.

4. Select File > Update in the home application.

5. Select File > Close & Return to Drawingx in the home application—here, x is the number of your Visio drawing.

    The home application closes and Visio reappears, showing the edits you've made to the embedded data.

And that completes working with embedded data.

CONVERTING FROM LINKED-TO OBJECTS TO EMBEDDED OBJECTS

What if you want to convert linked-to data to embedded data? Can you do that?

Yes you can, in Visio. Just follow these steps:

1. Open the Visio drawing that contains the linked object that you want to convert to an embedded object.

2. Select Edit > Links. Visio opens the Links dialog, as shown in Figure 8.37.

Figure 8.37
The Links dialog.

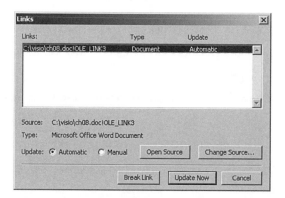

3. Select the link you want to break. You can see a link selected in Figure 8.37.

4. Click the Break Link button, and click OK in the confirmation dialog that opens. The entry for that link disappears from the Links dialog.

5. Click Close to close the Links dialog. Now the linked-to object has become an embedded object.

   The object still looks the same, but it's now an independent, embedded object, not a lined-to object.

CHANGING A LINKED-TO OBJECT'S SOURCE FILE

Can you change the source file for a linked-to object? Yes, you can do that as well. Here's how to go about it:

1. Open the Visio drawing that contains the linked object that you want to change.

2. Select Edit > Links. Visio opens the Links dialog.

3. Select the link you want to alter.

4. Click the Change Source button. Visio opens the Change Source dialog.

5. Browse to the new source file for the link.

6. Click Open. Visio closes the Change Source dialog and returns you to the Link dialog.

7. Click Close. Visio closes the Links dialog.

HANDLING PICTURES IN VISIO

There are many shapes in Visio, but sometimes you need more—such as when you want to embed your own photo into a drawing. Or what if you want to insert the company logo? Or some clip art?

Inserting pictures in Visio is a special case of embedding objects, and Visio is up to the task, including some strong tools for the purpose.

We'll start by inserting graphics files into Visio drawings.

INSERTING GRAPHICS FILES

Want to insert an image from a graphics file? Here's how that works:

1. Open the Visio drawing that you want to insert the image into.

2. Select Insert > Picture > From File. Visio displays the Insert Picture dialog shown in Figure 8.38.

Figure 8.38
The Insert Picture dialog.

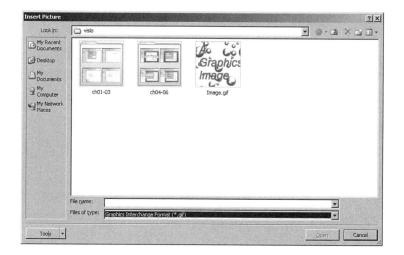

3. Browse to the graphics file you want to open and click Open. Visio inserts the picture, as shown in Figure 8.39.

Figure 8.39
Inserting a picture.

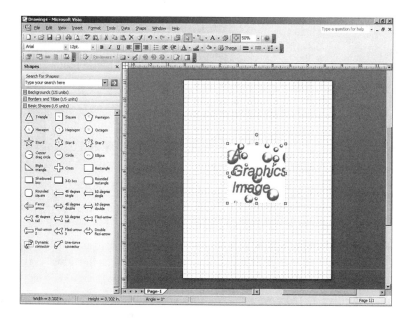

And that's it—now you can insert your photo, the company logo, or a photo of the big boss in your drawings.

INSERTING CLIP ART

Visio includes a great facility for searching for clip art to embed in your drawings—and it provides the clip art for you. A large selection of clip art is available, so the odds are good that you'll find what you're looking for without a problem.

Here's how to search for and insert clip art in Visio:

1. Open the Visio drawing that you want to insert the image into.

2. Select Insert > Picture > Clip Art. Visio displays the Clip Art task pane shown in Figure 8.40.

Figure 8.40
The Clip Art task pane.

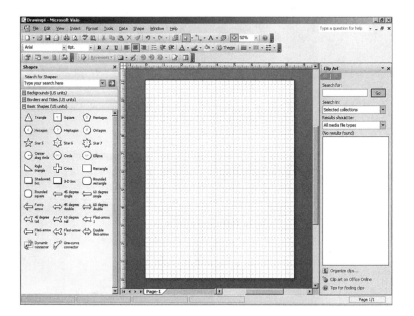

3. Enter your search term in the Search For box. You can see the search term "tiger" entered in Figure 8.41.

4. Select where to search in the Search In box. You can select from My Collections (selected by default), Office Collections, Selected Collections, Web Collections, and Everywhere (which selects all three collection types).

5. Select what media type you want the results to be in the Results Should Be box. This lets you select the media type that the search tries to locate. You can select from Clip Art, Photographs, Movies, Sounds, or All Media File Types.

6. Click the Go button next to the Search For box. Visio performs the search, and any matches appear in the lower box in the Clip Art task pane.

For example, we've found a tiger this way, as you see displayed in Figure 8.42.

Figure 8.41
Entering a clip art search term.

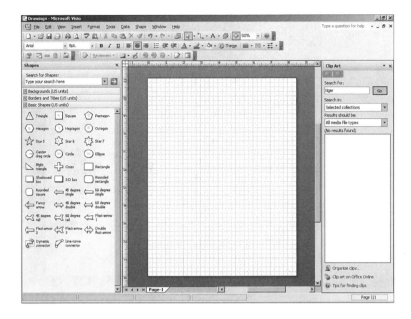

Figure 8.42
Finding a tiger.

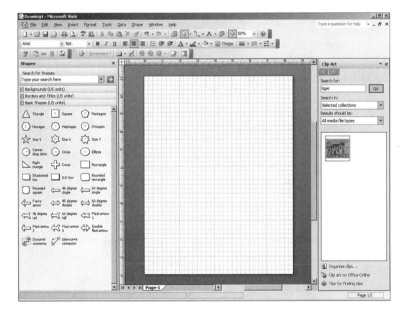

7. Hovering the mouse over a match displays a down arrow, which you can click to copy the image, save it in a collection, and so on. The most useful of the options displayed is Copy to Collection, which allows you to save the image to one of your local collections.

8. Drag the image you want onto the drawing surface. After you've dragged the image, you can resize it and move it, as shown in Figure 8.43.

Figure 8.43
A tiger in a drawing.

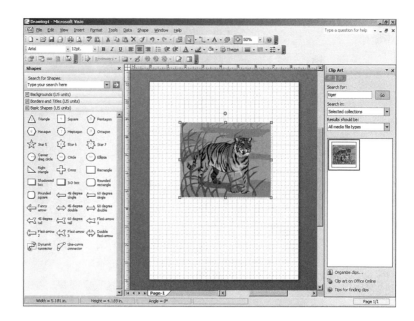

9. Click the × button in the Clip Art task pane. Visio closes the Clip Art task pane.

When you drag a clip art object onto a drawing, Visio makes it a full-fledged 2D shape. You can resize or rotate the image as you would any 2D shape.

TIP

> In previous versions of Visio, you used to be able to read images directly from scanners or digital cameras. That's no longer an option in Visio 2007; the way to import photos from scanners or cameras now is to save those photos to a file, then import that file.

CROPPING IMAGES

You can also use the Picture toolbar to manage pictures in Visio. For example, you can use it to crop images.

Here's how that works:

1. Insert an image into a drawing. For example, you can insert clip art as shown previously.

2. Display the Picture toolbar by right-clicking any toolbar and selecting Picture. You can see the Picture toolbar in Figure 8.44.

Figure 8.44
The Picture toolbar.

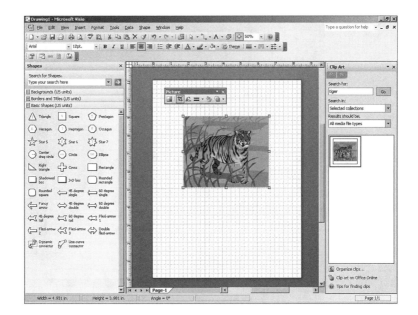

Here are the buttons in the Picture toolbar, from left to right:

> Insert Picture
>
> Crop Tool
>
> Rotate Left
>
> Line Weight
>
> Format Picture
>
> Transparency

3. Select the Crop tool.

4. Drag the selection handles to crop the image. When you drag selection handles to resize an image normally, using the Pointer tool, the image as a whole is resized.

    However, when you resize the image with the Crop tool, the image is cropped, not resized, as shown in Figure 8.45.

5. Release the mouse button. The image appears in its cropped form.

Besides cropping images with the Picture toolbar, you can also format graphics using this toolbar.

Figure 8.45
Cropping a tiger
image.

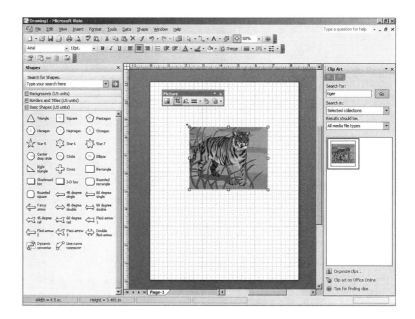

FORMATTING GRAPHICS

You can also format images that you import, changing their brightness and contrast, by using the Format Picture dialog.

Here's how that works:

1. Insert an image into a drawing.
2. Display the Picture toolbar by right-clicking any toolbar and selecting Picture. You can see the Picture toolbar in Figure 8.44.
3. Select the Format Picture button (second from the right), or select Format > Picture. That opens the Format Picture dialog, shown in Figure 8.46.

Figure 8.46
The Format Picture
dialog.

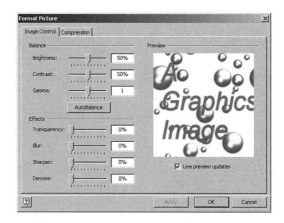

Use the following controls to format the image:

- **Brightness**—Lightens or darkens the image.
- **Contrast**—Adjusts the contrast of the image.
- **Gamma**—Adjusts the brightness of gray tones.
- **AutoBalance**—Adjusts the brightness, contrast, and gamma.
- **Transparency**—Adjusts the image's transparency; 100% makes the image totally transparent.
- **Blur**—Blurs the image.
- **Sharpen**—Sharpens the image.
- **Denoise**—Removes noise in the image, such as speckles.

The Compression tab lets you adjust the compression of the image.

4. Click OK. Visio closes the Format Picture dialog.

As you can see, the support for formatting pictures in Visio is good—but if you need more formatting capabilities, consider editing the image with editing software before importing it into Visio.

INSERTING CHARTS

Here's a cool one: You can insert pictures of charts using Visio, and you do that with the Insert > Picture > Chart menu item.

Here's what you do:

1. Open the drawing you want to insert a chart into.
2. Select Insert > Picture > Chart. That opens the Datasheet dialog, shown in Figure 8.47.

    Edit the data in the Datasheet dialog to reflect the data you want to insert into the chart.

    To delete rows, right-click the Datasheet dialog and select Delete.

    To insert rows, right-click the Datasheet dialog and select Insert.
3. Click the drawing. You can see the inserted chart, as shown in Figure 8.48.

Figure 8.47
The Datasheet dialog.

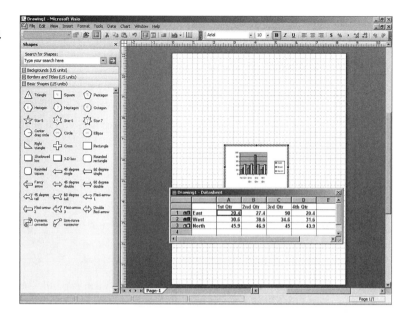

Figure 8.48
A new chart.

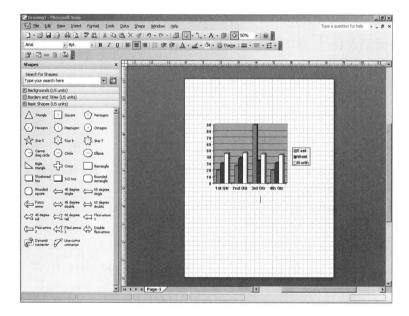

INSERTING EQUATIONS

Visio also includes the Office Equation Editor, to let you insert equations into drawings.

Here's what you do:

1. Open the drawing you want to insert an equation into.

2. Select Insert > Picture > Equation. That opens the Equation Editor, shown in Figure 8.49.

Figure 8.49
The Equation Editor.

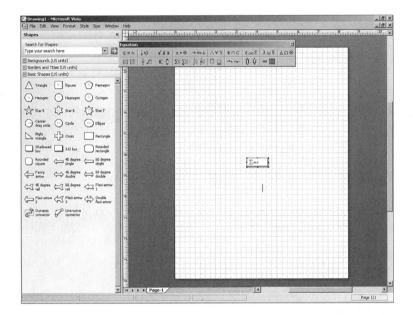

You can use the buttons in the Equation Editor and type standard characters on the keyboard to create equations.

3. Close the Equation Editor. Visio closes the Equation Editor, and you see the inserted equation, as shown in Figure 8.50.

If you want to edit the equation, just double-click it, which opens the equation in the Equation Editor.

Figure 8.50
A new equation.

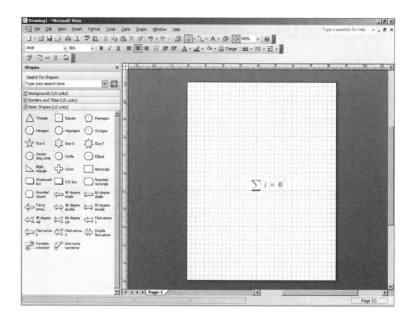

EXPORTING FROM VISIO

You can also explicitly export whole files in Visio. For example, here are the graphics formats that Visio exports:

- AutoCAD drawing (.dwg)
- AutoCAD Interchange Format (.dxf)
- Compressed Enhanced Metafile (.emz)
- Enhanced Metafile (.emf)
- Graphics Interchange Format (.gif)
- JPEG (.jpg)
- Portable Network Graphics (.png)
- Scalable Vector Graphics (.svg)
- Scalable Vector Graphics Compressed (.svgz)
- Tagged Image Format (.tif)
- Web page (.htm)
- Windows bitmap (.bmp, .dib)
- Windows Metafile (.wmf)

Want to export shapes or a drawing in graphic format? Here's how to do it:

1. Open the drawing you want to export from.
2. If you want to export shapes in the drawing, select those shapes.

3. Select File > Save As. In the Save As Type box, select the graphics format you want to export in, as shown in Figure 8.51, in which we're saving a drawing in JPEG format.

Figure 8.51
Saving in a selected graphics format.

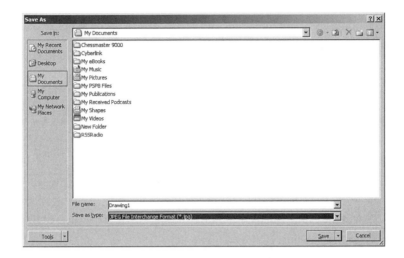

4. Enter the name you want to give to the saved image in the File Name box.
5. Click Save.

Visio opens an export options dialog if you save in any of these formats:

> GIF
>
> JPEG
>
> PNG
>
> TIFF

You can see the JPEG formatting options in Figure 8.52.

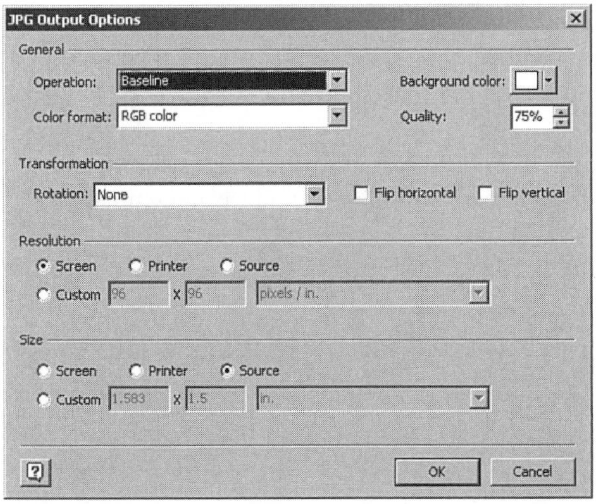

Figure 8.52
The JPEG options dialog.

8

6. Select the formatting options you want, if Visio displays an options dialog, and click OK. Visio saves the image.

That completes saving in graphics formats—how about saving in Adobe PDF format or XML Paper Specification (XPS) format?

EXPORTING IN PDF AND XPS FORMATS

You can set up Visio to export in PDF and XPS format. To do so, you first have to install an add-on; here's how to do that:

1. In a browser, navigate to www.microsoft.com/downloads.
2. Enter "PDF or XPS" in the search box and click Go. The Microsoft site displays matches to your search.
3. Select the "2007 Microsoft Office Add-in: Microsoft Save as PDF or XPS" match.
4. Download and install the add-on.

After the add-on has been installed, do this to save a drawing in PDF or XPS format:

1. Open the drawing you want to save in PDF or XPS format.
2. Select File > Publish as PDF or XPS. Visio opens the Publish as PDF or XPS dialog.
3. Navigate to the folder you want to save the file in.
4. Enter the name you want to save the file under in the File Name box.
5. In the Save As box, select either PDF or XPS format.
6. If you want to save the document in minimal size for web publishing, select the Minimize Size option.
7. Click the Publish button. Visio creates and saves the file. For example, you can see a Visio drawing saved in PDF format in Figure 8.53.

And that lets you save Visio drawings in PDF or XPS format. Cool.

Saving Visio drawings in PDF format in particular is useful when you want to publish drawings on the Web. In fact, that's a whole new topic, coming up next.

Figure 8.53
A Visio drawing in
PDF format.

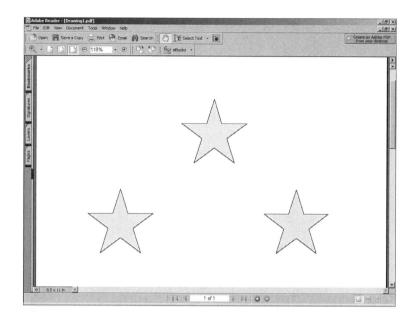

PUBLISHING TO THE WEB

Visio offers a lot of support when it comes to publishing drawings on the Web—you can even publish multipage drawings with hyperlinks between the pages.

Visio can generate HTML frame pages and controls to navigate between pages.

So how do you save a drawing as a web page? Follow these steps:

1. Open the drawing you want to save in PDF or XPS format.
2. Select File > Save As Web Page. Visio opens the Save As dialog, shown in Figure 8.54.
3. Navigate to the folder you want to save the HTML file in.
4. Enter the name of the HTML file you want to create in the File Name box.
5. To change the title of the HTML page, click the Change Title button. Visio opens the Set Page Title dialog; enter the new page title in the Page Title box.
6. To select publishing options, click the Publish button. Visio opens the Save As Web Page dialog, shown in Figure 8.55.
7. Select the pages of the drawing to publish. Make this selection in the Pages to Publish area.

Figure 8.54
Saving a drawing as a
web page.

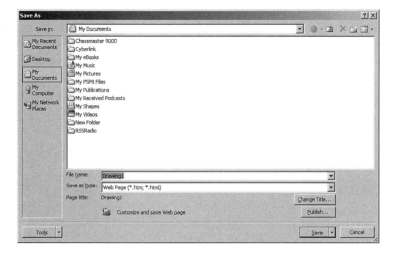

Figure 8.55
The Save As Web
Page dialog.

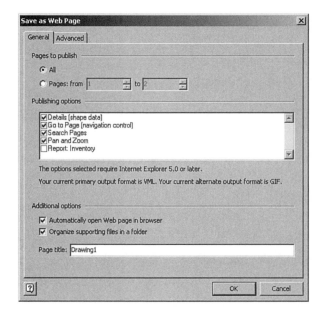

8. Select the options in the Publishing Options box. Here are the options and what they mean:

- **Details**—Displays shape data. To display shape data in a frame, click a shape to select it and press Ctrl+Enter.

- **Go to Page**—Displays navigational controls that let you navigate between pages.

- **Search Pages**—Lets you create a search page.

- **Pan and Zoom**—Displays a Pan and Zoom window that you can use to pan and zoom in a drawing. Available only when you use the VML Save option and Internet Explorer 5.0 or later.

- **Report**—Displays reports. Select each report you want to publish in the Publishing Options list.

9. To publish the drawing, click OK in the Save As Web Page dialog, or click Save in the Save As dialog. Visio saves the web page in the location you specified.

   Visio opens the web page in your default browser, as shown in Figure 8.56.

Figure 8.56
A drawing published to the Web.

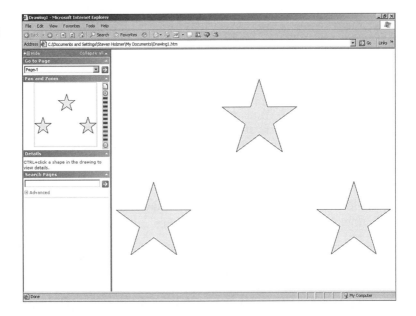

You can navigate between the pages of the drawing by selecting Page-2 in the Go To Page box shown in Figure 8.56, which gives you the results you see in Figure 8.57 (the pages are given the same names you give to the pages in your drawing).

So as you can see, there are plenty of options you can use when you publish to the Web.

If you don't want a frame on the left side, deselect the Details, Go to Page, Search Pages, and Pan and Zoom options in the Save As Web Page dialog.

Figure 8.57
Navigating to a new page.

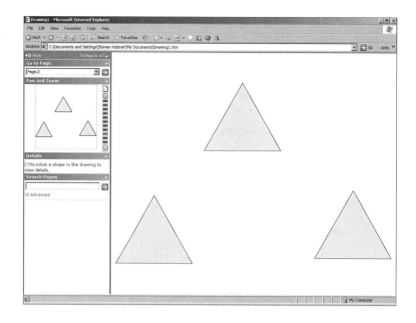

THE FILES THAT WERE CREATED

What files does Visio create when you save a drawing as a web page? That's important to know when you want to upload those files to a website.

Fortunately, Visio makes it easy for you. It stores an `.htm` file with the name you've specified, such as `Drawing1.htm`.

The support files appear in a folder with the name *xxxxxx*_files, where *xxxxxx* is the name of your web page. In the preceding example, the created folder is named Drawing1_files.

Here are the files that appear in the Drawing1_files folder:

arrow.gif	go.gif	toc.gif
data.xml	keys.js	toc2.gif
filelist.xml	maximize.gif	toolbar.htm
find.js	minimize.gif	visio.css
frameset.js	minus.gif	vml_1.emz
fullpage.gif	panminus.gif	vml_1.htm
gif_1.gif	panplus.gif	vml_1.js
gif_1.htm	plus.gif	vml_2.emz
gif_1.js	tick-foc.gif	vml_2.htm
gif_2.gif	tick-off.gif	widgets.htm
gif_2.htm	tick-on.gif	zoom.htm

By storing all these files in a folder, Visio makes it easy for you—just upload the main .htm file and the folder that contains all the other files, and you're set.

ADVANCED FORMATTING OPTIONS

You can set advanced web page publishing options in the Save As Web Page dialog if you click the Advanced tab, as shown in Figure 8.58.

Figure 8.58
Advanced web page options.

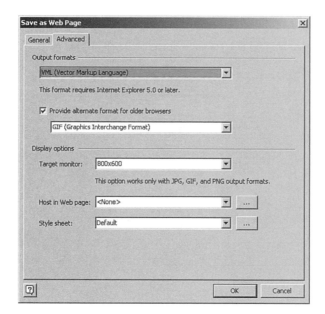

Here are the advanced options you can set:

- **Output formats**—Select the output format that you want. VML creates the best results, but that's workable only for Internet Explorer 5.0 and greater.

- **Provide Alternate Format for Older Browsers**—Because VML and SVG require Internet Explorer 5.0 or later, you can also specify a format for older browsers. The usual selection here is GIF format, which is selected by default.

- **Target Monitor**—Lets you set the targeted screen resolution for JPG, GIF, and PNG output.

- **Host in Web Page**—Select the web page in which you want to embed the generated web page.

- **Style Sheet**—Lets you supply your own style sheet for use in the generated style sheet.

SHAPESHEETS AND MACROS

In this chapter

9

SHAPESHEETS, MACROS, AND TOOLBARS

The underlying theme of this chapter is *customization*. Visio is an extensive application, and there are hundreds of techniques you can use to customize it. This chapter covers some advanced customization topics.

It all starts with ShapeSheets. When you take a look at a shape on a drawing surface, you see the shape visually. It may be a star shape, a resistor in an electrical circuit, a CEO in an organization chart—no matter what it is, you can see it visually on the drawing surface.

That's one way of viewing shapes—on the drawing surface. That shape is just a visual representation of the shape's data—its width, position, color, fill, and so on. Behind the scenes, that's what the shape is to Visio—a collection of data fields.

And a ShapeSheet is just the numeric representation of the same data. It's another way of looking at a shape—as a collection of data fields, arranged in spreadsheet form. In fact, that's the way Visio sees your shapes—as collections of data.

You have direct access to a shape's ShapeSheet in Visio, as you're going to see in this chapter. ShapeSheets are divided into sections, and you can access the section you want—and modify it as well, as you're going to see here.

Another advanced customization topic is macros, which you can use to automate common Visio tasks. Using macros, you can record series of actions and then "play" them back when you want.

Just about all Microsoft Office applications let you create macros, and Visio is no exception. Handling macros is one of the most common ways of automating Visio, as you're going to see.

This chapter also covers how to customize toolbars and menus in Visio. It turns out that you can create your own toolbars in Visio, and stock them with the buttons you want.

That capability turns out to be extremely useful as you become a Visio power user. Visio has many toolbars built in—16 of them—but displays only 3 of them by default, because when you start displaying more, the Visio window begins to get crowded.

But a power user might use six or more toolbars in normal, everyday use. So how do you reconcile that with the scarcity of screen space? You can create your own toolbar, placing the buttons you want into that custom toolbar. You might want buttons from four or more toolbars in your custom toolbar—and with Visio, that kind of customization is no problem at all.

You can also customize menus in Visio. And you're going to see how that works in this chapter.

All this and more is coming up in this chapter, so let's get started at once with ShapeSheets.

WORKING WITH SHAPESHEETS

There's a lot of information packed into each Visio element—shapes, guides, even the pages themselves. And you can view that information directly using ShapeSheets. As already mentioned, ShapeSheets are a view of shapes from Visio's point of view, in which you see a shape's data in numeric form, instead of that data being used to visually configure a shape.

TAKING A LOOK AT SHAPESHEETS

How do you get a look at a ShapeSheet? Follow these steps for shapes, groups, guides, guide points, or OLE objects:

1. Open the drawing that contains the shape, group, guide, guide point, or OLE object whose ShapeSheet you want to view in Visio.

2. Select the shape, group, guide, guide point, or OLE object and select Window > Show ShapeSheet. You can see an example in Figure 9.1.

   Note that the ShapeSheet opens in a separate window in Visio.

Figure 9.1
A ShapeSheet.

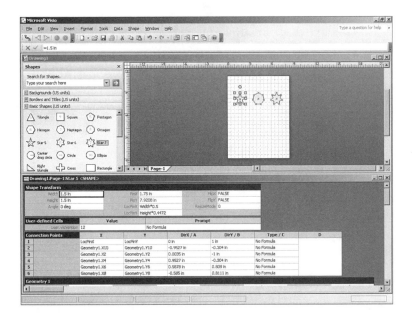

You can see that the ShapeSheet in Figure 9.1 is divided into various sections, and the sections you see in the figure are only the tip of the iceberg (as you can see by looking at the scrollbar in the ShapeSheet, which is indicating there are many more sections that you can't see directly in the ShapeSheet window).

The ShapeSheet in Figure 9.1 lists literally all the information that Visio has about the selected start shape. You saw earlier in this book how to add shape data to shapes, but this is different—this is all the internal data that Visio has on a graphic element.

You can also open a ShapeSheet for a shape in a group. Just follow these steps:

1. Open the drawing that contains the group that contains the shape you want to open a ShapeSheet for.

2. Select the group with the mouse.

3. Click the shape in the group to select it. You can see an example in Figure 9.2.

Figure 9.2
Selecting a shape in a group.

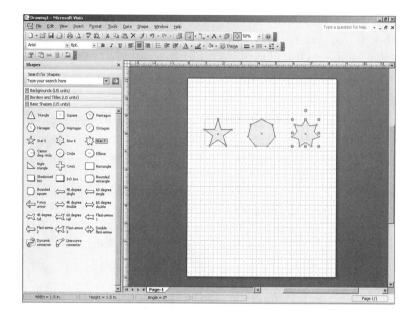

4. Select Window > Show ShapeSheet. This shows the ShapeSheet for the selected shape; you can see an example in Figure 9.3.

You can also display a ShapeSheet for a whole drawing page. Doing so displays the page properties, page layout, and so on.

Here's how you display a ShapeSheet for a whole page:

1. Open the drawing.

2. Make sure that no elements on the page are selected. If anything is selected, deselect it by clicking the page.

3. Select Window > Show ShapeSheet. This shows the ShapeSheet for the page, as shown in Figure 9.4.

Figure 9.3
A ShapeSheet for a selected shape in a group.

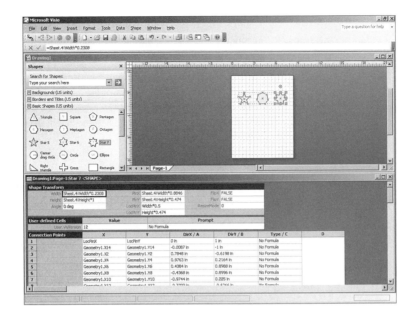

Figure 9.4
A ShapeSheet for a page.

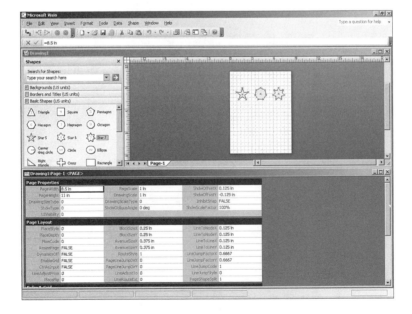

In fact, you can even display a ShapeSheet for a master shape in a custom stencil. Here's how that works:

1. Open the drawing containing the custom stencil.

2. Right-click the custom stencil's title bar and select Edit Stencil from the context menu.

3. Right-click the master shape and select Edit Master.

4. Select Window > Show ShapeSheet. This shows the ShapeSheet for the master shape.

TIP

Want to add the Show ShapeSheet command on every shape's context menu? Select Tools > Options, click the Advanced tab, and select the Run in Developer Mode check box.

You also have control over how each ShapeSheet is opened. By default, there's only one window for ShapeSheets, and as you open successive ShapeSheets, they appear in that window.

However, you can open each ShapeSheet in its own window. To do so, follow these steps:

1. Select Tools > Options.

2. Click the Advanced tab.

3. Deselect the Open Each ShapeSheet in the Same Window check box. You can see this check box in Figure 9.5 in the Options dialog.

Figure 9.5
The Advanced tab of the Options dialog.

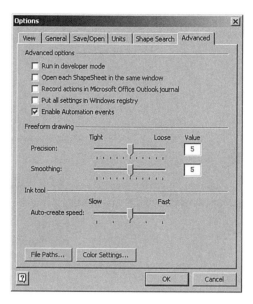

4. Click OK. Visio closes the Options dialog.

Okay, that's how to view ShapeSheets. Now let's take a look at what's inside them.

HANDLING SHAPESHEET SECTIONS

As you can see in the preceding figures, there are plenty of entries in ShapeSheets, divided into different sections. Here are some standard sections you'll see in ShapeSheets:

- **1-D Endpoints**—Displays the coordinates of the endpoints of a 1D shape.
- **Events**—Lists the events that the shape responds to, such as double-clicking.
- **Fill Format**—Lists settings for the fill formats in the shape.
- **Geometry**—Lists the geometry of the shape: coordinates for each vertex, fill information, and more.
- **Group Properties**—Lists group behavior, such as whether the group can be the target of dropped shapes.
- **Line Format**—Displays settings for lines, such as line thickness and format.
- **Miscellaneous**—Controls shape behaviors, involving selection handles, control handles, and so on.
- **Paragraph**—Lists the paragraph formatting used in the shape. You set this format by selecting Format > Text and then clicking the Paragraph tab.
- **Protection**—Lists what's locked in the shape. You can also see some ShapeSheet-specific lock options.
- **Shape Data**—Displays the labels and values of user-defined shape data.
- **Shape Layout**—Lists the layout settings for the shape, as specified on the File > Page Setup dialog's Layout and Routing tab.
- **Shape Transform**—Displays the position of the shape on the drawing page, the dimensions of the shape, pin positions, rotation information, and more.
- **Text Block Format**—Lists the text block formatting used in the shape. You set this format by selecting Format > Text and then clicking the Text Block tab.
- **Text Transform**—Displays the position and size of a shape's text block.
- **User-Defined Cells**—Displays user-defined values, such as keywords used to search for the shape.

There are dozens of sections like the preceding ones that you can see in ShapeSheets.

You also have some control over which sections appear in a ShapeSheet. Here's how you exercise that control:

1. Open the ShapeSheet that you want to configure.
2. Right-click the ShapeSheet (not its title bar) and select the View Sections item. Visio displays the View Sections dialog, shown in Figure 9.6.

Figure 9.6
The View Sections
dialog.

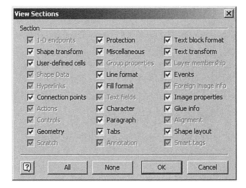

3. Select the check boxes for the sections you want to view, and deselect the check boxes for the sections you don't want to see. Note that in Figure 9.6, some sections are selected and grayed out, which means you don't have a choice—you have to view those sections.

4. Click OK. Visio closes the View Sections dialog.

PRINTING SHAPESHEETS

When you've got a ShapeSheet selected, Visio removes all the Print items from the File menu. And you can't select ShapeSheet entries en masse to copy them over to, say, Excel and print them that way.

So how do you print a ShapeSheet, or a ShapeSheet section? For that matter, how can you export a ShapeSheet or a ShapeSheet section to another program?

The way to do this is to use the Visio 2007 Software Development Kit (SDK), which includes a Print ShapeSheet tool.

To get the Visio 2007 SDK, navigate your browser to http://msdn.microsoft.com/office/program/visio/ and click the link to the Visio 2007 SDK. Download and install the SDK, and then follow these steps to print a ShapeSheet:

1. Select a drawing.

2. Select Tools > Add-ons > SDK > Tools > Print ShapeSheet. Visio starts the Print ShapeSheet tool.

3. Select the ShapeSheet type in the Print ShapeSheet dialog. You can select from among the Document, Styles, Page, and All Shapes options.

4. Select an entry in the Send To drop-down list. You can send the output to a printer, a file, or the Clipboard. If you send the ShapeSheet to the Clipboard, you can paste it into other applications like Excel.

5. Select the check boxes for the sections you want to print.

6. Click OK. Visio closes the Print ShapeSheet dialog.

That lets you print a ShapeSheet, or transfer its data to other applications like Excel.

UNDERSTANDING SHAPESHEET SECTIONS

There are hundreds of fields in the typical ShapeSheet, divided into sections. Most of these fields are self-explanatory. For example, the HideText field lets you hide the text associated with a shape, and it's set to FALSE by default.

But what about a field named ConFixedCode? What the heck does that mean in Visio?

You can let Visio give you the answer. All you have to do is select the field's value and press F1. Visio displays a Help window explaining what the particular field you've selected stands for, and what the possible values are.

You can see an example in Figure 9.7.

Figure 9.7
A ShapeSheet field's Help window.

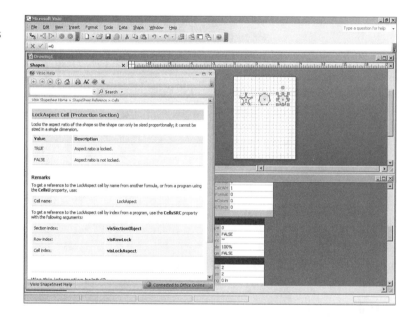

So what does the ConFixedCode field do? You can look it up this way, and you'll find that it specifies the behavior of connectors when a connector has to be rerouted, as when you move a shape.

Here are the possible values for the ConFixedCode field:

- 0 Reroute freely
- 1 Reroute as needed (manual reroute)
- 2 Never reroute
- 3 Reroute on crossover
- 4 For internal use only

- 5 For internal use only
- 6 For internal use only

You can browse the Microsoft Office Visio ShapeSheet Reference to find what every field in a ShapeSheet does.

To open the Microsoft Office Visio ShapeSheet Reference, follow these steps in Visio:

1. Select Help > Microsoft Office Visio Help. Visio displays the Help window shown in Figure 9.8.

Figure 9.8
The Help window.

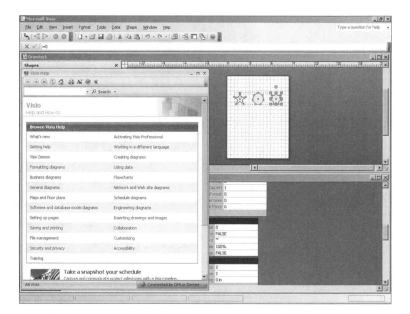

2. Click the down arrow in the Search button and select Visio ShapeSheet Help. You can see this item in Figure 9.9.

3. Enter "reference" in the Search box and press Enter.

4. Click the Welcome to the Microsoft Office Visio 2007 ShapeSheet Reference item in the search results. Visio opens the Microsoft Office Visio ShapeSheet Reference Welcome page, shown in Figure 9.10.

Figure 9.9
The Visio ShapeSheet Help options.

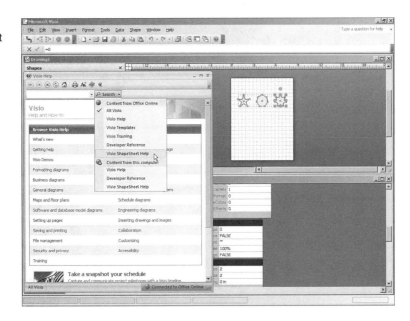

Figure 9.10
The Microsoft Office Visio ShapeSheet Reference's Welcome page.

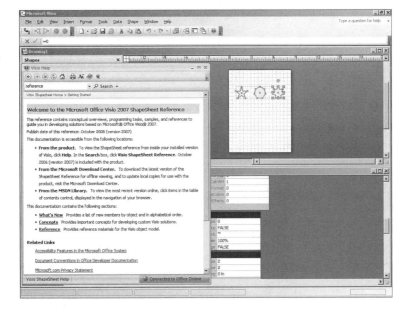

5. Click the Reference link to get to the Microsoft Office Visio ShapeSheet Reference. Visio opens the Microsoft Office Visio ShapeSheet Reference page shown in Figure 9.11.

Figure 9.11
The Microsoft Office
Visio ShapeSheet
Reference.

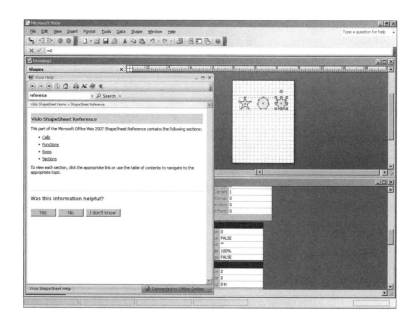

You can find information on just about everything ShapeSheet related in the ShapeSheet Reference.

How about taking a look at the most common fields in ShapeSheets and what they contain? Some common fields, arranged by ShapeSheet section, are coming up next.

THE SHAPE TRANSFORM SECTION

Here are the some of the fields in the Shape Transform section, which sets the position and orientation of shapes:

- **Angle**—Sets the angle by which shapes can rotate.
- **Height**—Sets a shape's height.
- **LocPinX**—Sets the X position of the rotation pin in a shape.
- **LocPinY**—Sets the Y position of the rotation pin in a shape.
- **Width**—Sets a shape's width.

THE GEOMETRY SECTION

Here are some of the fields in the Geometry section, which sets the coordinates of each vertex in a shape:

- **EllipticalArcTo**—Sets a new location to draw an arc to from the current position.
- **Geometry.NoFill**—Indicates whether you want to let a shape accept fill.
- **LineTo**—Sets a new location to draw a line to from the current position.
- **MoveTo**—Sets a new location to move to.

THE MISCELLANEOUS SECTION

Here are some of the fields in the Miscellaneous section, which sets various shape attributes, such as handle selection and visibility:

- **Comment**—Contains comment text that you might want to add to a shape.
- **DropOnPageScale**—Holds the percentage by which a shape is scaled when dropped on the drawing page.
- **NoAlignBox**—Sets whether the shape displays an alignment box. If set to TRUE, the shape will not display an alignment box. The default is FALSE.
- **NonPrinting**—Sets whether the shape prints. If set to TRUE, the shape will not print. The default is FALSE.
- **NoObjHandles**—Sets whether the shape can be resized. If set to TRUE, the shape cannot be resized. The default is FALSE.

THE PROTECTION SECTION

Here are some of the fields in the Protection section, which specifies the locking behavior for the shape:

- **LockCalcWH**—Locks a shape's selection frame so that it will stay locked when vertices are edited.
- **LockCrop**—Locks an OLE object so that you can't use the Crop tool on it.
- **LockCustProp**—Locks shape data properties.
- **LockGroup**—Locks a group so that it can't be ungrouped.
- **LockVtxEdit**—Locks the vertices so that they can't be edited using the vertex editing tools.

THE ACTIONS SECTION

Here are some of the fields in the Actions section, which specifies the items on a shape's context menu:

- **Action**—Sets the action that occurs when the user selects this context menu item.
- **Checked**—Specifies whether an item is supposed to appear checked.
- **Disabled**—Specifies whether an item is supposed to appear disabled.
- **Menu**—Specifies the name of a menu item.

THE SHAPE DATA SECTION

Here are some of the fields in the Shape Data section, which specifies the shape data associated with a shape:

- **Ask**—Specifies whether you want Visio to ask users for shape data when they drop shapes. If set to TRUE, Visio asks.

- **SortKey**—Specifies the order with which shapes are sorted.
- **Type**—Specifies the property's data type.

Okay, that introduces what's available—now how about making use of it?

EDITING SHAPESHEET DATA

Everything in ShapeSheet fields is actually a formula—even if it looks like pure data. You can treat the value in the fields of a ShapeSheet as pure data, however, changing values as you want them, if you follow these steps:

1. Open the drawing you want to work on.
2. Select the shape whose data you want to change. Visio draws a selection frame around the shape, as shown for the square in Figure 9.12.

Figure 9.12
A selection frame around a square.

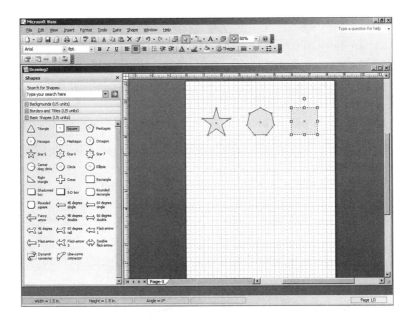

3. Select Window > Show ShapeSheet. Visio displays the ShapeSheet, as shown in Figure 9.13.
4. Select the Width field in the Shape Transform section. You can see this field selected in Figure 9.13.
5. Edit the value of the field by typing a new value. You can see 2.5 in entered in Figure 9.14.

   Note that for measurements like width measurements, you have to provide the units, so this value is 2.5 in for 2.5 inches.

Figure 9.13
The Microsoft Office Visio ShapeSheet window.

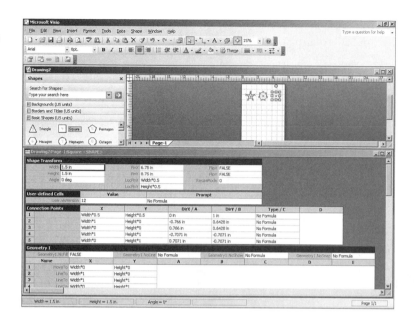

Figure 9.14
Editing a ShapeSheet field.

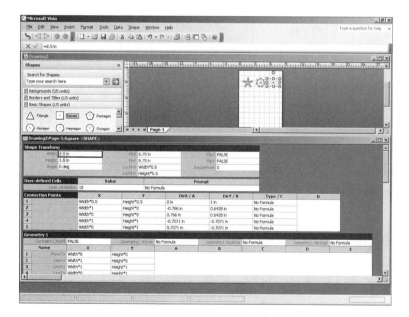

6. Press Enter. Visio removes the blinking cursor from the Width field and displays that field's new value, 2.5 in.

7. Close the ShapeSheet window by clicking its × button at the upper right. Visio removes the ShapeSheet window.

8. Maximize the drawing window by clicking its Maximize button (the square icon button). Visio displays the drawing window maximized, as shown in Figure 9.15.

Figure 9.15
A maximized drawing window.

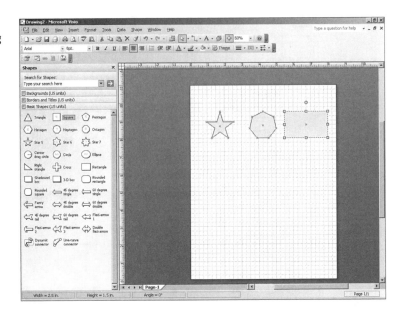

Note that the square now has a new width, as you can see in Figure 9.15.

Compare Figure 9.15 with Figure 9.12. You can see that the square's width really did increase—from 1.5 inches to 2.5 inches in this example.

As you can see, it's easy to change the data in a ShapeSheet's fields. But take a look at Figure 9.14, in the Connection Points section—you see fields containing values like `Width*0.5`. What's all that about?

That's an example of a Visio ShapeSheet formula, and that's our next topic, coming up now.

WORKING WITH VISIO SHAPESHEET FORMULAS

As already mentioned, every value you enter into a ShapeSheet field is considered a formula. Even when you enter a numeric value, like `2.5 in`, that's still considered a formula.

You can see this in Figure 9.14, by taking a look at the Visio formula bar, which appears below the other toolbars. The formula bar appears when you select a ShapeSheet in Visio (that is, when its title bar is darkened, indicating that it's been selected). While the value in the Width field simply reads `2.5 in`, you can see the formula nature of that value by looking in the formula bar, which reads `=2.5 in`.

That's a Visio formula, and it says that the Width value of the square shape is equal to 2.5 in. Visio adds the = sign if you don't enter it, and it's always there. As you can see, Visio is treating even your straight value, `2.5 in`, as part of a formula.

Visio formulas let you control just about everything there is about a shape—how it's resized, how it rotates, how the control handles move as it's resized, and more. You can learn a great deal more about Visio formulas if you go to the Visio developer's page, http://msdn.microsoft.com/visio (which currently redirects you to http://msdn2.microsoft.com/en-us/office/aa905478.aspx), and search for "ShapeSheet formula."

Visio formulas is a huge topic, and we'll get an introduction to it here. But we're only going to be able to scratch the surface.

There are four different entities you can use in Visio formulas: immediate values, operators, functions, and field references, and we'll take the time to discuss them next.

IMMEDIATE VALUES

You can insert immediate values into Visio formulas, as you've already seen with that `2.5 in`.

If you use only an immediate value, you should give it units if you're entering that value into a field that has units, such as Width or Height fields. Furthermore, you should restrict yourself to using the same type of units as the drawing itself uses—US units or metric units.

Some immediate values can use percent signs (%)—for example, Brightness fields can be set to percentage values, such as `50%`.

Not all values need units—for example, color values are simple numbers.

OPERATORS

You can use standard math operators like + and - in Visio formulas. Here are the most popular formula operators:

- **+** Addition
- **-** Subtraction
- ***** Multiplication
- **/** Division
- **^** Exponentiation

Here are a few examples (note that you can use parentheses to group operands):

```
=1.8 + 0.7
=2.9 * 4.5
=(1.5 - .03)/6.3
```

Here's how to use the exponentiation operator, ^, in squaring 7 to get 49:

```
=7^2
```

FUNCTIONS

There are hundreds of built-in functions in Visio, and you normally pass them data and they return a value.

For example, the RGB function returns color values. Here's how you would tell Visio that you want the color white, which has red, green, and blue values all set the maximum possible, 255:

```
RGB(255, 255, 255)
```

There are also math functions, which you pass data to, and they return a value. For example, you can use the SQRT function to calculate the square root of 49 like this:

```
SQRT(49)
```

Or here's how to take the tangent of 45°:

```
TAN(45 deg)
```

Here's how to take the inverse tangent (arc tangent) of 1.0:

```
ATAN(1.0)
```

Other functions perform some action. For example, the function

```
OPENTEXTWIN()
```

opens a shape's text window. You can use functions like OPENTEXTWIN() in the Events section of a ShapeSheet window; if you assign it to, for example, the EventDblClick field, then when the user double-clicks the shape, its text window opens.

There are also functions that emulate conditional statements from programming languages. For example, take a look at this Visio expression, which emulates an IF statement:

```
IF(AND(Angle>-60 deg,Angle<120 deg),0 deg,180 deg)
```

What does this mean? It uses the value in the ShapeSheet Shape Transform section's Angle field, and compares that value to –60° and to 120° using the AND function. If the value assigned to the Angle field is both greater than –60° and less than 120°, the AND function returns a value of TRUE.

You pass three values to the IF function: a TRUE/FALSE value, the value the IF function should return if the TRUE/FALSE value is TRUE, and the value IF should return if the TRUE/FALSE value is FALSE.

In other words, the expression IF(AND(Angle>-60 deg,Angle<120 deg),0 deg,180 deg) returns 0 deg if the value in the ShapeSheet section's Angle field is between –60° and 120°. On the other hand, if the value in the Angle field is outside the –60° to 120° range, the expression returns a value of 180 deg.

As you can see, Visio functions can be very powerful.

But what's this about referring to the contents of the Angle field? That's another very powerful part of Visio formulas—the capability to refer to the data held in other fields.

FIELD REFERENCES

When you're writing formulas, you frequently want to refer to the value in other fields. For example, you might want to relate the width of a shape to its height, which means you want to refer to the value in the Width field in the formula for the Height field.

For example, you might want to constrain the height to being half the width of a particular shape. If the ShapeSheet you're working with has a field named Width, for example, you might enter this for the formula for the Height field in a ShapeSheet:

```
=Width*0.5
```

That's how it works—if you're referring to another field in the same ShapeSheet, you can simply refer to it by name. Easy.

Some fields don't have names, however, but are specified by indexes. For example, take a look at the Connection Points and Geometry 1 sections in Figure 9.14. As you can see in that figure, the fields in those sections are stored in an Excel spreadsheet-like manner, with titles (X, Y, A, and so on) in the columns, and numbers (1, 2, 3, and so on) in the rows.

Those fields are called indexed fields, and instead of referring to them by name (they don't have any names) you refer to them using identifiers like X3 or Y2.

For example, if you wanted to refer to the data in the X3 field of the Geometry 1 section, you could do that like this:

```
Geometry1.X3
```

On the other hand, a reference from one shape to a field in another shape, page, master, or style requires a prefix that identifies the container of that field. You specify such a field by giving the container's name, followed by an exclamation point, and the field name, as shown here:

```
Couch1!Width
```

This reference specifies the Width in the Shape Transform section of the shape named Couch1.

Here's an example that takes the tangent of 90° minus the value in the Scratch section's A1 field (after converting the angle to radians), as well as using the MIN function to find the minimum of two values:

```
MIN((0.5*Height)*TAN(RAD(90-Scratch.A1)),0.45*Width)
```

MODIFYING AN ARROW SHAPE

Here's an example that uses ShapeSheets and formulas to correct a flaw you've found in arrow shapes. That is, when you resize an arrow shape, the arrowhead changes shape—and you might want to avoid that.

You can see this behavior of arrows in Figure 9.16—that's the arrow you start with.

When you resize the arrow, the shape of the arrow's head changes, as shown in Figure 9.17.

Figure 9.16
An arrow shape.

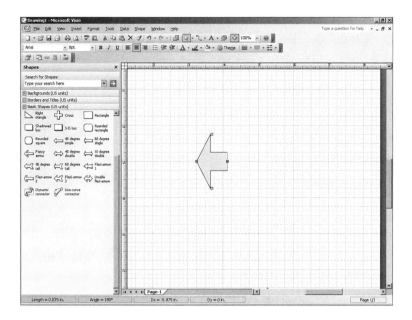

Figure 9.17
Resizing an arrow.

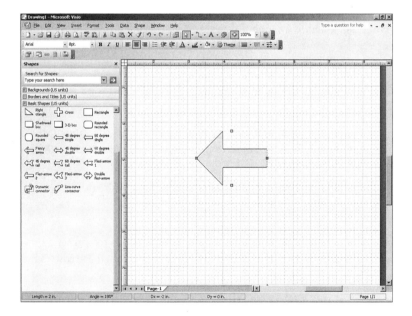

Now say that you don't want to tolerate this kind of behavior—you want to make sure that the arrowhead retains the same shape. How can you do that?

Just follow these steps:

1. Open a Visio drawing using the Basic Shapes template.

2. Open the Basic Shapes stencil.

3. Draw an arrow shape. You can see the new arrow shape in Figure 9.18.

Figure 9.18
Drawing an arrow shape.

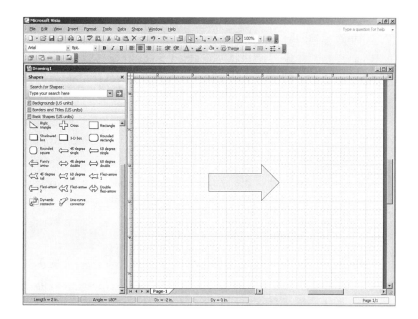

4. Select the arrow shape.
5. Select Window > Show ShapeSheet. Visio opens the ShapeSheet window, shown in Figure 9.19.

Figure 9.19
An arrow's ShapeSheet entries.

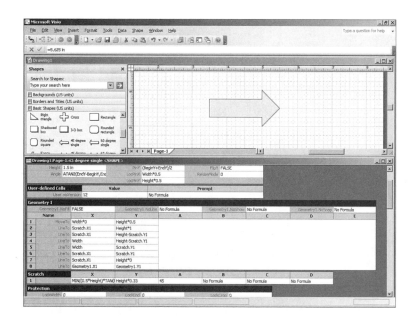

So far, this is a traditional arrow, which changes its head shape when resized. Now it's time to start editing the ShapeSheet formulas to alter the resizing behavior, which is done in the Geometry 1 section of the ShapeSheet.

6. Change the fields as specified here:

Change the X1 field of the Geometry 1 ShapeSheet section to Width*0.

Change the Y1 field of the Geometry 1 ShapeSheet section to Height*0.75.

Change the X2 field of the Geometry 1 ShapeSheet section to Width*0.

Change the Y2 field of the Geometry 1 ShapeSheet section to Height*0.25.

Change the X3 field of the Geometry 1 ShapeSheet section to Width-Height*0.5.

Change the Y3 field of the Geometry 1 ShapeSheet section to Height*0.25.

Change the X4 field of the Geometry 1 ShapeSheet section to Geometry1.X3.

Change the Y4 field of the Geometry 1 ShapeSheet section to Height*0.

Change the X5 field of the Geometry 1 ShapeSheet section to Width*1.

Change the Y5 field of the Geometry 1 ShapeSheet section to Height*0.5.

Change the X6 field of the Geometry 1 ShapeSheet section to Geometry1.X3.

Change the Y6 field of the Geometry 1 ShapeSheet section to Height*1.

Change the X7 field of the Geometry 1 ShapeSheet section to Geometry1.X3.

Change the Y7 field of the Geometry 1 ShapeSheet section to Height*0.75.

These edits give you the ShapeSheet shown in Figure 9.20.

Figure 9.20
An arrow's edited
ShapeSheet entries.

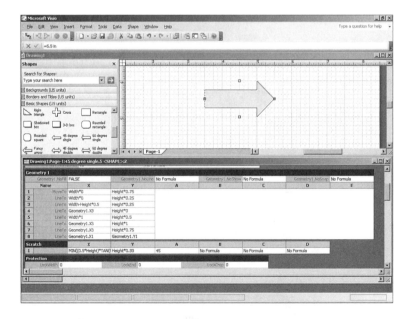

7. Now resize the arrow, as you see in Figure 9.21. Note that the head of the arrow stays the same.

Figure 9.21
Resizing the edited
arrow.

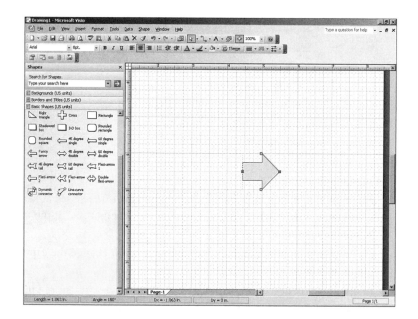

And that's it—now you've changed the resizing behavior of a Visio shape using Visio formulas.

Very cool.

MACROS

Macros give you a way of automating tasks in Visio. Using macros, you can automate common tasks.

For example, say that you have a set of toolbars that you customarily want to display for a particular type of drawing, but not for others. When you work on such a drawing, you might not want to take the time out to configure the toolbar just the way you want it.

Instead, you can create a macro. When you run that macro, Visio performs the task you want, adding the toolbars you want to the toolbar area. And it all happens automatically.

RECORDING MACROS

Want to create a macro? Follow these steps:

1. Open Visio.

2. Select Tools > Macro > Record New Macro. Visio opens the Record Macro dialog, shown in Figure 9.22.

3. Enter the name for your macro in the Macro name box. Visio starts by default with the name Macro1. The next macro is Macro2, and so on, by default, but you can enter your own name.

Figure 9.22
The Record Macro dialog.

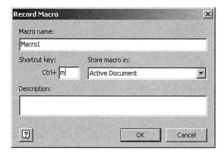

4. Enter a keyboard shortcut in the Ctrl+ box. This is the shortcut key that will launch your macro. For example, if you enter "m", as in Figure 9.23, the macro will run when you press Ctrl+m.

   If you enter a capital letter, such as "M", Visio will change the caption of the Ctrl+ box to Ctrl+Shift+.

5. Enter a document to store the macro in. Visio macros are stored in documents, and by default, the new macro is stored in the current document. You can select a document from the drop-down list box to store the macro where you want it.

6. Enter a description of the macro in the Description box. When you're looking for the right macro six months from now, it will help to be able to read the description you gave to your macros.

7. Click OK to start recording your macro. Visio closes the Record Macro dialog and starts recording the steps you take. Those steps will be recorded as your new macro.

   Visio next displays the Macro toolbar, as shown in Figure 9.23.

Figure 9.23
The Macro toolbar.

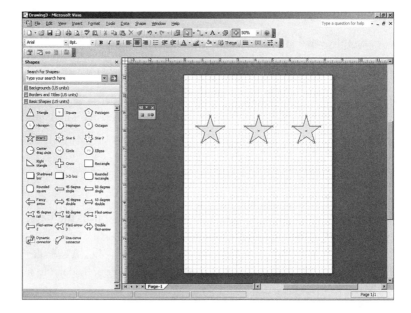

8. Perform the steps you want your macro to contain. For example, you might make Visio display the Drawing and Ink toolbars.

   Just follow your normal steps, executing those steps as you want Visio to execute them when you run your macro.

9. Click the Stop button on the Macro toolbar (the first button on the left) or select Tools > Macro > Stop Recording. Visio removes the Macro toolbar and stops recording.

10. To confirm that your new macro was created, select Tools > Macro > Macros. Visio displays the Macros dialog, shown in Figure 9.24.

Figure 9.24
The Macros dialog.

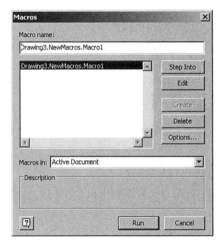

You can see the entry for the new macro in the Macros dialog, confirming that it was indeed recorded.

11. Click Cancel to close the Macros dialog (or click Run to run the macro).

That records your new macro. To run the macro, press your Ctrl-key shortcut.

For example, pressing Ctrl+m runs the macro you just created, displaying the Drawing and Ink toolbars, as shown in Figure 9.25.

You can also run a macro by selecting Tools > Macro > Macros, selecting the macro you want to run, and clicking the Run button.

You can also run macros by name. For example, the macro created in the preceding example was stored in the NewMacros folder, and it's named Macro1; so you can run it by selecting Tools > NewMacros > Macro1.

Figure 9.25
The result of running a macro.

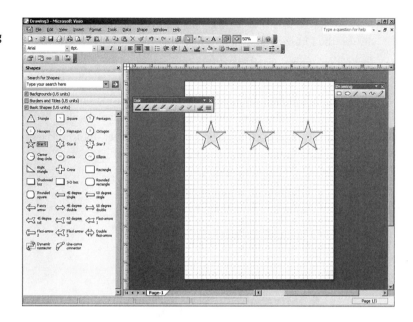

EDITING MACROS

If you know Visual Basic for Applications (VBA), you can edit and modify your macro directly.

Here's how to do that:

1. Open the drawing containing the macro you want to edit.
2. Select Tools > Macro > Macros. Visio displays the Macros dialog, shown in Figure 9.24.
3. Select the macro you want to edit and click the Edit button. Visio displays the Microsoft Visual Basic editor, shown in Figure 9.26.

   The Microsoft Visual Basic editor is made up of two panes:

   The Project Explorer pane at the left provides an overview of the project.

   The Code window at the right holds the VBA code to edit.
4. Make your edits in the Code window and select File > Close and Return to Visio. Visio closes the VBA editor and returns you to Visio.

You need to know VBA in order to make edits to macros in Visio. Here's how, for example, Macro1 is defined:

```
Sub Macro1()
' Keyboard Shortcut: Ctrl+m
'
    Application.CommandBars("Drawing").Visible = True
    Application.CommandBars("Ink").Visible = True

End Sub
```

Figure 9.26
The Microsoft Visual Basic editor.

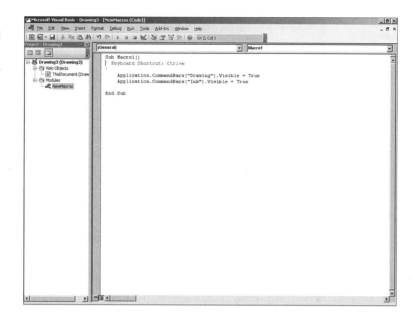

That is, Macro1 is defined as a subroutine here. Note that the keyboard shortcut here is defined in a comment: Keyboard Shortcut: Ctrl+m. And you can see how the toolbars are displayed—for example, to display the Drawing toolbar, you execute this VBA statement:

```
Application.CommandBars("Drawing").Visible = True
```

You can edit this macro if you know VBA. For example, to display the Reviewing toolbar as well, and to hide the Formatting toolbar, you might make these changes to Macro1:

```
Sub Macro1()
' Keyboard Shortcut: Ctrl+m
'
    Application.CommandBars("Reviewing").Visible = True
    Application.CommandBars("Drawing").Visible = True
    Application.CommandBars("Ink").Visible = True
    Application.CommandBars("Formatting").Visible = False

End Sub
```

RUNNING MACROS WITH DOUBLE-CLICKS

Want to set a shape's double-click behavior to run a macro? Just follow these steps:

1. Open the drawing containing the shape you want to have run a macro.
2. Select the shape.
3. Select Format > Behavior. Visio displays the Behavior dialog, shown in Figure 9.27.
4. Click the Double-Click tab. Visio displays the Double-Click tab, shown in Figure 9.27.
5. Select the Run Macro option's radio button.

Figure 9.27
The Behavior dialog.

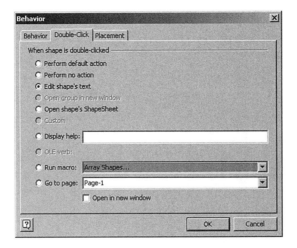

6. Select the macro you want to run when the shape is double-clicked. You make this selection in the drop-down list box next to the Run Macro radio button. Visio displays the macros accessible to the current document, and you can select one.

7. Click OK. Visio closes the Behavior dialog.

Now when you double-click the shape, the chosen macro will run.

USING VISIO'S PREDEFINED MACROS

Visio comes with a bunch of macros already defined, and you can run them easily. Curiously, you can't access these macros from the Tools > Macro set of menu items. You have to use the Behavior dialog instead.

Here are the predefined macros in Visio:

- Array Shapes
- Color by Values
- Convert CAD Drawings
- Convert CAD Library
- Database Export Wizard
- Database Refresh
- Database Settings
- Database Update
- Database Wizard
- Disable Space Plan
- Enable Space Plan
- Export Project Wizard

- Export to Database
- Import Project Wizard
- Import Data
- Label Shapes
- Link to ODBC Database
- Move Shapes
- Number Shapes
- Organization Chart Wizard
- Refresh Data
- Reports
- Shape Area and Perimeter
- Update Shapes

Want to use one of these predefined macros? Just do this:

1. Open the drawing containing the shape you want to have run a predefined macro.
2. Select the shape.
3. Select Format > Behavior. Visio displays the Behavior dialog.
4. Click the Double-Click tab. Visio displays the Double-Click tab.
5. Select the Run Macro option's radio button.
6. Select the predefined macro you want to run when the shape is double-clicked. You make this selection in the drop-down list box next to the Run Macro radio button.
7. Click OK. Visio closes the Behavior dialog.

For example, connecting a shape's double-click behavior to the Organization Chart Wizard launches that wizard when the shape is double-clicked, as shown in Figure 9.28.

Figure 9.28
Launching the
Organization Chart
Wizard.

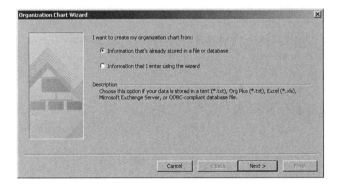

VIEW VISIO DRAWINGS WITH VISIO VIEWER 2007

If you want to share Visio drawings—not just images of those drawings—with others who don't actually have Visio on their machines, you can do it using the Visio Viewer.

The Visio Viewer is actually an ActiveX control that runs in Internet Explorer automatically when you launch a Visio Drawing, .vsd, file—if you don't have Visio on your machine.

You can get the Visio Viewer free from Microsoft at www.microsoft.com/downloads. Enter "Visio Viewer" in the search box, and follow the directions for downloading and installing the Visio Viewer. You can also save time if you have Internet Explorer 7+—the Visio Viewer is already built in.

TIP

If you do have Visio on your machine, and want to see the Visio Viewer at work, you'll need to temporarily disconnect Visio itself from opening files with the .vsd extension automatically. You can do that by opening Windows Explorer, selecting Tools > Folder Options, clicking the File Types tab, and editing the VSD entry so that Visio doesn't open .vsd files by default.

Using the Microsoft Office Visio Viewer 2007, you can open, view, or print Visio drawings—no need to have Visio installed. You cannot, however, edit, save, or create a new Visio drawing—you need Visio 2007 for that. The Visio Viewer can open Visio drawings from Visio 2000 and later—but note that drawings created by Visio 2007 can be opened only in the Visio Viewer 2007 ActiveX control.

TIP

You can also recommend to the people to whom you send Visio drawings that they download a free trial version of Visio. You can download free trial versions of Office Visio Standard 2007 or Office Visio Professional 2007. That's a handy solution if you want people to edit–as in adding markup to–your drawings.

VIEWING A DRAWING

If you want to open a Visio drawing in the Visio Viewer (and you don't have Visio on your machine), just double-click the Visio file. It will open in Internet Explorer.

Alternatively, you can drag the Visio file from Windows Explorer to Internet Explorer; or select File > Open in Internet Explorer, browse to the Visio file, select it, and click Open.

Note that the Visio Viewer doesn't display stencils, panes, rulers, guides, or guide points. Visio Viewer also doesn't display rotated pages, more than one hyperlink associated with a shape, hyperlinks associated with the drawing page, or drawing page properties.

And note that custom fill styles, line styles, and some line ends might not look the same in Visio Viewer as they do when you open the drawing with Visio itself.

MOVING AND ZOOMING A DRAWING

To move a drawing, just drag the drawing where you want it in the browser window. You can also use the scrollbars or press the arrow keys to move your drawing.

For that matter, you can also rotate the wheel button to move your drawing up and down, or press Shift and rotate the wheel button to move left and right.

Want to zoom a drawing in the Visio Viewer? Do any of these to zoom in:

- Right-click the drawing, and then click Zoom In.
- Click the Zoom In button on the Visio Viewer toolbar.
- Press Alt+F7.

- Press Ctrl+Shift and drag a rectangle around the area you want to zoom in on.
- Press Ctrl+Shift and click the point in the drawing you want to zoom in on.

To zoom out, you can perform any of these actions:

- Right-click the drawing, and then click Zoom Out.
- Click the Zoom Out button on the Visio Viewer toolbar.
- Press Alt+Shift+F7.
- Press Ctrl+Shift and right-click the point in the drawing you want to zoom in on.
- To zoom out and view the whole page in the Visio Viewer window, right-click the drawing, click Zoom, and then click Whole Page.

You can also zoom in or out of your drawing using a zoom percentage. To do that, follow these steps:

1. Right-click the drawing.
2. Select Zoom.
3. Select a zoom percentage, or choose a zoom percentage from the Zoom box on the Visio Viewer toolbar.

You can also center drawings in the Visio Viewer easily.

Just do one of the following:

- Right-click the drawing, click Zoom, and then click Whole Page.
- Click the Zoom Page button on the Visio Viewer toolbar.
- Drag your drawing to the center of the browser window.

MOVING TO A NEW PAGE

The Visio Viewer also has the capability to move from page to page. By default, only the first page is displayed, but you can move to other pages as well.

To do that, perform any of these actions:

- Click the page tab for the page you want to go to at the bottom of the drawing window.
- Right-click the drawing, click Go to Page, and then click the page you want.
- Drag your drawing to the center of the browser window.
- Press Ctrl+Page Down to move to the next page.
- Press Ctrl+Page Up to move to the previous page.

As you can see, the Visio Viewer supports multiple-page drawings, just as Visio itself does.

VIEWING SHAPE DATA

The Visio Viewer even lets you view—but not change—the shape data connected to shapes in Visio drawings.

Shape data appears in the Properties and Settings dialog on the Shape Properties tab. If this tab is blank, the shape doesn't include any data.

Note that you cannot add new data or modify existing shape data in the Visio Viewer. For that, you need Visio itself.

To view shape data, you can double-click a shape in the Visio drawing. You can also select a shape and press Enter.

In fact, you can even view shape data connected to shapes in a group, if you first select the individual shape you're interested in. To do that, follow these steps:

1. Ctrl-click the shape.
2. Ctrl-click the shape again.
3. Right-click the drawing and click Properties and Settings. The shape data appears.

PRINTING FROM THE VISIO VIEWER

You can print from the Visio Viewer—but note that you're actually printing from the Internet Explorer, not Visio itself.

To print a drawing, just click the Print button on the browser's toolbar.

Note that if you change any settings in the Print dialog box when printing from Internet Explorer, your drawing might print incorrectly. To avoid this, don't change any settings in the Print dialog box.

If you must change your printer settings, change them before you print, using the Page Setup dialog box.

When you print Visio drawings from your Web browser, the same zoom factor and center point used in your browser window are used on the printed page, so what you see on your monitor closely approximates what prints. You can check the Print Preview dialog (select File > Print Preview) before printing your drawing.

CUSTOMIZING THE VISIO VIEWER

There are various ways to customize the Visio Viewer. For example, you can make many changes in the Properties and Settings dialog.

To view that dialog, click the Properties and Settings button in the Visio Viewer toolbar. Or you can right-click the drawing, and then click Properties and Settings.

Here's what you can do in the Properties and Settings dialog:

- **Change the color of the drawing background**—Click the Display Settings tab, and then under Color Settings, select the color you want in the Drawing Background list.

- **Change the color of the drawing page**—Click the Display Settings tab, and then under Color Settings, select the color you want to use.

- **Hide a layer on the drawing page**—Click the Layer Settings tab, and then in the Show column, clear the check box for the layer you want to hide.

- **Change a layer color**—Click the Layer Settings tab, and then in the Color column, select the layer you want to display using color, and then select a layer color in the Layer Color list.

- **Hide all markup overlays for the drawing**—Click the Markup Settings tab, and then deselect the Show Markup Overlays check box.

- **Hide individual markup overlays for the drawing**—Click the Markup Settings tab, and then in the Show column, clear the check box for the markup overlay you want to hide.

- **Hide the Visio Viewer toolbar**—Click the Display Settings tab, and then under Show, deselect the Toolbar check box.

- **Hide the Visio Viewer page tabs**—Click the Display Settings tab, and then under Show, deselect the Page Tabs check box.

- **Hide the Visio Viewer scrollbars**—Click the Display Settings tab, and then under Show, deselect the Scroll Bars check box.

- **Show the page boundary for your drawing**—Click the Display Settings tab, and then under the Show area, select the Page check box.

- **Show the grid on the drawing page**—Click the Display Settings tab, and then under Show, select the Grid check box.

All of this is to say that the Visio Viewer is a powerful tool for use in distributing your drawings to people who don't have Visio—yet want to perform many of the (read-only) tasks you can perform with a full-fledged version of Visio.

And it's available to you free from Microsoft.

USING VISIO WITH SHAREPOINT

One good way of sharing Visio drawings with others is to use the Microsoft SharePoint server. You use that server through a Document Workspace in Visio, and the Document Workspace gives you a shared workspace that lets you share and work on files, as well as communicate with others.

If you have the appropriate permissions, you can create your own Document Workspace as a subsite of the SharePoint site. You can interact with others through the use of the Document Workspace.

9

CREATING A DOCUMENT WORKSPACE

How do you create a Document Workspace?

Follow these steps:

1. Open the drawing you want to share in Visio.
2. Select Tools > Document Management. Visio displays the Document Management pane, shown at right in Visio in Figure 9.29.

Figure 9.29
The Document
Management pane.

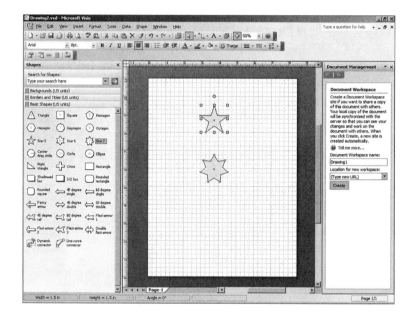

3. In the Document Workspace Name text box, enter a name for the new workspace.
4. In the Location for New Workspace box, enter the URL for the SharePoint site.
5. Click Create.
6. Click Members in the Document Management task pane, and click Add New Members.
7. Enter the names of the members you want to add to your workspace. Separate the names with semicolons.

You can also create a Document Workspace in a Windows SharePoint Services web site. Follow these steps:

1. Navigate to your SharePoint site in your Web browser.
2. Click Create on the site's Action menu.
3. Under Web Pages, click the Sites and Workspaces entry.

4. Enter a title, a description, and a URL.

5. In the Permissions section, select a permission setting.

6. In the Template Selection section, click the Collaboration tab and click Document Workspace.

7. Click Create.

HANDLING DRAWINGS WITH SHAREPOINT

How do you open a drawing when you're working with SharePoint?

Follow these steps:

1. Select File > Open.

2. In the Open dialog, click My Network Places.

3. Select the SharePoint site, and click Open.

4. Select the Visio file, and click Open. The drawing opens in Visio.

5. Make your changes to the drawing.

6. In the Document Updates task pane, click the Get Updates button. The drawing is in updated with changes made by other users.

You can also edit files directly from the SharePoint site. In the Document Workspace that holds the drawing you're interested in, right-click the drawing and select Edit.

CUSTOMIZING TOOLBARS AND MENUS

Visio gives you the option of customizing toolbars and menus, and you're going to see how that works now, starting with toolbars.

Being able to customize toolbars is great for power users, because they can make the buttons they want readily available.

Here's how to add a new button to a toolbar:

1. Open Visio.

2. Select Tools > Customize. Visio displays the Customize dialog, shown in Figure 9.30.

3. Click the Commands tab. Visio displays the Commands tab, shown in Figure 9.30.

   Toolbar buttons are taken from menu items. Visio displays the menus you can create buttons from in the left of the Commands tab, and the items in each menu on the right.

4. Select the menu you want to create a button from.

5. Drag the menu item to the toolbar you want to add it to. Visio displays an I-beam insertion caret in the toolbar where the new button is going to go, as you can see in Figure 9.31.

Figure 9.30
The Customize dialog.

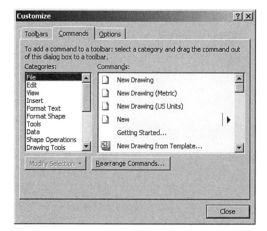

Figure 9.31
Dragging a new button to a toolbar.

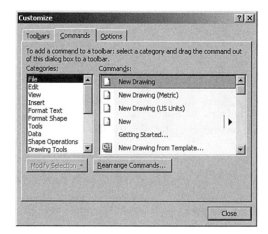

You can delete buttons from toolbars as well, following these steps:

1. Open Visio.

2. Select Tools > Customize. Visio displays the Visio Customize dialog.

3. Click the Commands tab.

4. Right-click the button (on the real toolbar, not in the Customize dialog) that you want Visio to remove from the toolbar.

5. Select Delete. Visio removes the button from the toolbar.

Note that you have to display the Customize dialog before removing a button from a toolbar—if you don't, you'll just see the normal selection of toolbars when you right-click a toolbar.

You can also rearrange buttons on existing toolbars. Just follow these steps:

1. Open Visio.

2. Select Tools > Customize. Visio displays the Customize dialog.

3. Click the Commands tab. Visio displays the Commands tab.

4. Drag the button you want to move on the toolbar to its new position. Visio displays the I-beam caret to show where the button will go, as shown in Figure 9.32.

5. Drop the button, which will appear in its new position in the target toolbar.

Figure 9.32
Moving a button in a toolbar.

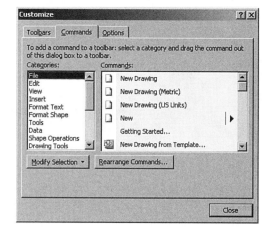

In fact, you can create your own toolbars. Open the Customize dialog and click the Toolbars tab to do that. Click the New button, and enter the name of your new toolbar. Click OK. Then add buttons to the new toolbar as discussed previously.

Okay, how about customizing menus?

Want to add a new command to a menu? Here's how you do that:

1. Open Visio.

2. Select Tools > Customize. Visio displays the Customize dialog.

3. Click the Commands tab. Visio displays the Commands tab, shown earlier in Figure 9.30.

   Visio displays the categories you can create menu items from in the left of the Commands tab, and the items in each category on the right.

4. Select the menu item you want to add to a menu.

5. Drag the menu item to the menu you want to add it to. Visio displays an I-beam insertion caret in the toolbar where the new menu item is going to go, as shown in Figure 9.33.

Figure 9.33
Dragging a new item
to a menu.

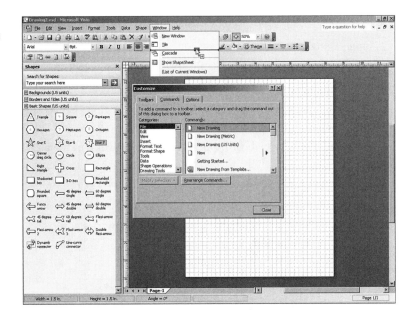

You can also delete menu items:

1. Open Visio.
2. Select Tools > Customize. Visio displays the Visio Customize dialog.
3. Click the Commands tab.
4. Right-click the menu item you want Visio to remove from the menu.
5. Select Delete. Visio removes the item from the menu.

And you can rearrange menu items on existing menus. Just follow these steps:

1. Open Visio.
2. Select Tools > Customize. Visio displays the Customize dialog.
3. Click the Commands tab. Visio displays the Commands tab.
4. Drag the item in the menu—or the menu in the menu bar—to its new position. Visio displays the I-beam caret to show where the menu or menu item will go, as shown in Figure 9.34.
5. Drop the menu or menu item, which then appears in its new position in the target menu bar or menu.

Figure 9.34
Moving an item in a menu.

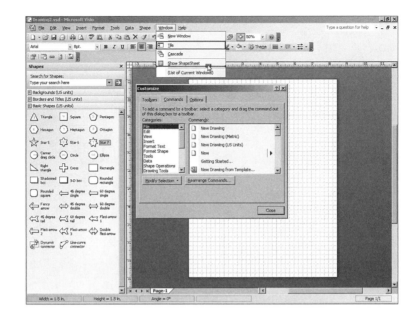

You can also create your own menus. Open the Customize dialog and click the Commands tab to do that. Select the New Menu category, and drag the New Menu item to the menu bar or toolbar. Finally, add menu items to the new menu as discussed previously.

Visio with Other Applications

10

IMPORTING AND EXPORTING DATA

Why import or export data in Visio? There are plenty of reasons. For example, you might already have data you want to display stored in a database file, or a spreadsheet. You might update that file and want to update your shapes based on that data.

You might also want to avoid errors, and working with external, checkable files can be the way to go here. If some external checks exist on your data, you've got a leg up on Visio.

There are many features built into Visio for importing and exporting data—data links, database wizards, export wizards, and the like. You're going to see those features in this chapter.

Some types of drawings have built-in techniques for importing and exporting data, and we'll start by taking a look at those—beginning with importing data into organization charts.

CREATING ORGANIZATION CHARTS FROM EXTERNAL DATA

Organization charts provide a good example of how to import data from external sources. You might, for example, maintain the organization data for your company in an Excel worksheet, or a Microsoft Access database file, and want to import it using Visio.

Because linking to external data is such a common thing to do for Visio organization charts, there's a special wizard that takes care of this process—the Organization Chart Wizard.

IMPORTING ORGANIZATION CHART DATA INTO VISIO

Say, for example, that you had this data in an Excel worksheet, `organization.xls`:

Unique_ID	Department	E-mail	Name	Telephone	Title	Reports_To	Master_Shape
ID1	Sales	george@ddrr.com	George	4552	CEO		0
ID2	Sales	sue@ddrr.com	Sue	4553	Director	ID1	1
ID3	Sales	ed@ddrr.com	Ed	4554	Director	ID1	1
ID4	Sales	james@ddrr.com	James	4555	Director	ID1	1

You can import this data and make an organization chart out of it by following these steps:

1. Open Visio.
2. Select File > New > Business Organization Chart Wizard. This opens the Organization Chart Wizard shown in Figure 10.1.

Figure 10.1
The Organization
Chart Wizard.

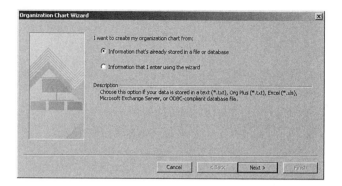

3. To import data, select the Information That's Already Stored in a File or Database radio button. You can see this radio button selected in Figure 10.1.

4. Click Next. Visio displays the next pane of the Organization Chart Wizard, as shown in Figure 10.2.

Figure 10.2
The Organization
Chart Wizard, second
pane.

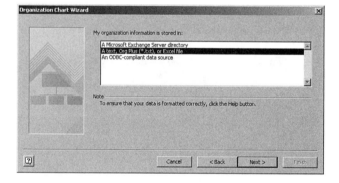

5. Select the type of data source you have. You can see the entry for Excel files selected in Figure 10.2.

   Select the data source appropriate for you:

   • **A Microsoft Exchange Server Directory.** Visio will look on your system to find matches, and let you select from among them.

   • **A Text, Org Plus (*.txt) or Excel File.** Use this option when you're reading data from text or Excel files.

   • **An ODBC-Compliant Data Source.** You can select any ODBC-compliant data source, such as Microsoft Access.

6. Click Next. Visio displays the next pane of the Organization Chart Wizard, as shown in Figure 10.3.

Figure 10.3
The Organization
Chart Wizard, third
pane.

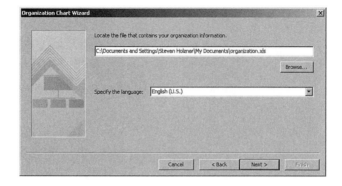

7. Follow the Wizard's steps to connect to the data source. The steps you follow will depend on the data source. For example, you can see in Figure 10.3 that the third pane of the Organization Chart Wizard asks for the location of the Excel worksheet, if you've indicated that you want to get your data from an Excel worksheet.

8. When you're done giving Visio the information it needs to connect to a data source, click Next. Visio displays the next pane of the Organization Chart Wizard, as shown in Figure 10.4.

Figure 10.4
The Organization
Chart Wizard, fourth
pane.

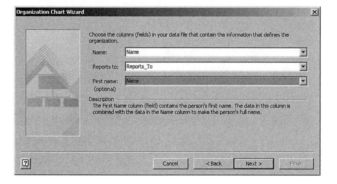

Here, Visio is trying to work with you to get the names of the people from your data and who they report to—needed information for an organization chart.

Because the sample Excel worksheet in this example already contains Name and Reports_To fields, Visio's job is easier here—it suggests those fields already, as shown in Figure 10.4.

9. Click Next. Visio displays the next pane of the Organization Chart Wizard, as shown in Figure 10.5.

Figure 10.5
The Organization Chart Wizard, fifth pane.

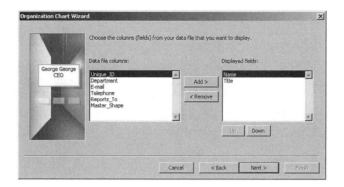

Here, Visio is asking which data you want to display. Organization charts usually display the person's name and title, so you can see those two items selected in the figure.

If you want to display any other fields, select them in the left box, labeled Data File Columns, and click the Add button.

To remove fields, select them in the Displayed Fields box and click Remove.

10. Click Next. Visio displays the next pane of the Organization Chart Wizard, as shown in Figure 10.6.

Figure 10.6
The Organization Chart Wizard, sixth pane.

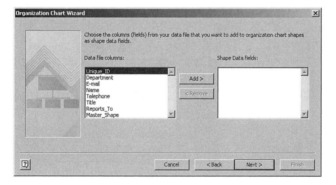

Here, Visio is asking which shape data you want to create.

You can use the data from your data source as shape data, if you want. Just select the fields you want to use as shape data and click the Add button to add them to the Shape Data Fields box.

We're not going to use any data from the Excel worksheet as shape data in this example, so no data has been added to the Shape Data Fields box in Figure 10.6.

11. Click Next. Visio displays the next pane of the Organization Chart Wizard, as shown in Figure 10.7.

Figure 10.7
The Organization
Chart Wizard, sev-
enth pane.

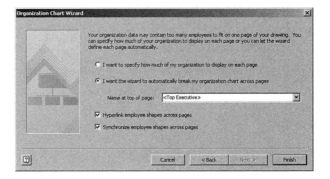

Now Visio is asking what to do if it needs to break up your chart among multiple pages. In this example, we'll just accept the defaults.

12. Click Finish. Visio displays the new organization chart, as shown in Figure 10.8.

Figure 10.8
The organization
chart.

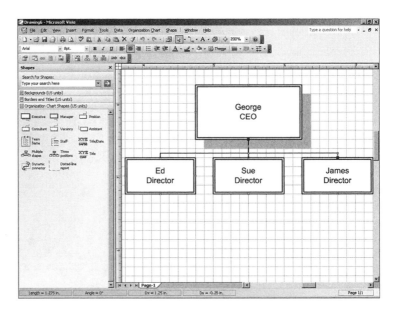

That's how the Organization Chart Wizard works—as you can see, it's a useful tool, letting you import organization data into Visio.

You can also open the Organization Chart Wizard when you're working on an organization chart by selecting Organization Chart > Import Organization Data.

EXPORTING ORGANIZATION CHART DATA FROM VISIO

The data in organization charts can go both ways: You can import it and you can also export it. That's handy when you've created an organization chart and want to export it to, say, Excel.

Here's how to export the data in an organization chart:

1. Open the organization chart you want to export.

2. Select Organization Chart > Export Organization Data. This opens the Export Organization Data dialog shown in Figure 10.9.

Figure 10.9
The Export Organization Data dialog.

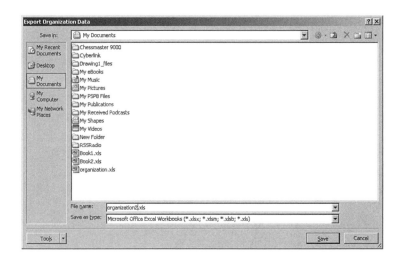

Visio lets you save organization chart data in Excel worksheets.

3. Enter the name of the Excel worksheet you want to create in the File Name box.

4. Click Save. Visio exports your data and saves it.

That saves the organization chart's data in an Excel worksheet something like this:

Unique_ ID	Depart- ment	E-mail	Name	Tele- phone	Title	Reports_ To	Master_ Shape
ID1	Sales	george@ddrr.com	George	4552	CEO		0
ID2	Sales	sue@ddrr.com	Sue	4553	Director	ID1	1
ID3	Sales	ed@ddrr.com	Ed	4554	Director	ID1	1
ID4	Sales	james@ddrr.com	James	4555	Director	ID1	1

CREATING GANTT CHARTS FROM EXTERNAL DATA

Gantt charts display schedules, and they're also a type of chart that you can import data into in Visio.

Say for example, that you had this Excel worksheet, `gantt.xls`:

Task #	Task Name	Duration	Start Date	Finish Date	Dependency	Resource	Outline Level	% Complete	Task Notes	Actual Start
1	Task 1	1	7/19/2007 8:00				1	0		7/19/2007 8:00
2	Task 2	1	7/19/2007 8:00				1	0		7/19/2007 8:00
3	Task 3	1	7/19/2007 8:00				1	0		7/19/2007 8:00
4	Task 4	1	7/19/2007 8:00				1	0		7/19/2007 8:00
5	Task 5	1	7/19/2007 8:00				1	0		7/19/2007 8:00

How would you use that data to create a Gantt chart in Visio?

IMPORTING GANTT CHART DATA INTO VISIO

All you need to do is to follow these steps:

1. Open Visio.
2. Select File > New > Schedule > Gantt Chart. This opens the Gantt Chart Options dialog, shown in Figure 10.10.

Figure 10.10
Creating a Gantt chart.

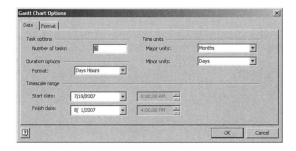

3. Select the options you want for the Gantt chart.

   Choose from the number of tasks, the units, the duration format, the start and end dates, and so on.
4. Click OK. Visio creates the new Gantt chart.
5. Select Gantt Chart > Import. Visio opens the Import Project Data Wizard, shown in Figure 10.11.
6. Select the Information That's Already Stored in a File option. You can see that option selected in Figure 10.11.
7. Click Next. Visio displays the second pane of the Import Project Data Wizard, as shown in Figure 10.12.

ctual nish	Actual Duration	User Defined Number	User Defined Time	User Defined Text 1	User Defined Text 2	User Defined Text 3	User Defined Text 4	User Defined Text 5	User Defined Decimal	User Defined Duration
		0	7/19/2007 10:40						0	0
		0	7/19/2007 10:40						0	0
		0	7/19/2007 10:40						0	0
		0	7/19/2007 10:40						0	0
		0	7/19/2007 10:40						0	0

10

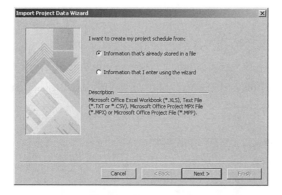

Figure 10.11
The Import Project Data Wizard.

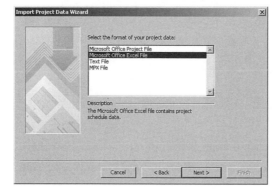

Figure 10.12
The Import Project Data Wizard, second pane.

In this pane, you select the format of the data you want to import from these options:

Microsoft Office Project File

Microsoft Office Excel File

Text File

MPX File

In this example, select Microsoft Office Excel File, as shown in Figure 10.12.

8. Click Next. Visio displays the third pane of the Import Project Data Wizard, as shown in Figure 10.13.

Figure 10.13
The Import Project Data Wizard, third pane.

The specifics in this pane are going to depend on what format your data is in. For Microsoft Excel worksheets, navigate to the worksheet in this pane.

9. Click Next. Visio displays the fourth pane of the Import Project Data Wizard, as shown in Figure 10.14.

Figure 10.14
The Import Project Data Wizard, fourth pane.

Here, Visio lets you set the time scale options for the Gantt chart. Set these options:

- **Major Units.** Select from these options: Days, Weeks, Months, Quarters, or Years.

- **Minor Units.** Select from these minor units options: Hours, Days, and Weeks.

- **Format.** Select from these format options: Weeks, Days, Hours, Days Hours, Weeks Days, and Weeks Hours.

10. Click Next. Visio displays the fifth pane of the Import Project Data Wizard, as shown in Figure 10.15.

Figure 10.15
The Import Project Data Wizard, fifth pane.

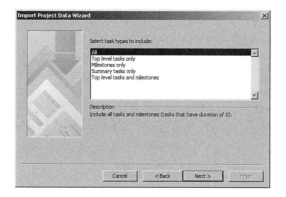

Here, Visio lets you set the task types to include for the Gantt chart. Select from these options:

> All
>
> Top Level Tasks Only
>
> Milestones Only
>
> Summary Tasks Only
>
> Top Level Tasks and Milestones

11. Click Next. Visio displays the sixth pane of the Import Project Data Wizard, as shown in Figure 10.16.

Figure 10.16
The Import Project Data Wizard, sixth pane.

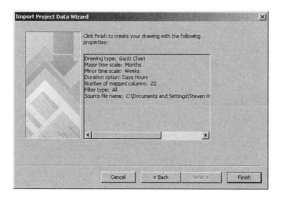

Visio displays a summary of your choices.

12. Click Finish. Visio creates the new Gantt chart for you, as shown in Figure 10.17.

And that's it—now you're able to import data to form Gantt charts.

Figure 10.17
A new Gantt chart

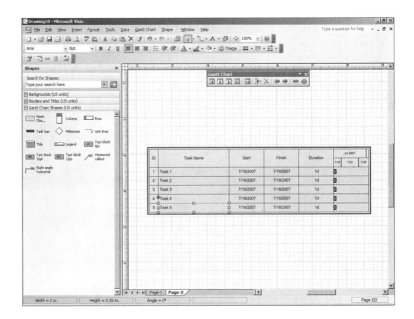

EXPORTING GANTT CHART DATA FROM VISIO

You can also export Gantt chart data from Visio in formats readable by other applications. Here's how to do that:

1. Open the Gantt chart in Visio. Visio creates the new Gantt chart for you, as shown in Figure 10.17.

2. Select Gantt Chart > Export. Visio opens the Export Project Data Wizard, as shown in Figure 10.18.

Figure 10.18
The Export Project Data Wizard.

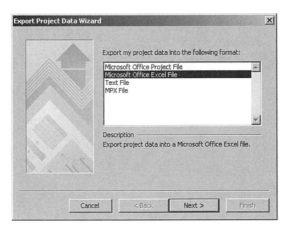

Select the format of the data you want to export:

Microsoft Office Project File

Microsoft Office Excel File

Text File

MPX File

3. Click Next. Visio opens the Export Project Data Wizard's second pane, as shown in Figure 10.19.

Figure 10.19
The Export Project Data Wizard, second pane.

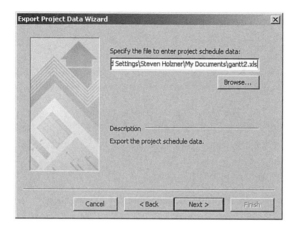

Specify the filename and path of the name of the file you want to save.

4. Click Next. Visio opens the Export Project Data Wizard's third pane, as shown in Figure 10.20.

Figure 10.20
The Export Project Data Wizard, third pane.

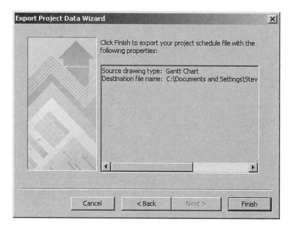

In this pane of the Export Project Wizard, Visio gives you a summary of the options you've selected.

5. Click Finish. Visio creates the export file and displays a dialog explaining that the file has been created.

6. Click OK to dismiss the dialog box.

And that's all you need—now you can export Gantt chart data.

There's another type of drawing that Visio enables importing and exporting with—calendars.

CREATING CALENDARS BY IMPORTING MICROSOFT OUTLOOK APPOINTMENTS

You can also import data from Microsoft Outlook or Vista's Calendar application to Visio, storing that data in a Visio calendar drawing. Doing so can give you a graphic display of your appointments.

Doing so gives you the ability to reformat the calendar data in a more pleasing way, as well as publish it to the Web, print it, and add special effects such as clip art.

IMPORTING CALENDAR DATA FROM OUTLOOK

You can only import calendar data in Visio—you can't export it. Here's how the importation process works:

1. Open Visio.

2. Select File > New > Schedule > Calendar. Visio creates a new calendar drawing, as shown in Figure 10.21.

Figure 10.21
A new calendar drawing.

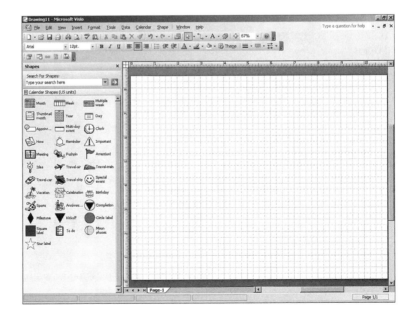

3. Select Calendar > Import Outlook Data Wizard. Visio displays the Import Outlook Data Wizard, as shown in Figure 10.22.

Figure 10.22
The Import Outlook Data Wizard.

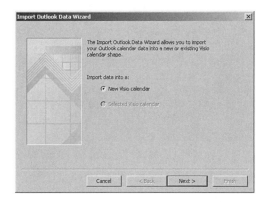

Select the New Visio Calendar radio button.

4. Click Next. Visio displays the Import Outlook Data Wizard's second pane, as shown in Figure 10.23.

Figure 10.23
The Import Outlook Data Wizard, second pane.

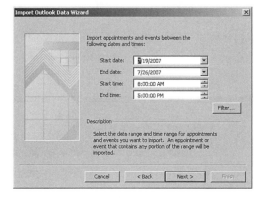

Select the starting and ending dates and times for the calendar you want to create.

5. Click Next. Visio displays the Import Outlook Data Wizard's third pane, as shown in Figure 10.24.

   Configure your Visio calendar in this pane, selecting calendar type, whether or not to shade weekends, and so on.

6. Click Next. Visio displays the Import Outlook Data Wizard's fourth pane, as shown in Figure 10.25.

   Visio displays a summary of your choices in this pane.

7. Click Finish. Visio creates the new calendar drawing, as shown in Figure 10.26.

10

Figure 10.24
The Import Outlook Data Wizard, third pane.

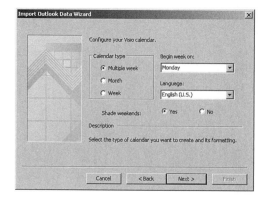

Figure 10.25
The Import Outlook Data Wizard, fourth pane.

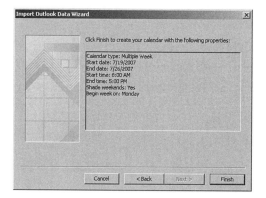

Figure 10.26
A new calendar.

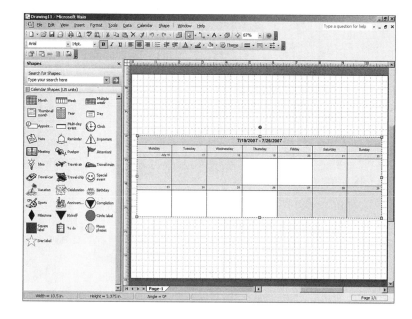

LINKING SHAPES TO DATA WITH DATA LINKS

Data links exist in Visio for one reason: to push data from external sources to your shapes. That is, data links provide shape data for your shapes from external sources.

They're more general than the examples you've already seen in this chapter—organization charts, Gantt charts, and calendars, each of which have specific import/export wizards. Data links let you link external data to shape data in a general way, no matter what the drawing you're creating is.

Using data links, you can connect data from these sources to shapes:

- Microsoft Office Excel workbook
- Microsoft Office Access database
- Microsoft Windows SharePoint Services list
- Microsoft SL Server database
- Other OLEDB or ODBC data source
- Previously created connection

10

> **TIP**
>
> Note that data links go only one way: directing data from external sources into your shapes. To go the other way—to send data from shapes to external data sources—you can use a database wizard in Visio, which is coming up.

CREATING DATA LINKS

Let's get started with data links. Say for example that you start with the organization chart shown in Figure 10.27. Without using the Organization Chart Wizard, how could you connect data from external sources to the various shapes in the figure?

Here's how to link data to the shapes shown in Figure 10.27, using the Visio data link feature:

1. Select Data > Link Data to Shapes. Visio displays the Data Selector dialog, as shown in Figure 10.28.
2. Select the type of your data source and click Next. Visio displays the second pane of the Data Selector dialog, as shown in Figure 10.29.

   What is actually displayed in the second pane depends on the data format you've selected in the first pane. Here's what you can expect to see, depending on the selection you made in the first pane of the Data Selector dialog:

   - **Microsoft Office Excel Workbook.** Select the workbook to use and click Next. In the next pane, you can select a range of cells—select the range and click Select Custom Range.
   - **Microsoft Office Access Database.** Select the Access database you want to use. In the What Tables Do You Want to Import drop-down list, select the table you want to work with and click Next. If your database has only one table, Visio selects that table automatically, by default.

Figure 10.27
A new organization chart.

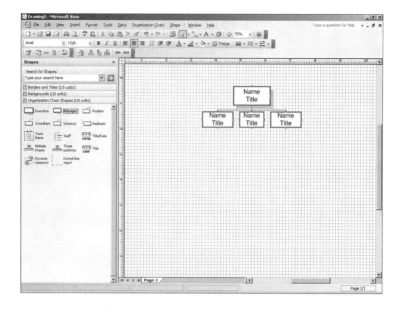

Figure 10.28
The Data Selector dialog.

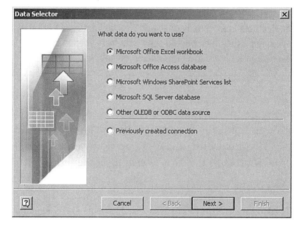

Figure 10.29
The Data Selector dialog, second pane.

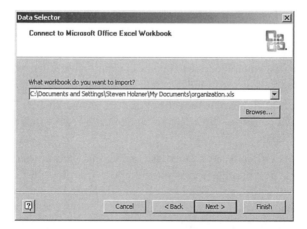

- **Microsoft Windows SharePoint Services List.** In the Site box, enter the SharePoint URL that holds the list you want to link to. Then click Next.

- **Microsoft SQL Server Database.** When you want to use a SQL Server database, you have to specify the location of the server, and your authentication credentials. You can use Windows authentication as well, which automatically uses your Windows username and password. After you've connected to the SQL server, select the database you want to use, and then select the table to use.

- **Other OLEDB or ODBC Data Source.** First, select the specific type of data source; then, select the file and database table.

- **Previously Created Connection.** Select the previously created connection from the drop-down list and click Next.

In this example, we'll use an Excel worksheet to supply data to the organization chart shapes, as shown in Figure 10.29.

After clicking Next, you can see the third pane of the Data Selector dialog, as shown in Figure 10.30, which asks you to select the worksheet or range of cells to use.

10

Figure 10.30
The Data Selector dialog, third pane.

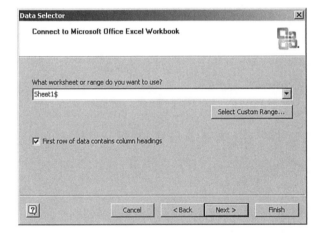

Make your selection and click Next, opening the fourth pane of the Data Selector dialog, as shown in Figure 10.31, which asks you to select the columns and rows to use.

3. Select the columns and rows to use and click Next. By default, Visio assumes you're going to use all columns and all rows, as shown in Figure 10.31.

To select rows or columns specifically, click the Select Rows or Select Columns button, and make your selection(s).

You can see the Select Columns dialog in Figure 10.32.

4. Click Next. Visio displays the fifth pane of the Data Selector dialog, as shown in Figure 10.33.

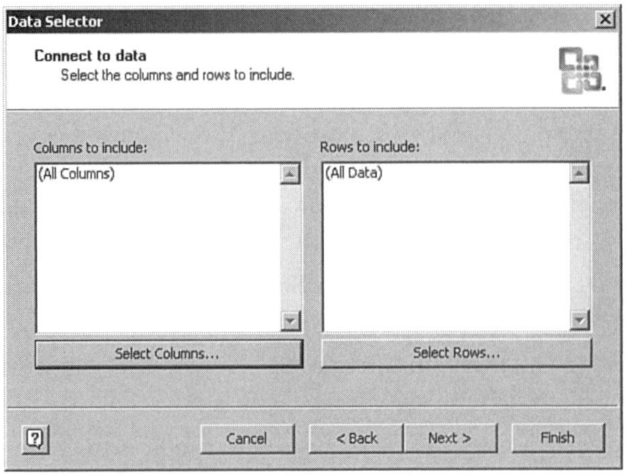

Figure 10.31
The Data Selector
dialog, fourth pane.

Figure 10.32
The Select Columns
dialog.

Figure 10.33
The Data Selector
dialog, fifth pane.

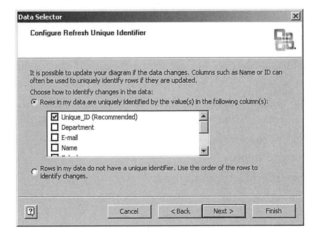

In this pane, you can select the fields that uniquely identify your records. When you tell Visio what the unique identifier is for each record, it can update the linked data.

5. Click Next. Visio displays the sixth pane of the Data Selector dialog, as shown in Figure 10.34.

Figure 10.34
The Data Selector dialog, sixth pane.

This pane tells you that you've been successful—or, if you haven't been successful, lets you know what the problem is.

6. Click Finish. Visio closes the Data Selector dialog, and opens the External Data window and the Data toolbar, as shown in Figure 10.35.

Figure 10.35
The External Data window.

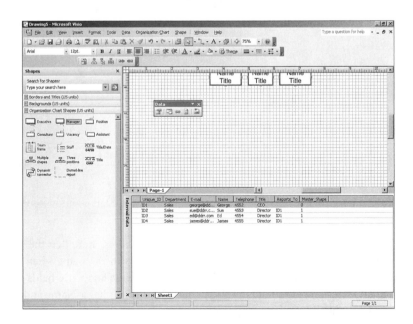

Okay, that makes the external data available to your drawing in the External Data window.

How do you actually connect the rows of data you see in the External Data window to the shapes on the drawing surface?

That's coming up next.

CONNECTING DATA TO SHAPES

There are two ways to link the data in an External Data window to the shapes in your drawings: manually and automatically.

LINKING DATA MANUALLY

Linking data manually is easy—just drag the row you want to link to a shape to the shape itself.

You can see an example in Figure 10.36, where the data for the CEO, George, has been dragged to the top (executive) shape.

Figure 10.36
Dragging data from the External Data window.

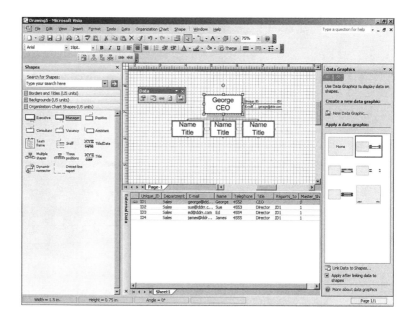

All you have to do is to drag a row from the External Data window to the shape you want to link it to.

There are a couple of things to note here. For one thing, note that the shape data that the shape is designed to use is automatically put to work in the shape when you drop a row onto the shape. In Figure 10.36, you can see the Name and Title fields reflected in the shape; because this is an organization chart, each shape has a Name and Title field, and the data from the dropped row appears in the shape.

That's the way it works: If a shape has a particular named field (check its ShapeSheet to find the names of a shape's fields) that's also a field in the dropped row, Visio attempts to assign the shape's field the value in the dropped row.

That works well with the text in the Name and Title fields in this example. You can see that the dropped data is put to work immediately: the Name and Title text appear in the target shape.

But there are all kinds of data you can drop onto shapes—for example, the color of the shape. Or its width, or height. When you drop a row with fields that have the same name as fields in the shape's data, Visio attempts to use that data in the shape.

Note also in Figure 10.36 that a link icon (a short length of chain) appears next to the top row in the External Data window. That icon appears anytime you drag a row onto a shape and a data link is created.

Finally, note that Visio opens the Data Graphics pane at right in Figure 10.36 when you drop a row onto a shape. Data Graphics help you visualize the data connected with a shape—more on Data Graphics is coming up in this chapter as well.

LINKING DATA AUTOMATICALLY

If you've got many shapes and many rows of data, you might want to link data to your shapes automatically. That works if you've got a shape data property for the field that uniquely identifies records in the external data source.

Here's how to link data to shapes automatically:

1. Open the drawing in which you want to set up automatic links in Visio.

2. Edit the shape data of the shapes you want to connect to the data source. When you do so, make sure that they each have a unique ID field, and a value for that field that matches the value in the same field of the data you're going to connect. To add data to shapes, select the shapes and then select the Data > Shape Data menu item.

   To create a new field of shape data, click the Define button and define your new field by setting its name, format type, and value.

   Then click OK.

   Next, select each of the other shapes you want to assign a similar ID to, and select Data > Shape Data, then enter the value for the field for each shape (if the shapes were selected when you added the unique ID field to the first shape, they will already have that field added to their shape data).

   Make sure that the value of the shape data field you've added for every shape matches the value in a field of the same name of the rows you're connecting to.

   For example, you might add a field named Unique_ID to every shape in a drawing, and assign a unique value to each shape's Unique_ID field. Then the data from the rows in the External Data window that have values in a field named Unique_ID that match the Unique_ID of the shapes will be assigned to those shapes.

3. Connect to an external data source using the Data Selector dialog, as discussed previously.

4. Select Data > Automatically Link, or click the Automatically Link button in the Data toolbar (the button third from the left in the Data toolbar). Visio opens the Automatic Link dialog shown in Figure 10.37.

Figure 10.37
The Automatic Link dialog.

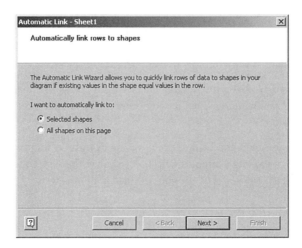

This pane asks what shapes you want to link automatically to your data.

If you've selected shapes in your drawing, Visio selects the Selected Shapes radio button. Otherwise, Visio selects the All Shapes on This Page radio button.

5. Click Next. Visio opens the Automatic Link dialog's second pane, shown in Figure 10.38.

Figure 10.38
The Automatic Link dialog, second pane.

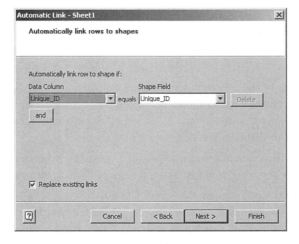

This pane lets you select the unique field that ties the data you're connecting to your shapes.

Select the unique field that ties the external data to the shapes in your drawing. The field need not have the same name in the external data and your shapes—you can select the name in the external data (that's the Data Column drop-down list box) and then select the name of the field in the shape data (that's the Shape Field) drop-down list box, as shown in the figure.

Visio will make a guess as to which field you want to connect to which field in the shape data.

Bear in mind that the shapes in your drawing should already have values assigned to this identifying field so that Visio knows which row to connect to which shape.

6. Click Next. Visio opens the Automatic Link dialog's third pane, shown in Figure 10.39.

Figure 10.39
The Automatic Link dialog, third pane.

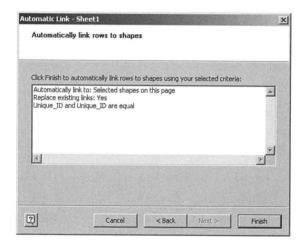

This pane gives you a summary of the options you've selected, such as making sure that the Unique_ID field values match in the row data and the target shape.

7. Click Finish. Visio closes the Automatic Link dialog.

You can see the results in Figure 10.40.

Note that every shape in the organization chart has been assigned data from a row in the External Data window—and that every row in that window now has a link icon displayed (this icon is a few links of chain).

And that's how automatic data linking works—as long as your shapes have a uniquely identifying field, and a unique value in that field (shared by no other shape), and each row in the data you're linking to has a unique value in that field as well, you're set.

You can also add new shapes to drawings with built-in data links.

Figure 10.40
Automatically linked data.

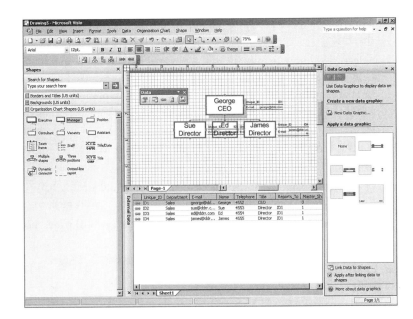

ADDING NEW SHAPES WITH BUILT-IN DATA LINKS

You can add new shapes—with built-in data links—to a drawing.

Just follow these steps:

1. Open the drawing you want to add new data-lined shapes to in Visio.
2. Select the shape you want to add in the stencil. Just select the shape—don't drag it.
3. Drag the data row to which you want to link data from the External Data window to the drawing surface.
4. Release the mouse button. Visio creates the newly linked shape for you on the drawing surface.

   The new shape will be of the type of shape that you've selected in the stencil, and will use the data from the row that you dragged to the drawing surface.

In fact, you can also create multiple shapes, using multiple rows of data at the same time.

Here's how to do it:

1. Open the drawing you want to add new data-lined shapes to in Visio.
2. Select the shape you want to add in the stencil. Just select the shape—don't drag it.
3. Select the data rows you want to create new shapes from. You can select multiple rows by holding down the Ctrl key and clicking them, or a range of rows by selecting one row, holding down the Shift key, and clicking the row at the other end of the range you want to select.

4. Drag the rows to which you want to link data from the External Data window to the drawing surface.

5. Release the mouse button. Visio creates the newly linked shapes for you on the drawing surface.

   The new shapes will be of the type of shape that you've selected in the stencil, and will use the data from the rows that you dragged to the drawing surface.

Very cool.

REFRESHING LINKED DATA

You can also refresh linked data. For example, say that someone edits the data in a linked-to source—you probably want that change to be reflected in your shape's data. Here's what to do:

1. Open the drawing in which you want to refresh the data connected to shapes in Visio.

2. Select Data > Refresh Data. The Refresh Data dialog appears, as shown in Figure 10.41.

Figure 10.41
The Refresh Data
dialog.

3. Select the data source that you want to use to refresh the linked-to data from.

4. Click Refresh. Visio refreshes the data and lists the Progress as Completed, as shown in Figure 10.42.

5. Click Close. Visio hides the Refresh Data dialog, and you're done—the data in your drawing has been refreshed.

You can also set up periodic data refreshes to happen automatically. That's useful if your data changes periodically and you want to be kept up-to-date.

Here's how to refresh linked-to data on a schedule:

1. Open the drawing in which you want to set up a data-refresh schedule in Visio.

2. Select Data > Refresh Data. The Refresh Data dialog appears, as shown in Figure 10.41.

Figure 10.42
The Refresh Data
dialog—refresh
completed.

3. Select the data source that you want to use to refresh the linked-to data from.

4. Click Configure. Visio displays the Configure Refresh dialog, shown in Figure 10.43.

Figure 10.43
The Configure
Refresh dialog.

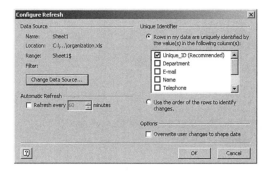

5. Select the Refresh Every check box.

6. Select a number of minutes from the drop-down list box. That lets you select the number of minutes between automatic refreshes.

7. If you want to override any of your changes to shape data with data from the data source, select the Overwrite User Changes to Shape Data check box.

8. Select the unique identifier that ties the shape data in the various shapes to the rows in the data source, unless you're satisfied with the selection Visio has made.

9. Click OK. Visio closes the Configure Refresh dialog and returns you to the Refresh Data dialog.

10. Click Close. Visio closes the Refresh Data dialog and returns you to the drawing you're working on.

The automatic refresh starts automatically, on the schedule you've specified.

USING DATA GRAPHICS

Data graphics are designed to help you visualize your data, and there are four kinds:

- **Text callout**—This type of data graphic just displays data as text.

- **Data bar callout**—Data bars let you visualize data with various controls, such as progress bars and speedometers.

- **Icon set callouts**—Using icon sets, you can display interpretations of your data; for example, a stop light can be shown if the data is out of bounds or otherwise a problem.

- **Color by value**—This lets you color shapes depending on the value of a particular item in their shape data.

Note that data graphics are built to display shape data, so if a shape doesn't have any data, you can't create a data graphic for it.

When you create data links for shapes, Visio automatically creates the first type of data graphics—text callouts, as shown in Figure 10.44.

Figure 10.44
Text callout data graphics.

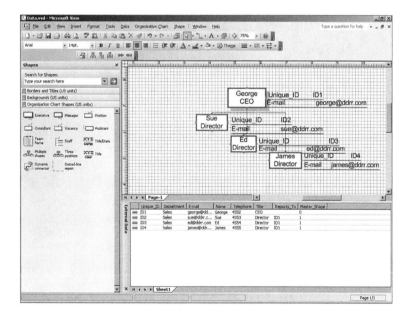

You can configure data graphics to be any of the four types listed previously.

Want to create a data graphic? First, make sure that your shapes have shape data. For example, all the stars in Figure 10.45 have been given names, using a Name property.

Figure 10.45
Named shapes.

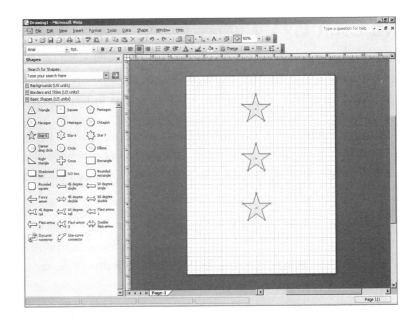

To add shape data to shapes that don't already have such data, use a data link, or follow these steps:

1. Right-click the shape you want to add data to.

2. Select Data > Shape Data.

   If there is no shape data connected with the shape yet, the Define Shape Data dialog appears. Give the new data item a new label, select a data format, and enter the shape data's value in the Value box. Then click OK.

   If there is shape data connected with the shape, the Shape Data dialog appears, and you can edit the shape data. To define a new shape data field, click the Define button and follow the previous steps in the Define Shape Data dialog. Click OK to close the Define Shape Data dialog, and then click OK again to close the Shape Data dialog.

When you've added shape data to a set of shapes, you can add data graphics to those shapes. Just follow these steps:

1. Open the Visio drawing that contains the shapes with the shape data you want to display using data graphics.

2. Open the Data Graphics task pane by selecting View > Task Pane and then selecting Data Graphics using the drop-down arrow. Alternatively, you can select Data > Display Data on Shapes. Visio displays the Data Graphics task pane, as shown at the right in Figure 10.46.

Figure 10.46
The Data Graphics
task pane.

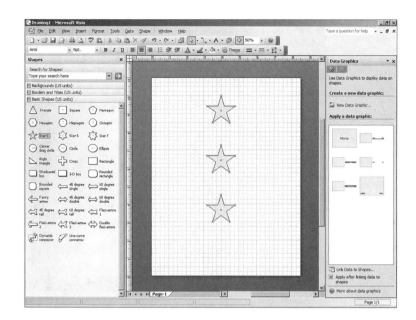

3. Select the shape or shapes you want to create data graphics for.

4. Move the mouse over the data graphic thumbnail that's closest to what you want. A down arrow appears next to the data graphic. You can edit the data graphic later to configure it.

5. Click the down arrow that appears next to the data graphic you've selected and select Apply to Selected Shapes. Visio applies the data graphics to the selected shapes.

6. Select a data graphic. The first time you click a data graphic, the associated shape is selected—you have to click the data graphic a second time to select it.

7. Right-click the data graphic and select the formatting options you want, such as Format > Text. Format the text in the data graphic the way you want it, as shown in Figure 10.47.

That's it—you've created a new set of data graphics, as shown in Figure 10.47.

As you can see in the figure, the Name shape data is represented in text callouts, and you can see the name of each shape displayed.

How about altering data graphics, editing them to appear as you want, and even switching types? Or selecting which data appears in text callouts, and which data is hidden?

That's coming up next.

10

Figure 10.47
Configuring a data graphic.

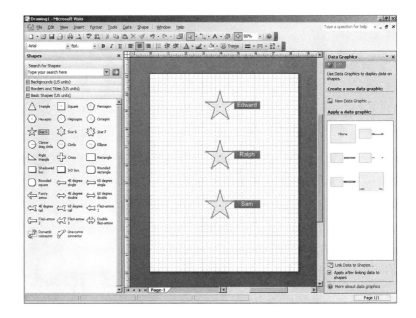

EDITING DATA GRAPHICS

You have a lot of control over data graphics, editing their types and whether or not they appear, and what data they use.

Want to configure the data displayed in a data graphic? Follow these steps:

1. Open the Visio drawing that contains the shapes with the shape data you want to display using data graphics.

2. Open the Data graphics task pane by selecting View > Task Pane and then selecting Data Graphics using the drop-down arrow. Alternatively, you can select Data > Display Data on Shapes.

3. Select the shape or shapes you want to edit the Data Graphics for.

4. Right-click the selected shape or shapes and select Data > Edit Data Graphic. The Edit Data Graphic dialog appears, as shown in Figure 10.48.

Figure 10.48
Editing a data graphic.

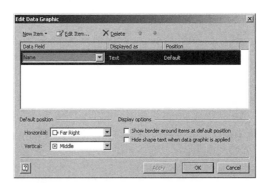

5. To make the Data Graphic display a different data field, select that data field from the drop-down list in the Data Field column. That's how you tie a data graphic to a different data field.

6. To alter the type of text callout the data graphic displays, click the Edit Item button. Visio displays an editing dialog box appropriate to the type of data graphic—for example, you can see the Edit Text dialog in Figure 10.49, which allows you to select the callout type. When you're done with the editing dialog, click OK.

Figure 10.49
Editing text callout types.

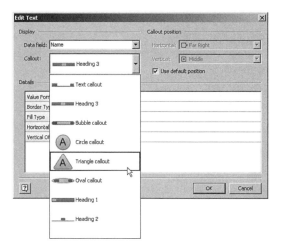

7. Click OK to close the Edit Data Graphic dialog.

How about deleting a data graphic? Follow these steps:

1. Open the Visio drawing that contains the shapes with the shape data you want to display using data graphics.

2. Open the Data graphics task pane by selecting View > Task Pane and then selecting Data Graphics using the drop-down arrow. Alternatively, you can select Data > Display Data on Shapes.

3. Select the shape or shapes you want to delete the data graphics for.

4. Right-click the selected shape or shapes and select Data > Edit Data Graphic. The Edit Data Graphic dialog appears.

5. To delete a data graphic, select it in the Edit Data Graphic dialog and click the Delete button. Visio deletes the data graphic.

6. Click OK to close the Edit Data Graphic dialog.

What if you want to change the type of data graphic connected to a shape or shapes entirely? For example, what if you want to switch from text callouts to color-based data graphics?

Follow these steps:

1. Open the Visio drawing that contains the shapes with the shape data you want to work with.

2. Open the Data graphics task pane by selecting View > Task Pane and then selecting Data Graphics using the drop-down arrow. Alternatively, you can select Data > Display Data on Shapes.

3. Select the shape or shapes you want to alter the data graphics for.

4. Right-click the selected shape or shapes and select Data > Edit Data Graphic. The Edit Data Graphic dialog appears.

5. Click the New Item's down arrow and select the new type of data graphic you want to use. Here are the choices:

   - **Text**—Creates a text callout data graphic.
   - **Data Bar**—Creates a data bar data graphic.
   - **Icon Set**—Creates an icon-based data graphic.
   - **Color by Value**—Colors shapes by data value.

   For example, selecting Color by Value in the three-star example we've been working with opens the New Color by Value dialog shown in Figure 10.50.

Figure 10.50
Creating a new Color by Value data graphic.

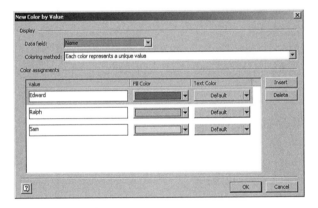

Select the data field whose value you want to display by color in the Data Field drop-down box.

Visio selects colors for the shapes automatically—you can change those colors by clicking the drop-down arrow next to the chosen colors and making a new selection.

Click OK to create the new data graphic.

6. If you want to delete the current data graphic associated with your shapes, select that data graphic and click the Delete button.

7. Click OK to close the Edit Data Graphic dialog. You can see the results in Figure 10.51, where you see the three stars colored by value (in glorious black and white in the book, of course).

Figure 10.51
Using color-by-value
data graphics.

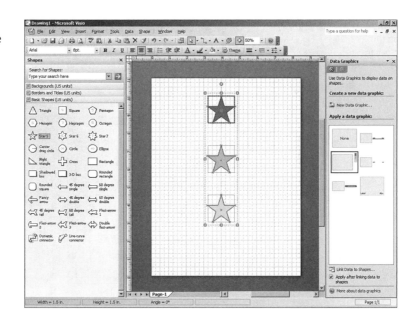

As you can see, data graphics are a cool feature that allows you to handle the display of additional data connected to shapes. From icons to text callouts to coloring, you can have Visio configure the appearance of shapes to make understanding and displaying shape data much easier.

WORKING WITH DATABASES

The data links you created earlier in this chapter go only one way—they read data from external sources. However, Visio has great tools for exporting data to databases, or maintaining two-way links to databases.

We'll take a look at those tools next, starting with the Export to Database dialog.

EXPORT TO DATABASE

The Export to Database dialog is perhaps the easiest way of sending data to databases. As with the other tools in this section, you can reach this dialog by using the Tools > Add-ons > Visio Extras menu item.

To export the data in a drawing, follow these steps:

1. Open the Visio drawing that contains the shapes with the shape data you want to export.
2. Select Tools > Add-ons > Visio Extras > Export to Database. Visio opens the Export to Database dialog, shown in Figure 10.52.

Figure 10.52
The Export to
Database dialog.

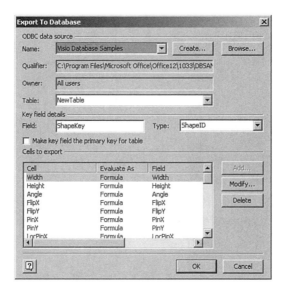

3. Select the type of database you want to export to by selecting an item in the drop-down list next to the Name box. Visio opens a dialog that asks you for the appropriate file, such as the Select Workbook dialog, shown in Figure 10.53, for exporting to Excel.

Figure 10.53
The Select Workbook
dialog.

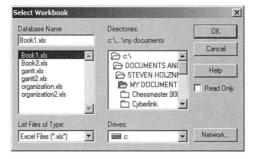

Select your database filename and click OK.

4. Configure the Owner, Table, and Key Field Details as needed. You can delete data fields by selecting them in the Cells to Export box and clicking Delete.

5. Click OK. Visio closes the Export to Database dialog, and updates the database file you've selected.

That's an easy way to export all the data in a drawing to a database. You can also use the Database Export Wizard.

DATABASE EXPORT WIZARD

The difference between the Database Export Wizard and the Export to Database dialog box is that through the wizard you can choose to export all shapes on a layer. If you do not need to export by layers, you might find that using the Export to Database dialog is more convenient.

To export the data using the Data Export Wizard, follow these steps:

1. Open the Visio drawing that contains the shapes with the data you want to export.

2. Select Tools > Add-ons > Visio Extras > Database Export Wizard. Visio opens the Database Export Wizard, shown in Figure 10.54.

Figure 10.54
The Database Export Wizard.

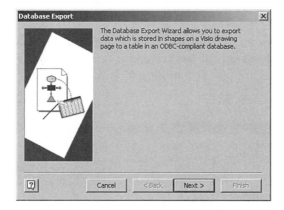

3. Click Next. Visio displays the second pane of the Database Export Wizard, as shown in Figure 10.55.

Figure 10.55
The Database Export Wizard, second pane.

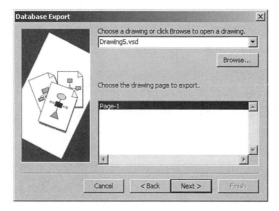

4. Select your drawing and page to export, and click Next. Visio displays the third pane of the Database Export Wizard, as shown in Figure 10.56.

Figure 10.56
The Database Export
Wizard, third pane.

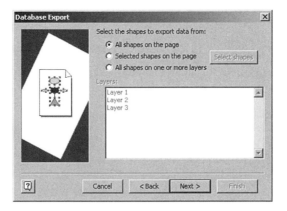

5. Select whether you want to export data from all shapes on the page, selected shapes, or shapes on one or more layers (if specifying layers, select the layers in the Layers box) and click Next. Visio displays the fourth pane of the Database Export Wizard, as shown in Figure 10.57.

Figure 10.57
The Database Export
Wizard, fourth pane.

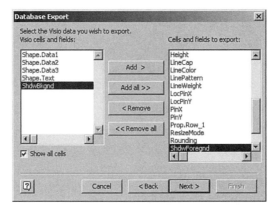

6. Select the Visio data you want to export and click Next. Visio displays the fifth pane of the Database Export Wizard, as shown in Figure 10.58.

7. Select the type of database file you want to export to and click Next. Visio displays a dialog box letting you choose the database file you want to export to; select that file and click OK.

   Visio displays the sixth pane of the Database Export Wizard, as shown in Figure 10.59.

8. Specify the details of the table you want to export to, or whether you want to export to a new table and click Next. Visio displays the seventh pane of the Database Export Wizard, as shown in Figure 10.60.

Figure 10.58
The Database Export Wizard, fifth pane.

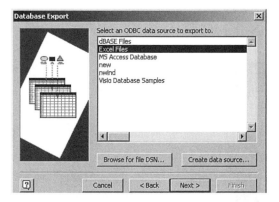

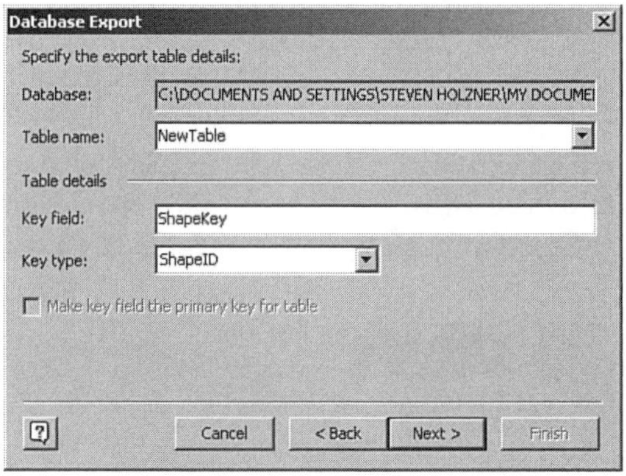

Figure 10.59
The Database Export Wizard, sixth pane.

10

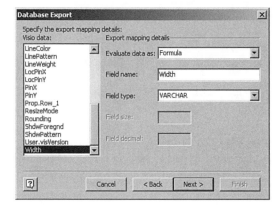

Figure 10.60
The Database Export Wizard, seventh pane.

9. Specify the export mapping details. In this pane, you can specify the format of each field to export.

When you're done specifying the data formats to export, click Next. Visio displays the eighth pane of the Database Export Wizard, as shown in Figure 10.61.

Figure 10.61
The Database Export Wizard, eighth pane.

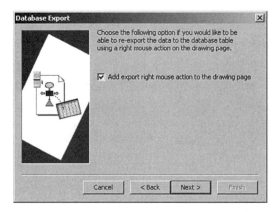

10. Specify whether you want to be able to add a context menu item to the drawing page to re-export the data to the database file with, and click Next. Visio displays the ninth pane of the Database Export Wizard, as shown in Figure 10.62.

Figure 10.62
The Database Export Wizard, ninth pane.

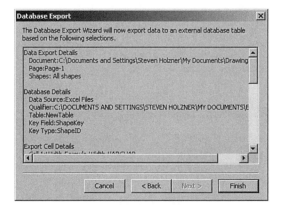

11. Click Finish to export your data. Visio displays a summary of your selections in the ninth pane of the Data Export Wizard—click Finish if you're satisfied. Otherwise, click Back to make changes in your selections.

When you click Finish, the Data Export Wizard exports your data to the selected database file. Nice.

DATABASE WIZARD

You can set up two-way links to database sources using the Database Wizard. You can link shapes to individual records in the database, create drawings that are visual representations of data fields in the database, and more.

To run the Database Wizard, follow these steps:

1. Open the Visio drawing that contains the shapes with the data you want to link to a database.

2. Select Tools > Add-ons > Visio Extras > Database Wizard. Visio opens the Database Wizard, as shown in Figure 10.63.

Figure 10.63
The Database Wizard.

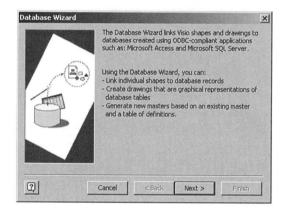

3. Click Next. Visio displays the second pane of the Database Wizard, as shown in Figure 10.64.

Figure 10.64
The Database Export Wizard, second pane.

4. Select what you want to do with the wizard. The Database Wizard gives you these options:

>   Link Shapes to Database Records
>
>   Create a Linked Drawing or Modify an Existing One
>
>   Generate New Masters from a Database

In this example, we'll link shapes in a drawing to database records. That radio button is selected by default, so click Next.

Visio displays the third pane of the Database Wizard, as shown in Figure 10.65.

Figure 10.65
The Database Wizard, third pane.

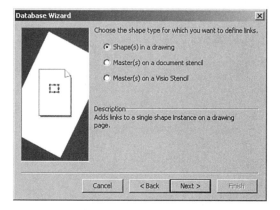

5. Select the shape type for which you want to create links and click Next. Visio displays the fourth pane of the Database Wizard, as shown in Figure 10.66.

Figure 10.66
The Database Wizard, fourth pane.

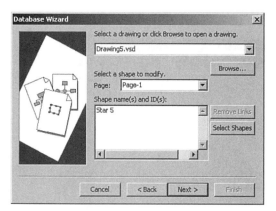

6. Select the drawing and shapes you want to create links for and click Next. Visio displays the fifth pane of the Database Wizard, as shown in Figure 10.67.

Figure 10.67
The Database Wizard,
fifth pane.

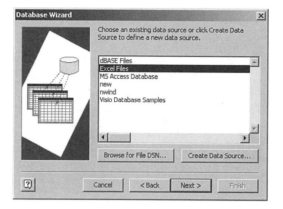

7. Select a data source and click Next. Visio displays a dialog box letting you choose the database file you want to export to; select that file and click OK.

   Visio displays the sixth pane of the Database Export Wizard, as shown in Figure 10.68.

Figure 10.68
The Database Wizard,
sixth pane.

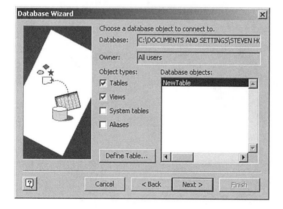

8. Specify the details of the table you want to connect to, or whether you want to connect to a new table and click Next. Visio displays the seventh pane of the Database Wizard, as shown in Figure 10.69.

9. Specify the number of fields that make up the primary key for the link and click Next. The primary key is the field or fields that you use to link records to shapes with. Specify the number of fields that the primary key uses (normally one) and click Next.

   Visio displays the eighth pane of the Database Wizard, as shown in Figure 10.70.

10. Select the primary key you want to use to relate the shape to the database table and click OK. Visio displays the ninth pane of the Database Wizard, as shown in Figure 10.71.

Figure 10.69
The Database Wizard,
seventh pane.

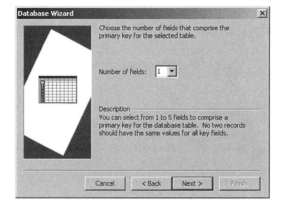

Figure 10.70
The Database Wizard,
eighth pane.

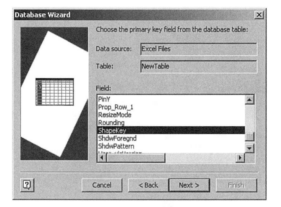

Figure 10.71
The Database Wizard,
ninth pane.

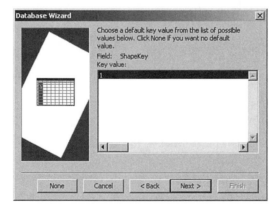

11. Choose a default primary key value and click OK. Visio displays the tenth pane of the
    Database Wizard, as shown in Figure 10.72.

Figure 10.72
The Database Wizard, tenth pane.

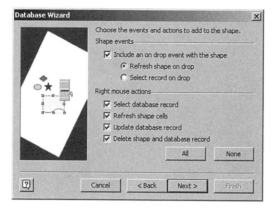

12. Select the events and mouse actions you want to add to the shape to maintain the two-way database link and click OK. Visio displays the 11th pane of the Database Wizard, as shown in Figure 10.73.

Figure 10.73
The Database Wizard, 11th pane.

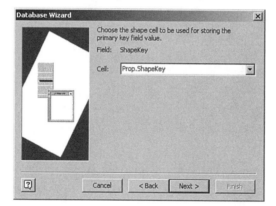

13. Select the shape cell used to store the primary key and click OK. Visio displays the 12th pane of the Database Wizard, as shown in Figure 10.74.

14. Connect the ShapeSheet cells to database cells and click OK. Visio displays the 13th pane of the Database Wizard, as shown in Figure 10.75.

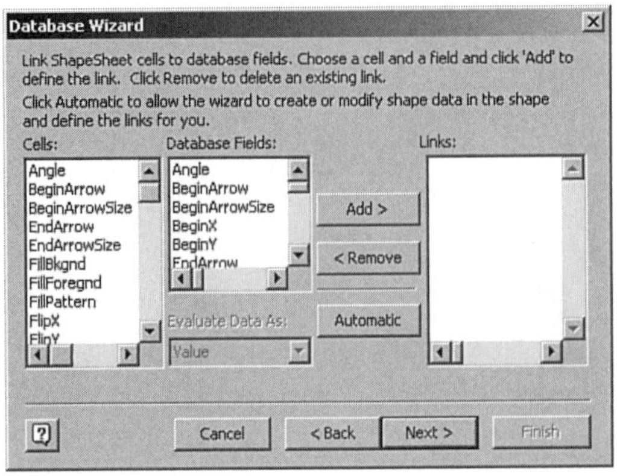

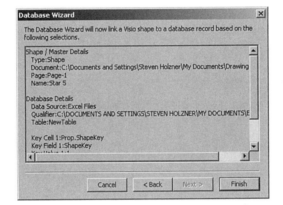

Figure 10.74
The Database
Wizard, 12th pane.

Figure 10.75
The Database Wizard,
13th pane.

15. If you accept the summary, click Finish; otherwise, click Back and make changes. When you click Finish, the Data Wizard connects your shape or shapes to the selected database file.

You can use the mouse actions you selected earlier to maintain the two-way link to the database. Very cool.

CHAPTER 11

CREATING BLOCK DRAWINGS AND CHARTS

In this chapter

BLOCK DRAWINGS

Block drawings are the easiest and probably the most common of all drawings, and in this chapter, you're going to get a good look at them. This is where most new Visio users turn first, creating drawings that put the block shapes to work.

Want a simple drawing with shapes, possibly showing text and connected with arrows? The block drawings are for you.

There are three templates involved here: Basic Diagram, Block Diagram, and Block Diagram with Perspective.

THE BASIC DIAGRAM TEMPLATE

The Basic Diagram template contains the Basic Shapes stencil, which appears in all its glory in Figure 11.1.

Figure 11.1
The Basic Shapes stencil.

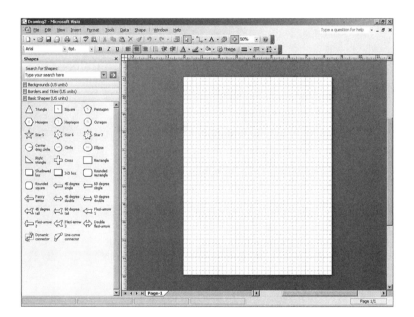

This is the most basic of the basic shapes, and the stencil that most new users use most. It has the essential shapes you can use to create block drawings, drawing and connecting blocks.

Here's an overview of what this stencil packs:

- **Arrows**—The Basic Shapes stencil also supports a number of arrow shapes, which you can use to connect the geometric shapes with, creating basic flowcharts and showing interconnectivity.
- **Flexi-arrows**—Flexi-arrows are, as their name implies, flexible, and using them, you can connect geometric shapes no matter what their position.

- **Geometric shapes**—From triangles to rounded squares, the Basic Shapes stencils has a wide variety of geometric shapes, as shown in Figure 11.1. That's its charm—many of the shapes you want are there.

THE BLOCK DIAGRAM TEMPLATE

The Block Diagram template is specially designed to contain blocks of all kinds. There are two stencils here—Blocks and Blocks Raised. You can see the shapes in the Blocks stencil in Figure 11.2, and the shapes in the Blocks Raised stencil in Figure 11.3.

Figure 11.2
The Blocks stencil.

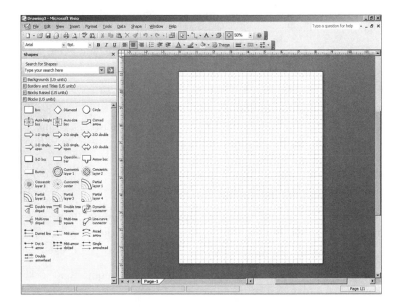

Figure 11.3
The Blocks Raised stencil.

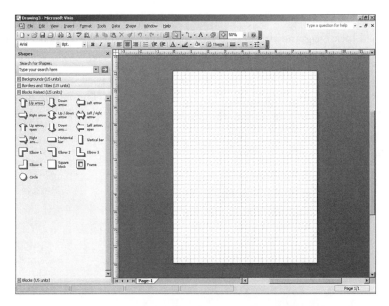

The Blocks stencil is the most comprehensive of all the block stencils. This is the stencil for blocks, tree diagrams, concentric diagrams, and others. Here's an overview of this stencil:

- **Arrow box**—This shape combines a box and an arrow to let you display a step in an operation, as well as the arrow pointing to the next step.

- **Arrows**—You can use the control points on the arrow to change the bend in this shape.

- **Auto-sizing boxes**—These boxes can contain text, and they size themselves automatically to contain the text you type, stretching up and down and left to right.

- **Concentric shapes**—These shapes let you create concentric ring shapes.

- **Connectors**—There's also a good selection of bendable connectors in the Blocks stencil.

- **Geometric shapes**—Shapes like the box, diamond, and circle shapes give you a good selection of block shapes.

- **Open/Close shapes**—These shapes can display borders or not. When they don't, the shapes appear to flow together; with a border, the shapes are distinct.

- **Tree shapes**—These shapes let you create tree drawings, connecting the leaves and branches to show interconnectivity between items.

The Blocks Raised stencil, which appears in Figure 11.3, contains shapes that appear to be raised from the drawing surface.

These kinds of shapes can make drawings more interesting; however, this stencil contains mostly arrows, with only a few geometric shapes. On the other hand, these shapes have no sense of perspective—they stay the same no matter how you resize them.

If you want true perspective, complete with vanishing point, the Block Diagram with Perspective template is a better choice.

THE BLOCK DIAGRAM WITH PERSPECTIVE TEMPLATE

The Block Diagram with Perspective template contains one stencil, the Blocks With Perspective stencil, shown in Figure 11.4.

These shapes are 3D, much like those in the Blocks Raised stencil, but there's a difference here—you can use a vanishing point with these shapes. The vanishing point is already in the drawing, as you can see in the drawing surface in Figure 11.4, marked as V.P.

The vanishing point is the point toward which the 3D appearance of shapes is directed, as shown in Figure 11.5.

Figure 11.4
The Blocks With
Perspective stencil.

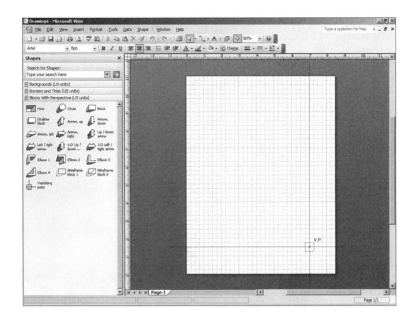

Figure 11.5
Using perspective.

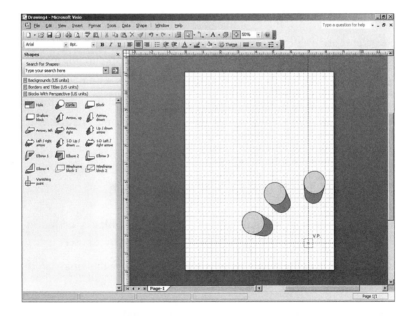

You can reorient the vanishing point as you like, and the 3D shapes will change their appearance to match, as shown in Figure 11.6.

Figure 11.6
Moving the vanishing
point.

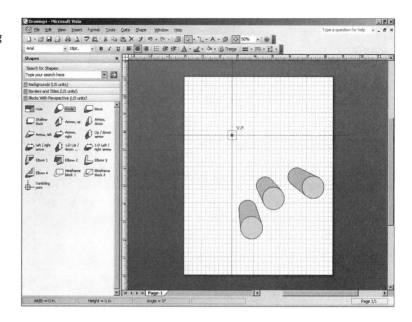

The Blocks With Perspective stencil contains these kinds of shapes:

- **Geometric shapes**—These shapes—block, circle, arrow, and elbow shapes—automatically orient themselves toward the vanishing point in the drawing.
- **Holes**—These shapes give you the appearance of a hole into the drawing surface.
- **Vanishing point**—You can drag multiple vanishing points onto the drawing surface.
- **Wireframe blocks**—These shapes are 3D wireframe boxes.

Okay, that gives us an overview of block drawings. Now let's put them to work in Visio.

CREATING BLOCK DRAWINGS

You can create block drawings with the Basic Shapes, Blocks, or Blocks Raised stencils. Every one of those stencils contains basic blocks for you to use.

Here's how to put these stencils to work creating block drawings:

1. Open Visio.
2. Select File > New > General > Block Diagram, or File > New > General > Basic Diagram. Visio opens the template you've selected and displays a drawing surface.
3. Drag shapes from the Basic Shapes, Blocks, or Blocks Raised stencils onto the drawing surface.
4. Select a shape and enter the text you want to appear in that shape.
5. Use AutoConnect to connect shapes, or drag arrow shapes or connectors to the drawing surface.

MODIFYING BLOCK SHAPES

There are plenty of ways to modify and customize block shapes after you've dragged them onto the drawing surface. You can do the following:

- **Add relationships**—Drag a connector or arrow shape onto the drawing and glue one of its endpoints to a connection point of a shape.
- **Add text**—To add text, just select a block shape and begin typing.
- **Bend shapes**—Select the Arc, Line, Pencil, or Freeform tool in the drawing bar, and select a shape; then drag an eccentricity handle to bend the shape.
- **Format shapes**—To format a shape right-click it, select Format from the context menu, and select one of the Format item's sub-items.
- **Modify shapes**—Select the Arc, Line, Pencil, or Freeform tool in the drawing bar, and select a shape; then drag a vertex to modify the shape.
- **Resize shapes**—Select a shape and use a green sizing handle to resize the shape.
- **Rotate shapes**—Select a shape and use the rotation handle to rotate the shape.

There are also some special techniques for handling some box shapes in these stencils:

- **3D box**—You can drag the control points on 3D boxes to change the direction and depth of the sides of the box.
- **Auto-height box**—You can enter text into auto-height boxes, and the height of the box will adjust automatically. If you want to adjust the width, however, you need to drag the sizing handles.
- **Auto-size box**—You can enter text into auto-size boxes, and the size of the box will adjust automatically to fit your text. Unlike auto-height boxes, both the height and width of the box will automatically adjust.

There are also special behaviors, control handles, and context menu items you can use to work with arrows in block drawings. Here are some of the salient points for arrows:

- **Arrows boxes**—You can drag the control point of an arrowhead to set its width. You can also drag the control point at the intersection of the arrow and the box to set the length of the arrow and the height of the box.
- **Curved arrows**—These arrows appear in the Blocks stencil. You can drag the control points on the arrowhead in order to move the arrowhead. You can also drag the curve's control point around to change the curvature, as shown in Figure 11.7.
- **Flexi-arrows**—These arrows appear in the Basic Shapes stencil. You can drag the arrowhead's control points to change the shape of the arrowhead, as well as the width of the arrow tail, as shown in Figure 11.8.

11

Figure 11.7
Working with curved arrows.

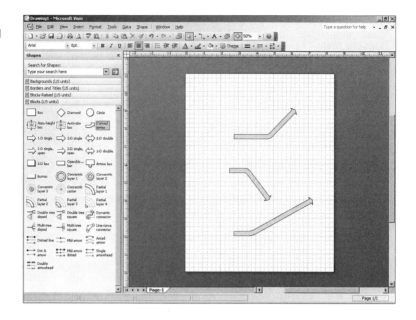

Figure 11.8
Working with flexi-arrows.

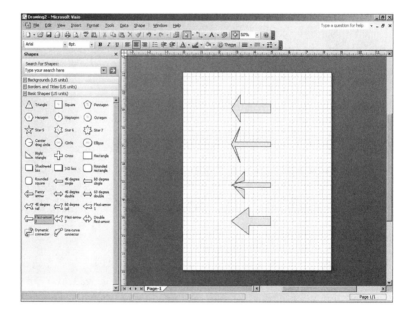

CREATING TREES

Tree drawings are used to represent a treelike dependency between items, such as an organization drawing or a genealogy chart. As you might expect, you can resize, reshape, and rearrange tree drawings on the fly.

Here's how to create a tree drawing:

1. Open Visio.

2. Select File > New > General > Block Diagram. Visio creates a new drawing, as shown in Figure 11.9.

Figure 11.9
Working with block drawings.

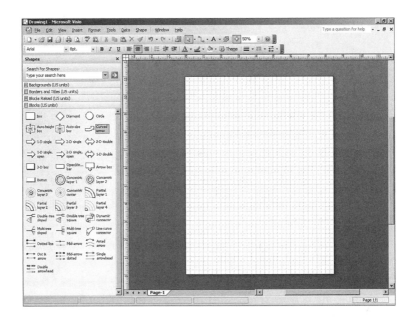

3. Open the Blocks stencil.

4. Drag the blocks you want to appear in the tree drawing to the drawing surface. You can see an example in Figure 11.10.

5. Drag a tree shape from the stencil to the drawing surface. You can select from these tree styles:

   • Double tree (two branches) with sloped branches

   • Double tree (two branches) with square branches

   • Multi-trees (multiple branches—up to six) with sloped branches

   • Multi-trees (multiple branches—up to six) with square branches

6. Rotate the tree shape as needed. You can rotate a tree shape by 90° by selecting it and pressing Ctrl+L. Or you can press Ctrl+H to flip it left to right.

7. Connect the tree's branches to the appropriate blocks. Simply drag a control handle at the end of a tree branch to a connection point on a block shape.

Figure 11.10
Dragging blocks.

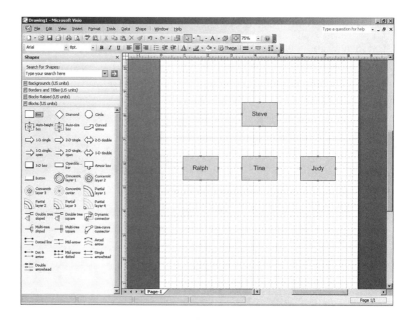

A red outline around the connection appears when the tree and the block are connected.

To create additional branches in a multi-tree, drag branches from the yellow control handle on the tree's trunk. You can see this control handle—a diamond shape—in Figure 11.11.

Figure 11.11
A completed tree.

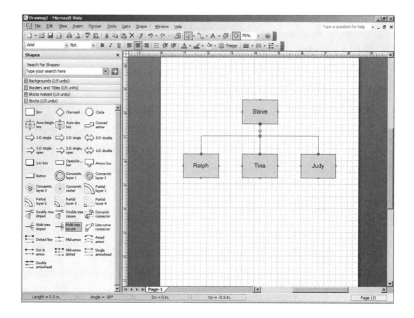

8. You can even add text to the tree's trunk—just select the tree and enter your text.

And that lets you create tree shapes. Cool.

You can also edit tree shapes using these techniques:

- **Adding a branch**—To add a branch to a tree, drag it from the yellow control handle that appears on the tree trunk. You can use a maximum of only six branches in a multi-tree shape, however. If you need more branches, try superimposing a second tree over the first—the trunks will overlap, giving the impression of a single trunk instead of two trunks.

- **Deleting a branch**—To delete a branch, drag the control handle at the end of the branch you want to delete on top of any other branch's control handle.

- **Moving a branch**—To move a branch, drag the control handle at the end of the branch to the new position.

- **Moving the trunk**—To move the trunk, drag the green box at the juncture of the trunk and the branches. You can also select the tree and use the arrow keys to move the trunk.

> **TIP**
>
> When you move a shape that's connected to a shape, the tree trunk rotates. If you want to keep the tree's trunk vertical or horizontal, select the shape you want to move, the tree, and any other shapes connected to the tree, and move everything en masse.

USING 3D BLOCKS

Using 3D shapes can be more visually exciting than using simple shapes. They are more eye-popping, yet Visio handles all the details of constructing them for you.

You can create simple 3D shapes using the Blocks Raised stencil by following these steps:

1. Open Visio.
2. Select File > New > General > Block Diagram. Visio creates a new drawing.
3. Open the Blocks Raised stencil.
4. Drag the 3D blocks you want to appear in the drawing to the drawing surface. You can see an example in Figure 11.12.

Figure 11.12
Raised block shapes.

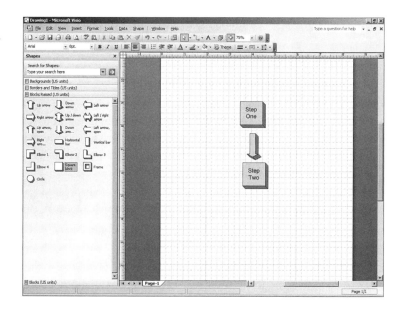

You can also create shapes with perspective. Follow these steps:

1. Open Visio.
2. Select File > New > General > Block Diagram with Perspective. Visio creates a new drawing.
3. Open the Blocks with Perspective stencil.
4. Drag the 3D blocks you want to appear in the drawing to the drawing surface. You can see an example in Figure 11.13.

Figure 11.13
3D shapes with perspective.

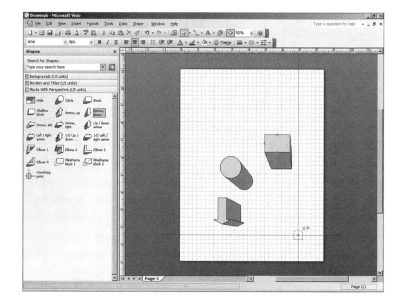

You can change the perspective of 3D shapes like this:

- **Change the entire drawing perspective**—Just drag the vanishing point with the mouse to a new location, as shown in Figure 11.14.

Figure 11.14
Changing a drawing's perspective.

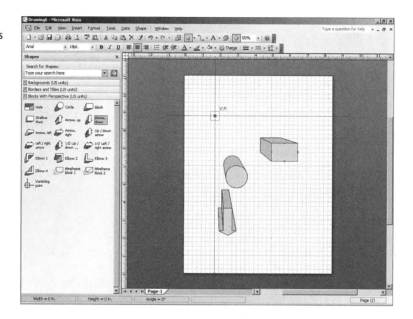

- **Change the perspective of a single shape**—You can change the perspective of single shapes as well. Select only the shape whose perspective you want to change, and drag the vanishing point to the shape's new vanishing point's location. A yellow diamond will mark the vanishing point for the shape—the vanishing point of the drawing as a whole is unchanged.

- **Alter a shape's depth**—Right-click a shape and select Set Depth from the context menu, opening the Shape Data dialog shown in Figure 11.15.

Set a new depth as a percentage of the distance from the shape to the vanishing point.

Figure 11.15
Changing a shape's depth.

■ **Associate a shape with the vanishing point**—Select the shape and drag the yellow diamond control handle that appears on the drawing page, connecting it to a connection point on the vanishing point.

You can also use multiple vanishing points in Visio drawings. Here's how to do that:

1. Open Visio.
2. Select File > New > General > Block Diagram with Perspective. Visio creates a new drawing.
3. Open the Blocks with Perspective stencil.
4. Drag a new vanishing point from the stencil to the drawing surface and position it where you want it.
5. Select a shape that you want to associate with the new vanishing point.
6. Drag the red control handle that appears in the drawing's vanishing point to the new vanishing point. Visio connects the shape to the new vanishing point.

CREATING CONCENTRIC DRAWINGS

Concentric shapes are circular, multilayered shapes, which build out from a central core. They illustrate enveloping data sets, such as levels of security in a corporation, starting with the big boss and extending out to the mailroom clerks.

Here's how to create a concentric drawing:

1. Open Visio.
2. Select File > New > General > Block Diagram. Visio creates a new drawing.
3. Open the Blocks stencil.
4. Drag a Concentric Layer 1 shape onto the drawing. This establishes the outer layer of the drawing.
5. Drag a Concentric Layer 2 shape onto the drawing. This sets the next inner layer of the drawing.
6. Drag a Concentric Layer 3 shape onto the drawing. This sets the next inner layer of the drawing.
7. Drag a Concentric Center shape onto the drawing. This sets the core of the drawing.
8. Add text to a ring by selecting a ring and typing the text.

You can see a concentric drawing in Figure 11.16.

Figure 11.16
A concentric shape.

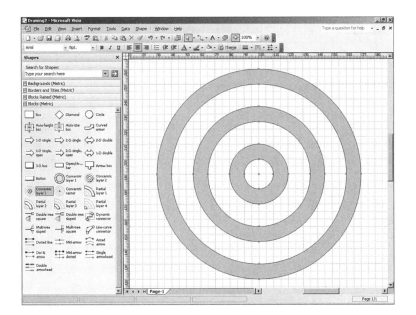

You can also divide a concentric layer into sections to show a number of components. Here's how to do that:

1. Open Visio.

2. Select File > New > General > Block Diagram. Visio creates a new drawing.

3. Open the Blocks stencil.

4. Drag a Partial Layer 1 shape onto the drawing. This establishes a partial outer layer of the drawing. Use the control handles to size and rotate the partial layer.

5. Repeat the preceding step to add other partial layers to the drawing.

6. Drag a Partial Layer 2 shape onto the drawing. This establishes a partial second layer of the drawing. Use the control handles to size and rotate the partial layer.

7. Repeat the preceding step to add other partial layers to the drawing.

8. Drag a Partial Layer 3 shape onto the drawing. This establishes a partial third outer layer of the drawing. Use the control handles to size and rotate the partial layer.

9. Repeat the previous step to add other partial layers to the drawing.

10. Drag a Concentric Center shape onto the drawing. This sets the core of the drawing.

11. Add text to each ring section by selecting a ring and typing the text.

That gives you the goods on concentric drawings. That also introduces the concept of creating charts and graphs, our next topic.

CREATING CHARTS AND GRAPHS

You can use charts and graphs to display quantitative data visually. The profits of your company over time can be seen at a glance with a bar chart, something that isn't as evident with a simple table of numbers. Temperatures rising or lowering over the past decade? A line graph will show you the answer.

Using Visio, you can create all kinds of graphs and charts: pie charts, line graphs, bar charts, and more. You can also use the Visio marketing shapes to indicate market share; strengths, weaknesses, opportunities, and threats (SWOT); sales prospects; and more.

Which template category do you use here? You use the Business category in Visio 2007, which contains the charts and graphs. The Charts and Graphs template in the Business category might sound like the one to use, but the fact is that the Marketing Charts and Diagrams template is even better, because it opens all three Visio charts and graphs stencils:

- Charting Shapes
- Marketing Shapes
- Marketing Diagrams

We'll start with a look at the Charting Shapes stencil.

THE CHARTING SHAPES STENCIL

You can see the Charting Shapes stencil in Figure 11.17—as you can see, it contains a large number of shapes.

Figure 11.17
The Charting Shapes stencil.

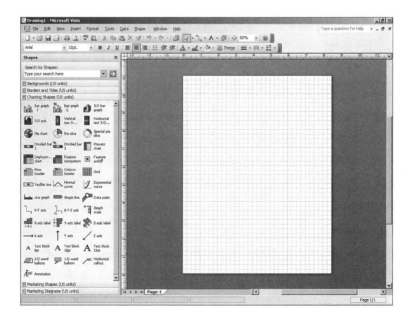

Here are the kinds of shapes you'll find in this stencil:

- **3D bar graphs**—These bar graphs compare data in two different dimensions, in a 3D way. You can use the X-Y-Z axis shape with these graphs.

- **Annotations**—Use these shapes to annotate your graphs and charts.

- **Bar graphs**—These bar graphs are the usual bar graphs. Bar graph 1 shows numbers, while Bar Graph 2 shows percentages. You can also add x- and y-axes by using the axis shapes.

- **Distribution graphs**—Using the normal curve shape, you can display distribution graphs.

- **Divided bars**—Divided bars divide bars into rectangles—sort of like rectangular pie charts. The Divided Bar 1 shape divides bars using numbers, and the Divided Bar 2 shape uses percentages.

- **Feature comparison charts**—The feature comparison shape can compare up to 10 features of up to 10 products.

- **Grids**—These shapes produce tables. You can combine the grid, row header, and column header shapes here.

- **Line graphs**—Line graphs are like bar graphs, except they display connected points, rather than bars. They're better for displaying data when you have many sets of data in the same graph.

- **Pie charts**—You can use pie charts to make relative values apparent at a glance. These are the standard pie charts that you've seen time and time again.

- **Tabular charts**—The deployment chart is a table that lets you track deployment for up to six departments, in five phases. The process chart contains up to 10 steps of a process.

THE MARKETING SHAPES STENCIL

You can see the Marketing Shapes stencil in Figure 11.18.

As you see, the Marketing Shapes stencil contains what's effectively clip art, for use in creating marketing drawings.

The clip-art images range from people icons to dogs, stars, and factories. They're useful, but chances are you'll have to search farther afield for any real drawing that uses clip art (note the tombstone clip-art icon in this stencil—one wonders what that's doing here; it doesn't look promising if someone's going to use it for marketing reports).

There are some intriguing shapes here—the variable building shape, for example, adds new floors as you stretch the building vertically.

Figure 11.18
The Marketing
Shapes stencil.

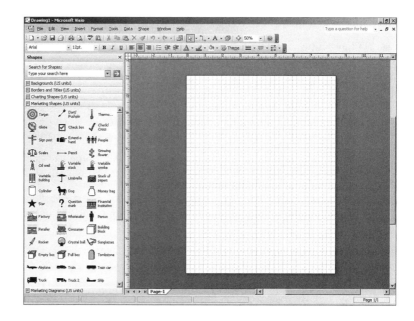

THE MARKETING DIAGRAMS STENCIL

You can see the Marketing Diagrams stencil in Figure 11.19.

Figure 11.19
The Marketing
Diagrams stencil.

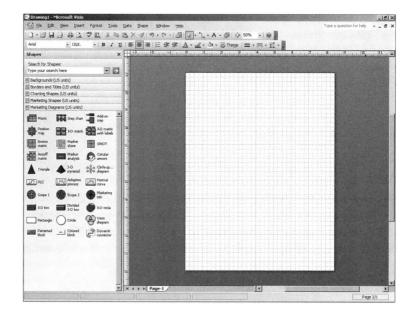

Here are the kinds of shapes you'll find in this stencil:

- **Matrices**—Matrices let you divide your data up into a matrix of cells, with X and Y headers for labeling.

- **Strengths, weaknesses, opportunities, and threats (SWOT)**—This shape creates a matrix with four sections: strengths, weaknesses, opportunities, and threats.

- **Triangles and pyramids**—These create triangle and pyramid shapes, with sections you can add text to.

- **Curves**—The PLC, adoption curve, and normal curve shapes all let you create curve graphs.

- **Scope**—The scope 1 and scope 2 shapes let you compare market scope with sections for product, place price, promotion, and so on, as well as a target market central icon.

- **3D shapes**—The 3D shapes are much like the bar charts in the Charting Shapes stencil.

- **Venn diagrams**—Venn diagrams let you illustrate overlapping relationships with circles.

Okay, that's an overview of what's available. Now let's put it to work.

CREATING BAR, LINE, AND PIE GRAPHS

There is good support for bar graphs in Visio—the 2D bar graph shapes can display up to 12 bars and the 2D bar graph shapes can display up to 5 3D bars.

CREATING 2D BAR GRAPHS

Want to create a 2D bar graph? Follow these steps:

1. Open Visio.
2. Select File > New > Business > Charts and Graphs, or File > New > Business > Marketing Charts and Diagrams. Visio creates a new drawing.
3. Select the Charting Shapes stencil.
4. Drag a 2D bar graph shape onto the drawing surface.

   Visio opens the Shape Data dialog shown in Figure 11.20, asking for the number of bars in the graph.

Figure 11.20
The Shape Data dialog.

Set the number of bars and click OK. Visio displays the new 2D bar graph, as shown in Figure 11.21.

Figure 11.21
A new bar chart.

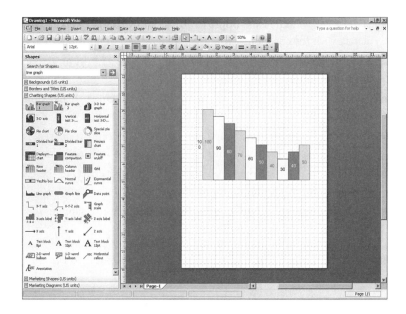

5. To set the height of the bar chart, drag the yellow control handle (it's diamond shaped) on the largest bar vertically.

6. To set the width of the bars, drag the control handle that appears at the lower left of the first bar. All the other bars' widths will be resized to match.

7. To set the value for a bar, select the bar chart, click the bar whose value you want to set, and type the new value. You can see a new value being entered for the first bar shown in Figure 11.22.

Figure 11.22
Setting a bar's value.

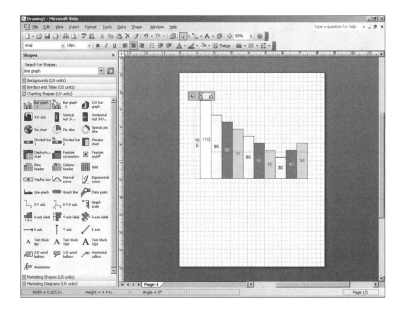

When you're done setting the bar's value, click outside the bar graph.

When you're setting values for bar graphs that display percentages, include the percent sign (%) after your values. If you don't, Visio multiplies your value by 100—so a value of 5, where you meant 5%, would appear as 500%.

Want to change the color of the bars? Do this:

1. Open the drawing containing the bar graph in Visio.

2. Select the bar whose color you want to change. First click the 2D bar graph, then the bar.

3. Right-click the selected bar and select Format > Fill. Visio displays the Fill dialog, shown in Figure 11.23.

Figure 11.23
Setting a bar's fill.

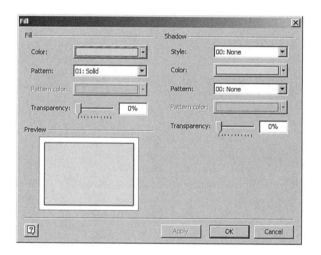

4. Set the appropriate fill options and click OK.

How about changing the number of bars in the bar graph? Follow these steps:

1. Open the drawing containing the bar graph in Visio.

2. Right-click the bar graph and select the Set Number of Bars menu item. Visio displays the Shape Data dialog.

3. Select the new number of bars from the Number of Bars drop-down box and click OK.

What about adding x- and y-axes? Just follow these steps:

1. Open the drawing containing the bar graph in Visio.

2. Drag the X-Y axis shape until the origin of the shape snaps to the origin of the 2D bar graph.

3. Click the X-Axis or Y-Axis text boxes and enter the new text to label those axes.

CREATING 3D BAR GRAPHS

You can also create 3D bar graphs in Visio—it's almost as easy as creating 2D bar graphs.

Here's how to create a 3D bar graph:

1. Open Visio.

2. Select File > New > Business > Charts and Graphs, or File > New > Business > Marketing Charts and Diagrams. Visio creates a new drawing.

3. Select the Charting Shapes stencil.

4. Drag a 3D bar graph shape onto the drawing surface.

    Visio opens the Shape Data dialog shown in Figure 11.24, asking for the data in the graph.

Figure 11.24
Using the Shape Data dialog.

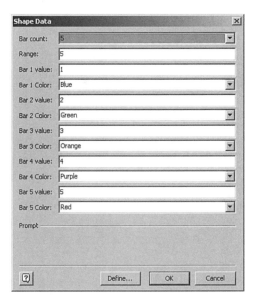

Select the bar count. Unfortunately, Visio limits the number of bars to five.

Set the range of the graph—that's the full extent of the y-axis.

Set the value for the bars in the Bar x value boxes, where x is the number of the bar.

Set the color for the bars in the Bar x color drop-down lists, where x is the number of the bar.

Click OK.

Visio displays the new 3D bar graph shape, as shown in Figure 11.25.

5. Select the 3D bar graph and type the text you want to label the shape with.

6. To set the height of the bar chart, drag the green sizing handle at the top or bottom of the shape.

Figure 11.25
A new 3D bar graph.

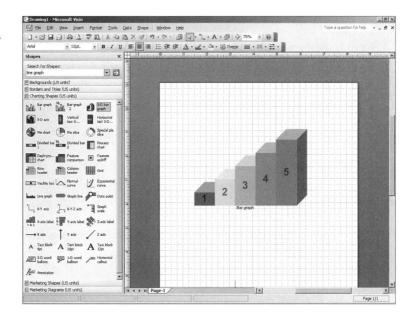

7. To set the width of the bars, drag the control handle that appears at the lower left of the first bar. All the other bars' widths are resized to match.

If you want to change the colors of the bars, do this:

1. Open the drawing containing the bar graph in Visio.
2. Select the bar whose color you want to change. First click the 3D bar graph, then the bar.
3. Right-click the selected bar and select Format > Fill. Visio displays the Fill dialog.
4. Set the appropriate fill options and click OK.

You can also change the number of bars in the bar graph. Follow these steps to do that:

1. Open the drawing containing the bar graph in Visio.
2. Right-click the bar graph and select the Bar Count and Range menu item. Visio displays the Shape Data dialog.
3. Select the new number of bars from the Bar Count drop-down box and click OK.

And you can change the range of the bars in the bar graph this way:

1. Open the drawing containing the bar graph in Visio.
2. Right-click the bar graph and select the Bar Count and Range menu item. Visio displays the Shape Data dialog.
3. Enter the new range for the bar graph in the Range box and click OK.

You can also reset the height of a bar this way:

1. Open the drawing containing the bar graph in Visio.

2. Right-click the bar graph and select the Bar Properties menu item. Visio displays the Shape Data dialog.

3. Set the value for the bar in the Bar *x* value boxes, where *x* is the number of the bar you're interested in.

CREATING LINE GRAPHS

You can use line graphs to display the same kinds of data you use bar graphs for; you can see an example in Figure 11.26.

Figure 11.26
A line graph.

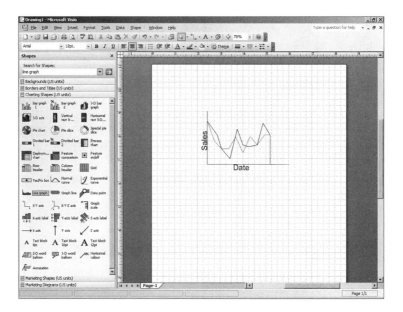

Unfortunately, the line graph shape lets you draw only a single line graph. So why do you see two lines in Figure 11.26? Figure 11.26 was made by superimposing two line graph shapes, after setting the fill of each shape to "none."

How do you create a line graph? Follow these steps:

1. Open Visio.

2. Select File > New > Business > Charts and Graphs, or File > New > Business > Marketing Charts and Diagrams. Visio creates a new drawing.

3. Select the Charting Shapes stencil.

4. Drag a line graph shape onto the drawing surface.

Visio opens the Shape Data dialog shown in Figure 11.27, asking for the data in the graph.

Figure 11.27
The Shape Data dialog.

Select the number of data points in the Shape Data dialog.

Visio displays the new line graph shape, as shown in Figure 11.28.

Figure 11.28
A new line graph.

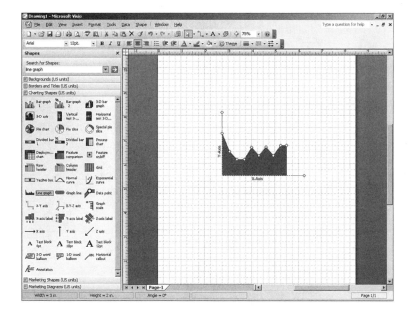

5. To change the height of the graph, drag the yellow diamond control handle at the top of the y-axis.

6. To change the width of the graph, drag the yellow diamond control handle at the right end of the x-axis.

7. To set the value of a data point, drag its yellow diamond control handle to the correct height. Oddly, Visio doesn't have any way for you to type in the values directly—you have to drag the data points to their correct position by yourself.

8. To set the fill under the graph, including removing the fill entirely, right-click the graph and select Format > Fill. Visio opens the Fill dialog, shown in Figure 11.29.

If you want to remove the fill altogether, select None in the Pattern drop-down box.

After making the changes you want to the line graph's fill and fill pattern, click OK.

11

Figure 11.29
The Fill dialog.

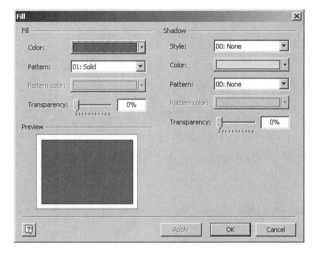

By default, Visio doesn't make the data points appear in any special way in a line graph; they're just vertices on the line that connects them.

However, you can change that with the data point shape. Just drag data point shapes from the Charting Shapes stencil to the vertices of a line graph, and you get the results shown in Figure 11.30.

Figure 11.30
Using data point shapes.

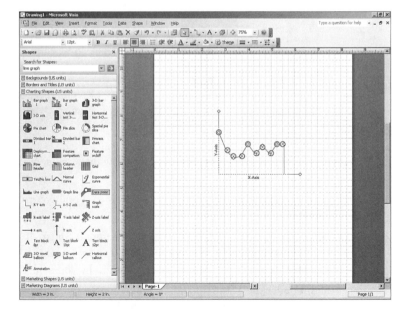

CREATING PIE CHARTS

Visio also supports pie charts—those round graphs divided into radial segments.

If you want to create a pie chart, follow these steps:

1. Open Visio.

2. Select File > New > Business > Charts and Graphs, or File > New > Business > Marketing Charts and Diagrams. Visio creates a new drawing.

3. Select the Charting Shapes stencil.

4. Drag a pie chart shape onto the drawing surface.

   Visio opens the Shape Data dialog shown in Figure 11.31, asking for the number of slices in the chart.

Figure 11.31
The Shape Data dialog.

Select the number of slices and click OK.

Visio displays the new pie chart, as shown in Figure 11.32.

Figure 11.32
A new pie chart.

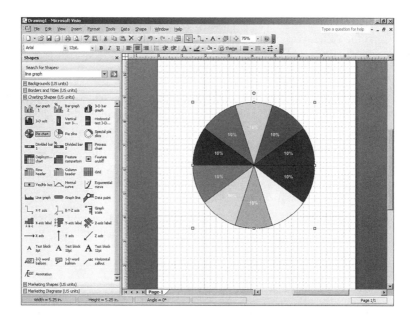

To change the dimensions of the pie chart, drag the resizing handles on the chart.

5. To set the size of each slice, right-click the pie chart and select the Set Slice Sizes item.

Visio opens the Shape Data dialog shown in Figure 11.33, asking for the value of each slice.

Figure 11.33
The Shape Data
dialog.

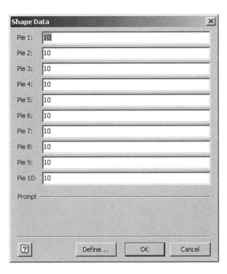

Visio opens the Shape Data dialog shown in Figure 11.33, asking for the value of each slice.

Enter the value for each slice as a percentage and click OK.

If the values you specify don't add up to 100%, Visio adds an empty pie slice to make up the difference.

6. To enter text for a slice, select the slice and type your text.

What if you want to create a pie with more than the 10 slices that the pie shape allows you? Or what if you want to create a pie with "exploded" slices, such as that shown in Figure 11.34?

You can create a pie with more than 10 slices or with exploded slices by using the pie slice shape. Here's how to create pie charts with the pie slice shape:

1. Open Visio.

2. Select File > New > Business > Charts and Graphs, or File > New > Business > Marketing Charts and Diagrams. Visio creates a new drawing.

3. Select the Charting Shapes stencil.

4. Drag a pie slice shape onto the drawing surface. Color the slice by right-clicking it, selecting Format > Fill, and using the Fill dialog.

   Adjust the size of the slice with the yellow diamond control handle.

5. Drag another pie slice shape onto the drawing surface. Color the slice by right-clicking it, selecting Format > Fill, and using the Fill dialog.

   Adjust the size of the slice with the yellow diamond control handle.

Figure 11.34
An "exploded" pie slice.

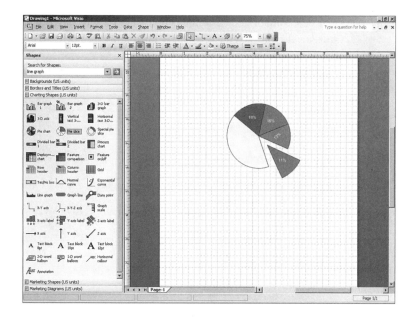

6. Glue the green control handle on one end of the circumference of the new pie slice to a noncenter vertex of the original pie slice, as shown in Figure 11.35.

Figure 11.35
Connecting pie slices.

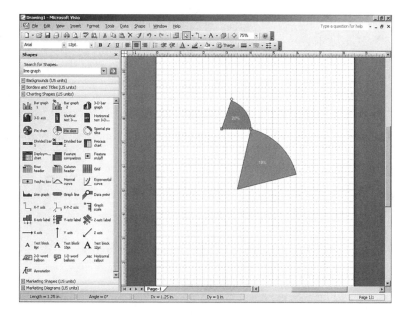

If you need to, rotate the new slice so that its control handle may be connected to the original slice using Shape > Rotate or Flip > Flip Vertical.

7. Drag the green control handle at the center of curvature of the new slice to the center of curvature of the original slice, as shown in Figure 11.36.

Figure 11.36
Aligning pie slices.

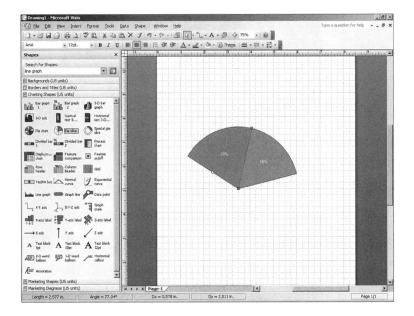

8. Repeat the preceding steps to add more slices.

You can also create exploded pie slices by simply positioning the slices as you want them.

CREATING MARKETING DRAWINGS

There are plenty of business shapes, and we'll take a look at some of them here, starting with triangle and pyramid drawings.

These kinds of drawings indicate a hierarchical relationship between their segments, such as the parts of a marketing program, or the command levels of an organization.

CREATING TRIANGLE AND PYRAMID DRAWINGS

To create a triangle or pyramid drawing, follow these steps:

1. Open Visio.

2. Select File > New > Business > Marketing Charts and Diagrams. Visio creates a new drawing.

3. Select the Marketing Diagrams stencil.

4. Drag a triangle or pyramid shape to the drawing surface. Visio opens a Shape Data dialog.

For triangles, the Shape Data dialog asks for the number of levels (the maximum is five) you want in the triangle. Fill that in and click OK.

For pyramids, the Shape Data dialog asks for the number of levels you want in the pyramid (the maximum is six), and the color of the pyramid. Make your selections and click OK.

Visio creates the triangle or pyramid, as shown in Figure 11.37.

Figure 11.37
A new pyramid.

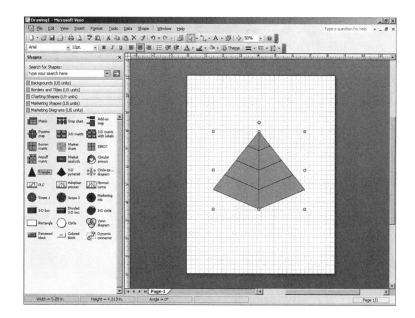

5. Use the sizing handles to resize the triangle or pyramid to the size you want. Visio resizes the triangle or pyramid to match the mouse movements.

6. Add text to the triangle or pyramid; click the shape to select it, then click it again to select the level of the triangle or the face of the pyramid you want to add text to—then simply type your text, as shown in Figure 11.38.

As you can see, triangles and pyramids are some of the simplest of the business drawings available.

How about some circle-spoke drawings?

Coming up next.

Figure 11.38
Adding text to a
pyramid.

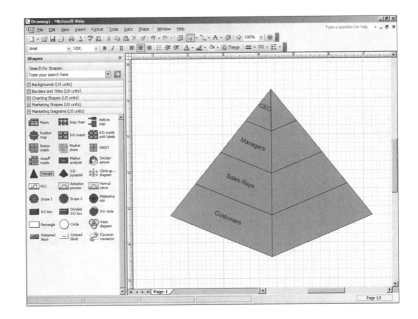

CREATING CIRCLE-SPOKE DRAWINGS

Circle-spoke drawings also represent relationships—this time a one-to-many relationship. These drawings have a central circle that is connected with spokes to a set of other, satellite circles.

For example, you might use a circle-spoke drawing to illustrate a vice-president's responsibilities, listing the various departments the VP is in charge of.

Here's how to create a circle-spoke drawing:

1. Open Visio.
2. Select File > New > Business > Marketing Charts and Diagrams. Visio creates a new drawing.
3. Select the Marketing Diagrams stencil.
4. Drag a circle-spoke to the drawing surface. Visio opens a Shape Data dialog.

   This Shape Data dialog asks for the number of circles you want in the drawing—it's important to note that this refers to the number of circles surrounding the central circle, and does not include the central circle that the spokes radiate from.

   Select the number of circles you want (the maximum is eight) and click OK.

   Visio creates the circle-spoke drawing, as shown in Figure 11.39.
5. Use the sizing handles to resize the shape to the size you want. Visio resizes the circle-spoke shape to match the mouse movements.

Figure 11.39
A new circle-spoke
drawing.

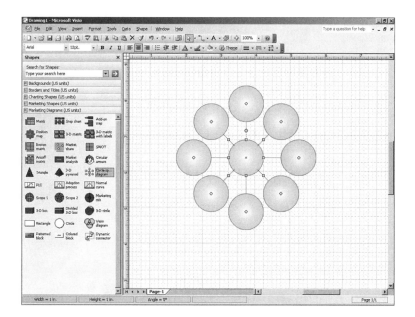

6. To rearrange the circles, drag the yellow diamond control handles in the center of each circle. Visio moves the circles to match your mouse movements.

7. To add text to a circle, just select that circle and type your text.

Not bad.

CREATING NORMAL CURVES

Normal curves are bell-shaped curves, and you can draw them with the Visio normal curve shape.

This shape isn't designed to let you reshape the curve exactly to fit a set of data—it's just a bell-shaped curve that you can resize in only two ways: in height and in width.

These curves are used to illustrate any process that is bell-shaped, such as demographics curves. They're mostly good for predictions, because you can't configure the curve to match actual data.

Here's how to create a normal curve drawing:

1. Open Visio.

2. Select File > New > Business > Marketing Charts and Diagrams. Visio creates a new drawing.

3. Select the Marketing Diagrams stencil.

4. Drag a normal curve shape to the drawing surface. Visio creates the normal curve shape, as shown in Figure 11.40.

Figure 11.40
A new normal curve drawing.

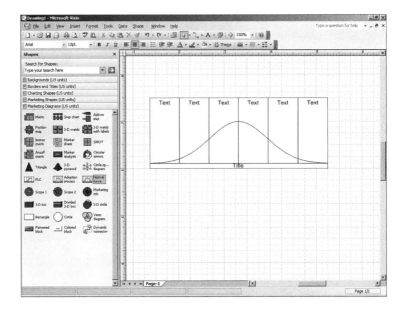

5. Use the sizing handles to resize the shape to the size you want. Visio resizes the normal curve shape to match the mouse movements.

6. Add text to a sector of the curve; select that text (currently all sectors show the text "Text" as shown in Figure 11.40) by selecting the shape and then selecting the text in the sector you want, and typing your text.

You can see an example in which text has been added to the curve's sectors in Figure 11.41.

Figure 11.41
Text added to a normal curve drawing.

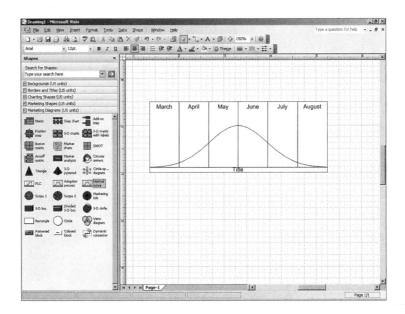

7. Add text to the title of the normal curve. (Currently the title shows the text "Title" as shown in Figure 11.40.) Select the normal curve shape, then select the title text and type the new title.

You can see an example in which text has been added to the curve's title in Figure 11.42.

Figure 11.42
Text added to a normal curve drawing's title.

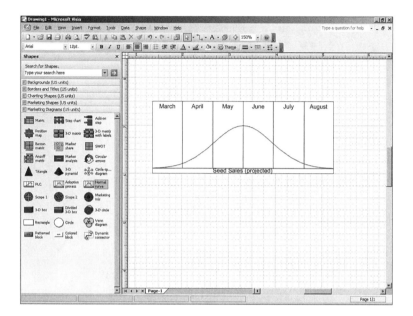

That's how to create a normal curve. As mentioned, normal curves aren't configurable, except for changes in their width and height, so they're not good for graphing your data. But they are good for anything that you need a bell-shaped curve for.

CREATING VENN DIAGRAMS

Venn diagrams are used to illustrate overlapping relationships. They use overlapping circles to do that. Here's how to create a Venn diagram drawing in Visio:

1. Open Visio.
2. Select File > New > Business > Marketing Charts and Diagrams. Visio creates a new drawing.
3. Select the Marketing Diagrams stencil.
4. Drag a Venn diagram shape to the drawing surface. Visio creates the Venn diagram shape, as shown in Figure 11.43.
5. Use the sizing handles to resize the shape to the size you want. Visio resizes the Venn diagram shape to match the mouse movements.

Figure 11.43
A new Venn diagram drawing.

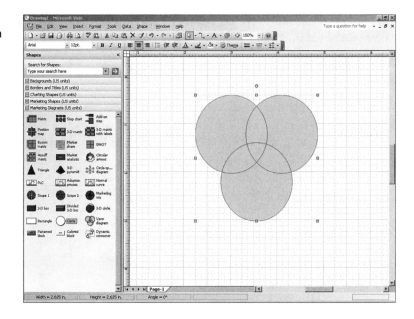

6. Add text to a sector of the Venn diagram. Select that sector by selecting the shape and then selecting the sector you want, and typing your text.

   You can see an example in which text has been added to the Venn diagram's sectors in Figure 11.44.

Figure 11.44
Text added to a Venn diagram drawing.

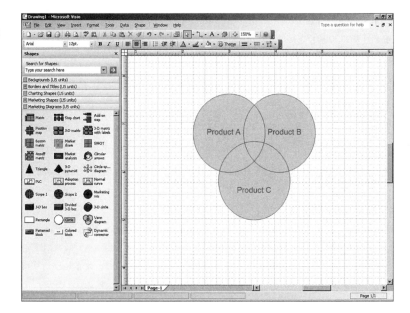

Unfortunately, Visio's Venn diagrams have a serious drawback—they're not configurable at all. What you see in Figure 11.43 is what you get—you can't add circles, and you can't change the way they intersect.

If you want to create your own Venn diagrams, with the number of circles you want, intersecting the way you want, try using circles, coming up next.

CREATING VENN DIAGRAMS WITH CIRCLES

You can use the circle shape to create your own Venn diagrams; here's how:

1. Open Visio.
2. Select File > New > Business > Marketing Charts and Diagrams. Visio creates a new drawing.
3. Select the Marketing Diagrams stencil.
4. Drag a circle shape to the drawing surface. Visio creates the circle shape, as shown in Figure 11.45.

Figure 11.45
A new circle drawing.

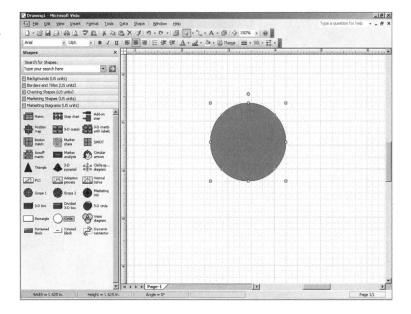

5. Use the sizing handles to resize the shape to the size you want. Visio resizes the circle shape to match the mouse movements.
6. Right-click the circle shape and select Format > Fill, then set the color of the circle. Visio colors the circle shape to match.
7. Right-click the circle shape and select Format > Fill, then set the transparency of the circle to 50%.
8. To add text to a circle, select that circle, and then type your text.

9. Repeat the preceding steps for additional circles in your Venn diagram.

You can see an example of using circles to make a Venn diagram in Figure 11.46.

If you want to create your own Venn diagrams, using circles is usually a better way to go.

Figure 11.46
A Venn diagram drawing made of circles.

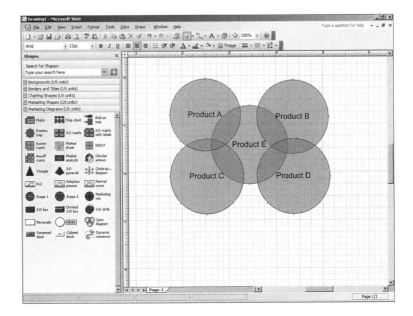

CREATING MATRIX SHAPES

You can use the matrix shapes to illustrate breakdowns of your data in two dimensions. For example, you might want to show how a number of colors mix, and display that data something like this:

```
     ¦ yellow         green
------------------------------------------
red  ¦ orange         brown
blue ¦ green          cyan
```

There are a number of matrix shapes in the Marketing Diagrams stencil:

- Matrix
- 3D matrix
- 3D matrix with labels
- Boston matrix

Here's how to create a matrix—in particular, a 3D matrix with labels shape in Visio:

1. Open Visio.

2. Select File > New > Business > Marketing Charts and Diagrams. Visio creates a new drawing.

3. Select the Marketing Diagrams stencil.

4. Drag a 3D matrix with labels shape to the drawing surface. Visio creates the matrix shape, as shown in Figure 11.47.

Figure 11.47
A new 3D matrix with labels drawing.

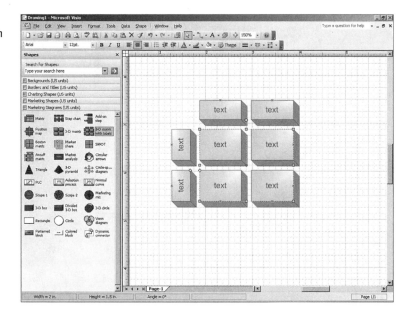

5. Use the sizing handles to resize the shape to the size you want. Visio resizes the matrix shape to match the mouse movements.

6. To add text to a block in the matrix, select that block, and then type your text.

7. Repeat the preceding steps for additional blocks in the 3D matrix with labels shape.

You can see an example in Figure 11.48, in which the matrix shows what the results are of mixing colors.

Unfortunately, the matrix shapes have the same drawback as the Venn diagram shape in Visio—they're not configurable.

The matrix shapes are great as long as you want a 2×2 matrix, but what if you want a 3×3? Or a 4×6 matrix?

As with Venn diagrams, the best way to create your own custom matrices is to create them yourself. You can do that with the rectangle or 3D box shape in the Marketing Diagrams stencil, dragging as many of those shapes as you need to the drawing surface to create your own matrix.

There's another type of drawing that we should cover while discussing the Business category—PivotDiagrams, and they're coming up next.

Figure 11.48
Text added to a 3D matrix.

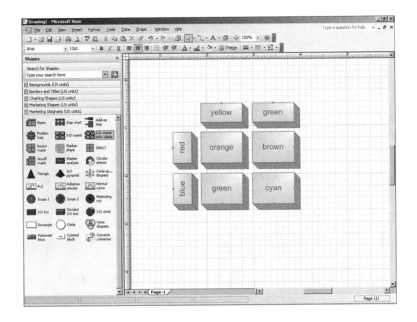

PIVOTDIAGRAMS

PivotDiagrams are all about displaying your data—from any of a variety of perspectives. They're as sophisticated a shape as you get in Visio.

The best way to get started with PivotDiagrams is to create one. Follow these steps:

1. Open Visio.
2. Select File > New > Business > PivotDiagram. Visio creates a new drawing and opens the Data Selector Wizard, shown in Figure 11.49.

Figure 11.49
The Data Selector Wizard, first pane.

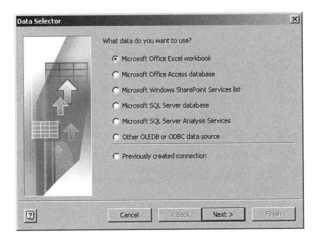

3. Select your data source and click Next. Visio opens the second pane of the Data Selector wizard, shown in Figure 11.50.

Figure 11.50
The Data Selector wizard, second pane.

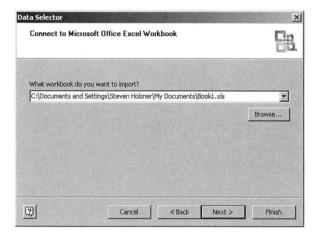

4. Select the data to work with and click Next. Visio opens the third pane of the Data Selector wizard, shown in Figure 11.51.

Figure 11.51
The Data Selector wizard, third pane.

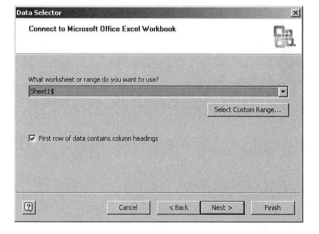

5. Select the rows and columns to work with and click Next. Visio opens the fourth pane of the Data Selector wizard, shown in Figure 11.52.

6. If the summary displayed in the fifth pane of the wizard is okay, click Next; otherwise, click Back and make changes. You can see the fifth pane of the Data Selector wizard in Figure 11.53.

Figure 11.52
The Data Selector wizard, fourth pane.

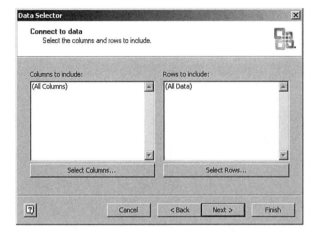

Figure 11.53
The Data Selector wizard, fifth pane.

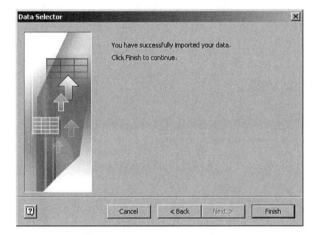

This creates a new PivotDiagram, as shown in Figure 11.54.

There are three parts of PivotDiagrams:

- **The PivotDiagram window**—You can see this window at the left in Figure 11.54. This window is how you access your data.

- **Pivot nodes**—These display data in the PivotDiagram; you can see that Visio creates one pivot node to get you started when you create a PivotDiagram, as shown in Figure 11.54.

- **The PivotDiagram toolbar**—You can see this toolbar in Figure 11.54; it gives you buttons for common PivotDiagram actions.

Now that you've created a PivotDiagram, you're ready to look at your data from different perspectives.

Figure 11.54
A new PivotDiagram.

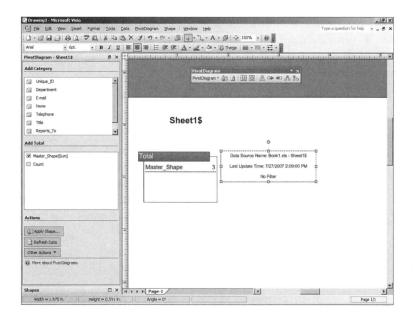

How can you do that? Follow these steps:

1. Select a pivot node. This is the node that your data will be categorized under.

2. In the PivotDiagram window, click the category of data you want displayed. Visio displays the data items in this category under the node you selected.

   You can see an example in Figure 11.55, where the nodes are displaying Name data.

Figure 11.55
Displaying Name
data in a
PivotDiagram.

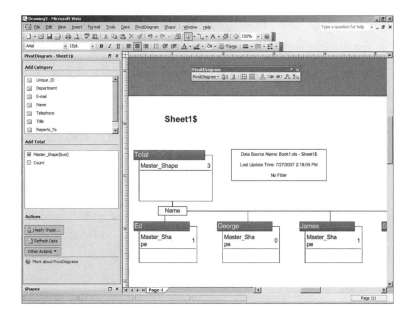

Want to view your data in a different way? That's what PivotDiagrams are all about. To pivot the diagram, select the node whose displayed data you want to change, and select a new data category. Visio displays a new breakdown of the category's data under the node.

You can see an example in Figure 11.56, in which the nodes are displaying Title data.

Figure 11.56
Displaying Title data in a PivotDiagram.

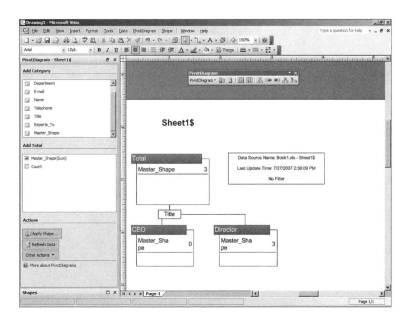

Note that the PivotDiagram is indicating that there are three shapes with Director status in Figure 11.56. How can you find out who those three are?

You can do that by selecting the Director pivot node and then selecting the Name category to add, resulting in a breakdown of the three directors, as shown in Figure 11.57.

You can also use the items in the PivotDiagram menu to sort nodes, merge or unmerge them, and collapse or expand them.

The items in PivotDiagrams are data graphics, and you can edit their appearance. Here's how to do that:

1. Select the pivot node whose data graphic you want to change.

2. Select PivotDiagram > Edit Data Graphic. Visio opens the Edit Data Graphic dialog, listing the data graphics associated with each pivot node.

3. Select the data graphic to edit and click Edit Item. Visio opens the Edit Text dialog, shown in Figure 11.58.

Figure 11.57
Breaking out data in a PivotDiagram.

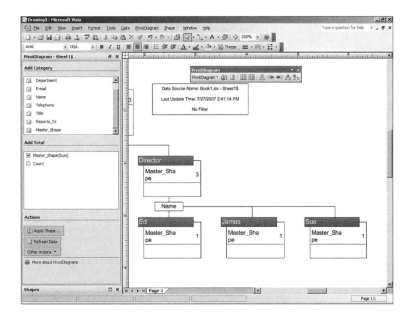

Figure 11.58
Editing a data graphic in pivot nodes.

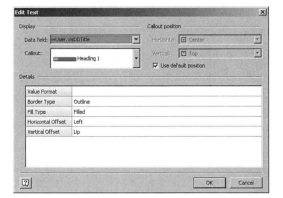

Make the changes you want in the data graphic and click OK twice to close the two dialogs.

The new data graphics are displayed in the PivotDiagram, as shown in Figure 11.59.

Figure 11.59
New data graphics in pivot nodes.

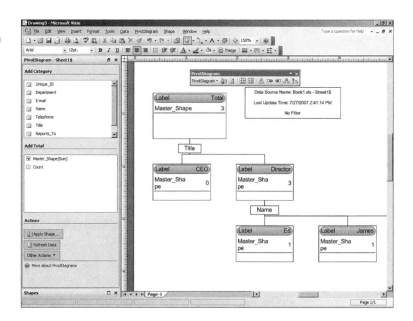

You can also get sums or averages of data in PivotDiagrams. Here are the steps to follow:

1. Select the pivot nodes that you want to include in the calculation.

2. Select the operation you want to perform by letting the mouse hover over the items in the Add Totals box of the PivotDiagram window, and making a selection from the drop-down list whose arrow appears. You can choose from these types of calculations:

   Sum

   Average

   Min

   Max

   Count

   Visio adds the calculation results to the boxes for each pivot node.

CHAPTER 12

CREATING ORGANIZATION CHARTS AND FLOWCHARTS

In this chapter

ORGANIZATION CHARTS

Like it or not, most businesses are built on formal hierarchies—and that's what Visio's organization charts exist to document.

Organization charts make visual the hierarchical structure of a business, laying out the tiers and dependencies of that business. There are many ways that Visio helps you create organization charts, and you're going to see all the tricks in this chapter.

Organization charts are one of those specialized drawings that let you connect to a data source automatically and keep synchronized with that data source as well.

Note that there are additional uses for organization charts beyond just reporting on business structures—another major use of organization charts is to document genealogy relationships.

We'll start now with creating basic organization charts.

CREATING ORGANIZATION CHARTS

The organization chart template is a serious one in Visio, and it supports a number of tools.

First are the organization chart shapes themselves, which are SmartShapes. They connect themselves—no need to add your own connectors. And they can be moved between hierarchy layers as well.

When you create an organization chart, an Organization Chart menu appears in the Visio menu bar. This is the menu that does just about everything you need when it comes to organization charts—lay them out, run the Organization Chart Wizard, and more.

Speaking of the Organization Chart Wizard, that's a tool that lets you import data from other programs to build your organization charts—very useful if you keep track of your organization in, say, an Excel worksheet.

The Organization Chart toolbar offers six buttons, giving you speedy access to the most common layout commands. There are three layout options, a re-layout button, and two buttons for moving shapes around.

You can see the Organization Chart template's Organization Chart Shapes stencil—which is where the action is when it comes to organization charts—in Figure 12.1.

Figure 12.1
The Organization
Chart Shapes stencil.

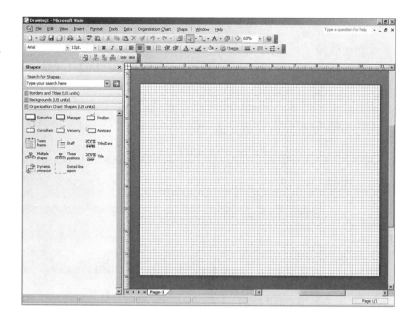

Here's an overview of the kinds of shapes you'll find in this stencil:

- **Executive**—The Executive shape is a little larger than the other shapes, and it has a heavier border.

- **Manager**—The Manager shape is a normal-sized box, and it has a heavier border.

- **Position**—The Position box is a normal-sized box with a single border.

- **Consultant**—The Consultant shape is a normal-sized box, and it has a dotted border.

- **Assistant**—The Assistant shape appears like the Position shape, but positions itself in an offset way.

- **Vacancy**—The Vacancy shape is a normal-sized box, with a dotted border.

- **Multiple shapes**—If you drop this shape on a superior shape, Visio connects the number of shapes you specify to the superior shape automatically.

- **Three positions**—If you drop this shape on a superior shape, Visio connects three positions to the superior shape automatically.

- **Team frame**—Displays graphically that people are the members of a team.

- **Dynamic connector**—Lets you add connectors to an organization chart besides the ones that Visio adds itself.

So what about actually creating an organization chart?

12

That's coming up now. To create an organization chart, just follow these steps:

1. Open Visio.

2. Select File > New > Business > Organization Chart. Visio opens a new drawing, as shown in Figure 12.1.

3. Drag an executive shape to the drawing. Visio opens a new dialog, telling you that organization charts are special, and you can connect shapes merely by dropping them onto a superior shape.

   When you dismiss this dialog by clicking OK, the new Executive shape appears, as shown in Figure 12.2.

Figure 12.2
A new organization chart with an executive shape.

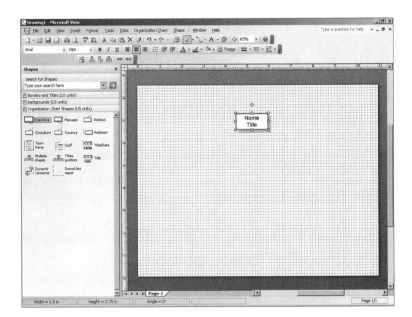

The Executive shape will be selected, so it's ready for you to enter text into.

4. Enter the name of the new executive, press Enter, then enter his or her title. When you're done entering the person's name and title, click outside the shape, deselecting it.

   The result appears in Figure 12.3.

   Note that Visio lets you enter the person's name and title this way, as a shortcut—that is, entering the name, pressing Enter, and then entering the title.

   Visio does separate those two items into the Name and Title shape fields, as shown in Figure 12.4, where the Shape Data dialog for the Executive shape appears.

Figure 12.3
Adding a name and title to an executive shape.

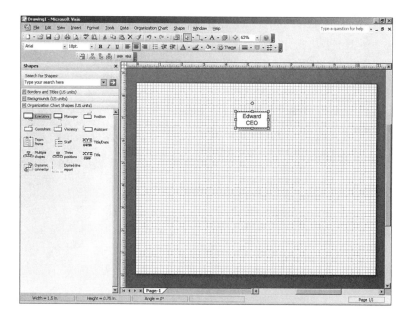

Figure 12.4
An Executive shape's data.

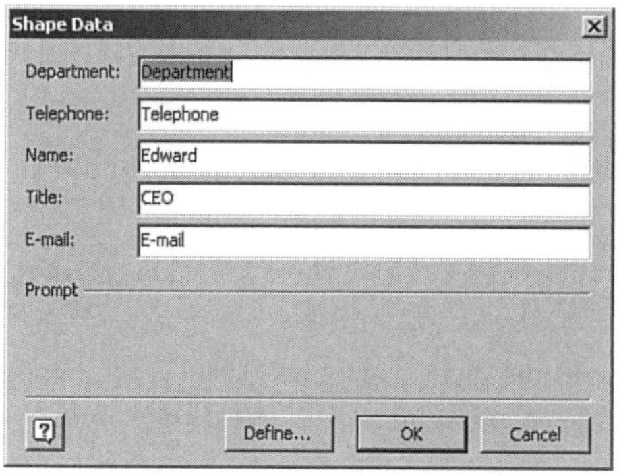

Add the other data you want connected to the executive shape by displaying the Shape Data dialog shown in Figure 12.4, by right-clicking the shape and selecting Data > Shape Data.

After you've added other shape data to the Executive shape as needed, such as Department and Telephone, click OK to dismiss the Shape Data dialog.

5. Drag a Manager shape onto the Executive shape. Visio arranges the Manager shape under the Executive and adds a connector, as shown in Figure 12.5.

Enter the name of the new manager, press Enter, and then enter the title. When you're done entering the person's name and title, click outside the shape, deselecting it.

Add the other data you want connected to the Manager shape by displaying the Shape Data dialog, by right-clicking the shape and selecting Data > Shape Data.

Figure 12.5
Adding a Manager shape.

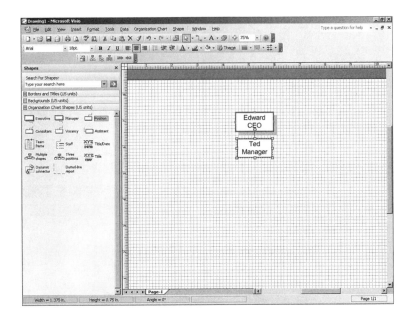

After you've added other shape data to the Manager shape as needed, such as Department and Telephone, click OK to dismiss the Shape Data dialog.

6. Drag additional shapes onto the chart as needed. Visio arranges the shapes under the superior shape you've dropped them on and adds a connector.

Enter the name of the new person, press Enter, then enter the title. When you're done entering the person's name and title, click outside the shape, deselecting it.

Add the other data you want connected to the person's shape by displaying the Shape Data dialog, by right-clicking the shape and selecting Data > Shape Data.

After you've added other shape data to the person's shape as needed, such as Department and Telephone, click OK to dismiss the Shape Data dialog.

You can see a sample organization chart in Figure 12.6.

That's one way of building an organization chart—manually. But there are other ways, such as using the Organization Chart Wizard.

Figure 12.6
A sample organiza-
tion chart.

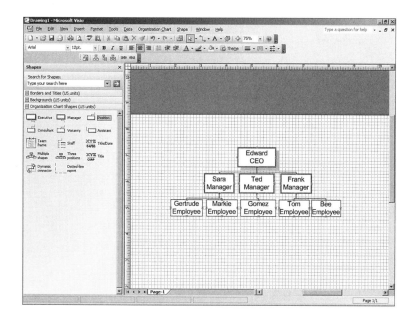

USING THE ORGANIZATION CHART WIZARD

There are two main ways of using the Organization Chart Wizard—if you don't have data already stored for your organization, and if you do.

We'll take a look at the first case—in which you don't have external stored data—first.

ENTERING YOUR OWN DATA

Here's how to build an organization chart if you don't have any stored data to work with, using the Organization Chart Wizard:

1. Open Visio.
2. Select File > New > Business > Organization Chart Wizard. Visio opens the Organization Chart Wizard, as shown in Figure 12.7.

Figure 12.7
The Organization
Chart Wizard, first
pane.

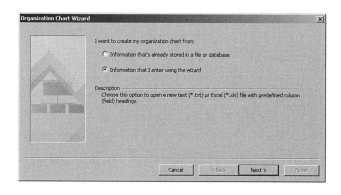

3. Select the option labeled Information That I Enter Using the Wizard, and click Next. You can see this option selected in Figure 12.7.

Visio opens the second pane of the Organization Chart Wizard, shown in Figure 12.8.

Figure 12.8
The Organization
Chart Wizard, second
pane.

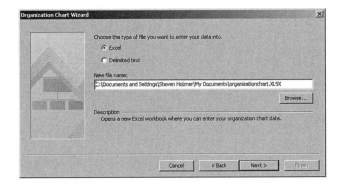

4. Select the type of file you want to save your data in, enter a name, and click Next. Visio then displays a dialog telling you to type over the sample data that appears and close the file. Click OK to dismiss this dialog.

For example, if you've elected to save your data in a comma-delimited file, Visio displays the sample text in Notepad, as shown in Figure 12.9.

Figure 12.9
Using Notepad.

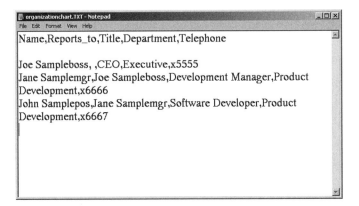

Enter your data and select File > Exit.

If, however, you've chosen to store your data in Excel, Visio opens Excel with a sample template. Enter your data and select File > Exit.

Visio displays the fourth pane of the Organization Chart Wizard, shown in Figure 12.10.

5. Specify how to break your chart over pages and click Finish. Visio displays the new organization chart, as shown in Figure 12.11.

Figure 12.10
The Organization
Chart Wizard, fourth
pane.

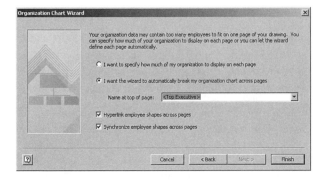

Figure 12.11
The Organization
Chart Wizard, fifth
pane.

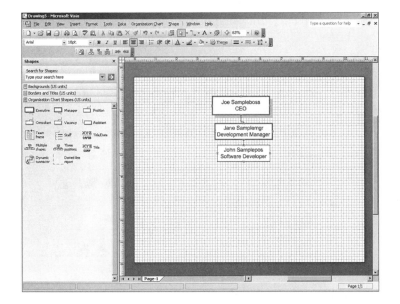

That's how you create a file to store your organization data using the Organization Chart Wizard, and how you put that data to work creating an organization chart.

USING EXISTING DATA

If you already have your data stored in an external data source, however, you can also use the Organization Chart Wizard. For example, you might have this data to import from an Excel worksheet:

Unique_ID	Name	Title	Reports_To	Master_Shape
ID1	Mark	CEO		0
ID2	Toni	Director	ID1	1
ID3	Sam	Director	ID1	1
ID4	Cathy	Director	ID1	1

12

The Organization Chart Wizard will let you import that data.

Note that the column headers above—Unique_ID, Name, Title, and so on—are tailored to organization charts. You might wonder how Visio can be expected to know which columns should correspond to what shape data in an organization chart if your data isn't set up this way. The wizard solves this problem by letting you connect columns to shape data yourself.

Here's how to build an organization chart if you do have stored data to work with, using the Organization Chart Wizard:

1. Open Visio.

2. Select File > New > Business > Organization Chart Wizard. Visio opens the Organization Chart Wizard.

3. Select the option labeled Information That's Already Stored in a File or Database, and click Next.

    Visio opens the second pane of the Organization Chart Wizard, shown in Figure 12.12.

Figure 12.12
The Organization Chart Wizard, second pane.

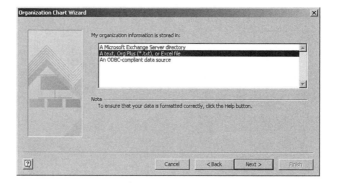

4. Select the source of your data and click Next.

    Visio opens the third pane of the Organization Chart Wizard, shown in Figure 12.13.

Figure 12.13
The Organization Chart Wizard, third pane.

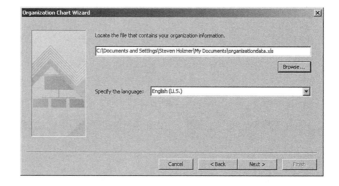

Browse to your data file and click Next.

Visio displays the fourth pane of the Organization Chart Wizard, shown in Figure 12.14.

Figure 12.14
The Organization Chart Wizard, fourth pane.

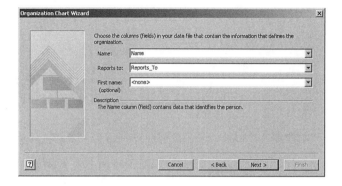

5. Specify which columns to use in your data for the Name and Reports To shape data, and, optionally, select a First Name column; click Next. Visio displays the fifth pane of the Organization Chart Wizard, as shown in Figure 12.15.

Figure 12.15
The Organization Chart Wizard, fifth pane.

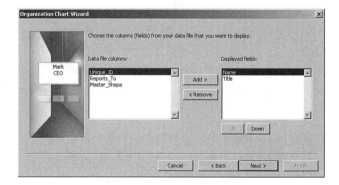

6. Specify which additional columns to display and click Next. By default, Visio displays only the person's name and title, but you might have additional columns storing the person's telephone, email address, and so on, and you can display that additional data using this pane.

   When you click Next, Visio displays the sixth pane of the Organization Chart Wizard, shown in Figure 12.16.

7. Specify which additional columns to store as shape data and click Next. Visio lets you import your data and store it as shape data.

   When you click Next, Visio displays the seventh pane of the Organization Chart Wizard, shown in Figure 12.17.

12

Figure 12.16
The Organization
Chart Wizard, sixth
pane.

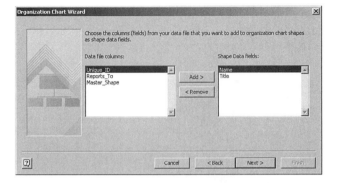

Figure 12.17
The Organization
Chart Wizard,
seventh pane.

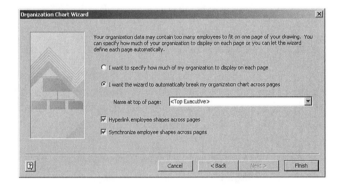

8. Specify how to break your data across pages and click Finish.

When you click Finish, Visio displays the new organization chart, as shown in Figure 12.18.

Figure 12.18
The new organization
chart.

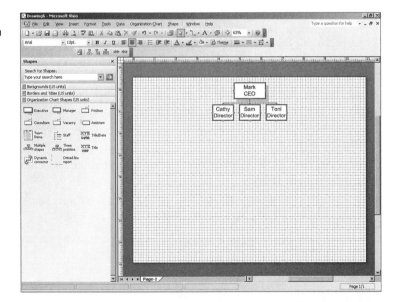

Cool.

Note in particular the options available in the last pane of the Organization Chart Wizard (shown in Figure 12.17), which contains some options that are worth discussing.

Here's what those options let you do:

- **If** you want to hyperlink the same employee shapes across pages, select the Hyperlink Employee Shapes Across Pages option—This connects the same employee across pages using hyperlinks.
- **If** you want to synchronize changes to a particular shape across all copies of that shape in your drawing, select the Synchronize Employee Shapes Across Pages option—If you select this option, changes to an employee's shape that you make in one location are made automatically to every copy of the shape on any page in the drawing.
- **If** you want to control how Visio displays your shapes across pages, select the I Want to Specify How Much of My Organization to Display on Each Page option—When you select this option, the Finish button on the pane changes into a Next button.

    Clicking the Next button displays the Organization Chart Wizard's Page Break dialog, shown in Figure 12.19.

Figure 12.19
The Organization Chart Wizard's Page Break dialog.

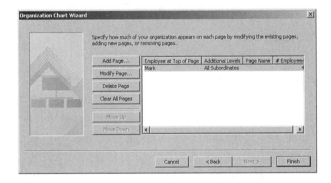

To specify the levels to display on the first page, click the Modify Page button. Visio displays the pane shown in Figure 12.20.

Figure 12.20
The Organization Chart Wizard's Modify Page pane.

Here's what you can do on this pane:

You can select the number of additional levels you want to appear on the first page as an executive summary in the Number of Additional Levels drop-down list.

To name the first page, such as "Executive Summary," type that name into the Page Name box.

Click OK to close the Organization Chart Wizard's Modify Page pane.

To add additional pages to the organization chart, such as a sub-organization, click the Add Page button in the Organization Chart Wizard's Page Break dialog. Visio displays the pane shown in Figure 12.21.

Figure 12.21
The Organization Chart Wizard's Add Page pane.

Here's what you can do on this pane:

Select the name that appears on the first level of the new page. For example, you might select a manager whose organization you want to break out on this new page.

Select the number of additional levels. You can choose 0–8, or All Subordinates (which is the default choice).

To name the new page, type that name into the Page Name box.

Click OK to close the Organization Chart Wizard's Modify Page pane.

CONTROLLING THE LAYOUT

The Organization Chart toolbar gives you control over the layout of organization charts. Say that you start off with the organization chart shown in Figure 12.22.

Now say that you've decided that your chart doesn't look quite right. The Organization Chart toolbar has three layout options available:

- Horizontal layout
- Vertical layout
- Side by side

Figure 12.22
An organization
chart.

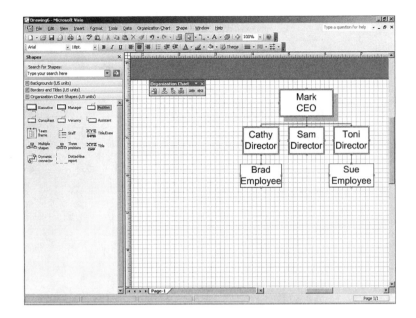

Each of these options has suboptions as well.

To change the layout of the chart shown in Figure 12.22, just follow these steps:

1. Open Visio.
2. Open the Visio drawing containing the organization chart in which you want to alter the layout.
3. Click the top shape in the layout to select it.
4. Click the other shapes in the layout to select them and create a group.
5. Click the button you want in the Organization Chart toolbar—Horizontal Layout, Vertical Layout, or Side by Side. A context menu opens, as shown in Figure 12.23. Select the layout you want.

   Visio lays out your selected group to match, as shown in Figure 12.24.

12

Figure 12.23
The Organization
Chart toolbar.

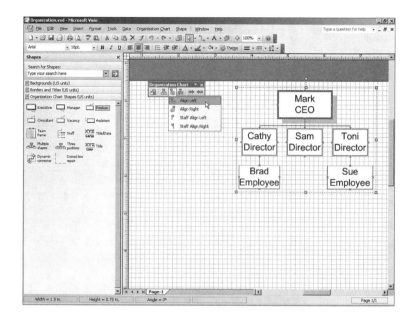

Figure 12.24
A new organization
chart layout.

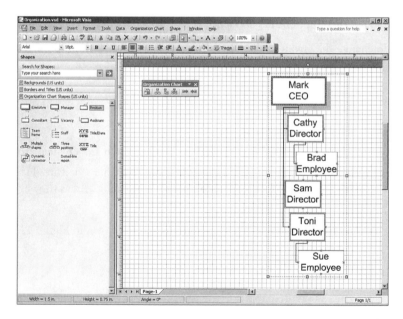

You can also access all the submenu items for the layout buttons of the Organization Chart toolbar by selecting Organization Chart > Arrange Subordinates, which opens the Arrange Subordinates dialog, shown in Figure 12.25.

Figure 12.25
The layout options.

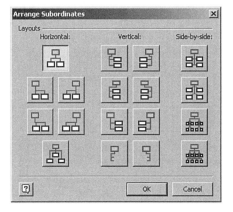

As you can see, laying out organization charts does work, but you might not like the results (see Figure 12.24). In my opinion, you're better off laying out the shapes in an organization chart yourself, adding more shapes or removing them as time and the needs of the organization dictate.

You can also have Visio move the subordinates of a person: Just select that person and then select Organization Chart > Move Subordinates, then select Left/Up or Right/Down from the submenu. Once again, this does work, but I recommend simply using the mouse.

FORMATTING ORGANIZATION CHARTS

There are many options in Visio for formatting organization charts. For example, organization chart text is, by default, 8-point, very small when you want to present information in a legible way. Using the formatting options, you can set the default font in your organization chart, among other formatting options.

To display the formatting options, select Organization Chart > Options, which displays the Options dialog, shown in Figure 12.26.

Figure 12.26
The formatting options.

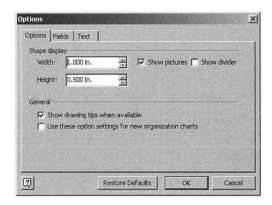

Here are the options on the default Options tab, shown in Figure 12.26:

- Set the height and width of shapes in the Shape Display region—Use the Width and Height boxes to set the default dimensions of shapes in the chart.

- Select whether you want to show pictures in the organization chart shapes with the Show Pictures check box—You can insert pictures into organization chart shapes by right-clicking them and selecting the Insert Picture menu item. That's cool when, for example, you want to show pictures of all employees.

- Select whether you want to show dividers in the organization chart shapes with the Show Divider check box—You can have Visio draw a horizontal dividing line in each organization chart shape, separating each displayed field—for example, if you select this option, a dividing line will appear between the Name and Title fields.

The Fields tab of the Options dialog lets you format where in the shape the various field data is displayed. You can see this tab in Figure 12.27.

Figure 12.27
The formatting options in the Fields tab.

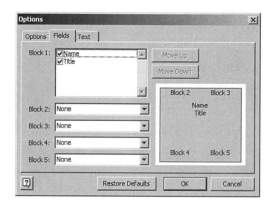

Using this tab, you can add or rearrange fields to display in organization chart shapes. As you see in Figure 12.27, you can set fields in the four corners of organization chart shapes.

For example, rearranging the Name and Title fields can give you the results shown in Figure 12.28.

The Text tab of the Options dialog lets you format the text in organization shapes; you can see this tab in Figure 12.29.

You can use the controls in this tab to format text, but you have to select each field (for example, Name, Title) you want to format separately.

Figure 12.28
Formatting organization shapes.

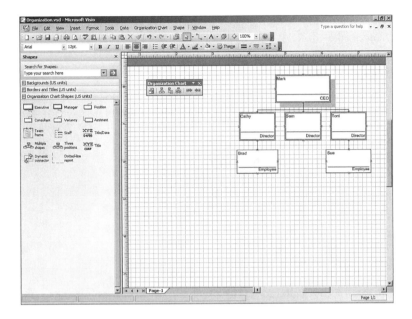

Figure 12.29
The Options dialog, Text tab.

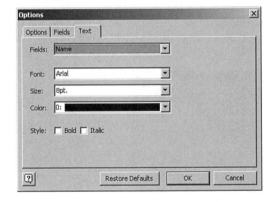

Here are the controls in this tab of the Options dialog:

- **The Fields box**—Lets you select the field in organization chart shapes to format, such as the Name or Title field.

- **The Font box**—Lists the fonts installed on your machine. Select a font from the list.

- **The Size box**—Lets you select a font size. For example, use this box to enlarge the font.

- **The Color box**—Lets you select a font color. Select the color of each font you want to use.

- **The Bold and Italic check boxes**—Let you specify whether the font should be bold or italic.

When you're done with the Options dialog, click OK to dismiss that dialog and make your changes take effect.

MODIFYING SPACING

You can also modify the shape spacing in organization charts. You do that with the Organization Chart > Change Spacing menu item, which opens the Spacing dialog, shown in Figure 12.30.

Figure 12.30
The Spacing dialog.

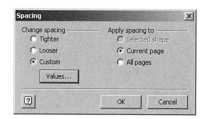

You can use this dialog to set the spacing between shapes looser or tighter, as shown in Figure 12.30.

You can also set the spacing to your own custom spacing if you select the Custom radio button and click the Values button. Selecting that option and clicking the Values button opens the Custom Spacing Values dialog, shown in Figure 12.31.

Figure 12.31
The Custom Spacing Values dialog.

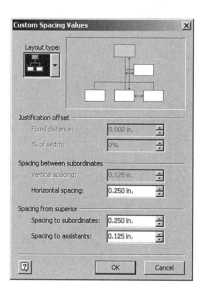

The Custom Spacing Values dialog lets you select the spacing, both vertically and horizontally, for shapes in organization charts. You can change the spacing between superiors and subordinates in the units you've selected for the organization chart (US or metric) using this dialog.

When you're done with the Custom Spacing Values dialog, click OK twice to make your changes take effect.

In this discussion of formatting, it's also worth noting that you can hide subordinate shapes. That can help in complex charts. To hide the subordinates of a shape, right-click the shape and select Hide Subordinates.

To make the subordinate shapes visible again, right-click the superior shape and select Show Subordinates.

CHANGING SHAPES

If someone gets a promotion—or a demotion—you can change the type of that person's shape. For example, if someone goes from the standard employee shape (Position) to the Manager shape, you can alter the shape type.

You can change someone's shape type by selecting Organization Chart > Change Position Type, which opens the Change Position Type dialog, shown in Figure 12.32.

Figure 12.32
The Change Position Type dialog.

You can use this dialog to promote or demote any shape in an organization chart. Just select the new type of shape you want and click OK.

COMPARING CHARTS

Visio organization charts can get pretty involved, and you might even lose track of the changes you've made to various versions of a chart across different files.

That's no problem because, believe it or not, Visio will compare organization chart files for you. That's pretty impressive, given the number of different drawing types there are in Visio—organization charts are actually supported in such depth that Visio will compare charts for you.

For example, say that you changed the employee Sue (see Figure 12.32) to Edna in a new version of the file, as shown in Figure 12.33.

Figure 12.33
A changed organization chart.

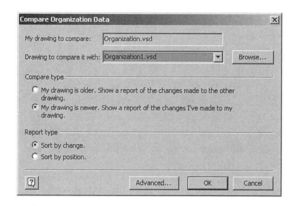

Let's see whether Visio will pick up the change. Follow these steps:

1. Select Organization Chart > Compare Organization Data. This opens the Compare Organization Data dialog, shown in Figure 12.33.
2. Select the other version of the file in the Drawing to Compare It With box.
3. Select the My Drawing Is Older or the My Drawing Is Newer radio button. Make the choice depending on which version of the drawing is newer—the one currently open, or the one whose file you've indicated in the preceding step.

   You can see the My Drawing Is Newer radio button selected in Figure 12.33.
4. Select the report type in the Report Type area of the dialog. You can choose from two selections: Sort by Change or Sort by Position.
5. If you want to perform an advanced comparison, click the Advanced button. In the Advanced dialog, you can select which fields (Name, Title, and so on) to compare.
6. Click OK. Visio makes the comparison and opens the report in Internet Explorer, as shown in Figure 12.34.

   As you can see, Visio did indeed pick up the change from Sue to Edna in its report.

12

Figure 12.34
A change report.

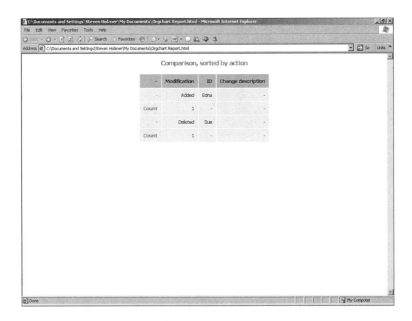

CREATING MULTIPAGE ORGANIZATION CHARTS

In larger organizations, organization charts can spread over multiple pages. Visio has some tools that let you break up charts among several pages, and we'll take a look at that capability next.

In particular, you can select any shape to be copied, along with any of its subordinates, to another page to break it out. When that shape is on its own page, you can add additional structure and details to it.

Here's how to copy a shape to a new page, and keep it synchronized with the original—that is, when you make a change to the original, the copy is changed as well:

1. Open Visio.

2. Open the drawing that contains the organization chart you want to work with.

3. Select the shape that you want to copy, along with its subordinates.

4. Select Organization Chart > Synchronize > Create Synchronized Copy. This opens the Create Synchronized Copy dialog, shown in Figure 12.35.

5. Select the New Page or Existing Page option. The New Page option creates the synchronized copy on a new page, and the Existing Page option lets you specify an existing page on which to create the copy.

6. Select the Hide Subordinates option if you want to hide the subordinates of the copy.

12

Figure 12.35
The Create
Synchronized Copy
dialog.

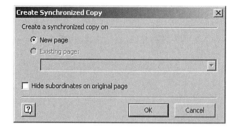

7. Click OK. Visio creates the synchronized copy of the shape you selected, along with its subordinates if you've set things up that way, on the new page or an existing page, as shown in Figure 12.36 (note the page tabs at the bottom of the drawing, indicating that what's displayed is really page 2).

Figure 12.36
A synchronized copy.

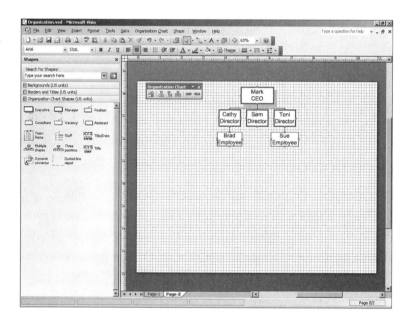

Now you can make the additions or changes you want to the synchronized copy, on its own page.

Creating new pages like this helps you break out the structure of a organization chart drawing.

That completes our look at organization charts. Next up are flowcharts.

CREATING FLOWCHARTS

Flowcharts are all about showing the flow of processes. That's one of Visio's fortes—creating flowcharts.

Flowcharts are an extraordinarily popular type of drawing, because they diagram just how a process works, and what types of decisions you can make inside the process.

There are many type of flowcharts in Visio:

- **Audit diagram**—Tracks audit information, such as for accounting purposes. In the Business template category.
- **Basic flowchart**—Shows the flow of a process, such as information flow and cost flow. In the General, Flowchart, and Business template categories.
- **Brainstorming**—Charts idea flows from brainstorming sessions. In the Business template category.
- **Cause and Effect diagram**—Models cause-and-effect processes, also called fishbone diagrams, in business terms. In the Business template category.
- **Cross-Functional flowchart**—Shows the relationship between a flowchart and the departments responsible for the steps in the chart. In the Flowchart and Business template categories.
- **Data Flow diagram**—Shows the flow of data. In the Flowchart and Business template categories.
- **EPC diagram**—Creates Event-driven Process Chains (a SAP concept), which model processes as chains of events. In the Business template category.
- **Fault Tree Analysis diagram**—Charts the behavior of processes that might fail, and indicates where their failures are. In the Business template category.
- **IDEF0 diagram**—Models processes according to the Structured Analysis and Design Technique (SADT). In the Flowchart template category.
- **ITIL diagram**—Documents management procedures, especially when it comes to IT operations. In the Business template category.
- **Organization chart**—Charts organization hierarchies. In the Business template category.
- **Project timeline**—Charts project timelines. In the Business template category.
- **SDL diagram**—Models event-driven processes, such as communication processes. In the Flowchart template category.
- **TQM diagram**—Documents quality control, reengineering, and continuous improvement processes. In the Business template category.
- **Work Flow diagram**—Charts work flow for business and management purposes. In the Flowchart and Business template categories.

Okay, that's what's available.

How about creating some flowcharts?

12

CREATING A BASIC FLOWCHART

We'll start by creating a basic flowchart drawing, to get the ball rolling with flowcharts.

To create a basic flowchart, follow these steps:

1. Open Visio.

2. Select File > New > General > Basic Flowchart, or File > New > Business > Basic Flowchart, or File > New > Flowcharts > Basic Flowchart. That creates a new flowchart drawing, as shown in Figure 12.37.

Figure 12.37
A new basic flowchart.

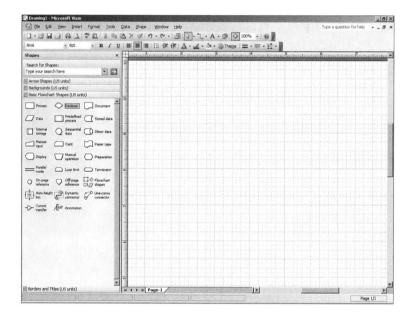

3. Drag a process shape onto the drawing surface. The process shapes are the basic building blocks of these kinds of drawings, the ones that appear most frequently in them.

4. Drag a decision shape onto the drawing surface. Position the decision shape under the process shape.

5. Select the decision shape and hover the mouse under the process shape until you see a downward autoconnect blue arrow. You can see this downward arrow under the mouse cursor in Figure 12.38.

6. Click the downward autoconnect blue arrow. Visio connects the process shape with the decision shape with a downward arrow, as shown in Figure 12.39.

Figure 12.38
An autoconnect arrow.

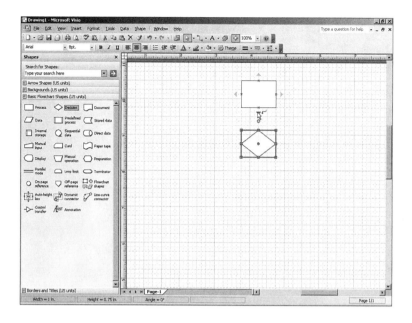

Figure 12.39
Connecting shapes in a flowchart.

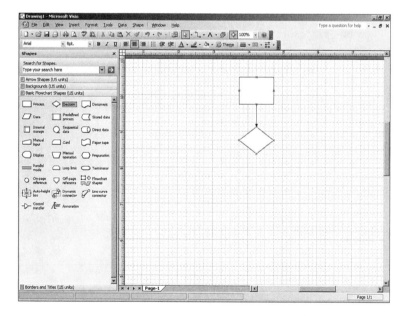

7. To add another process shape, select the process shape in the Basic Flowchart Shapes stencil, let the mouse hover over a vertex of the decision shape until an autoconnect arrow appears, and click the arrow. Visio adds a process shape, as shown in Figure 12.40.

Figure 12.40
Creating a new process shape in a flowchart.

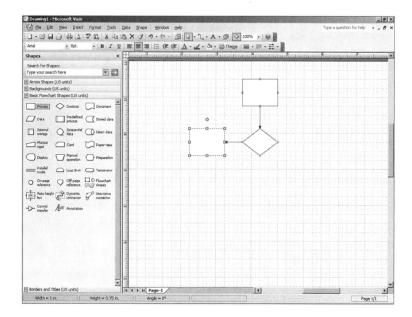

8. To add other shapes using autoconnect, follow the previous steps. Visio adds the new shapes, as shown in Figure 12.41.

Figure 12.41
Creating a new flowchart.

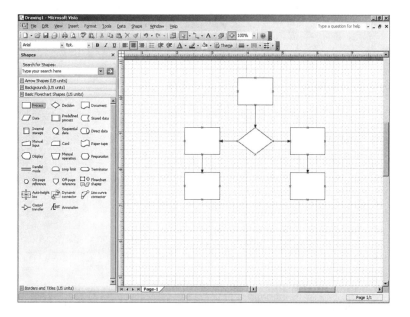

9. To add text to the drawing, select a shape and enter your text. You can see sample results in Figure 12.42.

Figure 12.42
Adding text to a new flowchart.

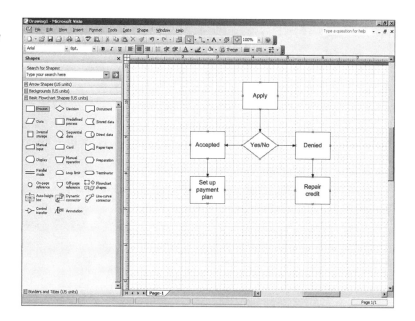

That shows how to create a basic flowchart. It also shows one way of connecting flowchart shapes: using autoconnect.

There are other ways as well, and they're worth looking at before we proceed to other flowcharts.

CONNECTING SHAPES IN FLOWCHARTS

There are several ways of connecting flowchart shapes:

- **Autoconnect version one**—To use autoconnect, select the shape to connect to, hover the mouse over the shape to connect from, and click the blue autoconnect arrow that appears.

- **Autoconnect version two**—Select the shape to connect from, select the type of shape you want to connect to in a stencil, and then click the blue autoconnect arrow that appears in the shape that you want to connect from.

- **Dragging**—Click the Connector tool on the standard toolbar, then drag your shapes onto your flowchart in sequence.

- **Connect Shapes command**—Drag all the shapes you want to connect onto the flowchart. Select them in the order in which they should be connected, and select Shape > Connect Shapes. Visio then connects the shapes for you.

That's the way to connect elements in a flowchart. Now we'll turn to more specific types of flowcharts, starting with Cause and Effect flowcharts.

12

CREATING CAUSE AND EFFECT FLOWCHARTS

Cause and Effect flowcharts let you explore the underlying reasons for a process. They're also called fishbone diagrams, because they look like fishbones.

Here's how to create a Cause and Effect flowchart:

1. Open Visio.

2. Select File > New > Business > Cause and Effect Diagram. Visio creates a new Cause and Effect drawing, as shown in Figure 12.43.

Figure 12.43
A new Cause and Effect flowchart.

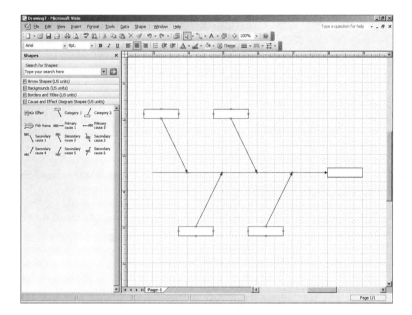

Note that Visio creates an Effect shape and four Category shapes, as you can see in the figure.

3. To enter the problem or effect you're charting, select the horizontal arrow in the drawing or the effect box at right, and type your text. Visio automatically adds that text to the Effect shape, as shown in Figure 12.44.

4. To enter the name of the categories, select a diagonal arrow in the drawing, or a category box, and type your text. Visio automatically adds that text to the Category shape, as shown in Figure 12.45.

5. To add more category shapes, drag a Category 1 or Category 2 shape onto the drawing, and position the shape so that its arrowhead touches the horizontal arrow in the drawing. Visio adds the new shape to the drawing.

6. To show a primary cause, drag a primary cause shape to the drawing and let its arrowhead snap to a category arrow. Enter the text for the shape by selecting the shape and typing.

Figure 12.44
Adding text to a new Cause and Effect flowchart.

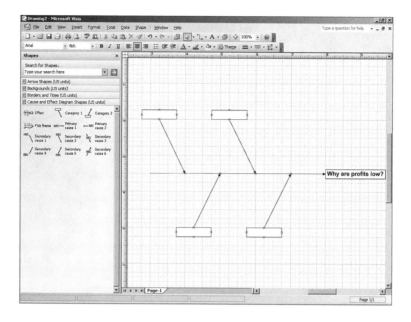

Figure 12.45
Adding text to the Category shape.

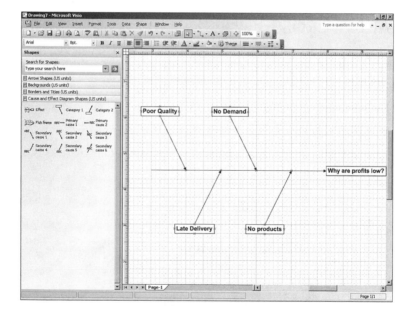

12

You can see an example in Figure 12.46.

7. To show a secondary cause, drag a secondary cause shape to the drawing and let its arrowhead snap to a primary cause arrow. Enter the text you want into the secondary cause shape.

And that's how to create Cause and Effect diagrams.

Figure 12.46
Adding a primary
cause shape.

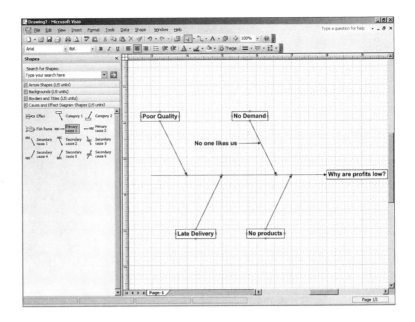

CREATING CROSS-FUNCTIONAL FLOWCHARTS

Cross-Functional flowcharts are useful when you want to indicate the units or departments that contribute to a process. You can list each department with a band that indicates what process they're involved with, as you're going to see.

Here's how to create a Cross-Functional flowchart:

1. Open Visio.
2. Select File > New > Business > Cross-Functional Flowcharts. Visio creates a new drawing, as shown in Figure 12.47.

Figure 12.47
Setting up a new
Cross-Functional
flowchart.

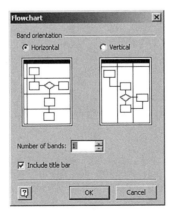

In the Flowchart dialog, Visio asks whether you want horizontal or vertical bands. Make your selection (if you're unsure, just accept the default horizontal bands).

Also select the number of bands to create—these bands correspond to the departments you're tying to the process being illustrated, so Visio is asking you about the number of departments you want to display in the flowchart.

If you want the flowchart to include a title bar, leave the Include Title Bar check box selected.

Click OK.

Visio creates the Cross-Functional flowchart for you, as shown in Figure 12.48. This particular flowchart has, as you can see, four horizontal bands in it.

Figure 12.48
A new Cross-Functional flowchart.

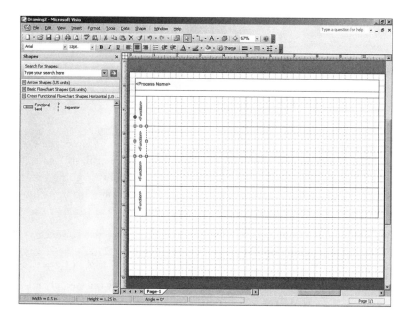

3. Select the title bar and enter your text for the flowchart's title bar.

4. Select each band's label and enter text for that band.

5. Open the Basic Flowchart Shapes stencil and drag flowchart shapes onto the drawing. When you want to span several departments with a process step, size the process shape accordingly, or use connectors to connect two process steps from completely different bands.

You can see an example in Figure 12.49.

That's the way it works—you create a Cross-Functional flowchart, and then use the basic flowchart shapes to add a process or processes to that flowchart.

You can use process shapes, as shown in Figure 12.49, as well as decision shapes, data shapes, and all the shapes that can appear in flowcharts.

Figure 12.49
Using flowchart shapes.

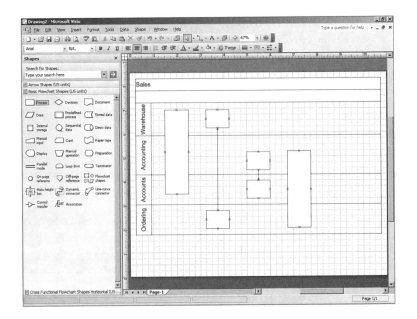

When you want to show the department association of a step in the process, you can stretch a process shape, as shown in Figure 12.49, to span one or more bands. Stretching a process shape is good when it works, but your bands are not always going to arrange themselves to match—you'll end up with cases in which the bands you want to include in a process are not adjacent.

In cases like that, you have a couple of choices. You can use connectors, as shown in Figure 12.49, to connect processes across nonadjacent bands. That's the most common solution. You can also, however, use multipage drawings, in which the bands on a new page might be next to each other, when they're not next to each other on the current page.

CREATING WORK FLOW DRAWINGS

Here's a fun one: the Work Flow diagram. This one comes packed with engaging icons that you can arrange to indicate the work flow of a department or departments.

The Work Flow Diagram template comes with three stencils:

- **Department stencil**—This stencil is the most fun one, and contains what amounts to clip art for all different types of departments that may exist in your organization—accounting, payroll, packaging, and so on.

- **Work Flow Objects stencil**—This stencil contains icon shapes for some generic work flow items—CD-ROMs, people, mail, document, and so on.

- **Work Flow Steps stencil**—Contains icons that represent work flow verbs, like Analyze, Approve, and Submit.

You connect shapes from these stencils using connectors, or the arrow shapes from the Arrow Shapes stencil, which is also part of the Work Flow Diagram template.

Here's how to create a work flow drawing:

1. Open Visio.
2. Select File > New > Business > Work Flow Diagram. Visio creates a new drawing, as shown in Figure 12.50.

Figure 12.50
A new work flow drawing.

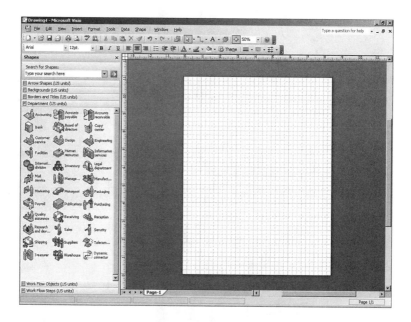

You can see the work flow stencils—Department, Work Flow Objects, Work Flow Steps—at left in the figure.

3. Using the three stencils available, drag the shapes you want to the drawing. You can see an example in Figure 12.51.
4. Using autoconnect or the Connector tool, or the arrows in the Arrow Shapes stencil, connect your shapes in the drawing. You can see an example in Figure 12.52.

Figure 12.51
Dragging shapes to a new work flow drawing.

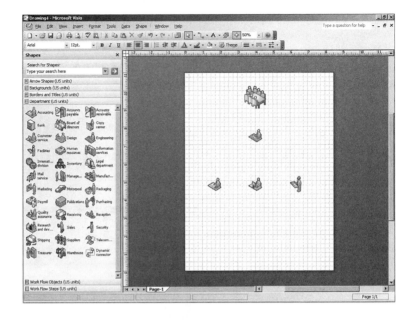

Figure 12.52
Adding connectors to a new work flow drawing.

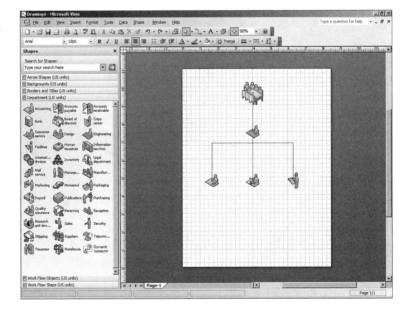

5. Add text to the shapes by selecting them and entering your text. You can see an example in Figure 12.53.

Figure 12.53
Adding text to a new work flow drawing.

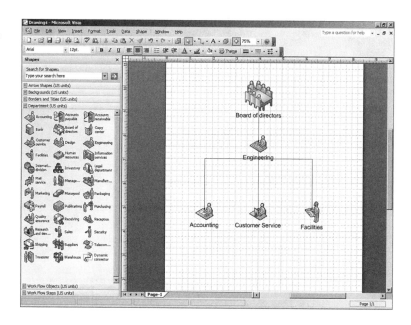

CREATING VALUE STREAM MAPPING DRAWINGS

Value stream mapping drawings are a descendant of the lean manufacturing process pioneered by Toyota. This kind of drawing can help you streamline processes by pinpointing waste.

The Process shape in the Value Stream Map Shapes stencil includes shape data for such items as Cycle Time and so on. You can use data graphics to make that kind of shape data visible in the drawing.

Here's how to create a value stream mapping drawing:

1. Open Visio.

2. Select File > New > Business > Value Stream Map. Visio creates a new drawing, as shown in Figure 12.54.

3. Using the Value Stream Map Shapes stencil, drag the shapes you want to the drawing. You can see an example in Figure 12.55.

12

Figure 12.54
A new value stream mapping drawing.

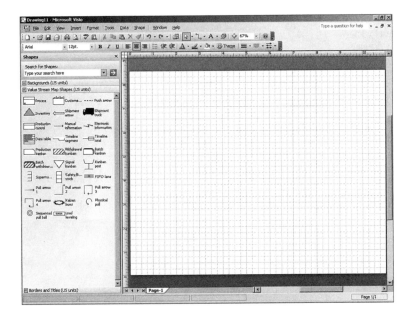

Figure 12.55
Dragging shapes to a new value stream mapping drawing.

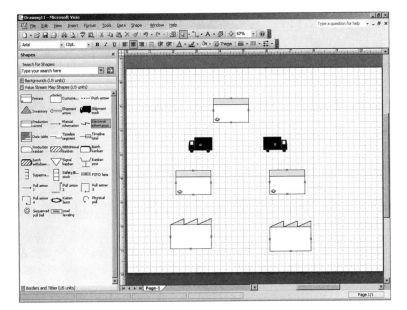

4. Using autoconnect or the Connector tool, or the arrows in the Value Stream Map Shapes stencil, connect your shapes in the drawing. You can see an example in Figure 12.56.

5. Add shape data to your shapes and create data graphics. You can see the shape data associated with a process shape in Figure 12.57.

Figure 12.56
Adding connectors to
a new value stream
mapping drawing.

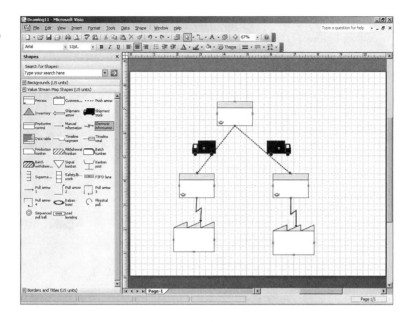

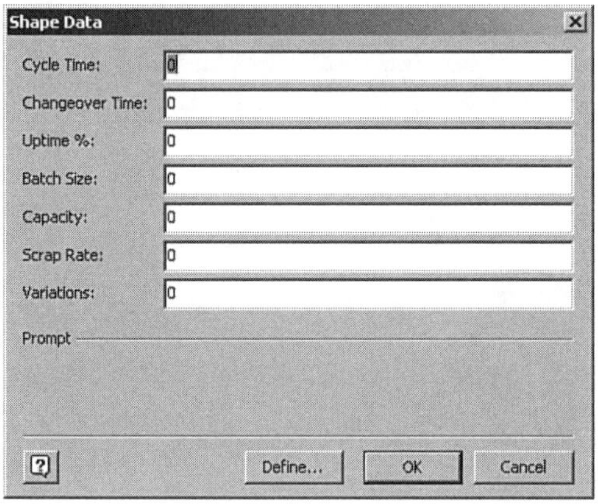

Figure 12.57
Shape data for a
process shape.

6. Add text to the shapes by selecting them and entering your text. You can see an example in Figure 12.58.

Note also the data graphic that's been added to the top process shape in the figure.

Figure 12.58
Adding text to a new value stream mapping drawing.

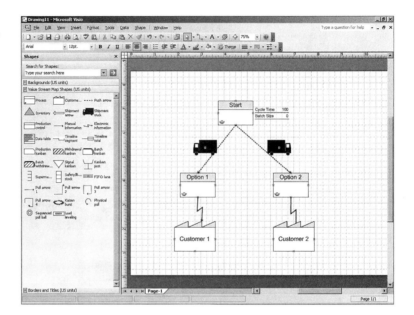

CHAPTER 13

SCHEDULING PROJECTS AND HANDLING BRAINSTORMING SESSIONS

In this chapter

SCHEDULING PROJECTS

Schedules are a big part of business, and Visio helps out here too. Schedules and timelines let people plan how projects are going to go, and what milestones they're going to attempt to meet.

Visio has good support for this kind of planning process built in, with calendars, timelines, Gantt charts, and more. Here are the templates to use in Visio:

- **Calendar**—Visio lets you create your own calendars by the week, month, or year for scheduling purposes. This template includes the Calendar Shapes stencil.
- **Timeline**—This template lets you create timelines that spell out just where milestones in your project are. This template includes the Timeline Shapes stencil.
- **Gantt charts**—You can create Gantt charts by dragging shapes in Visio, but you can also import data. This template includes the Gantt Chart Shapes stencil.
- **PERT charts**—Visio also lets you create PERT charts. This template includes the PERT Chart Shapes stencil.

We'll start by taking a look at calendars.

CREATING CALENDARS

Calendars are great for tracking events and appointments, and Visio is up to the task. When you create a calendar in Visio, a dialog box appears first to let you configure the calendar the way you want it—and there are plenty of options.

The calendar shapes are in the Calendar Shapes stencil of the Calendar template, which is in the Schedule template category.

CREATING DAY CALENDARS

Want to create a calendar in Visio? Here's how to do it, starting by creating a daily calendar:

1. Open Visio.
2. Select File > New > Schedule > Calendar.
3. Open the Calendar Shapes stencil.
4. Drag a Day shape onto the drawing. Visio opens the Configure dialog, shown in Figure 13.1.

Figure 13.1
The Configure dialog.

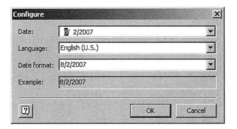

The Day shape creates a calendar item for only a single day, which means you're responsible for adding multiple days yourself to the drawing, if that's what you want.

Configure the Day shape this way:

Select the date for the day in the Date box.

Select the language for the day in the Language box.

Select the date format for the day in the Date Format box; you can choose from a wide variety of U.S. and European formats.

Click OK. When you do, Visio opens the new Day shape on the drawing surface, as shown in Figure 13.2.

Figure 13.2
A new Day shape.

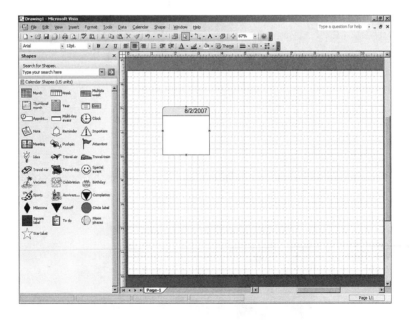

5. Select the shape and type the text for that day. The Day shape displays your text.

6. Repeat the preceding steps for the other days you want to create. You can see an example in Figure 13.3.

Figure 13.3
New Day shapes.

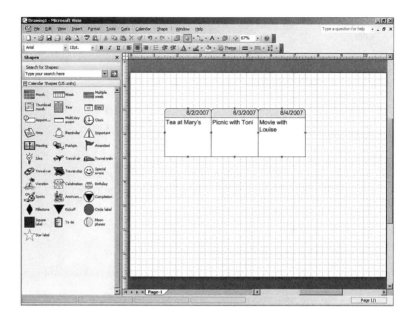

That's how to assemble a calendar from Day shapes.

CREATING WEEK CALENDARS

Creating calendars the previous way is a little awkward, however. You have to assemble the whole thing from individual shapes. A better option is usually the Week shape, which works like this:

1. Open Visio.
2. Select File > New > Schedule > Calendar.
3. Open the Calendar Shapes stencil.
4. Drag a Week shape onto the drawing. Visio opens the Configure dialog, as shown in Figure 13.4.

Figure 13.4
The Configure dialog for the Week shape.

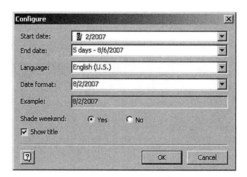

The Week shape creates a calendar item for a week.

Configure the Week shape this way:

Select the start date for the week in the Start Date box.

Select the end date for the week in the End Date box. You can select from two to eight days.

Select the language for the week in the Language box.

Select the date format for the week in the Date Format box; you can choose from a wide variety of U.S. and European formats.

Click OK. When you do, Visio opens the new Week shape on the drawing surface, as shown in Figure 13.5.

Figure 13.5
A new Week shape.

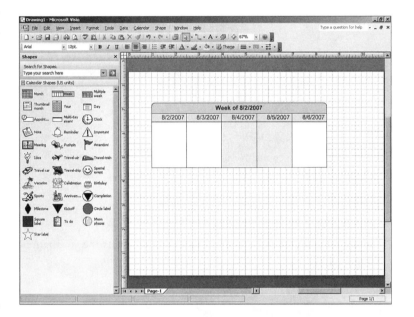

5. Select a day and type the text for that day. The shape displays your text.

You can see an example in Figure 13.6.

13

Figure 13.6
A new Week calendar.

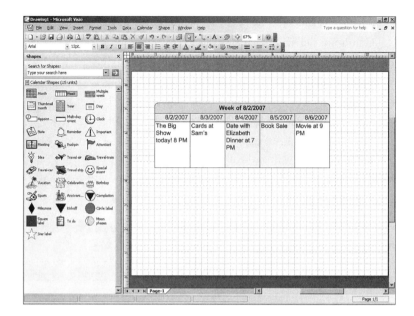

CREATING MONTH CALENDARS

You can also create a monthly calendar:

1. Open Visio.
2. Select File > New > Schedule > Calendar.
3. Open the Calendar Shapes stencil.
4. Drag a Month shape onto the drawing. Visio opens the Configure dialog, as shown in Figure 13.7.

Figure 13.7
The Configure dialog for the Month shape.

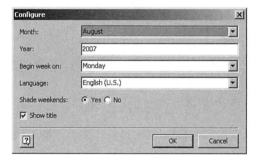

13

The Month shape creates a calendar item for a month.

Configure the Month shape this way:

Select the month you want in the Month box.

Select the year you want in the Year box.

Select the day of the week you want to start the week on in the Begin Week On box.

Select the language for the month in the Language box.

Select whether you want to shade weekends with the Shade Weekends radio buttons.

Select whether you want to show the shape's title with the Show Title check box.

Click OK. When you do, Visio opens the new Month shape on the drawing surface, as shown in Figure 13.8.

Figure 13.8
A new Month shape.

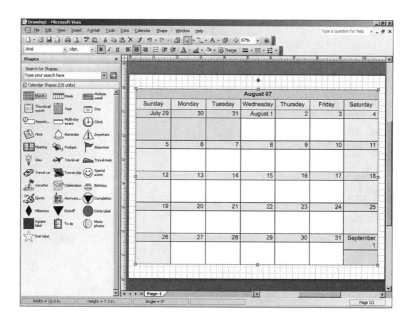

5. Select a day and type the text for that day. The shape displays your text. You can see an example in Figure 13.9.

13

Figure 13.9

A new Month calendar.

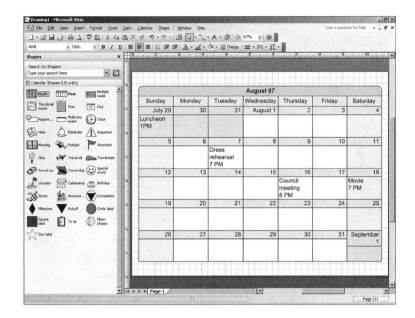

CREATING YEAR CALENDARS

You can also create annual calendars. Here's how:

1. Open Visio.

2. Select File > New > Schedule > Calendar.

3. Open the Calendar Shapes stencil.

4. Drag a Year shape onto the drawing. Visio opens the Shape Data dialog, as shown in Figure 13.10.

Figure 13.10

The Shape Data dialog for the Year shape.

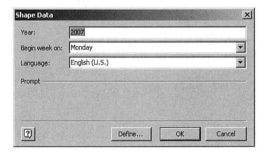

Configure the Year shape this way:

Select the year you want in the Year box.

Select the day of the week you want to start each week on in the Begin Week On box.

Select the language for the year in the Language box.

Click OK. When you do, Visio opens the new Year shape on the drawing surface, as shown in Figure 13.11.

Figure 13.11
A new Year shape.

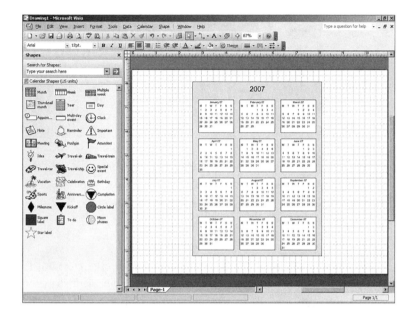

By default, year calendars fill the whole page; if you want another calendar, add another page to your drawing.

If you want to, you can reconfigure a calendar at any time by right-clicking it and selecting the Configure item.

ADDING APPOINTMENTS TO CALENDARS

The Calendar Shapes stencil also contains an Appointment shape that you can use to install appointments in calendars.

Here's how it works:

1. Open Visio.
2. Select File > New > Schedule > Calendar.
3. Open the Calendar Shapes stencil.
4. Drag a Week shape onto the drawing. Visio opens the Configure dialog.

   Configure the Week shape.

   Click OK.

   Visio displays the new Week shape.
5. Drag an Appointment shape onto a day. Visio opens the Configure dialog for Appointment shapes, as shown in Figure 13.12.

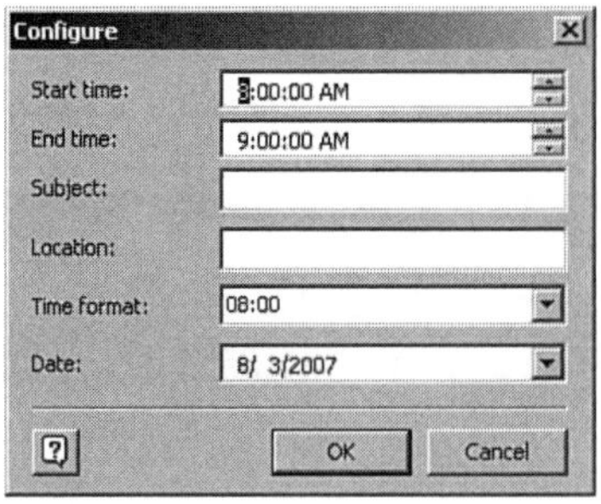

Figure 13.12
Configuring an
Appointment shape.

Configure the Appointment shape this way:

Select the start time you want in the Start Time box.

Select the end time you want in the End Time box.

Enter the subject of the appointment in the Subject box.

Enter a location in the Location box.

Select the time format in the Time Format box.

If you want to, select a date for the appointment in the Date box (Visio will have already entered a date if you've dropped the Appointment shape onto a date).

Click OK. When you do, Visio displays the new Appointment shape, as shown in Figure 13.13.

Figure 13.13
A new Appointment
shape.

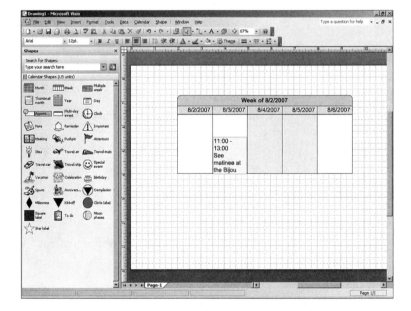

ADDING MULTIDAY EVENTS TO CALENDARS

Besides appointments, the Calendar Shapes stencil also a Multi-Day Event shape that you can use in calendars.

Here's how you do it:

1. Open Visio.
2. Select File > New > Schedule > Calendar.
3. Open the Calendar Shapes stencil.
4. Drag a Week shape onto the drawing. Visio opens the Configure dialog.

   Configure the Week shape.

   Click OK.

   Visio displays the new Week shape.
5. Drag a Multi-Day Event shape onto the calendar. Visio opens the Configure dialog for Multi-Day Event shapes, as shown in Figure 13.14.

Figure 13.14
Configuring a Multi-Day Event shape.

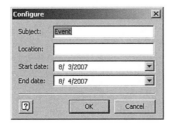

Configure the Multi-Day Event shape this way:

Enter the subject of the multiday event in the Subject box.

Enter a location in the Location box.

Select the start date you want in the Start Date box.

Select the end date you want in the End Date box.

Click OK. When you do, Visio displays the new Multi-Day Event shape, as shown in Figure 13.15.

Want to edit an appointment or event? Just right-click it and select Configure.

13

Figure 13.15
A new Multi-Day
Event shape.

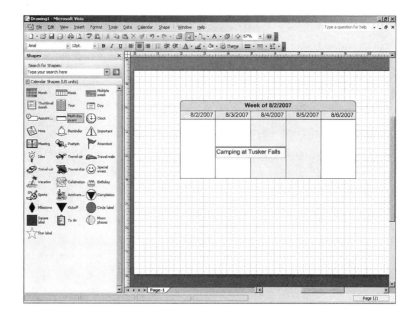

ADDING ART TO CALENDARS

The Calendar Shapes stencil also comes with clip art that you can use in calendars—stars, idea icons, birthday cakes, and so on.

You can drag these icons to calendars to embellish them. An example appears in Figure 13.16.

Figure 13.16
Adding calendar art
shapes to a calendar.

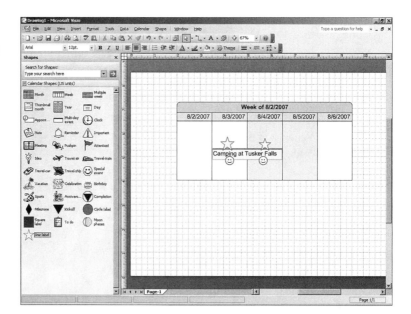

IMPORTING DATA TO CALENDARS

You can import data from Microsoft Outlook into calendars, which is useful if you've got a lot of data to transfer. Here's how it works:

1. Open Visio.
2. Select File > New > Schedule > Calendar.
3. Open the Calendar Shapes stencil.
4. Drag a calendar shape onto the drawing. Visio opens the Configure dialog; configure your calendar.
5. Select the calendar shape.
6. Select Calendar > Import Outlook Data Wizard. Visio opens the Import Outlook Data Wizard, shown in Figure 13.17.

Figure 13.17
The Import Outlook Data Wizard.

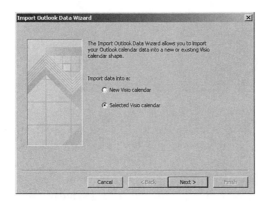

7. Select the radio button indicating whether you want to start a new calendar, or to work with an old one, and click Next. Visio opens the second pane of the Import Outlook Data Wizard, shown in Figure 13.18.

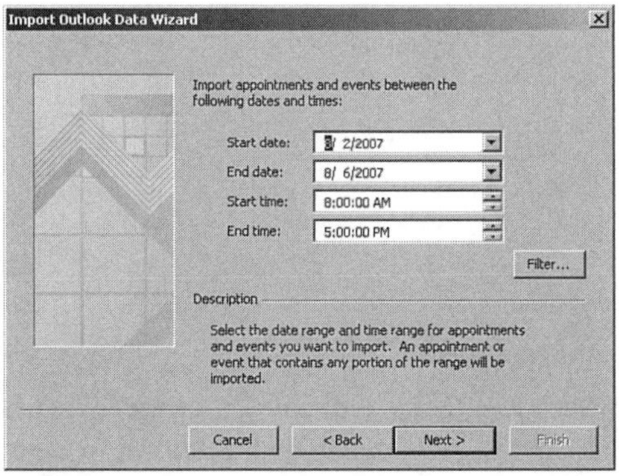

Figure 13.18
The Import Outlook Data Wizard, second pane.

13

Select the start date you want in the Start Date box.

Select the end date you want in the End Date box.

Select the start time you want in the Start Time box.

Select the end time you want in the End Time box.

Click OK. When you do, Visio displays the third pane of the Import Outlook Data Wizard, shown in Figure 13.19.

Figure 13.19
The Import Outlook Data Wizard, third pane.

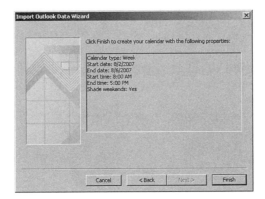

Visio displays a summary of your choices in the third pane of the wizard. If everything looks correct, click Finish; otherwise, click Back and make changes.

That's it—Visio adds appointments to your calendar, matching the appointments in your Outlook data. If there are too many appointments for a given day, they'll overlap—resize the calendar to separate them.

That completes our coverage of calendars in Visio—next are project timelines in Visio.

CREATING PROJECT TIMELINES

Timelines are especially useful for illustrating schedules. They show tasks, intervals, and milestones. Timelines are vertical or horizontal bars showing dates or times in Visio, and you can add your own shapes to them, as you'll see here.

Here's how to create a timeline in Visio:

1. Open Visio.
2. Select File > New > Schedule > Timeline.
3. Open the Timeline Shapes stencil.
4. Drag a timeline shape, such as a Block Timeline or a Line Timeline, to the drawing surface. Visio opens the Configure Timeline dialog, shown in Figure 13.20.

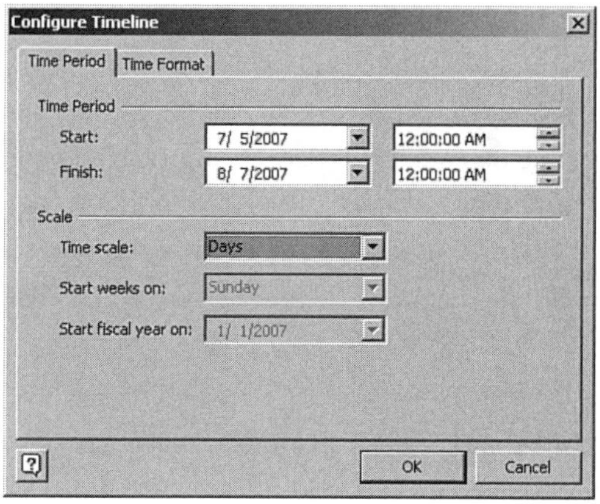

Figure 13.20
Configuring a
timeline.

Configure the timeline like this:

Select the start date and time you want in the Start boxes.

Select the end date and time you want in the Finish boxes.

Select the time scale, such as days, hours, weeks, or months, in the Time Scale box.

Select the end time you want in the Finish box.

Select the day of the week you want to start the weeks on in the Start Weeks On box.

Select the day you want to start the fiscal year on in the Start Fiscal Year On box.

Click OK. When you do, Visio displays the timeline, as shown in Figure 13.21.

Figure 13.21
Creating a timeline.

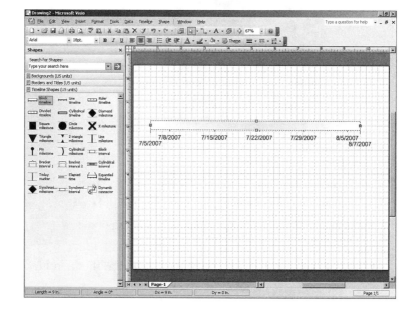

13

Resize the timeline as needed.

If your timeline shows a mass of overlapping dates, right-click the timeline and select Configure Timeline.

In the Configure Timeline dialog's Time Period tab, try lengthening the time scale—from days to weeks, for example.

If all else fails, select the Time Format tab and deselect the check box labeled Show Interim Time Scale Markings on Timeline to remove the markings altogether.

ADDING INTERVALS TO TIMELINES

Now that you have a basic timeline, you can add interval shapes to it. Doing so helps add structure to your timeline.

To add intervals to your timeline, do the following:

1. Open Visio.
2. Open the drawing with the timeline.
3. Open the Timeline Shapes stencil.
4. Drag an interval shape, such as a Block Interval or a Cylindrical Interval shape, to the timeline. Visio opens the Configure Interval dialog, shown in Figure 13.22.

Figure 13.22
Configuring an interval.

Configure the interval like this:

Select the start date and time you want in the Start boxes.

Select the end date and time you want in the Finish boxes.

Enter the description of the interval in the Description box.

Select the date format.

Click OK. Visio adds the interval to the timeline, as shown in Figure 13.23.

Cool.

Figure 13.23
Adding an interval to
a timeline.

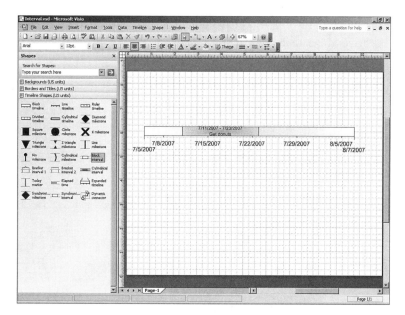

ADDING MILESTONES TO TIMELINES

Milestones in timelines represent those dates that are deadlines of some sort—a project has
to deliver through a certain phase, for example, or a marketing study has to be complete.

To add milestones to your timeline, do the following:

1. Open Visio.
2. Open the drawing with the timeline.
3. Open the Timeline Shapes stencil.
4. Drag a Milestone shape to the timeline. You can use X Milestones, Triangle
   Milestones, Double Triangle Milestones, Line Milestones, Pin Milestones, or
   Cylindrical Milestones.

   Visio opens the Configure Milestone dialog, shown in Figure 13.24.

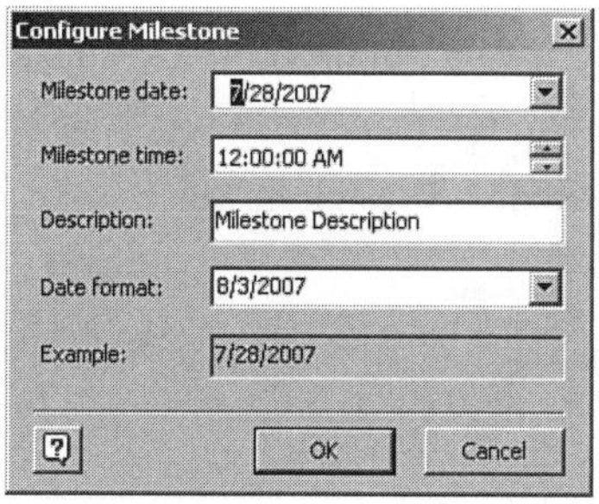

Figure 13.24
Configuring a
milestone.

Configure Milestone	
Milestone date:	7/28/2007
Milestone time:	12:00:00 AM
Description:	Milestone Description
Date format:	8/3/2007
Example:	7/28/2007

OK   Cancel

Configure the milestone like this:

Select the date in the Milestone Date box.

Select the time in the Milestone Time box.

Enter the description of the milestone in the Description box.

Select the date format.

Click OK. Visio adds the milestone to the timeline, as shown in Figure 13.25.

Figure 13.25
Adding a milestone to a timeline.

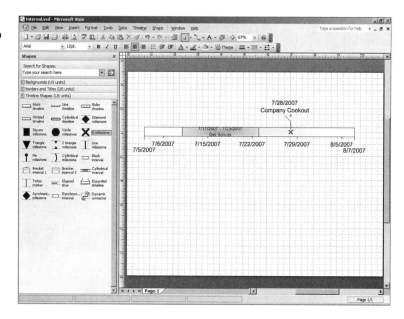

As you can see, milestones are represented by special graphics in timelines—they represent special events in a Visio timeline that you especially want to keep track of.

EXPANDING TIMELINES

Timelines can get pretty crowded in Visio, and the individual events can get very hard to see. You can fix that with expanded timelines, which are subsets of your main timeline.

The expanded timeline is actually a shape—you can drop the Expanded Timeline shape onto your drawing, and set the interval that the shape shows as expanded.

To add an expanded timeline to your timeline, do the following:

1. Open Visio.

2. Open the drawing with the timeline.

3. Open the Timeline Shapes stencil.

4. Drag an Expanded Timeline shape to the timeline. Visio opens the Configure Timeline dialog, shown in Figure 13.26.

Figure 13.26
Configuring an expanded timeline.

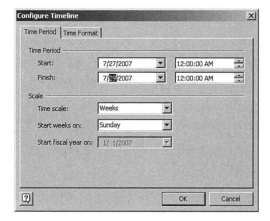

Configure the interval like this:

Select the start date and time you want in the Start boxes.

Select the end date and time you want in the Finish boxes.

Select the time scale, such as days, hours, weeks, or months, in the Time Scale box.

Select the day of the week you want to start the weeks on in the Start Weeks On box.

Click OK. Visio adds the expanded timeline to your timeline, as shown in Figure 13.27.

Figure 13.27
Adding an expanded timeline to a timeline.

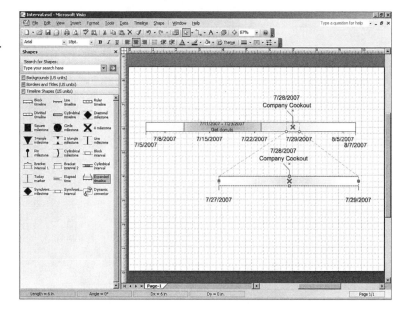

13

IMPORTING AND EXPORTING TIMELINES TO MICROSOFT PROJECT

Microsoft Project is all about timelines and scheduling projects. If you have access to Project, you can import and export timeline data to and from Visio with it.

Here's how to import timeline data from Project into Visio:

1. Open Visio.
2. Open the drawing with the timeline.
3. Select Timeline > Import Timeline Data. Visio opens the Import Timeline Wizard, shown in Figure 13.28.

Figure 13.28
The Import Timeline Wizard.

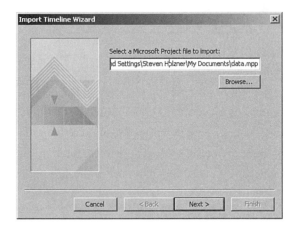

4. Enter or browse to the name of the Project file to import and click Next. Visio opens the second pane of the Import Timeline Wizard, shown in Figure 13.29.

Figure 13.29
The Import Timeline Wizard, second pane.

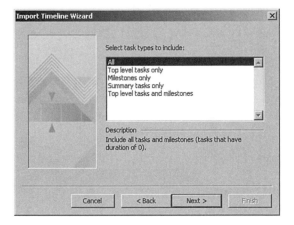

13

5. Select the types of tasks to import in the Select Task Types to Include box, and click Next. Visio opens the third pane of the Import Timeline Wizard, shown in Figure 13.30.

Figure 13.30
The Import Timeline
Wizard, third pane.

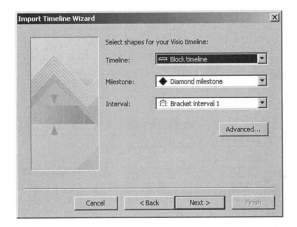

6. Select the Timeline, Milestone, and Interval shapes and click Next. Visio opens the fourth pane of the Import Timeline Wizard, shown in Figure 13.31.

Figure 13.31
The Import Timeline
Wizard, fourth pane.

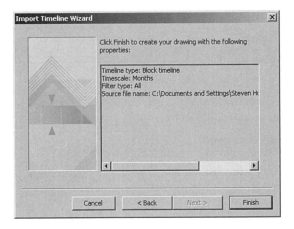

7. Check the summary; if everything is okay, click Finish; otherwise, click Back and make changes. Visio imports the Project data and creates a new timeline to match.

   Note that the new timeline will be created on a new page.

That's how to import Microsoft Project data into Visio.

What about exporting Visio timeline data to Project? Coming up next.

Here's how to export timeline data from Visio to Project:

1. Open Visio.

2. Open the drawing with the timeline.

3. Select the timeline to export.

4. Select Timeline > Export Timeline Data. Visio asks whether you want to export all markers on the timeline with a dialog.

5. Click Yes or No. Visio asks you for the name of the exported Microsoft Project file, as shown in Figure 13.32.

Figure 13.32
Storing a timeline as a Project file.

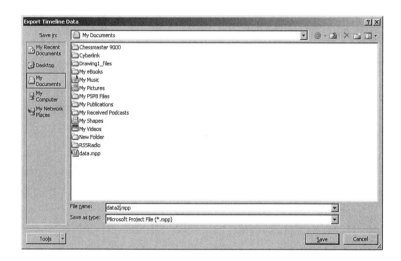

6. Enter the name of the Project file to export and click Save. Visio saves the file and lets you know it's done so with a dialog box.

   Click OK to dismiss the dialog.

That completes our work with Visio timelines—now it's time to turn to Gantt charts.

CREATING GANTT CHARTS

You use Gantt charts to schedule projects along timelines. In fact, Gantt charts are the most popular way of scheduling projects in business environments.

Let's see this at work. To create a Gantt chart, follow these steps:

1. Open Visio.

2. Select File > New > Schedule > Gantt Chart. Visio opens the Gantt Chart Options dialog, shown in Figure 13.33.

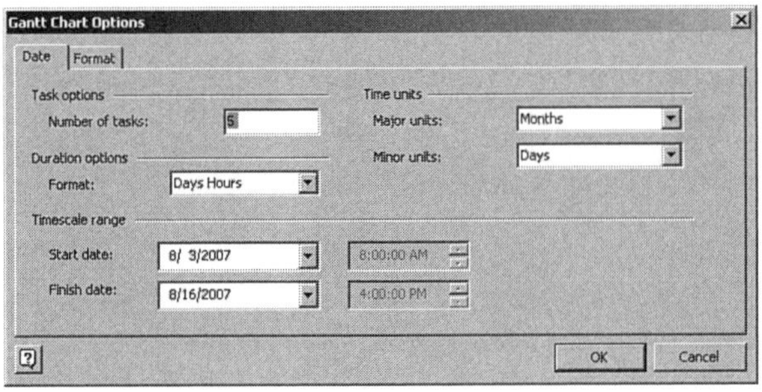

Figure 13.33
The Gantt Chart
Options dialog.

Configure the Gantt chart like this:

Select the number of tasks you want to chart in the Number of Tasks box.

Select the time units in the Time Units region—select the major units and minor units.

Select the format—the default is Days Hours.

Select a time-scale range, setting the start date and time, as well as the end date and time.

Click OK. Visio creates the new Gantt chart, as shown in Figure 13.34.

Figure 13.34
A new Gantt chart.

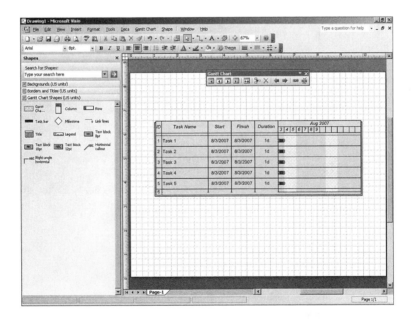

13

CONFIGURING GANTT CHARTS

Now that you've got a Gantt chart, you can configure it:

1. Open Visio.

2. Open the drawing with the Gantt chart.

3. Customize the Gantt chart:

Select the Task Name box and enter the name of the task you want to configure.

Select the Start date and enter the new start date.

Select the Finish date and enter the new finish date.

Select the Duration box and enter the new duration of the task.

You can also drag the task bar in the chart using the mouse, as shown in Figure 13.35. If you do, the start and end date are also adjusted automatically.

Figure 13.35
Altering task bars.

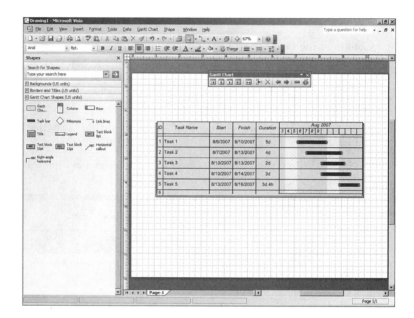

ADDING MILESTONES

You can also add milestones to Gantt charts. Milestones act like they do in timelines—they represent target dates for deadlines or events.

To add milestones to a Gantt chart, follow these steps:

1. Open Visio.

2. Open the drawing with the Gantt chart.

3. Drag a Milestone shape onto the task bar that you want the milestone to appear under. Visio creates a new task at the left in the chart—milestones are treated as tasks with a duration of 0 days in Visio.

Select the Start box for the new task and enter its date. Because milestones have zero duration, Visio automatically makes the end date the same as the start date.

Visio draws the new milestone, as you can see under the second task bar in Figure 13.36.

Figure 13.36
Adding a milestone.

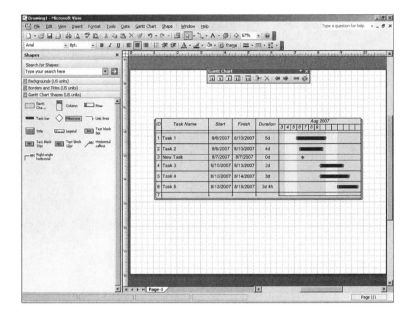

CREATING SUBTASKS

You can organize the tasks in a Gantt chart as tasks and subtasks. That can be useful for larger projects whose tasks can themselves have subtasks, as is often the case.

To make a task a subtask of the task above it in a Gantt chart, follow these steps:

1. Open Visio.
2. Open the drawing with the Gantt chart.
3. Select the first task's name that you want to make into a subtask. Visio displays green sizing handles around the task name.
4. Select Gantt Chart > Indent or click the Indent button in the Gantt Chart toolbar.

   Visio indents the selected task, making it a subtask of the task above it.

   Visio bolds the task above the subtask, making it into a *summary* task. Summary tasks contain subtasks.

   Visio adds triangular endpoints to the summary task's task bar, to indicate that it is a summary task.

   You can see the results in Figure 13.37.

13

Figure 13.37
Adding a subtask.

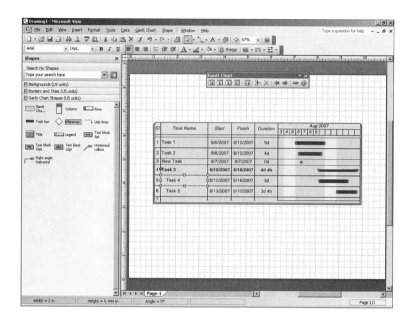

LINKING TASKS

You can link tasks in Gantt charts. Linking tasks indicates their relationship—one shouldn't start until the previous one is finished, for instance. An example would be that you can't start plastering a house until the drywall is up.

In Visio, you can create finish-to-start links, but you can't create any other kind (start-to-start, finish-to-finish, or start-to-finish links).

Here's how to link tasks in Gantt charts:

1. Open Visio.
2. Open the drawing with the Gantt chart.
3. Select the first task to be linked.
4. Select the second task to be linked by pressing Ctrl and clicking the mouse button on the task.
5. Click the Link button in the Gantt Chart toolbar (the button with the chain icon) or select Gantt Chart > Link Tasks.

    Visio links the tasks in a finish-to-start relationship. You can see the results in Figure 13.38.

Figure 13.38
Linking tasks.

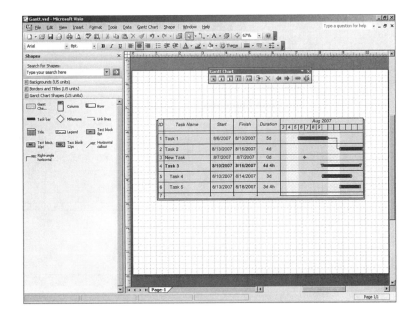

You can see in the figure how Visio indicates a finish-to-start relationship—with a connector.

You can link as many tasks as you want this way.

To unlink tasks, select the two linked tasks and select Gantt Chart > Unlink Tasks, or click the Unlink Tasks button in the Gantt Chart toolbar.

ADDING AND DELETING TASKS

Projects change—and their Gantt charts should change with them. That's why you can add and delete tasks at any time.

Here's how to add or delete tasks in Gantt charts:

1. Open Visio.
2. Open the drawing with the Gantt chart.
3. Select the task that you want to delete, or above which you want to add a new task.
4. To add a new task, select Gantt Chart > New Task, or click the New Task button in the Gantt Chart toolbar.

   Visio adds a new task, as shown in Figure 13.39.

13

Figure 13.39
Adding a task.

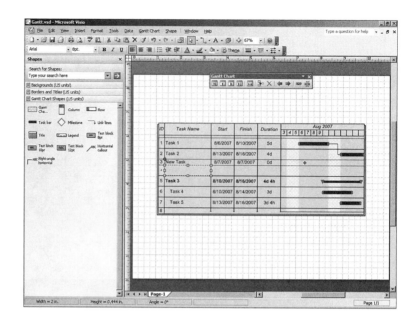

Configure the new task this way:

Select the Task Name box and enter the name of the task you want to configure.

Select the Start date and enter the new start date.

Select the Finish date and enter the new finish date.

Select the Duration box and enter the new duration of the task.

You can also drag the task bar in the chart using the mouse.

5. To delete a task, select Gantt Chart > Delete Task, or click the Delete Task button in the Gantt Chart toolbar.

ADDING AND DELETING COLUMNS

You can also add or delete a column in a Gantt chart. Doing so allows you to configure custom columns in Gantt charts.

Here's how to add or delete columns in Gantt charts:

1. Open Visio.

2. Open the drawing with the Gantt chart.

3. Select the column that you want to delete, or to the left of where you want to add a new column.

4. To add a new column, select Gantt Chart > Insert Column.

Visio asks you what type of column you want, as shown in Figure 13.40.

Figure 13.40
The Insert Column dialog.

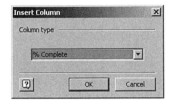

Select the new column type and click OK.

Visio adds a new column, as shown in Figure 13.41.

5. To delete a column, select Gantt Chart > Hide Column.

Figure 13.41
Adding columns.

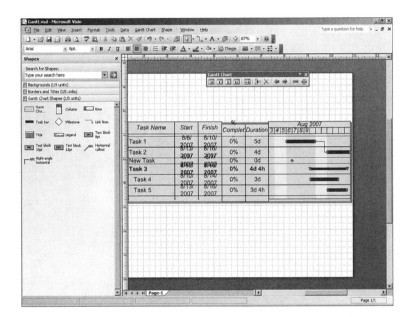

IMPORTING AND EXPORTING GANTT CHARTS

Visio makes it easy to import and export data to and from Gantt charts.

Here's how to import Gantt chart data if you want to enter your data yourself:

1. Open Visio.

2. Select File > New > Schedule > Gantt Chart.

3. Select Gantt Chart > Import.

    Visio opens the Import Project Data Wizard, shown in Figure 13.42.

4. Select the Information That I Enter Using the Wizard radio button and click Next.

13

Figure 13.42
The Import Project
Data Wizard.

Visio opens the second pane of the Import Data Wizard, shown in Figure 13.43.

Figure 13.43
The Import Project
Data Wizard, second
pane.

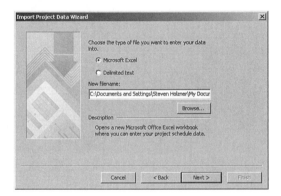

5. Select a file type and name and click Next. Visio opens a sample set of data in Notepad if you selected the Delimited Text option, or in Excel if you selected the Microsoft Excel option.

You can see the sample data in Excel in Figure 13.44.

6. Enter your data and select File > Exit.

Visio opens the third pane of the Import Data Wizard, shown in Figure 13.45.

7. Select the major and minor units in the Time Scale area, as well as the format in the Duration Options area, and click Next. Visio opens the fourth pane of the Import Data Wizard, shown in Figure 13.46.

Figure 13.44
Sample data in Excel.

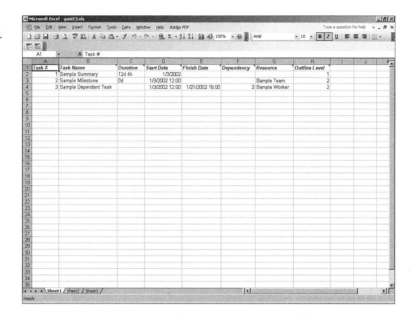

Figure 13.45
The Import Project
Data Wizard, third
pane.

Figure 13.46
The Import Project
Data Wizard, fourth
pane.

13

8. Select the type of tasks you want to include and click Next. Visio opens the fifth pane of the Import Data Wizard, shown in Figure 13.47.

Figure 13.47
The Import Project Data Wizard, fifth pane.

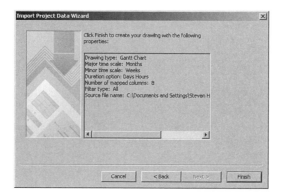

9. If the summary looks okay, click Finish; otherwise, click Back and make changes.

Visio creates and opens the new Gantt chart, as shown in Figure 13.48.

Figure 13.48
A new Gantt chart.

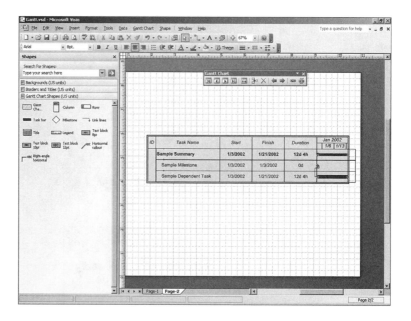

Here's how to import Gantt chart data if your data is already stored in a file:

1. Open Visio.

2. Select File > New > Schedule > Gantt Chart.

3. Select Gantt Chart > Import.

Visio opens the Import Project Data Wizard, shown in Figure 13.49.

Figure 13.49
The Import Project
Data Wizard.

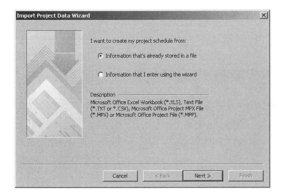

4. Select the Information That's Already Stored in a File option, and click Next.

Visio displays the next pane of the Import Project Data Wizard, shown in Figure 13.50.

Figure 13.50
The Import Project
Data Wizard, second
pane.

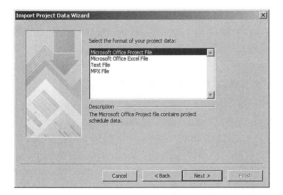

5. Select the type of file you're importing and click Next.

Visio displays the next pane of the Import Project Data Wizard, shown in Figure 13.51.

Figure 13.51
The Import Project
Data Wizard, third
pane.

13

6. Select the file you're importing and click Next.

   Visio displays the next pane of the Import Project Data Wizard, shown in Figure 13.52.

Figure 13.52
The Import Project Data Wizard, fourth pane.

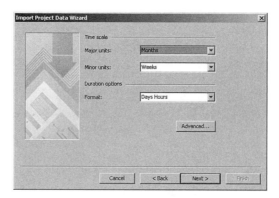

7. Select the major and minor units in the Time Scale area, as well as the format in the Duration Options area, and click Next. Visio opens the fifth pane of the Import Data Wizard, shown in Figure 13.53.

Figure 13.53
The Import Project Data Wizard, fifth pane.

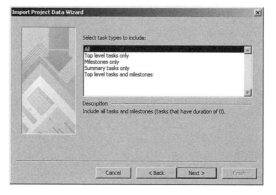

8. Select the type of tasks you want to include and click Next. Visio opens the sixth pane of the Import Data Wizard, shown in Figure 13.54.

9. If the summary looks okay, click Finish; otherwise, click Back and make changes.

   Visio creates and opens the new Gantt chart

Figure 13.54
The Import Project
Data Wizard, sixth
pane.

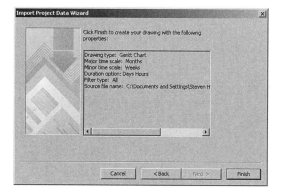

How about exporting Gantt charts to Project?

To do that, follow these steps:

1. Open Visio.
2. Open the drawing that contains the Gantt chart you want to export.
3. Select the Gantt chart to export.
4. Select Gantt Chart > Export. Visio opens the Export Project Data Wizard, shown in Figure 13.55.

Figure 13.55
The Export Project
Data Wizard.

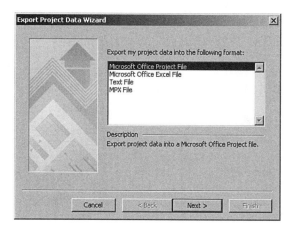

You can export to these data formats:

       Microsoft Project

       Microsoft Excel

       Text files

       MPX files

5. To export to Microsoft Project, select the line that says Microsoft Office Project File and click Next.

Visio opens the second pane of the Export Project Data Wizard, shown in Figure 13.56.

Figure 13.56
The Export Project Data Wizard, second pane.

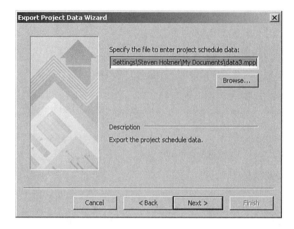

6. Select the Microsoft Project file to export to and click Next.

Visio opens the third pane of the Export Project Data Wizard, shown in Figure 13.57.

Figure 13.57
The Export Project Data Wizard, third pane.

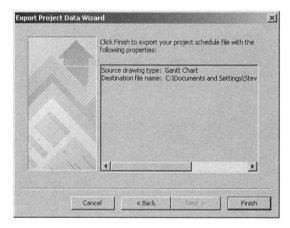

7. If everything looks good in the summary, click Finish; otherwise, click Back and make changes.

Open the saved file in your target application. For example, you can see a Gantt chart exported from Visio in Microsoft Project in Figure 13.58.

Figure 13.58
A Gantt chart
exported from Visio
to Microsoft Project.

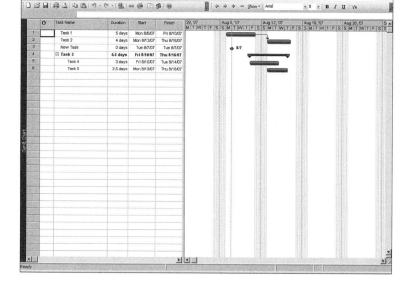

CREATING PERT CHARTS

What does PERT stand for? Project Evaluation and Review Technique. These types of charts provide an alternative to Gantt charts.

PERT charts are built from nodes, connected in a network. Each node can contain information about an individual task.

Here's how to create a PERT chart in Visio:

1. Open Visio.
2. Select File > New > Schedule > PERT chart. Visio creates a new PERT chart, but there's nothing in it yet.
3. Open the PERT Chart Shapes stencil and drag a node, such as PERT 1 or PERT 2, onto the drawing surface.
4. Repeat the dragging process until you have enough nodes for your project. You can see an example in Figure 13.59.
5. Select a text box in a node and enter your text—you can enter text in every text box this way. You can see an example in Figure 13.60.

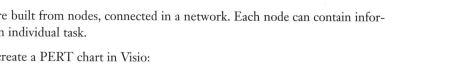

13

Figure 13.59
A new PERT chart.

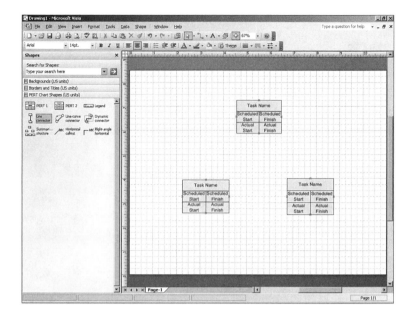

Figure 13.60
A new PERT chart with text.

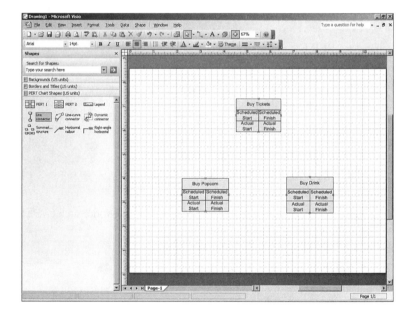

6. To add connectors, click the Connector tool on the standard toolbar, and connect the nodes. Or you can select the Line Connector, Line-Curve Connector, or Dynamic Connector shape in the PERT Chart Shapes stencil, and connect the nodes. You can see an example in Figure 13.61.

Figure 13.61
A new PERT chart
with connectors.

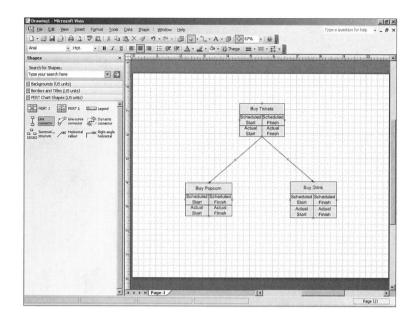

7. You can also drag legends to the PERT chart with the Legend shape. Visio allows you the option of labeling parts or the whole chart with legends, using the Legend shape.

As you can see, the support for scheduling and charting projects is great in Visio.

Time to turn to a new topic, and it's a popular one in Visio: brainstorming.

BRAINSTORMING

You can also use Visio to make brainstorming drawings, of the kind shown in Figure 13.62.

Brainstorming drawings are designed to be assembled quickly, following the brainstorming process. There are only two main shapes here: Main Topic and Topic.

Main Topic shapes are enclosed in an ellipse, as shown in Figure 13.62. You can have multiple main topics per brainstorming drawing, but you usually want to restrict those to a minimum.

The Topic shapes make up the bulk of the shapes in a brainstorming drawing. These shapes aren't boxes, as you might expect, but are thick lines, and you can see three of them in Figure 13.62. They're easy to drag onto a brainstorming drawing, and easy to customize with text—just select them and type.

You can also use the dynamic connectors that appear in the Brainstorming Shapes stencil to connect main topics, as well as topics. These connectors twist and turn as you drag them, so they're good for making rapid drawings as well.

13

Figure 13.62
A brainstorming drawing.

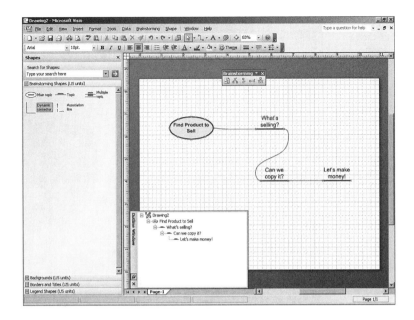

Let's take a look at creating a brainstorming drawing:

1. Open Visio.
2. Select File > New > Business > Brainstorming Diagram. Visio creates a new brainstorming drawing—but there's nothing in it just yet.
3. Open the Brainstorming Shapes stencil and drag a Main Topic shape onto the drawing surface.
4. Select the Main Topic shape and enter text for the shape. You can see an example in Figure 13.62, in which the main topic has the text "Find Product to Sell."
5. Drag a Topic shape onto the drawing.
6. Select the Topic shape and enter text for the shape. You can see several examples in Figure 13.62.
7. Select a Dynamic Connector shape and drag it to the drawing; connect the shapes as appropriate. You can see examples in Figure 13.62.

That completes an elementary brainstorming drawing. You can also add multiple topics at once to save time:

1. Open Visio.
2. Open the brainstorming drawing you want to work with.
3. Open the Brainstorming Shapes stencil and drag a Multiple Topic shape onto the drawing surface. Visio opens the Add Multiple Topics dialog, shown in Figure 13.63.

Figure 13.63
Adding multiple topics to a brainstorming drawing.

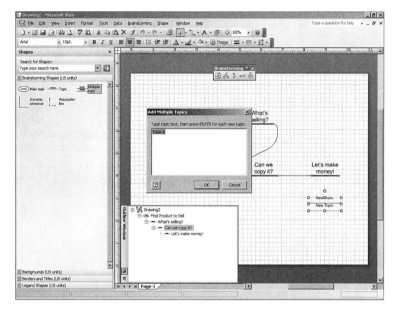

4. Enter the topics you want to add and click OK. Visio adds the topics you've created, as shown in Figure 13.64.

Figure 13.64
Multiple topics added to a brainstorming drawing.

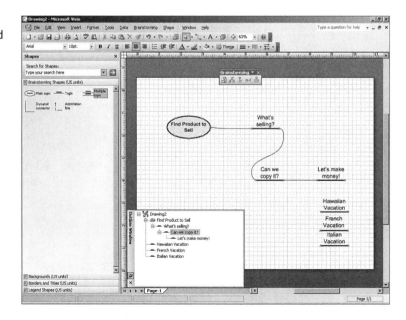

5. Select a Dynamic Connector shape and drag it to the drawing; connect the shapes as appropriate.

Want to neaten up a brainstorming drawing? Visio lets you do that automatically:

1. Open Visio.

2. Open the brainstorming drawing you want to work with.

3. Select Brainstorming > Auto-Arrange Topics. Visio arranges the topics for you, as shown in Figure 13.65.

Figure 13.65
Auto-arranging topics in a brainstorming drawing.

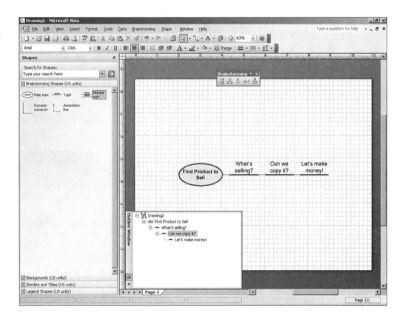

As you can see, you can indeed create brainstorming sessions in Visio. On the other hand, so far, they're pretty basic, with a mere total of five shapes in the Brainstorming Shapes stencil—and that's including two connectors.

Isn't there anything else you can do with brainstorming drawings? Yep, there is—you can add some excitement with the Legend stencil, which includes some fun shapes that catch the excitement of brainstorming sessions.

You can access the legend icons in the Legend Shapes stencil, shown in Figure 13.66.

13

Figure 13.66
Adding legend icons to a brainstorming drawing.

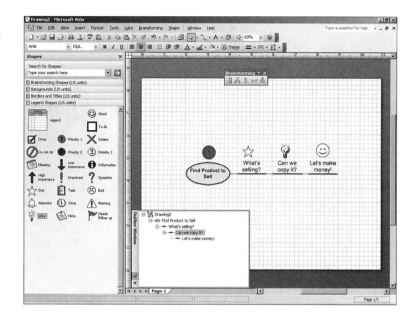

CHAPTER 14

CREATING SOFTWARE DEVELOPMENT DRAWINGS

In this chapter

CREATING UML DRAWINGS

As you might expect, the Unified Modeling Language (UML) support in Visio is strong. There are several stencils that have to do with UML, and you can find them in the Software and Database template category's UML Model Diagram template:

- UML Activity
- UML Collaboration
- UML Component
- UML Deployment
- UML Sequence
- UML Statechart
- UML Static Structure
- UML Use Case

We'll take a look at the UML support in Visio by creating a state machine drawing first.

CREATING STATE MACHINE DRAWINGS

Here's how to create a state machine drawing:

1. Open Visio.
2. Select File > New > Software and Database > UML Model Diagram. Visio creates a new UML drawing, as shown in Figure 14.1.

Figure 14.1
A new UML drawing.

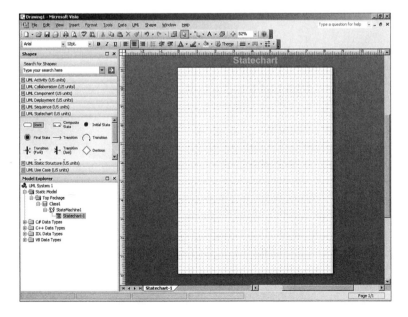

3. Open the UML Statechart stencil.

4. Drag an Initial State shape onto the drawing.

5. Drag the State shapes you want onto the drawing. Visio displays the State shapes, as shown in Figure 14.2.

Figure 14.2
State shapes in a UML state machine drawing.

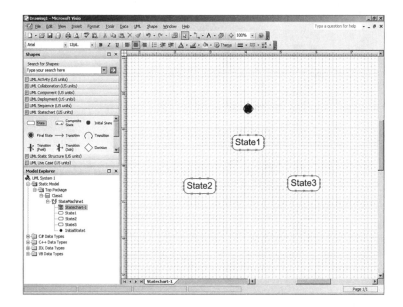

6. Drag the Transition shapes you want onto the drawing. Visio displays the Transition shapes, as shown in Figure 14.3.

Figure 14.3
Connecting State shapes in a UML state machine drawing.

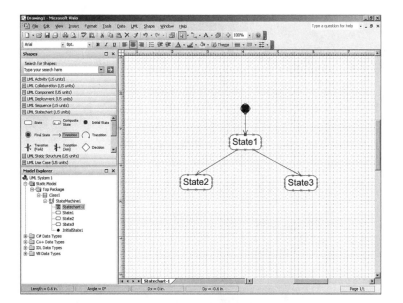

You can use the Transition shape to connect state, the arc-like Transition shape when a state transitions back to itself, the Transition (Fork) shape when a transition can go to multiple states, or the Transition (Join) shape when you want to join several transitions to the same state.

7. Add text to each State shape by selecting it and entering your text. You can see an example in Figure 14.4.

Figure 14.4
Entering text into State shapes.

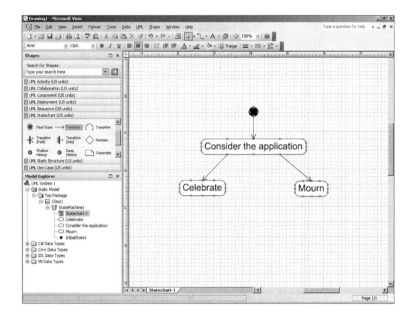

8. Double-click a transition to open the UML Transition Properties dialog. This dialog is shown in Figure 14.5.

Figure 14.5
The UML Transition Properties dialog.

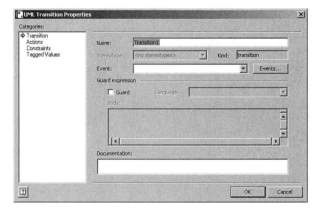

9. Click the Events button to open the UML Events dialog. This dialog is shown in Figure 14.6.

Figure 14.6
The UML Events dialog.

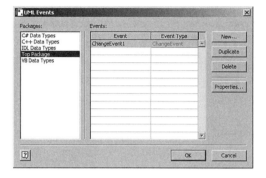

10. Select the Top Package item in the Packages box and click New to open the New Event Type dialog. This dialog is shown in Figure 14.7.

Figure 14.7
The New Event Type dialog.

11. Select the Change Event item and click OK. Visio opens the UML Change Event Properties dialog, shown in Figure 14.8.

Figure 14.8
The UML Change Event Properties dialog.

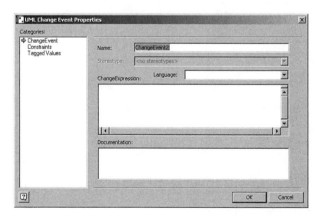

14

12. Enter the text for the transition in the ChangeExpression box and click OK twice. Visio displays the UML Transition Properties dialog, shown earlier in Figure 14.5.

13. In the UML Transition Properties dialog's Event box, select TopPackage::ChangeEvent1 and click OK. Visio displays the text that you've assigned to the transition, as shown in Figure 14.9.

Figure 14.9
Adding text to a transition.

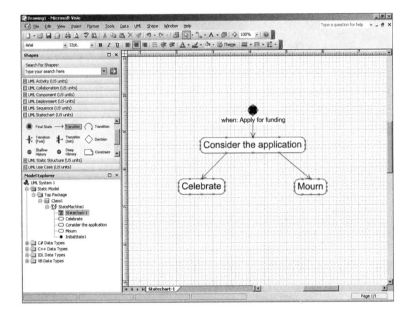

14. Repeat the preceding steps to add text to the other transitions. You can see an example in Figure 14.10.

Figure 14.10
Adding text to transitions.

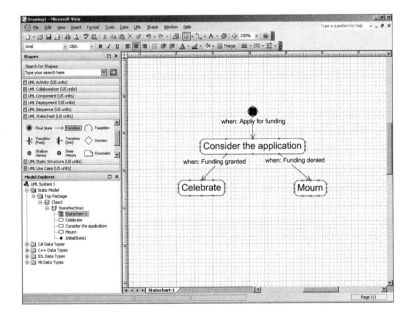

Note also the Model Explorer, which you can see at the lower left in Figure 14.10. As your UML models increase in size, the Model Explorer provides you with an overview of your state drawing.

CREATING USE CASE DRAWINGS

How about creating a UML Use Case drawing? Just follow these steps:

1. Open Visio.
2. Select File > New > Software and Database > UML Model Diagram. Visio creates a new UML drawing.
3. Open the UML Use Case stencil.
4. Drag an Actor shape onto the drawing. You can see an example in Figure 14.11.

Figure 14.11
A new UML Use Case drawing.

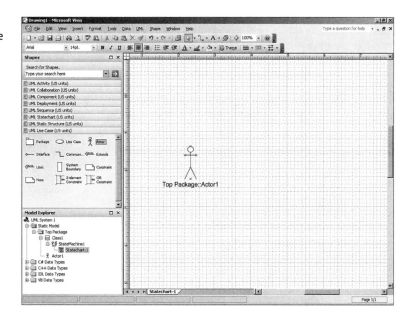

5. Drag a System Boundary shape onto the drawing. Visio displays the System Boundary shape, as shown in Figure 14.12.

   Resize the System Boundary shape as you want it; originally, it extends from top to bottom of the drawing.
6. Drag the Use Case shapes you want onto the drawing. Visio displays the Use Case shapes, as shown in Figure 14.13.

14

Figure 14.12
A System Boundary shape.

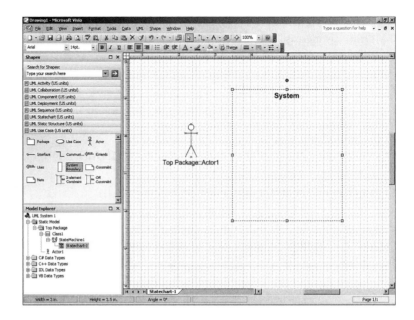

Figure 14.13
Adding Use Cases.

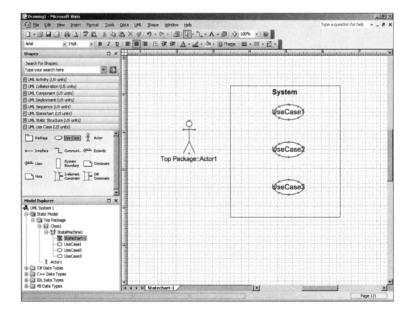

7. Double-click a Use Case shape, opening the UML Use Case Properties dialog. This dialog is shown in Figure 14.14.

8. Enter the text for the Use Case in the Name box and click OK.

9. Repeat the preceding steps for the other Use Cases. You can see an example for an ATM in Figure 14.15.

Figure 14.14
Entering text for Use Cases.

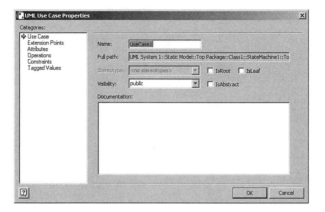

Figure 14.15
Adding text to Use Cases.

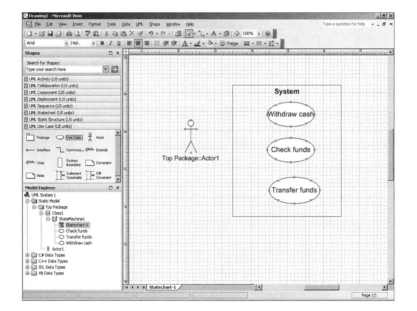

10. Select the System Boundary shape and enter the name for the system. You see an example in Figure 14.16, in which the system has been named ATM.

11. Connect the Actor to Use Case shapes using the Communicates connector from the UML Use Case stencil. You can see an example in Figure 14.17.

Draw relations between the Use Cases as needed using the Extends and Uses connectors from the UML Use Case stencil.

14

Figure 14.16
Naming a system.

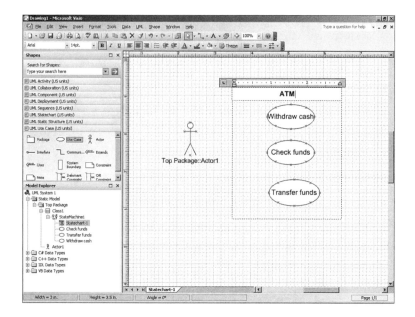

Figure 14.17
Connecting the Actor
to Use Cases.

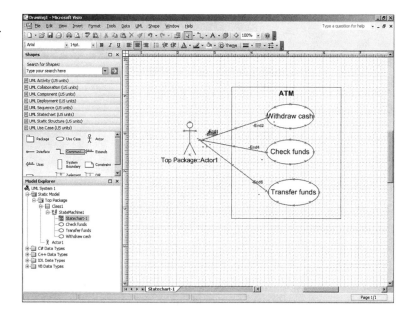

12. To change the endpoint text in a Communicates connector, double-click a connector, opening the UML Association Properties dialog. This dialog is shown in Figure 14.18.

Figure 14.18
The UML Association
Properties dialog.

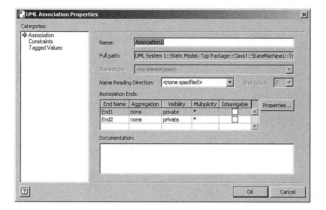

13. Select an association end in the Association Ends box and click Properties. Visio
    displays the UML Association End Properties dialog, shown in Figure 14.19.

Figure 14.19
The UML Association
End Properties dialog.

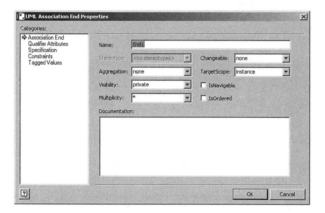

14. Enter the new name for the endpoint. You can also clear the name if you don't want
    labeled endpoints, as shown in Figure 14.20.

14

Figure 14.20
A UML Use Case
drawing.

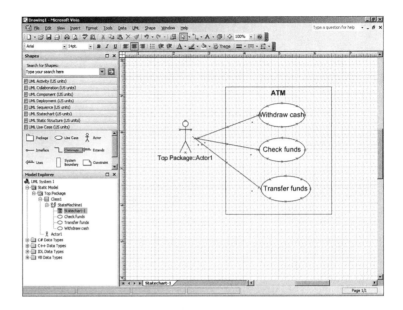

CREATING SEQUENCE DRAWINGS

You can also create UML Sequence drawings using Visio. Here's how:

1. Open Visio.

2. Select File > New > Software and Database > UML Model Diagram. Visio creates a new UML drawing.

3. Open the UML Sequence stencil.

4. Drag an Object shape onto the drawing. You can see an example in Figure 14.21.

Figure 14.21
A new UML
Sequence drawing.

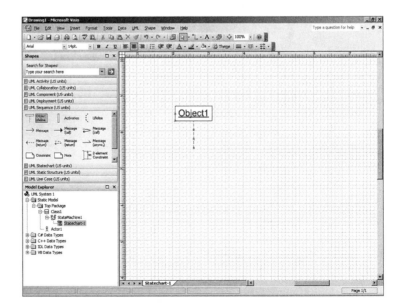

5. Drag other Object shapes onto the drawing. You can see an example in Figure 14.22.

Figure 14.22
A new UML
Sequence drawing
with two objects.

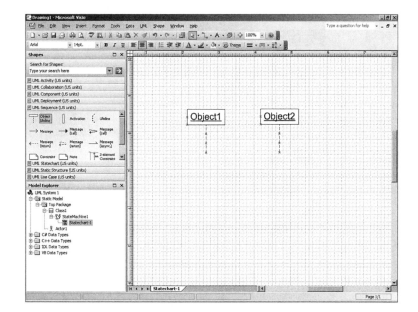

6. Drag the control handles on the object's lifelines to the length you want them.

7. Drag Activation shapes onto the drawing. Activation shapes indicate when the objects are active.

   Visio displays the Activation shapes, as shown in Figure 14.23.

Figure 14.23
Adding Activation
shapes.

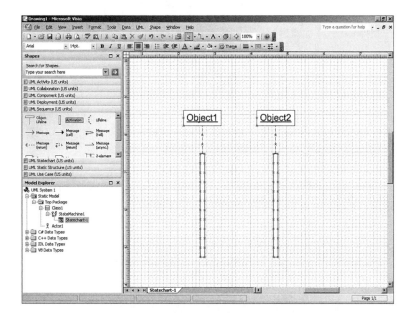

14

8. Drag Message, Message (Call), Message (Return), and Message (Async) connectors to connect Activation shapes as needed. You can see an example in Figure 14.24.

Figure 14.24
Adding Message connectors.

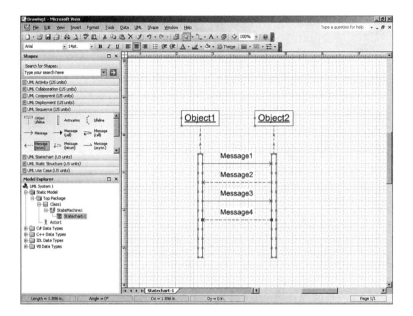

9. To customize the message names, double-click a message to open the UML Message Properties dialog. This dialog is shown in Figure 14.25.

Figure 14.25
The UML Message Properties dialog.

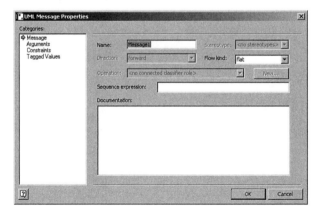

10. Enter the name you want to display for the message and click OK. You see an example in Figure 14.26, in which the messages have been named.

Figure 14.26
Naming messages.

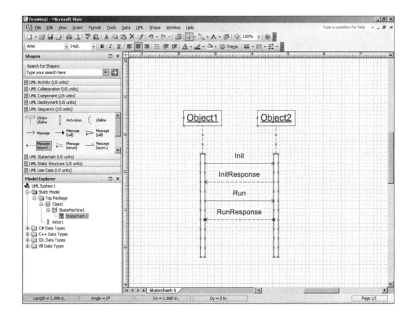

11. Add other Object shapes, Activation shapes, and Message connectors as needed. You can see how this might look in Figure 14.27.

Figure 14.27
Adding more objects, activations, and messages.

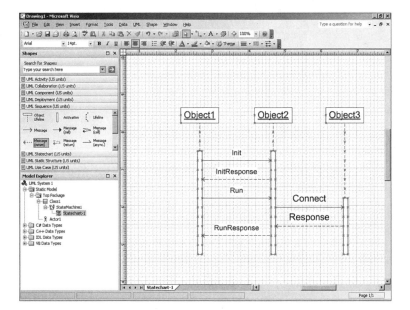

CREATING DEPLOYMENT DRAWINGS

You can also create UML deployment drawings using Visio. These drawings are meant to indicate how a complete system looks when fully deployed and installed.

Here's how to create a UML deployment drawing:

1. Open Visio.
2. Select File > New > Software and Database > UML Model Diagram. Visio creates a new UML drawing.
3. Open the UML Deployment stencil.
4. Drag a Node shape onto the drawing. You can see an example in Figure 14.28.

Figure 14.28
A new UML Deployment drawing.

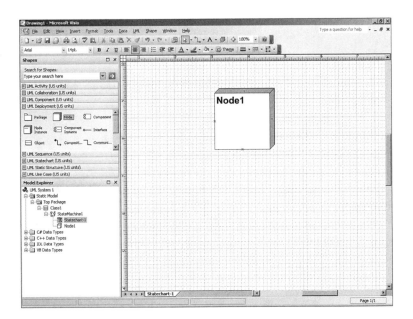

5. Drag other Node shapes onto the drawing as needed. You can see an example in Figure 14.29.
6. Select each node and enter its text. You can see how this might look in Figure 14.30.

Figure 14.29
A new UML Deployment drawing with three nodes.

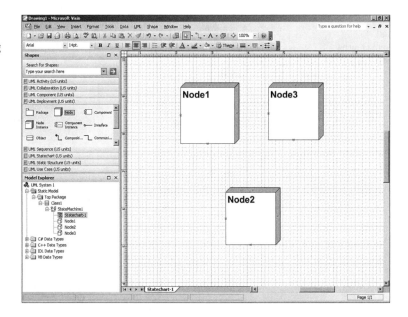

Figure 14.30
A new UML Deployment drawing with three customized nodes.

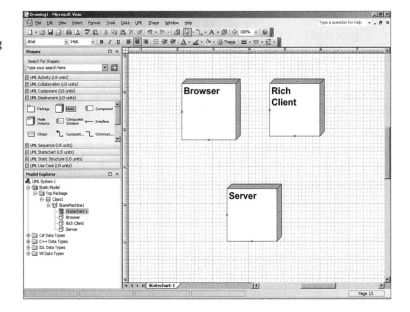

7. Drag Composition connector shapes onto the drawing to show how the nodes are connected. Visio displays the Composition shapes, as shown in Figure 14.31.

14

Figure 14.31
A new UML Deployment drawing with connectors.

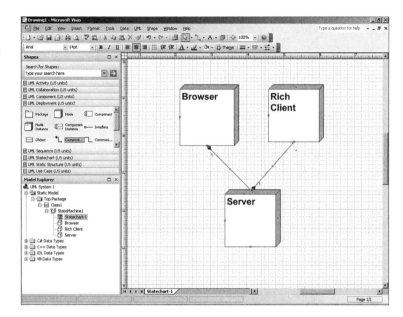

8. Drag Component shapes into Node shapes as needed. You can see an example in Figure 14.32.

Figure 14.32
A new UML Deployment drawing with components.

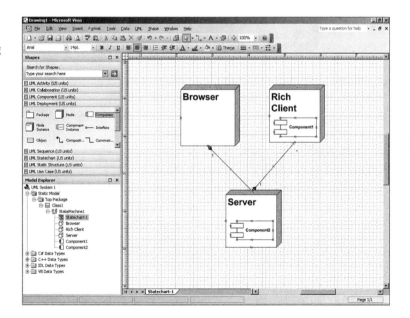

9. To customize the component names, select a new component and enter the name. Visio automatically capitalizes the name of each component (even if you don't want it to).

You can see how this might look in Figure 14.33.

Figure 14.33
A new UML
Deployment drawing
with customized com-
ponents.

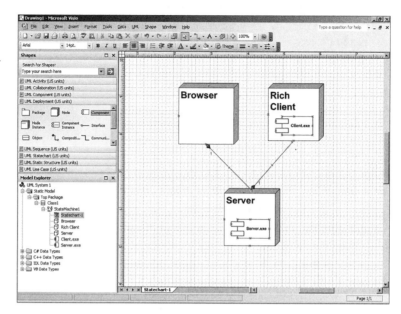

REVERSE-ENGINEERING MICROSOFT STUDIO PROJECTS TO UML

You can even reverse-engineer Microsoft Visual C++ or Microsoft Visual Basic code into UNL drawings. That's very useful if, for example, you've inherited a large application and want to see what's going on in it.

Here are the Microsoft languages you can reverse-engineer into Visio UML drawings:

- Visual C++ 6.0
- Visual C++ 7.0
- Visual Basic 6.0
- Visual Basic .NET
- Visual C++ .NET
- Visual C#

You have to customize Visual C++ and Visual Basic in order to reverse-engineer them with Visio.

Here's how to reverse-engineer Visual C++:

1. Select Tools > Customize in Visual C++. This opens the Customize dialog.
2. Select the Add-ins and Macro Files tab.
3. Select the Visio UML Add-in in the Add-in and Macro files list and click Close. The Visio UML Add-in toolbar appears in Visual C++.

14

You need to create a Browse Information file for your Visual C++ project.

4. Open the Visual C++ project you want to reverse-engineer, and select Project > Settings. Visual C++ opens the Visual C++ Project Settings dialog.

5. In the Project Settings dialog, select the build configuration you want.

6. Select the C/C++ tab, and click the Generate Browse Info button.

7. Select the Browse Info tab, and give the name and location of the Browse Info file you want to create. Visual C++ displays your settings.

8. Click OK.

9. Build your project in Visual C++. Visual C++ compiles the project and builds the output files.

10. In Visual C++, locate the Visio UML Add-in toolbar and click the Reverse Engineer UML Model button. Visio opens a blank static structure UML drawing.

    The UML Model Explorer will be stocked with the objects that Visual C++ reverse engineered for you.

11. Create a static structure drawing by dragging elements from the UML Model Explorer to the drawing surface. Drag only the elements you want to see in the drawing.

If there were errors in the reverse-engineering process, Visio writes them to a log file, which is located at `c:\Temp\project.txt` by default. If you're not getting the results you want (and sometimes, class names get garbled), check for that file.

You can also reverse-engineer Visual Basic projects—the process is similar to reverse-engineering Visual C++ projects.

Want to reverse-engineer a Visual Basic project? Follow these steps:

1. In Visual Basic, select Add-ins > Add-in Manager. Visual Basic opens its Add-in Manager.

2. In the Add-in Manager dialog, select the Visio UML Add-in.

3. In the Load Behavior section, select Loaded/Unloaded and Load on Startup.

4. Click OK to close the Add-in Manager. The Visio UML Add-in toolbar appears.

5. Open the project you want to reverse-engineer in Visual Basic.

6. Build your Visual Basic project in Visual Basic. Visual Basic compiles the project and builds the output files.

7. In Visual Basic, locate the Visio UML Add-in toolbar and click the Reverse Engineer UML Model button. Visio opens a blank static structure UML drawing.

    The UML Model Explorer will be stocked with the objects that Visual Basic reverse-engineered for you.

8. Create a static structure drawing by dragging elements from the UML Model Explorer to the drawing surface. Drag only the elements you want to see in the drawing.

That completes our UML work—now we'll take a look at the Program Structure template.

CREATING PROGRAM STRUCTURE DRAWINGS

You can create flowcharts to chart program structure in Visio—in particular, you can use the Program Structure template to create such flowcharts in Visio.

The Program Structure template includes two stencils:

- **Memory Objects**—These shapes represents objects in memory more than flowcharts; stacks, arrays, pointers, and so on are well-represented here.
- **Language Level Shapes**—This stencil contains the usual software flowchart members that you think of when sketching software flowcharts: functions, subroutines, flowchart shapes, invocation shapes, and so on.

We'll take a look at creating a program structure drawing now:

1. Open Visio.
2. Select File > New > Software and Database > Program Structure. Visio creates a new program structure drawing.
3. Open the Language Level stencil.

   Here's where things get a little weird. For some reason, Visio has lumped the usual flowchart shapes—Process, Decision, Document, Input/Output—into a single shape, rather than leaving them as separate shapes.

   To use these shapes, you have to drag a Flowchart Shapes shape onto your drawing surface and then configure it into the shape you actually want.

4. Drag a Flowchart Shapes shape onto the drawing. Visio creates a Process shape, as you can see in Figure 14.34.

Figure 14.34
A new program
structure drawing.

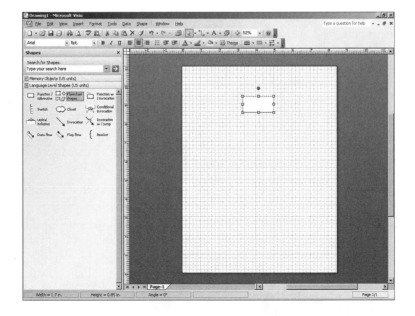

5. Select the Process shape and enter text. You can see an example in Figure 14.35.

Figure 14.35
A new program structure drawing, with text.

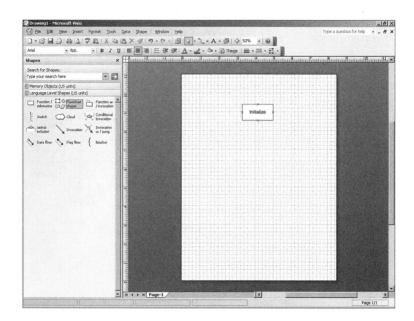

6. Drag another Flowchart Shapes shape onto the drawing surface.

7. To configure the new Flowchart Shapes shape, right-click it and select from Process, Decision, Document, and Input/Output.

For example, you can see a Decision shape in Figure 14.36.

Figure 14.36
A new program structure drawing, with a Decision shape.

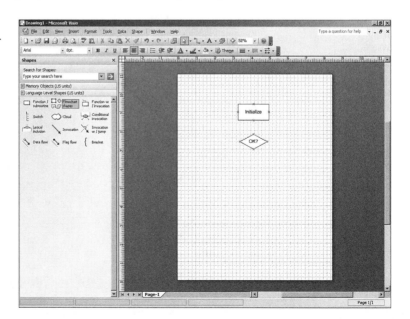

8. Add additional Flowchart Shapes shapes to the drawing, right-click them, and select from Process, Decision, Document, and Input/Output to configure them.

9. Add text to the new Flowchart Shapes shapes.

   For example, the result might look like what is shown in Figure 14.37.

Figure 14.37
A new program structure drawing, with various shapes.

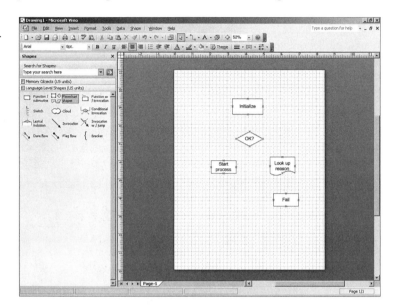

10. Drag Conditional Invocation, Invocation, Invocation w/Jump, Data Flow, and/or Flag Flow connectors to the drawing as needed.

    You can see an example in Figure 14.38.

Figure 14.38
A new program structure drawing, with connectors.

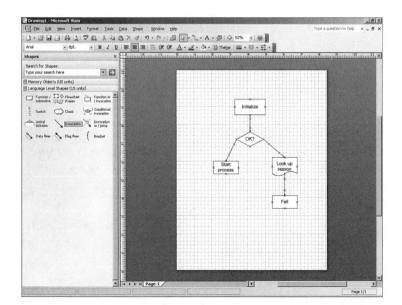

14

As you can see, the basic flowchart shapes are all here.

You can also go into more detail on the data flow in your application with data flow model drawings.

CREATING DATABASE MODEL DRAWINGS

Database model drawings chart the flow of data in software applications. Use this kind of drawing when your application is data-intensive.

Here's how to create a database model drawing:

1. Open Visio.
2. Select File > New > Software and Database > Database Model Diagram. Visio creates a new database model drawing, as shown in Figure 14.39.

Figure 14.39
A new database
model drawing.

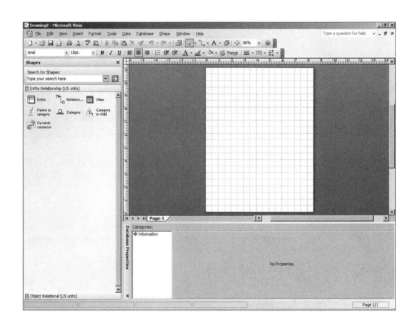

3. Open the Entity Relationship stencil.
4. Drag an Entity shape onto the drawing. Visio displays information in the Database Properties window at the bottom of the drawing surface, as you can see in Figure 14.40.
5. Fill in the physical and conceptual names of the new data table.
6. Select the other categories in the Database Properties window—Columns, Primary ID, Indexes, Triggers, Check, Extended, and Notes—and fill in information about the table.

   For example, the result might look like what is shown in Figure 14.41.

Figure 14.40
A new database model drawing with an entity.

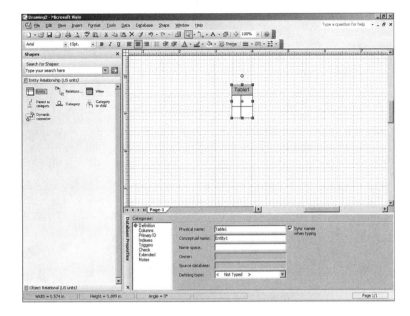

Figure 14.41
A new database model drawing with a configured entity.

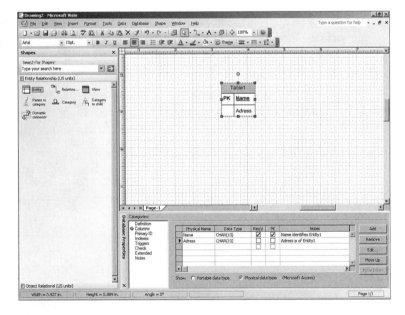

7. Drag other Entity shapes onto the drawing.

8. Fill in the physical and conceptual names of the new data table.

9. Select the other categories in the Database Properties window—Columns, Primary ID, Indexes, Triggers, Check, Extended, and Notes—and fill in information about the table.

The result might look like what is shown in Figure 14.42.

Figure 14.42
A new database model drawing with configured entities.

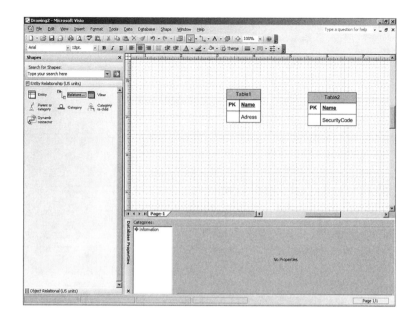

10. To indicate relations between table rows, drag a Relationship connector onto the drawing surface. Connect the Relationship connector between tables.

The results appear in Figure 14.43.

Figure 14.43
A new database model drawing with connectors.

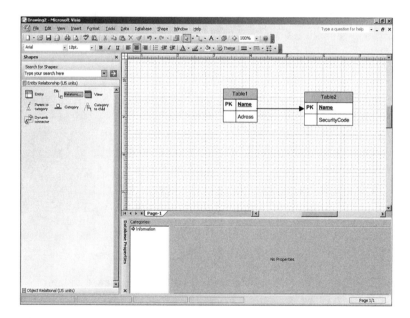

11. Add more database tables and relationships as needed.

CREATING DATA FLOW MODEL DRAWINGS

As their name suggests, data flow model drawings chart the flow of data in applications; they're based on Gane-Sarson terminology.

Here's how to create a representative data flow model drawing in Visio:

1. Open Visio.
2. Select File > New > Software and Database > Data Flow Model Diagram. Visio creates a new data flow model drawing, as shown in Figure 14.44.

Figure 14.44
A new data flow model drawing.

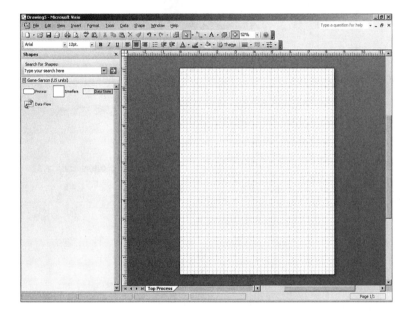

3. Open the Gane-Sarson stencil.
4. Drag an Interface shape onto the drawing.
5. Select the Interface shape and enter your text for the shape.
   For example, the result might look like what is shown in Figure 14.45.
6. Drag a Process shape onto the drawing.
7. Select the Process shape and enter your text for the shape.
   For example, the result might look like what is shown in Figure 14.46.
8. Drag a Data Store shape onto the drawing.

14

Figure 14.45
A new data flow model drawing with an interface.

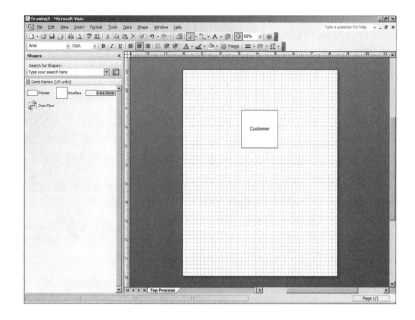

Figure 14.46
A new data flow model drawing with a Process shape.

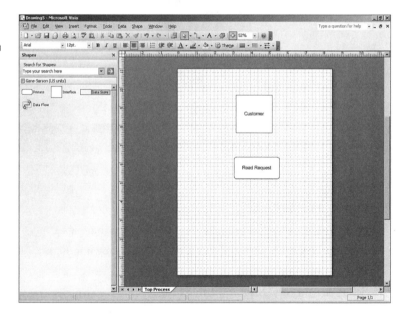

9. Select the Data Store shape and enter your text for the shape.

   The result might look as shown in Figure 14.47.

10. Drag Data Flow connectors onto the drawing to indicate the flow of data.

    The result might look like what is shown in Figure 14.48.

Figure 14.47
A new data flow model drawing with a Data Store shape.

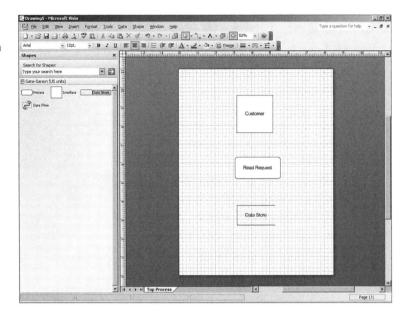

Figure 14.48
A new data flow model drawing with Data Flow connectors.

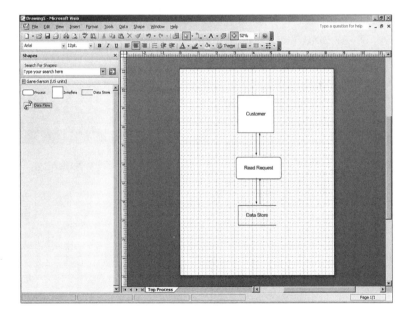

11. Repeat the preceding steps to add other Interface, Process, and Data Store shapes, as well as Data Flow connectors, to the drawing.

How about modeling the user interface? Coming up next.

14

MODELING THE USER INTERFACE

Here's a cool one—you can model Windows XP user interfaces using Visio.

You can model new Windows XP interfaces with the File > New > Software and Database > Windows XP User Interface template. That template contains these stencils:

- Common Controls
- Icons
- Toolbars and Menus
- Wizards
- Windows and Dialogs

Let's take a look at this template with an example.

Here's how to build a sample user interface for Windows XP:

1. Open Visio.
2. Select File > New > Software and Database > Windows XP User Interface. Visio creates a new Windows XP User interface drawing.
3. Open the Windows and Dialogs stencil.
4. Drag a Blank Form shape onto the drawing surface. You can see an example in Figure 14.49.

Figure 14.49
A new Windows XP user interface drawing.

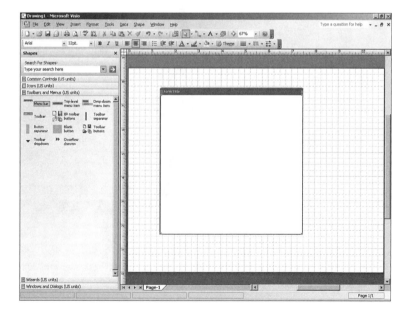

5. Select the Blank Form shape and enter text; the text is displayed in the title bar.

6. Right-click the blank form and select the kind of background you want—white, gray, or custom. Selecting Custom Background lets you choose the color, pattern, and shadow of the background for the window.

7. To display title bar buttons such as Close and Minimize buttons, drag a Toolbar Buttons shape to the title bar of the blank form.

   The Shape Data dialog opens, letting you select the type of title bar buttons you want to add. You can select from these buttons:

   > Restore
   >
   > Close
   >
   > Minimize
   >
   > Maximize
   >
   > Help

   The usual order of these buttons is Minimize, Maximize, and Close, as shown in Figure 14.50.

Figure 14.50
A new Windows XP user interface drawing with title bar buttons.

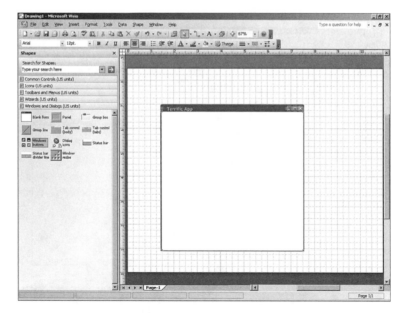

8. Drag a Status Bar shape onto the form. Select the Status Bar shape and enter any text you want. You can see an example in Figure 14.51.

9. Drag a Menu Bar shape onto the form.

10. To add menus to the menu bar, drag Top-Level Menu Item shapes onto the form. Select the items and enter their text. You can see an example in Figure 14.52.

Figure 14.51
A new Windows XP user interface drawing with a status bar.

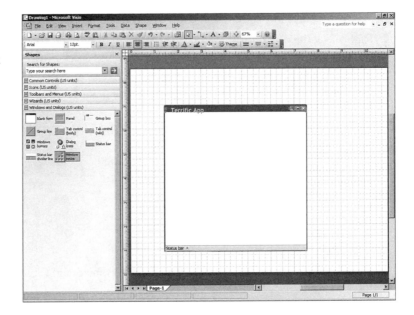

Figure 14.52
A new Windows XP user interface drawing with a menu bar.

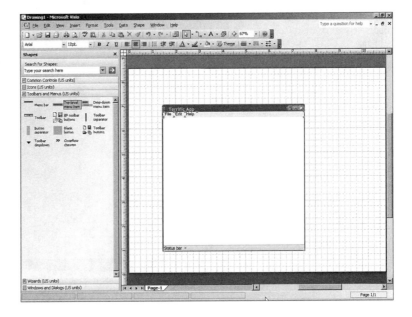

To add menu items to the menus, Drop-Down Menu Item shapes onto the menus.

To add gripper dots at the left end of a menu to let the user move the bar, right-click the bar and deselect the Lock Menu Bar check box that appears.

11. To add a toolbar, drag a Toolbar shape onto the form.

12. To add toolbar buttons, drag an XP Toolbar Buttons shape onto the toolbar. Visio opens the Shape Data dialog, asking you to select the type of button. Make your selection, and right-click the new button and select the Large Buttons menu item for maximum visibility.

You can see an example in Figure 14.53.

Figure 14.53
A new Windows XP user interface drawing with a toolbar.

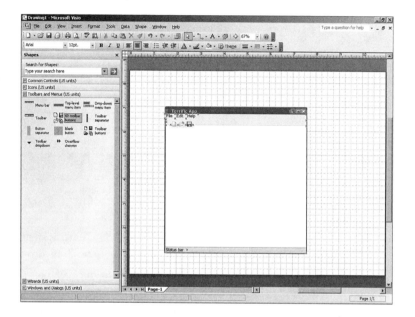

You can also drag other controls, such as scrollbars, onto the new form from the Common Controls stencil.

Want to create a dialog box? Follow these steps:

1. Open Visio.

2. Select File > New > Software and Database > Windows XP User Interface. Visio creates a new Windows XP user interface drawing.

3. Open the Windows and Dialogs stencil.

4. Drag a Blank Form shape onto the drawing surface.

Do not add title bar buttons, except for an optional Close button.

To add a Close button, drag a Windows Buttons shape onto the right end of the title bar, and select Close from the Button Type drop-down box in the Shape Data dialog that opens.

5. To display a dialog icon, drag a Dialog Icons shape onto the form. Visio displays a Shape Data dialog; select the type of icon from the Icon Type drop-down list.

You can see an example in Figure 14.54.

14

Figure 14.54
A new Windows XP
dialog box with
an icon.

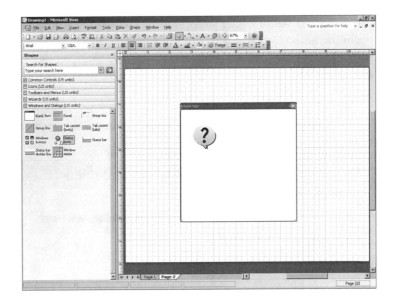

Additional icons are available in the Icons stencil.

6. Drag controls for the dialog box from the Common Controls stencil. Visio displays a Shape Data dialog; select the type of icon from the Icon Type drop-down list.

The Common Controls stencil contains controls from check boxes to progress bars to multilevel trees.

7. To display text in the dialog box, use the Visio text tool (click the down arrow next to the toolbar button marked with a capital A and select Text Tool.

You can see an example in Figure 14.55.

Figure 14.55
A new Windows XP
dialog box with text
and controls.

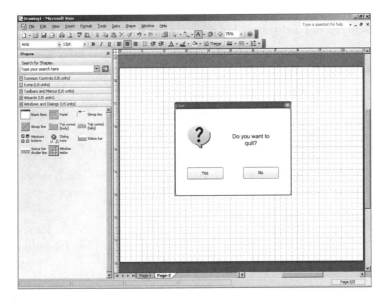

You can also create Windows XP Wizards using Visio—just use the Wizards stencil. Your wizards can contain multiple pages, and can include navigation from page to page. Very cool.

Next up—planning websites.

CREATING CONCEPTUAL WEBSITES

You can also plan and model websites using Visio. That involves drawing the website conceptually—not actually putting together mock-ups of the web pages.

Here's an example:

1. Open Visio.

2. Select File > New > Software and Database > Conceptual Web Site. Visio creates a new Conceptual Web Site drawing.

3. Open the Conceptual Web Site Shapes stencil.

4. Drag a Home or Home Page shape onto the drawing surface.

    You can see an example in Figure 14.56.

Figure 14.56
A new conceptual website drawing with a Home shape.

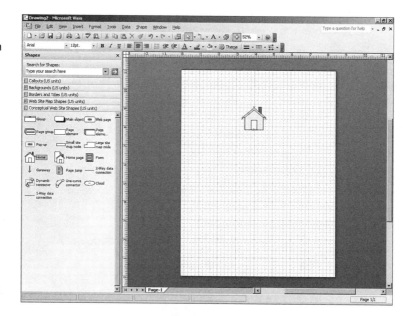

5. Drag a Web Page shape, or other shapes, such as the Form shape, onto the drawing surface.

    Select a shape and enter the text label for the shape. You can see an example in Figure 14.57.

14

Figure 14.57
A new conceptual website drawing with Web Page shapes.

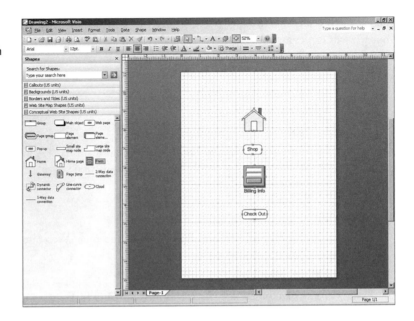

6. Drag connectors, such as 2-Way Data Connection, Dynamic Connector, or the Line-Curve Connector, onto the drawing surface to connect web elements.

The result might look like what is shown in Figure 14.58.

Figure 14.58
A new conceptual website drawing with connected Web Page shapes.

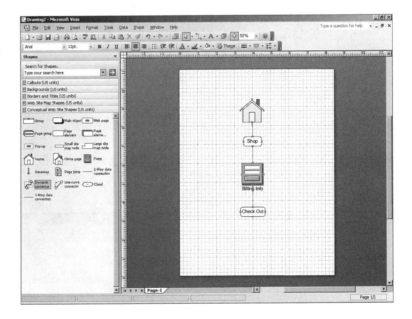

7. Drag additional shapes, such as Pop-up, Page Group, and Gateway shapes, to your conceptual website as needed.

You can also create website maps with Visio—a topic that's coming up next.

CREATING WEBSITE MAPS

Here's another cool one—you can map existing websites using Visio. In particular, you use the Web Site Map template in Visio—and it will connect to the Internet and map your site for you.

Here's an example:

1. Open Visio.
2. Select File > New > Software and Database > Web Site Map. Visio creates a new Conceptual Web Site drawing.
3. Enter the URL of the website's main page that you want to map in the Generate Site Map dialog's Address box.

   You can see an example in Figure 14.59.

Figure 14.59
Asking for a new website map.

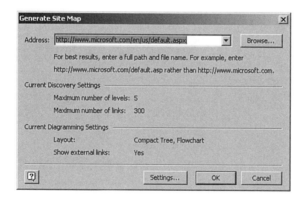

You can configure the website map by clicking the Settings button to specify the number of levels deep to go, the maximum number of links to map, and so on.

Visio maps the website and generates a website map for you, as shown in Figure 14.60.

Figure 14.60
A new website map.

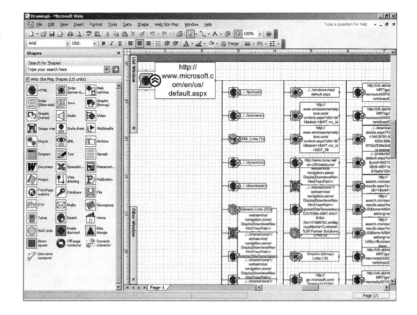

Very cool.

INDEX

P

Q-R

T